Cloud–Based Big Data Analytics in Vehicular Ad–Hoc Networks

Ram Shringar Rao
Ambedkar Institute of Advanced Communication Technologies and Research, India

Nanhay Singh
Ambedkar Institute of Advanced Communication Technologies and Research, India

Omprakash Kaiwartya
School of Science and Technology, Nottingham Trent University, UK

Sanjoy Das
Indira Gandhi National Tribal University, India

A volume in the Advances in Systems Analysis, Software Engineering, and High Performance Computing (ASASEHPC) Book Series

Published in the United States of America by
    IGI Global
    Engineering Science Reference (an imprint of IGI Global)
    701 E. Chocolate Avenue
    Hershey PA, USA 17033
    Tel: 717-533-8845
    Fax: 717-533-8661
    E-mail: cust@igi-global.com
    Web site: http://www.igi-global.com

Library of Congress Cataloging-in-Publication Data

Names: Rao, Ram Shringar, 1973- editor. | Singh, Nanhay, 1973- editor. |
  Kaiwartya, Omprakash, 1981- editor. | Das, Sanjoy, 1979- editor.
Title: Cloud-based big data analytics in vehicular ad-hoc networks / Ram
  Shringar Rao, Nanhay Singh, Omprakash Kaiwartya, and Sanjoy Das,
  editors.
Description: Hershey, PA : Engineering Science Reference, an imprint of IGI
  Global, [2020] | Includes bibliographical references and index. |
  Summary: "This book covers a range of new concepts in emerging VANETs
  including the integration with cloud computing and big data analytics,
  emerging wireless networking concepts, and computing models"-- Provided
  by publisher.
Identifiers: LCCN 2019043468 (print) | LCCN 2019043469 (ebook) | ISBN
  9781799827641 (hardcover) | ISBN 9781799827658 (paperback) | ISBN
  9781799827665 (ebook)
Subjects: LCSH: Vehicular ad hoc networks (Computer networks) | Big data. |
  Cloud computing. | Quantitative analysis.
Classification: LCC TE228.37 .C56 2020 (print) | LCC TE228.37 (ebook) |
  DDC 388.3/12--dc23
LC record available at https://lccn.loc.gov/2019043468
LC ebook record available at https://lccn.loc.gov/2019043469

This book is published in the IGI Global book series Advances in Systems Analysis, Software Engineering, and High Performance Computing (ASASEHPC) (ISSN: 2327-3453; eISSN: 2327-3461)

British Cataloguing in Publication Data
A Cataloguing in Publication record for this book is available from the British Library.

For electronic access to this publication, please contact: eresources@igi-global.com.

Advances in Systems Analysis, Software Engineering, and High Performance Computing (ASASEHPC) Book Series

Vijayan Sugumaran
Oakland University, USA

ISSN:2327-3453
EISSN:2327-3461

MISSION

The theory and practice of computing applications and distributed systems has emerged as one of the key areas of research driving innovations in business, engineering, and science. The fields of software engineering, systems analysis, and high performance computing offer a wide range of applications and solutions in solving computational problems for any modern organization.

The **Advances in Systems Analysis, Software Engineering, and High Performance Computing (ASASEHPC) Book Series** brings together research in the areas of distributed computing, systems and software engineering, high performance computing, and service science. This collection of publications is useful for academics, researchers, and practitioners seeking the latest practices and knowledge in this field.

COVERAGE

- Parallel Architectures
- Human-Computer Interaction
- Network Management
- Virtual Data Systems
- Computer Graphics
- Performance Modelling
- Enterprise Information Systems
- Computer Networking
- Computer System Analysis
- Software Engineering

IGI Global is currently accepting manuscripts for publication within this series. To submit a proposal for a volume in this series, please contact our Acquisition Editors at Acquisitions@igi-global.com or visit: http://www.igi-global.com/publish/.

Titles in this Series

For a list of additional titles in this series, please visit:
https://www.igi-global.com/book-series/advances-educational-technologies-instructional-design/73678

Balancing Agile and Disciplined Engineering and Management Approaches for IT Services and Software Products
Manuel Mora (Universidad Autónoma de Aguascalientes, Mexico) Jorge Marx Gómez (University of Oldenburg, Germany) Rory V. O'Connor (Dublin City University, Ireland) and Alena Buchalcevová (University of Economics, Prague, Czech Republic)
Engineering Science Reference • © 2021 • 354pp • H/C (ISBN: 9781799841654) • US $225.00

Urban Spatial Data Handling and Computing
Mainak Bandyopadhyay (DIT University-Dehradun, India) and Varun Singh (MNNIT-Allahabad, India)
Engineering Science Reference • © 2020 • 300pp • H/C (ISBN: 9781799801221) • US $245.00

FPGA Algorithms and Applications for the Internet of Things
Preeti Sharma (Bansal College of Engineering, Mandideep, India) and Rajit Nair (Jagran Lakecity University, Bhopal, India)
Engineering Science Reference • © 2020 • 257pp • H/C (ISBN: 9781522598060) • US $215.00

Advancements in Instrumentation and Control in Applied System Applications
Srijan Bhattacharya (RCC Institute of Information Technology, India)
Engineering Science Reference • © 2020 • 298pp • H/C (ISBN: 9781799825845) • US $225.00

Cloud Computing Applications and Techniques for E-Commerce
Saikat Gochhait (Symbiosis Institute of Digital and Telecom Management, Symbiosis International University, India) David Tawei Shou (University of Taipei, Taiwan) and Sabiha Fazalbhoy (Symbiosis Centre for Management Studies, Symbiosis International University, India)
Engineering Science Reference • © 2020 • 185pp • H/C (ISBN: 9781799812944) • US $215.00

Soft Computing Methods for System Dependability
Mohamed Arezki Mellal (M'Hamed Bougara University, Algeria)
Engineering Science Reference • © 2020 • 293pp • H/C (ISBN: 9781799817185) • US $225.00

Grammatical and Syntactical Approaches in Architecture Emerging Research and Opportunities
Ju Hyun Lee (University of New South Wales, Australia) and Michael J. Ostwald (University of New South Wales, Australia)
Engineering Science Reference • © 2020 • 351pp • H/C (ISBN: 9781799816980) • US $195.00

701 East Chocolate Avenue, Hershey, PA 17033, USA
Tel: 717-533-8845 x100 • Fax: 717-533-8661
E-Mail: cust@igi-global.com • www.igi-global.com

Table of Contents

Preface xiv

Acknowledgment xix

Chapter 1
An Approach Towards Intelligent Traffic Environment Using Machine Learning Algorithms 1
> *Kavita Pandey, Jaypee Institute of Information Technology, Noida, India*
> *Akshansh Narula, Jaypee Institute of Information Technology, Noida, India*
> *Dhiraj pandey, JSS Academy of Technical Education, Noida, India*
> *Ram Shringar Raw, Ambedkar Insitute of Advanced Communication Technologies and*
> *   Research, India*

Chapter 2
Geocast Routing Protocols for Ad-Hoc Networks: Comparative Analysis and Open Issues 23
> *Indrani Das, Assam University, India*
> *Sanjoy Das, Indira Gandhi National Tribal University, India*

Chapter 3
Evaluation of Topology-Based Routing Protocols for Dissemination of Emergency Messages in
Urban Vehicular Traffic Scenarios in India 46
> *Pawan Singh, Indira Gandhi National Tribal University, Amarkantak, India*
> *Suhel Ahmad Khan, Indira Gandhi National Tribal University, Amarkantak, India*
> *Pramod Kumar Goyal, Department of Training and Technical Education, Aryabhatt Institute*
> *   of Technology, India*

Chapter 4
Survey on VANET and Various Applications of Internet of Things 75
> *Nithiavathy R., Arjun College of Technology, Coimbatore, India*
> *Udayakumar E., Kalaignarkarunanidhi Institute of Technology, Coimbatore, India*
> *Srihari K., Department of CSE, SNS College of Engineering, India*

Chapter 5
Two-Stage Non-Cooperative Game Model for Vertical Handoffs in Heterogeneous Wireless
Networks 90
> *Pramod Kumar Goyal, Department of Training and Technical Education, Government of Delhi, India*
> *Pawan Singh, Indira Gandhi National Tribal University, Amarkantak, India*

Chapter 6
A Fuzzy Multi-Criteria Decision-Making Method for Managing Network Security Risk
Perspective 115
> *Suhel Ahmad Khan, Indira Gandhi National Tribal University, Amarkantak, India*
> *Waris Khan, Babasaheb Bhimrao Ambedkar University, Lucknow, India*
> *Dhirendra Pandey, Babasaheb Bhimrao Ambedkar University, Lucknow, India*

Chapter 7
Software-Defined Vehicular Adhoc Network: A Theoretical Approach 141
> *Ram S. Raw, Ambedkar Institute of Advanced Communication Technologies and Research, India*
> *Manish Kumar, Ambedkar Institute of Advanced Communication Technologies and Research, India*
> *Nanahay Singh, Ambedkar Institute of Advanced Communication Technologies and Research, India*

Chapter 8
Vehicle Monitoring and Surveillance Through Vehicular Sensor Network 165
> *Pooja Singh, CSE/IT Department, Amity School of Engineering and Technology, Noida, India*

Chapter 9
Routing in Vehicular Delay Tolerant Networks: A Comparision 191
> *Anamika Chauhan, Delhi Technological University, India*
> *Kapil Sharma, Delhi Technological University, India*
> *Alka Aggarwal, Delhi Technological University, India*

Chapter 10
Energy Harvesting for Wireless Sensor Nodes Using Rectenna 204
> *Sanjeev Kumar, Ambedkar Institute of Advanced Communication Technologies and Research, India*
> *Jyotsna Sharma, Ambedkar Institute of Advanced Communication Technologies and Research, India*
> *Arvind Kumar, Ambedkar Institute of Advanced Communication Technologies and Research, India*

Chapter 11
Cloud Computing Technologies 233
    Shweta Kaushik, JIIT Sector 128, Noida, India
    Charu Gandhi, JIIT Sector 128, Noida, India

Compilation of References 254

Related References 285

About the Contributors 306

Index 311

Detailed Table of Contents

Preface xiv

Acknowledgment xix

Chapter 1

An Approach Towards Intelligent Traffic Environment Using Machine Learning Algorithms 1

    Kavita Pandey, Jaypee Institute of Information Technology, Noida, India
    Akshansh Narula, Jaypee Institute of Information Technology, Noida, India
    Dhiraj pandey, JSS Academy of Technical Education, Noida, India
    Ram Shringar Raw, Ambedkar Insitute of Advanced Communication Technologies and
        Research, India

To make an optimal movement of vehicles and to reduce the accident rate, the government has installed traffic lights at almost every intersection. Traffic lights are intended to decrease congestion. However, the dynamic nature of traffic movement causes congestion always. This congestion leads to increased waiting times for every vehicle. In this chapter, two machine learning-based approaches used to improve in the congested traffic environment. The first part of the work is Deep-Learning based traffic signaling, which identifies the congestion on all sides of the intersection with the help of image processing techniques. By analyzing the congestion, the algorithm proposes dynamic green-light times rather than the traditional fixed lighting system. In the second part, a Q-learning-based approach has been suggested in which an agent decides the state of the traffic light based on a cumulative reward. Further, these algorithms have been tested on different traffic simulated environments using SUMO, and detailed analysis has been carried out.

Chapter 2

Geocast Routing Protocols for Ad-Hoc Networks: Comparative Analysis and Open Issues 23

    Indrani Das, Assam University, India
    Sanjoy Das, Indira Gandhi National Tribal University, India

Geocasting is a subset of conventional multicasting problem. Geocasting means to deliver a message or data to a specific geographical area. Routing refers to the activities necessary to route a message in its travel from source to the destination node. The routing of a message is very important and relatively difficult problems in the context of Ad-hoc Networks because nodes are moving very fast, network load or traffic patterns, and topology of the network is dynamical changes with time. In this chapter, different geocast routing mechanisms used in both Mobile Ad-hoc Networks and Vehicular Ad-hoc Networks. The authors have shown a strong and in-depth analysis of the strengths and weaknesses of each protocol.

For delivering geocast message, both the source and destination nodes use location information. The nodes determine their locations by using the Global Positioning System (GPS). They have presented a comprehensive comparative analysis of existing geocast routing protocols and proposed future direction in designing a new routing protocol addressing the problem.

Chapter 3
Evaluation of Topology-Based Routing Protocols for Dissemination of Emergency Messages in Urban Vehicular Traffic Scenarios in India...46

Pawan Singh, Indira Gandhi National Tribal University, Amarkantak, India
Suhel Ahmad Khan, Indira Gandhi National Tribal University, Amarkantak, India
Pramod Kumar Goyal, Department of Training and Technical Education, Aryabhatt Institute of Technology, India

VANET is a subclass of MANET that makes the dream of intelligent transportation systems come true. As per the report of the Ministry of Road Transport and Highways, India, 1.5 million people were killed in road accidents in 2015. To reduce casualty and provide some kind of comfort during the journey, India must also implement VANETs. Applicability of VANET in Indian roads must be tested before implementation in reality. In this chapter, the real maps of Connaught Place, New Delhi from Open Street maps websites is considered. The SUMO for traffic and flow modeling is used. Many scenarios have been used to reflect real Indian road conditions to measure the performance of AODV, DSDV, and DSR routing protocols. The CBR traffic is used for the dissemination of emergency messages in urban vehicular traffic scenarios. The throughput, packet delivery ratio, and end-to-end delay are considered for performance analysis through the NS-2.35 network simulator.

Chapter 4
Survey on VANET and Various Applications of Internet of Things 75

Nithiavathy R., Arjun College of Technology, Coimbatore, India
Udayakumar E., Kalaignarkarunanidhi Institute of Technology, Coimbatore, India
Srihari K., Department of CSE, SNS College of Engineering, India

The user of the cloud storage can store an enormous amount of the data without any worries of the local maintenances of hardware and software. The user outsources the data and takes security control in order to maintain the reliability of the data. The data deposited in the cloud server is under frequent audit to the user to check the correctness of the service provider using wireless networks. The user can service a third-party checker to do the security audit on behalf of them for managing time constraints. The confidentiality of the data outsourced is preserved as of the third-party checker also. The system should be more efficient build for securing the data from various vulnerabilities. The proposed audit mechanism satisfies the user by providing integrity of the data stored simultaneously effectively and efficiently using VANET.

Chapter 5

Two-Stage Non-Cooperative Game Model for Vertical Handoffs in Heterogeneous Wireless
Networks 90

*Pramod Kumar Goyal, Department of Training and Technical Education, Government of
Delhi, India*

Pawan Singh, Indira Gandhi National Tribal University, Amarkantak, India

In a heterogeneous wireless network (HWN) environment, performing an efficient vertical handoff requires the efficient qualitative evaluation of all stakeholders like wireless networks (WN) and mobile users (MU) and mutual selection of best WN-MU. In the literature, most of the work deals with both these requirements jointly in the techniques proposed by them for the vertical handoffs (VHO) in HWNs, leaving very little scope to manipulate the above requirements independently. This may result in inefficient vertical handoffs. Hence, this chapter proposed a generalized two-stage two players, iterative non-cooperative game model. This model presents a modular framework that separates the quantitative evaluation of WNs and MUs (at Stage 1) from the game formulation and solution (at Stage 2) for mutual selection of best WN-MU pair for VHO. The simulation results show a substantial reduction in the number of vertical handoffs with the proposed game theory-based two-stage model as compared to a single-stage non-game theory method like multiple attribute decision making.

Chapter 6

A Fuzzy Multi-Criteria Decision-Making Method for Managing Network Security Risk
Perspective 115

Suhel Ahmad Khan, Indira Gandhi National Tribal University, Amarkantak, India

Waris Khan, Babasaheb Bhimrao Ambedkar University, Lucknow, India

Dhirendra Pandey, Babasaheb Bhimrao Ambedkar University, Lucknow, India

Security threats evaluation accepts a pivotal part in network security management. In this chapter, the author has depicted the significant measures and parameters with respect to huge industry/organizational prerequisites for building up a secure network. The existing fuzzy model is a combination of fuzzy techniques and expert's opinions. The work aims to manage network security risks during D2D data communication through the network to optimize security assurance. The idea is to provide a means of security risk assessment during D2D data communication through the network. Security risks are those that prevent the accomplishment of the objectives specified by developers as well as organizations. The basic idea of the proposed work is to identify and prioritize the security risks methods, which is used to find the problems and fix them only to minimize cost, rework, and time. The work examines the effect of multi-criteria decision analysis methods for security risk assessment.

Chapter 7

Software-Defined Vehicular Adhoc Network: A Theoretical Approach 141

> Ram S. Raw, Ambedkar Institute of Advanced Communication Technologies and Research,
>   India
> Manish Kumar, Ambedkar Institute of Advanced Communication Technologies and
>   Research, India
> Nanahay Singh, Ambedkar Institute of Advanced Communication Technologies and
>   Research, India

Vehicular adhoc networks (VANETs) and software-defined networking (SDN) are the key enablers of 5G technology in developing intelligent vehicle networks and applications for the next generation. In recent years, many studies have been concentrated on SDN and VANET incorporation, and many researchers worked at various architecture-related issues along with the advantages of software-defined VANET services and features to adapt them. This chapter discusses the current state of the art of SD-VANET with the directions of future research work. This chapter presents a theoretical approach of architectures of software-defined VANET for its networking infrastructure design, functionalities, benefits, and challenges of future generation networks.

Chapter 8

Vehicle Monitoring and Surveillance Through Vehicular Sensor Network 165

> Pooja Singh, CSE/IT Department, Amity School of Engineering and Technology, Noida,
>   India

There are a lot of prospects of the vehicular network, including the artificial neural networks incorporating a wireless sensor network. Its number comes after the mobile communication network and the internet. The network is characterized by more through measure and sense and exhibits more comfortable operability and intelligence. A wireless sensor network can be simply defined as "a network of wireless devices using sensors to monitors and recording the physical conditions of the environment and organizing the collected data at a central location." WSNs measure environmental conditions like temperature, sound, pollution levels, humidity, wind speed and direction, pressure, etc. Thus, wireless sensor networks are widely used for fulfilling the essential needs of environmental sensing applications. These applications show the broad ranges in precision agriculture, monitoring of the vehicle, and video surveillance.

Chapter 9

Routing in Vehicular Delay Tolerant Networks: A Comparision 191

> Anamika Chauhan, Delhi Technological University, India
> Kapil Sharma, Delhi Technological University, India
> Alka Aggarwal, Delhi Technological University, India

With the ever-escalating amount of vehicular traffic activity on the roads, the efficient management of traffic and safety of the drivers and passengers is of paramount gravity. Vehicular ad-hoc networks (VANETs) have emerged as the systems where vehicles would be perceptive of the locality and can supply the driver with required inputs to take necessary actions to alleviate the various issues. The system is designed to detect and identify essential traffic events and inform all concerned entities and take appropriate action. The characteristics of VANET are the topology is highly mobile, depends on city infrastructure, and the high speed of vehicles. These challenges result in frequent disruption of connections, long delays in delivering the messages. The challenges are overcome through the vehicular delay-tolerant network

(VDTN) routing protocols are used that can facilitate communication under these network challenges. In this chapter, the authors evaluate the effect of the node density and message sizes on the performance of the various VDTN routing protocols.

Chapter 10

Energy Harvesting for Wireless Sensor Nodes Using Rectenna...204

Sanjeev Kumar, Ambedkar Institute of Advanced Communication Technologies and Research, India

Jyotsna Sharma, Ambedkar Institute of Advanced Communication Technologies and Research, India

Arvind Kumar, Ambedkar Institute of Advanced Communication Technologies and Research, India

Wireless sensor nodes generally operate using energy from source line batteries, which need to be replaced or recharge from time to time. The connection of electromagnetic energy to DC energy, which is called radiofrequency (RF) energy harvesting, is one of the best techniques to act as an energy source for this equipment. An ambient amount of RF energy is present in our environment radiated from numerous sources so that it can act as a much predictable source of energy as compared to other techniques of energy harvesting. This system eliminates the periodic replacement of energy batteries for these sensor nodes. Despite the enormous RF energy present in the environment, the power per unit area is quite low. Hence, the major barrier is to increase the output of the rectifier circuit, even though the power density is low.

Chapter 11

Cloud Computing Technologies 233

Shweta Kaushik, JIIT Sector 128, Noida, India

Charu Gandhi, JIIT Sector 128, Noida, India

In today's world, cloud computing and e-commerce are complementary to each other in terms of their vast effectiveness. E-commerce allows the business to move and grow on the internet without having or buying any physical space. Cloud computing helps e-commerce by securing the investment of IT infrastructure. That is the only reason why most of the organizations are moving their business towards cloud computing. Many organizations are getting much more benefit from the usage of cloud computing. But before adopting this, they must understand its trade-off also. In this chapter, the authors present the requirements of e-commerce organizations for adoption of cloud computing, benefit after the adoption of cloud computing in the e-commerce business, and what difficulties e-commerce organizations feel after the usage of this technology.

Compilation of References 254

Related References 285

About the Contributors 306

Index 311

Preface

According to World Health Organizations (WHO), millions of people around the world die and injured every year due to vehicular traffic accidents, and billions of hours of our time is lost because of traffic accidents and traffic jams, which causes a global loss of domestic productivity. Optimizing traffic management operations is a big challenge due to a massive increase in the number of vehicles, traffic congestions, and road accidents. Therefore, to reduce a large number of traffic accidents, improve the performance of transportation systems, enhance road safety, and protect the environment, the concept of Vehicular Ad-Hoc Network (VANET) was introduced. VANET has been developed for Intelligent Transportation Systems (ITS), and it is the future direction for the road transportation system. Current development in wireless communication, computing paradigms, big data, and cloud computing fetched the enhancement of intelligent devices equipped with wireless communication capabilities and high-performance processing tools.

In the recent development, cloud computing, big data, and Internet of Things (IoT) based services and concepts have been introduced in improved VANET with advanced cellular networks such as 5G networks and vehicular cloud concepts. Big data and cloud computing are becoming emerging research areas in VANETs, which can be seen in many projects worldwide. Vehicular communication systems will produce a large amount of data. Nowadays, these data are placed on cloud called cloud data and described as Big Data. Researchers and data scientists using IoT includes rapidly growing data that can be handled by using big data. Big data refers to a large amount of structured and unstructured data that can be analyzed using various applications software. Using big data analytics, we can get the gain from data. Therefore, the big data on the cloud will have profound impacts on the implementation of VANETs, which makes transportation systems much safer, efficient, and effective.

Further, VANETs have been studied intensively due to their uniqueness and a wide variety of applications and services, such as reduced traffic accidents, passenger safety, improved traffic efficiency, and entertainment, and infotainment. Big data analytics can improve traffic efficiency, congestion control, and safety level during transportation. Although applications of big data analytics in VANET have a great vision, many critical research issues, future scopes, and significant challenges are discussed. Cloud computing or mobile cloud computing is a style of new computing paradigm that can store, access, manipulate, share data, files, and programs on-demand basis through the internet. Cloud computing is considered a key element to satisfy these requirements in VANETs. It is a network access model that aims to exchange a large number of computing resources and services. Cloud computing and big data both include the various heterogeneous technologies that work together and provide real-time solutions for VANET. There will be some cloud service providers, they will provide cloud-based services to the vehicular node users on a payment basis, and some are free services.

With the development of wireless technologies, big data, IoT, cloud computing, and rapid growth in the number of smart vehicles, where the need to connect smart devices such as smartphones, PDAs, smartwatch, smart TV, laptop, etc. with the cloud through the internet has raised and demanded. Further, conventional VANETs face several technical challenges in deployment due to less flexibility, poor connectivity, and inadequate intelligence. Cloud computing, big data analytics, vehicular cloud computing, IoT, and VANET are the significant components in the current Intelligent Transport System (ITS). Various research on VANET, cloud concepts and big data analytics shows that these have significant effects in the smart transportation system of VANET.

Moreover, VANETs have been emerging concepts and gained popularity in recent years. Vehicular traffic accidents, safety, road congestion, parking, and environmental pollution due to a large number of vehicles have become severe global issues—the primary focus of current solutions to these problems provided by intelligent transportation systems. Therefore, to overcome these issues, the cloud and big data-based future VANET will have unique requirements of autonomous vehicles with high efficiency, better connectivity, low latency, and real-time applications, which may not be resolved by traditional VANET. Hence, integration of cloud computing, big data, vehicular cloud computing, and IoT with the traditional VANETs is discussed.

TARGET AUDIENCE

The book addressed various issues related to VANETs from routing to security and the latest technologies, i.e., cloud computing, the Internet of Things. Applications of machine learning techniques are also included. So, the book is expecting broad target audiences from different stakeholders, i.e., academicians, researchers, undergraduate, and postgraduate students, as well as industries.

ORGANIZATION OF THE BOOK

The book consists of a total of 11 chapters. The glimpses of each chapter given below:

Chapter 1 discusses the uses of machine learning techniques and how they will be useful for Intelligent Traffic environments. To make an optimal movement of vehicles and to reduce the accident rate, the government has installed traffic lights at almost every intersection. Traffic lights are intended to decrease congestion. However, the dynamic nature of traffic movement causes congestion always. This congestion leads to increased waiting times for every vehicle. In this chapter, two machine learning-based approaches used to improve in the congested traffic environment. The first part of the work is Deep-Learning based traffic signaling, which identifies the congestion on all sides of the intersection with the help of image processing techniques. By analyzing the congestion, the algorithm proposes dynamic green-light times rather than the traditional fixed lighting system. In the second part, a Q-learning based approach has been suggested in which an agent decides the state of the traffic light based on a cumulative reward. Further, these algorithms have been tested on different traffic simulated environments using SUMO, and detailed analysis has been carried out.

Chapter 2 discusses various location-based routing algorithms that exist for Ad hoc Networks. Geocasting is a subset of conventional multicasting problem. Geocasting means to deliver a message or data to a specific geographical area. Routing refers to the activities necessary to route a message in its travel from source to the destination node. The routing of a message is very important and relatively difficult problems in the context of Ad-hoc Networks because nodes are moving very fast, network load or traffic patterns, and topology of the network is dynamical changes with time. In this chapter, different geocast routing mechanisms used in both Mobile Ad-hoc Networks and Vehicular Ad-hoc Networks. We have shown a strong and in-depth analysis of the strengths and weaknesses of each protocol. For delivering geocast message, both the source and destination nodes use location information. The nodes determine their locations by using the Global Positioning System (GPS). We have presented a comprehensive comparative analysis of existing geocast routing protocols and proposed future direction in designing a new routing protocol addressing the problem.

Chapter 3 discusses the evaluation of various topology-based routing protocols in the context of Urban Vehicular Traffic Scenarios in India. VANET is a subclass of MANET that makes the dream of Intelligent Transportation Systems comes true. As per the report of the Ministry of Road Transport & Highways, India, 1.5 million people were killed in road accidents in 2015. To reduce casualty and provide some kind of comfort during the journey, India must also implement VANETs. Applicability of VANET in Indian Roads must be tested before implementation in reality. In this chapter, the real maps of Connaught Place, New Delhi from Open Street maps website is considered. The SUMO for traffic and flow modeling is used. Many scenarios have been used to reflect real Indian road conditions to measure the performance of AODV, DSDV, and DSR routing protocols. The CBR traffic is used for the dissemination of emergency messages in Urban Vehicular Traffic Scenarios. The throughput, packet delivery ratio, and end-to-end delay considered for performance analysis through the NS-2.35 network simulator.

Chapter 4 discusses the various applications of internet of things in Vehicular Ad hoc Networks. The user of the cloud storage can store an enormous amount of the data without any worries of the local maintenances of hardware and software. The user outsources the data and takes security control in order to maintain the reliability of the data. The data deposited in the cloud server is under frequent audit to the user to check the correctness of the service provider using wireless networks. The user can service a third-party checker to do the security audit on behalf of them for managing time constraints. The confidentiality of the data outsourced is preserved as of the third-party checker also. The system should be more efficient build for securing the data from various vulnerabilities. The proposed audit mechanism satisfies the user by providing integrity of the data stored simultaneously effectively and efficiently using VANET.

Chapter 5 discusses novel game theory-based vertical handoffs in Heterogeneous Wireless Networks. In a Heterogeneous Wireless Network (HWN) environment, performing an efficient vertical handoff requires the efficient qualitative evaluation of all stakeholders like Wireless Networks (WN) & Mobile Users (MU), and mutual selection of best WN-MU. In the literature, most of the work deals with both these requirements jointly in the techniques proposed by them for the Vertical Handoffs (VHO) in HWNs, leaving very little scope to manipulate the above requirements independently. This may result in inefficient vertical handoffs. Hence, this chapter proposed a generalized two-stage two players, iterative non-cooperative game model. This model presents a modular framework that separates the quantitative evaluation of WNs and MUs (at stage 1) from the game formulation and solution (at stage 2) for mutual selection of best WN-MU pair for VHO. The simulation results show a substantial reduction in the number of vertical handoffs with the proposed game theory-based two-stage model as compared to a single-stage non-game theory method like Multiple Attribute Decision Making.

Chapter 6 discusses various security risks and uses of a fuzzy multi-criteria decision-making method to manage risks. Security threats evaluation accepts a pivotal part in network security management. In this chapter, the author has depicted the significant measures and parameters with respect to huge industry/ organizational prerequisites for building up a secure network. The existing fuzzy model is a combination of fuzzy techniques and expert's opinions. The proposed work aims to manage network security risks during D2D data communication through the network to optimize security assurance. The idea is to provide a means of security risk assessment during D2D data communication through the network. Security risks are those that prevent the accomplishment of the objectives specified by developers as well as organizations. The basic idea of the proposed work is to identify and prioritize the security risks methods, which is used to find the problems and fix them only to minimize cost, rework, and time. The work examines the effect of multi-criteria decision analysis methods for security risk assessment.

Chapter 7 includes an extensive discussion on theoretical approaches on software-defined vehicular Ad hoc network. Vehicular Ad hoc Networks (VANETs) and Software Defined Networking (SDN) are the key enablers of 5G technology in developing intelligent vehicle networks and applications for the next generation. In recent years, many studies have been concentrated on SDN, and VANET incorporation and many researchers worked at various architecture-related issues along with the advantages of software-defined VANET services and features, to adapt them. This chapter discusses the current state of the art of SD-VANET with the directions of future research work. This chapter presents a theoretical approach of architectures of Software Defined VANET for its networking infrastructure design, functionalities, benefits, and challenges of future generation networks.

Chapter 8 discusses the monitoring and surveillance of vehicles through the vehicular sensor network. There are a lot of prospects of the vehicular network, including the artificial neural networks incorporating a wireless sensor network. Its number comes after the mobile communication network and the internet. The network is characterized by more through measure and sense and exhibits more comfortable operability and intelligence. A Wireless Sensor Network can be simply defined as "A network of wireless devices using sensors to monitors and recording the physical conditions of the environment and organizing the collected data at a central location." WSNs measure environmental conditions like temperature, sound, pollution levels, humidity, wind speed and direction, pressure, etc. Thus, wireless sensor networks are widely used for fulfilling the essential needs of environmental sensing applications. These applications show the broad ranges in precision agriculture, monitoring of the vehicle and the video surveillance, etc.

Chapter 9 discusses the comparison of routing in vehicular delay tolerant networks. With the ever-escalating amount of vehicular traffic activity on the roads, the efficient management of traffic and safety of the drivers and passengers is of paramount gravity. Vehicular Ad-hoc networks (VANETs) have emerged as the systems where vehicles would be perceptive of the locality and can supply the driver with required inputs to take necessary actions to alleviate the various issues. The system is designed to detect and identify essential traffic events and inform all concerned entities and take appropriate action. The characteristics of VANET are - the topology is highly mobile, depends on city infrastructure, and the high speed of vehicles. These challenges result in frequent disruption of connections, long delays in delivering the messages. The challenges are overcome through the vehicular delay-tolerant network (VDTN) routing protocols are used that can facilitate communication under these network challenges. In this paper, we evaluate the effect of the node density and message sizes on the performance of the various VDTN routing protocols.

Chapter 10 includes energy harvesting for WSNs using Rectenna. Wireless sensor nodes generally operate using energy from source line batteries, which need to be replaced or recharge from time to time. The connection of electromagnetic energy to DC energy, which is called Radiofrequency (RF) energy harvesting, is one of the best techniques to act as an energy source for this equipment. An ambient amount of RF energy is present in our environment radiated from numerous sources so that it can act as a much predictable source of energy as compared to other techniques of energy harvesting. This system eliminates the periodic replacement of energy batteries for these sensor nodes. Despite the enormous RF energy present in the environment, the power per unit area is quite low. Hence, the major barrier is to increase the output of the rectifier circuit, even though the power density is low.

Chapter 11 discusses the various cloud computing technologies. In today's world, cloud computing and e-commerce are complementary to each other in terms of their vast effectiveness. E-commerce allows the business to move and grow on the internet without having or buying any physical space. The cloud computing helps e-commerce by securing the investment of IT infrastructure. That is the only reason why most of the organizations are moving their business towards cloud computing. Many organizations are getting much more benefit from the usage of cloud computing. But before adopting this, they must understand its trade-off also. In this chapter we are going to present that what are the requirement of e-commerce organization for adoption of cloud computing, benefit after the adoption of cloud computing in the e-commerce business and what difficulties e-commerce organizations feels after the usage of this technology.

CONCLUSION

The chapters furnished in the book have tremendous scope for further explore the various domains of VANETs. The modern advancement in machine learning, fuzzy theory, the internet of things, and cloud computing are included in the book. These techniques enrich further research. The chapters contributed on cloud computing, internet of things, delay torrent network, and big data analytics in VANETs context. Extensive simulation works on various topology based, location-based routing is also addressed. The challenges, security, and applications of modern technologies are included for insight understanding of the area.

We hope this book will give ample space to the research communities to explore various aspects of VANETs and associate its networks.

Ram Shringar Rao
Ambedkar Institute of Advanced Communication Technologies and Research, India

Nanhay Singh
Ambedkar Institute of Advanced Communication Technologies and Research, India

Omprakash Kaiwartya
School of Science and Technology, Nottingham Trent University, UK

Sanjoy Das
Indira Gandhi National Tribal University, India

Acknowledgment

We are express our sincere thanks to Dr. Jan Travers, IGI-Global, for allowing us to convene the book in his esteemed publishing house, and Ms. Courtney Tychinski, IGI-Global for her kind cooperation in the completion of this book. We are thankful to Maria Rohde, Assistant Development Editor, the Book Development Team, IGI-Global for constant support. We thank our esteemed authors for having shown confidence in the book and considering it as a platform to showcase and share their original research work. We would also wish to thank the authors whose papers were not included in this book, probably because of their minor shortcomings. We are thankful to our editorial advisory board members for their valuable inputs. We also highly appreciate the contribution made by numerous reviewers for evaluating the various chapters. We are also thankful to our colleagues, friends for their constant support and encouragement in the completion of the book. Finally, we are grateful to all the family members for their support and love.

Ram Shringar Rao
Ambedkar Institute of Advanced Communication Technologies and Research, India

Nanhay Singh
Ambedkar Institute of Advanced Communication Technologies and Research, India

Omprakash Kaiwartya
School of Science and Technology, Nottingham Trent University, UK

Sanjoy Das
Indira Gandhi National Tribal University, India

Chapter 1
An Approach Towards Intelligent Traffic Environment Using Machine Learning Algorithms

Kavita Pandey

Jaypee Institute of Information Technology, Noida, India

Akshansh Narula

Jaypee Institute of Information Technology, Noida, India

Dhiraj pandey

https://orcid.org/0000-0001-5969-6071

JSS Academy of Technical Education, Noida, India

Ram Shringar Raw

Ambedkar Insitute of Advanced Communication Technologies and Research, India

ABSTRACT

To make an optimal movement of vehicles and to reduce the accident rate, the government has installed traffic lights at almost every intersection. Traffic lights are intended to decrease congestion. However, the dynamic nature of traffic movement causes congestion always. This congestion leads to increased waiting times for every vehicle. In this chapter, two machine learning-based approaches used to improve in the congested traffic environment. The first part of the work is Deep-Learning based traffic signaling, which identifies the congestion on all sides of the intersection with the help of image processing techniques. By analyzing the congestion, the algorithm proposes dynamic green-light times rather than the traditional fixed lighting system. In the second part, a Q-learning-based approach has been suggested in which an agent decides the state of the traffic light based on a cumulative reward. Further, these algorithms have been tested on different traffic simulated environments using SUMO, and detailed analysis has been carried out.

DOI: 10.4018/978-1-7998-2764-1.ch001

INTRODUCTION

To improve the living standards of citizens, smart cities are the future of any country across the globe. This concept is prospering step by step to accomplish the infrastructure advancements and facilities levels, above and beyond (Smart city definition, 2019) (Smart city mission, 2019). To make a city or country smart, the idea is to integrate ICT in all our daily routine life services. Services such as water supply, energy consumption, waste management, healthcare, traffic and transportation, education, agriculture, road infrastructure, surveillance systems and security of citizens are few among many more that can be integrated.

The Internet of things (IoT), sensors can gather information from gadgets, peoples and their belongings. This information would be further assessed using data analytics tools and intelligence could be added using Artificial Intelligence techniques. It could be utilized towards ongoing environmental challenges, for resource optimization, service administration and many more. City authorities can screen real-time information about the ongoing activities of the city. This could be one of the ways where government or the board individuals can keep a track about the troubles faced by their citizens and improve the quality standards. Active participation of citizens and governments is widely expected which will lead to a positive change in the general public standards (Smart city, 2019). A solution development towards designing it should be done by keeping in mind the two important objectives: sustainability and citizen-friendly.

Urbanization growth is also one of the important factors which depict the need for smart cities. Due to very few facilities in rural areas, more and more people are migrating towards urban areas. As per the UN report, two out of every three people will live in cities by 2050 (UN report, 2019). To handle this much of urban population, detailed planning of urban areas concerning to resource constraints, economic and environmental demands concerning air, water resources; health, education and transportation services, etc. is highly required.

From all these highlighted areas and current need to cater population and governance, it can be concluded that smart cities are the need for the development of any growing country. Thus all over the world, government officials are spending huge money to drive social transformation and make these projects realistic in upcoming times. Across the globe, Governments launched several projects. Smart city strategy is adopted by many cities such as Manchester, Dubai, Singapore, New York, Taipei, Amsterdam, City of Columbus and many more. If we talk about India, Prime Minister Narendra Modi announced his mission in 2015, about making 100 smart cities across the country (Smart Cities Mission, 2016). Government prepared a budget of approx. Rs 201,981 crore on various projects under this mission and it was expected that 20 cities would accomplish the objective of the smart city by 2021 (Hindustan Times, 2019). Not only government bodies, researchers and academicians also wanted to be the part of this success story of transformation. Some solutions in terms of digitization of data, online education, e-health services, affordable housing, better road connectivity, mobile computing, etc. are already developed but still there is a need of more adaptive and sustainable solutions (Features, 2019) (Rana, 2018) (Yin, 2015).

Transportation is one of the important sectors that need to be looked into for development of smart cities. Lee's report also recommends that **Intelligent Transportation System (ITS)** is an important stepping stone for completion of smart cities mission (Lee, 2014). One of the goals of ITS is to provide better public conveyance, efficient connectivity and better road infrastructure to the citizens (Mehta, 2019). However, this is just the basic requirement, on top of that, the main objective of ITS is to create and provide a digital platform which will effectively manage the traffic and transportation system. Travelers' wellbeing and their connectivity among themselves, can be guaranteed up to certain extent with ITS.

ITS can provide prior information about traffic, which saves the travelling time of the user. An efficient parking management system, one payment policy for all toll payments of city, guidance about the short and less congested routes in real-time, dynamic traffic lights, traffic awareness and prediction for a better driving experience, Wi-Fi support and a good internet connection while driving, safe driving and many more has been expected from ITS. Proficient use of infrastructure and connectivity among the vehicles provide useful information. This information is helpful for all kinds of travelers either by buses or by their own vehicles. Daily commuters can become acquainted about the bus timings, availability of seats in a bus, and the present location of the bus, etc. Government has taken various initiatives, reserved funds and grants for the improvement of this sector while automotive ventures are paying special attention to their research cell so that they can come up with some intelligent, adaptive and smart traffic solutions.

We have already achieved a level in terms of a variety of applications such as accessing the real-time maps to judge a route on various metrics such as congestion, distance, time and many more. The artificial intelligence-enabled vehicles can guide the driver about wearing of seat belt, fuel availability, opening of door, road conditions, etc. All this innovation is feasible due to the integration of technology and automobiles. Now, we have onboard units through which vehicles communicate with each other as well as with the infrastructure units. These all provides lots of benefits in many terms such as reducing the accidents rate, saving the commuter's time, locating the vehicle, reduction of fuel consumption, safety and many more. In some urban communities of the world, cameras have been installed to screen the traffic movement and regulate traffic flow. Still there is need of more intelligence in the cameras, so that it can differentiate among the pedestrians, privately owned vehicles, and public conveyance, etc.

A smart tag helps in toll collection and makes the traffic movement easy and fast (Rodrigo, 2015). Smart centers are also in the development phases which can help in saving the life of a person by alarming the nearby hospitals and police authorities in an emergency. Other passerby could be informed about the incident so that they can help in re-route the traffic (VDOT, 2019). There are smart highways which detect the violation of traffic signal by a vehicle, over speeding of a vehicle, etc.; issues a challan and inform the traffic management authorities for suitable action. One of the systems which maintain the information about travelers and their drivers so that users can decide about their trip based on the mode of travel and departure timings (ITS, 2019).

There are navigation apps by which the user can plan their trip and avoid the congested route. Even with the use of navigation apps, sometimes the user stuck in a situation where no possible alternative routes are available. **Traffic congestion** is a major issue in cities all over India and worsening day by day (Traffic, 2015). The traffic congestion leads to carbon dioxide emissions which have a direct impact on air quality. Due to this, many parameters are getting compromised like our health, time and money.

In India, the person spends approximately 90 minutes in travelling. This time depicts only to and fro time from house to the office. It does not include travelling time for eating out, shopping, etc. If that would be included then the average time spent by a person would be too large. One of the reports says that the four cities (Delhi, Mumbai, Kolkata and Bangalore) collectively cost 22 billion a year in traffic jams (Traffic, 2018). India is not the only country affected by this problem. Rather all over the world, this problem is becoming a giant and harming the life of people. One of the statistics of the U.S. shows that 1.9 billion gallon fuel gets wasted due to traffic jams. It is more than the worth of five days of fuel consumption (Sitting & fuming: traffic congestion statistics, 2019).

There are several reasons of traffic congestion such as poor road infrastructure, less number of traffic police personnel's for regulating the traffic, the high volume of vehicles, less public transportation, fixed duration of traffic signals, etc. (Shamsher, 2015). The quantity of vehicles has additionally expanded due

Figure 1. Traffic congestion scenario (News, 2019)

to the increasing population. Almost all the families have a vehicle in their home. To maintain societal stature and sometimes needs also, some families have more than one vehicle. A statistics show that approximately 54K vehicles were bought every day in 2018 in comparison to 18K a decade ago (News, 2019).

The ever-increasing nature of vehicles has caused even small intersections to be equipped with traffic lights. In India, at almost every intersection, traffic lights have been installed. These lights, intended to decrease congestion by managing movement and also decrease accident risk. In cities, traffic lights are one of the reasons for traffic jams (Driving, 2019). Too much traffic on one side of the road could not pass through because of fixed traffic light timings. The very dynamic nature of traffic movement causes congestion to form around an intersection easily. This congestion leads towards increased **waiting time** for every vehicle. Waiting for the signal to turn green, a person loses its precious time and the vehicle loses fuel. The waiting time would be a major problem for emergency vehicles where every second matter. Owing to these situations, sometimes the people missed out their flight or train. Even in some situations, we are unable to provide the aid on time to a patient and we have to bear this by the cost of the patient's life.

Majority of the **traffic signaling systems** are based on fixed-time approach. The fixed green-time is calculated as a result of surveys done over a period. These methods assume a predetermined time for aside. This is quite helpful when the traffic conditions match those of the average conditions calculated via the surveys. This approach becomes inefficient with increasing traffic and its dynamic nature. It does not manage traffic efficiently. This inefficiency of the fixed traffic light system brought the need for some kind of dynamic approach. Thus, bringing in real-time traffic control systems has become necessary to solve the issue. The concept of dynamic traffic light not only just takes into account the volume of traffic at every side; it also considers the unexpected situations such as any accident, emergency vehicle presence, etc. Dynamic traffic signaling can handle the traffic in an optimized way which reduces the vehicles waiting time. This effective managing of traffic also saves fuel which in turn saves money and makes the economical prosperous.

Our main objective is to make the intersections more attentive about the presence of nearby traffic. This will optimize the traffic flow which indirectly minimizes the vehicles waiting time at the intersection.

Traffic environment can behave more intelligently with the machine learning algorithms. The primary aim of this work is to explore the machine learning algorithms to provide an intelligent traffic environment where the objective is to manage traffic signals efficiently and thus reducing traffic congestion.

To fulfill the stated purpose, the chapter presents two algorithms, Deep-Learning based Traffic Signaling (DLTS) and Q-Learning based Traffic Signaling (QLTS). DLTS algorithm identifies the presence of vehicles on each side of the intersection using image processing. By analyzing the situation, the algorithm proposes dynamic green-light timings rather than fixed timings. While in the QLTS algorithm, there is an agent who decides the state of the traffic light based on a cumulative reward. The performance of the algorithms has been compared in different scenarios. These algorithms also take into account the presence of an emergency vehicle. Thus, the priority is also given to the emergency vehicle, without green light delay.

The rest of the article is structured as follows. The following section 2 presents the findings of various researchers on the highlighted issue. Section 3 and 4 discuss about the proposed work and technologies used for implementing the proposed approach respectively. The implementation details and results have been discussed in the section 5. Lastly, section 6 presents the conclusion of the chapter.

RELATED WORK

To alleviate the issue of traffic congestion, researchers put their hands together and connecting various technologies for providing the solution. Numerous techniques like neural network, image processing, genetic algorithm, reinforcement learning, fuzzy logic and many more has been applied either individually or in combination to assign the green light timings at an intersection. These findings are summarized as follows:

In (Hawi, 2017), authors built up a smart traffic light for an individual intersection roundabout. Authors started with the idea of deploying sensors on the road to collect the continuous traffic information. However, in simulation, they utilized the synthetic data. This information is being processed and then this data in terms of traffic amount and average waiting time is being fed into the fuzzy logic controller. It provides the output in terms of priority degree, which gives the green light timings for a specific lane. In another work done by Araghi et al. for minimizing the travelling delay (Araghi, 2014), they have applied the neural network as well as fuzzy logic. Authors proved that both, neural network and fuzzy logic, performed equally well but surely better than fixed light timings. Both the approaches used the genetic algorithm to find the optimal values of parameters.

Some authors have combined neural network with fuzzy logic for controlling of the traffic signal. In (Zang, 2006), authors developed a fuzzy model based on expert's knowledge. This model has been tuned and transformed into fuzzy neural network model by optimizing the system parameters with the proposed learning technique. Soh et al. (Soh, 2011) proposed an Adaptive Neural-Fuzzy Inference System controller by consolidating the advantages of both fuzzy logic and neural network. This controller was simulated on a model developed using M/M/1 queuing theory. The proposed controller has been compared with the fuzzy and other traditional controllers on various metrics such as average waiting time, queue length and delay time. Royani et al. (Royani, 2013) have also applied fuzzy neural network for controlling the traffic light timings. They have also used the genetic algorithm for setting the parameters. They simulated their FNN based approach in MATLAB and compared it with the fixed timing approach and found that the proposed one is better.

In another research (Chao, 2008), Chao et al. have tried to solve the problem of congestion using extension neural network. Extension neural network combines extension theory into neural network. Extension theory is used for classification of traffic as high, medium and low traffic flow at a particular crossroad. Based on this diagnosis, next cycle green light timings were predicted.

Maheswari et al. (Maheshwari, 2015) have discussed the wastage of two important resources, time and fuel due to increase in traffic congestion at the intersections. Authors proposed the idea of installing the cameras on red lights. Then, these feeds would be analyzed to get the traffic density count using image processing techniques. This information is further utilized to set the traffic light timings. Here, all type of vehicles is treated as same which can make a question mark on the proposed concept. In this article (Maheshwari, 2015), authors just discussed their idea; they have not shown any results.

Bui et al. (Bui, 2016) proposed the dynamic traffic light control based on theory of synchronization. The controller at the every intersection has been considered in the article for traffic flow. Whenever vehicle crosses the intersection, it contacts the controller at the intersection. Vehicles communicate among themselves so that their average waiting time would be reduced. In this article (Chen, 2016), based on the historical traffic data future traffic has been predicted. An optimized traffic light signaling based on this predicted traffic has been suggested in the article.

Abdoos et al. (Abdoos, 2011) have clarified the need of dynamic traffic light timings as per the traffic situation. They represented the network of traffic lights as a system of intelligent agents, where each agent controls an individual intersection. They employed Q-learning technique for adjusting the traffic light timings. In (Moghaddam, 2015), authors used fuzzy along with Q-learning. Fuzzy logic is used to set the states and actions of Q-learning variables. In (Araghi, 2013), authors compared the proposed NN approach for traffic signal control with Q-learning approach proposed by Abdoos et al. (Abdoos, 2011) and fixed timing approach. Araghi et al. shown that Q-learning is impractical in traffic light control and NN approach is superior (Araghi, 2013).

Researchers have also applied deep convolutional neural network for vehicle recognition (Adu-Gyamfi, 2017). They claimed that finer level vehicle classification is possible with the proposed model. From the surveyed literature, it can be said that the traffic congestion is an important issue that needs attention. By adjusting the different traffic light timings, this problem can be solved till some level. However, the various issues such as algorithms for multi intersections, synchronization of traffic lights, consideration of emergency vehicles by giving priority to them, exploration of machine learning algorithms for traffic light timings, different traffic scenarios such as peak hours, diversified traffic during different hours of the day, are still missing in the research work.

PROPOSED WORK

The major goal of the work is to limit the waiting time at an intersection. To achieve this objective, two techniques Deep learning and Q-Learning have been applied to implement dynamic traffic signaling. Deep learning based traffic signaling (DLTS) algorithm works on the concept of density score. The density is calculated at each junction based on volume of the traffic and classified as high, medium or low. The Greedy approach was used to decide the green times of individual sides of an intersection. Q-learning based traffic signaling (QLTS) algorithm view each intersection as an intelligent agent. The position and speed of approaching vehicles are known to the agent. During learning, the agent is able to learn about the current state and action required to perform. This helps the agent to change the traffic signals based on the current state. Both the proposed algorithms detect the quantity of vehicles, as well as presence of emergency vehicles at an intersection. It changes the traffic signals based on the priority and congestion level of all sides of an intersection. For more clarity about the intelligent traffic management, the proposed work is divided into three subsections, which are explained as follows:

DLTS Algorithm

DLTS algorithm works on the basis of density score. The first task is to detect the number of vehicles at any four way intersection. In this work, a tensor flow based model, using the SSD technique has been used for detecting the number of vehicles at the intersection. Merely taking into account the number of vehicles is not sufficient to decide about density at any intersection. A broader road with 100 vehicles would be less congested than a narrow road with 100 vehicles. Thus, there is a need of calculating density score. To calculate the density score, a weight to every vehicle with respect to size of vehicle has been assigned. To calculate the score, each detected object weight is considered as

{"car": 2, "bus": 4,"truck": 4, "person": 0.5, "bicycle": 0.5, "motorcycle": 1}

After the detection of objects, score would be calculated. All the four sides score would be classified as 'high', 'medium' or 'low'. Based on this classification, timings of traffic signal would be determined in a cyclic manner. Any side of the lane can be taken as a starting point. This has been tested and verified with the experiments because it does not effect on efficiency. Thus, for further analysis, our experiments are restricted with the following order, east side has been chosen first followed by south lane. Then west lane and north lane has been chosen.

Figure 2 depicts the work flow diagram of DLTS algorithm. As it can be seen in the top left of the figure that a live feed has been provided to the neural network. Top right part of the figure shows vehicle detection using single shot multibox detection. Average density score would be calculated based on the equation provided in bottom right part of the figure. In the equation, n and w represents the total number of vehicles and weight assigned to vehicle respectively. x_i represents the count of a particular type of vehicle. Greedy approach has been used for changing the traffic signals.

DLTS Algorithm with Emergency Vehicle Detection

DLTS algorithm decides the traffic light timings in accordance with the congestion on all sides of the network. There may be a scenario in which one side of the lane has low frequency of vehicles in comparison to all other sides of the intersection. Assuming a situation where an emergency vehicle ambulance or fire emergency vehicle waiting on that side. Priority should be given to the emergency vehicle in such a scenario. Thus, DLTS algorithm has been modified as per the need of emergency vehicle detection. HAAR Cascades has been used for detecting the emergency vehicles in the live feed. If an emergency vehicle is present, then higher priority is given to them. That particular side becomes green until it passes. Step by step procedure of DLTS algorithm with emergency vehicle detection has been provided in figure 3. The algorithm runs till the live feed is coming. Live feed is stored as a video and processed frame by frame. DLTS algorithm changes the traffic signals in accordance with the Classify_density function.

Figure 2. Work Flow Diagram of DLTS Algorithm

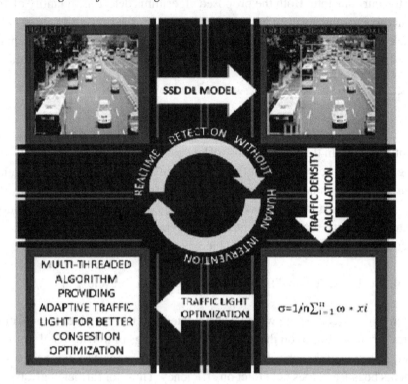

QLTS Algorithm

QLTS algorithm considers the velocity of vehicles along with the position of vehicles. The first two steps of Q-learning are mainly the defining of agent and its action. The agent would choose an action in the environment, so that the reward would be maximized. Here, the intersection is considered as an agent. This agent would chose an action based on calculating the total time for which the vehicles waited on the red signal. Agent will look at the current state and decide the next action. Here, two states have been considered, horizontal lanes as one state and vertical lanes as another state. Agent will decide about the change in the state on the basis of predicted Q-value. Either it will keep the state same or it would be changed. Agent either makes the light green with respect to horizontal lane or vertical lane. Agent will chose any of the following

(i)   Turn the green light on for the roads which are horizontal. It is represented as numeric zero.
(ii)   Turn the green light on for roads which are vertical. It is represented as numeric one.

Whenever the agent decide about the change i.e. suppose vertical is green and agent decides that horizontal will now become green, vertical become red or vice-versa. Traffic light has to undergo the green-yellow-red transition and it will function as follows:

(i)   The light changes to yellow for vehicles going straight.
(ii)   The light changes to red for vehicles going straight.

Figure 3. DLTS Algorithm with Emergency Vehicle Detection

```
While video playing

Fetch a frame of the video

Set density  score=[0,0,0,0] ([E, S, W,N])

        Initialize 'E' green_time = 30sec, 'S' green_time=60sec, 'W' green_ time=90sec and 'N' green_time=120sec.

Present_lane='E'

Next_lane ='S'

LABEL: Subtract 1sec from each side.

While (Present_lane green time != 0),   /*Check if there is an emergency vehicle currently present in the frame. */

                if( emergencyVehicle=present)

                        while( emergencyVehicle==present)

                                Keep the signal green

                else if( emergencyVehicle!=present)

                        Skip this step and follow next step.

Calculate density_score of the Next  lane   /* using SSD object detection */

Call Fn_Classify_density()

Present_lane='S'

Next_lane ='W'    /*Present_lane and Next_lane variables would be changed in the cyclic order */

GO TO LABEL


Fn_Classify_density()

                if density_score>40

                        traffic=high

                        green_time=40

                elseif density_score>30

                        traffic=medium

                        green_time=30
```

(iii) The light changes to yellow for vehicles turning towards left.
(iv) The light changes to red for vehicles turning towards left.

   Here, green light duration is considered as 10 seconds and yellow light duration is considered as 6 seconds. The state consists of a position vector, velocity vector and the light state. It is passed to the neural network as inputs. Neural network has been initialized with some random weights. The output of the neural network is a Q value which is predicted considering the reward to be maximized. Step by step procedure of QLTS algorithm is defined in figure 4.

As explained before, agent decides the action to achieve the goal. Based on its decision, either it has to be rewarded or punished. If the waiting time is decreased in comparison to the previous iteration, then agent gets a reward else it would be punished. At each iteration, two observations with respect to waiting time of the vehicles, $r1$ and $r2$ has been recorded, one at the beginning of the time stamp and one at the end. Finally, the total reward would be $R=r1-r2$.

Figure 4. Working of QLTS Algorithm

```
positionMatrix = [ ]
velocityMatrix = [ ]

While video playing
        Populate values in position matrix with 1 and 0
        Populate values in velocity matrix with the present velocity of the vehicle
        Pass both the matrix to the neural network as input
        Initialize the neural network with random weights
        Add convolution plus relu layers for accurate results
        Neural network selects a Q state for which the reward is maximized
        if Q value > previous Q value
                Agent does a traffic signal transition
                        -The light changes for vehicles going straight to yellow
                        -The light changes for vehicles going straight to red
                        -The light changes for vehicles turning left to yellow
                        -The light changes for vehicles turning left to red
        else
                No need to do traffic signal transition
```

The following section gives a brief overview about the technologies used for implementing the proposed idea.

TECHNOLOGIES USED

The following technologies have been used to implement the proposed idea for changing the traffic signals dynamically as per the real time traffic appearing at any busy road intersection.

OpenCV

A library, OpenCV has been designed to solve the issues of computer vision. Mat object is the essential data structure in OpenCV. It stores pictures and their segments. OpenCV provides simple and helpful approaches for reading and writing the images. It supports wide variety of computer programming languages. To save or show an image in OpenCV, the image needs to be either in BGR or Grayscale, else there are undesirable effects. OpenCV python is a wrapper for the original C++ openCV implementation. OpenCV contains numerous useful and simple functions for applying linear algebra on images. In openCV, all the images are converted to numpy arrays. It makes the integration with the matplotlib and sklearn libraries of python simpler. Figure 5 gives an idea of processing frames using OpenCV for object detection.

Figure 5. Usage of OpenCV for object detection

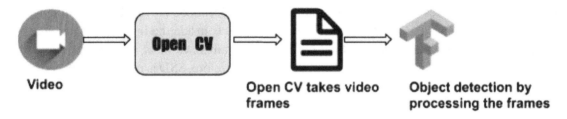

Neural Network

The inspiration of Neural Networks (NN) is the human brain. A NN is made up of two components, a neuron and a network. A neuron is a something that stores a numeric digit which is more than 0 but less than 1. Neurons collectively made a layer of the network. Zero signifies black image whereas one signifies a white image. The number inside the neuron is called its activation. Each neuron fires up when its activation number has a greater value (Neural, 2019). Figure 6 depicts the working behavior of a neural network.

Figure 6. Functioning of Neural Network

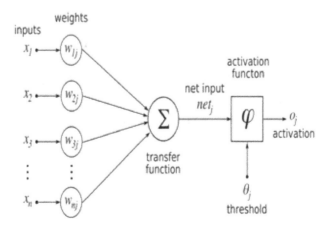

Actually, training a model means an optimization problem is to be taken into consideration that is the weights inside the model need to be optimized. Here, a widely used optimizer, stochastic gradient descent (SGD) has been used. Stochastic Gradient Descent (SGD) is a modified version of standard gradient descent algorithm which computes the gradient and updates the weight matrix on small batches of training data. It does not take into account the entire training set in one go. Its main purpose is to minimize the loss function. The loss function is the error between the predicted data and the original data. SGD would be assigning the weights such that the loss function would be minimized. During training, the data would be supplied with labels attached to it.

SingleShot MultiBox Detection

Single shot multibox detection is a popular algorithm for object identification. It works on the basis of a small set of default boxes of varying aspect ratios at various locations is evaluated. By utilizing SSD, we just need to take one single shot to identify multiple objects inside the image, while regional pro-posal network (RPN) based approaches like R-CNN series requires two shots, one for generating region proposals, one for recognizing the object of each proposal. Therefore, SSD is much faster in comparison to two-shot RPN-based approaches.

The SSD detector differs from others single shot detectors due to the usage of multiple layers that provide a finer accuracy on objects with different scales. Object localization and classification is done in single forward pass of network. This Single Shot Multibox Detection (SSD) framework can be used with Kalman filter for vehicle tracking and detection in autonomous vehicles. For each box, the shape offset and confidences of the object categories are predicted by comparing to the training values.

Figure 7. Working of Single Shot Multibox Detection

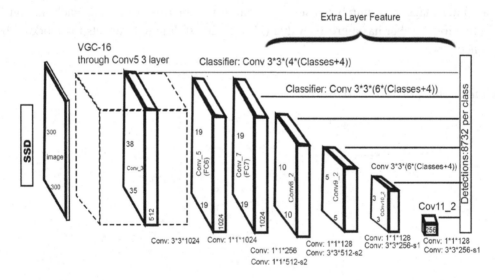

Haar Cascades

Haar Cascades are classifiers that are based on haar features. Let us take an example of detection of human faces. Generally, the areas around the eyes are darker than the areas on the cheeks. One example of a Haar-like feature for face detection is therefore a set of two neighboring rectangular areas above the eye and cheek regions (Viola, 2001). A cascade classifier is a combination of a set of weak classifiers used to create a stronger classifier. Weak classifiers are those whose performances are not so good in prediction. They don't have the ability to reach limits of state of the art classification models. Strong classifiers on the other hand are really good at classifying data correctly (Face, 2019). Figure 8 shows how HAAR Cascades are trained.

Haar cascades are trained on haar features. Haar features are simply a summation of rectangles and differences of those areas across the image.

Figure 8. Working of HAAR Cascades

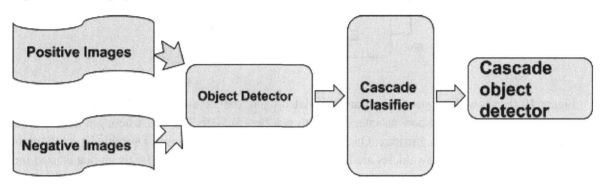

Reinforcement Learning

Reinforcement Learning (RL) is one of the stirring subjects of Artificial Intelligence. All goals can be described by maximizing expected cumulative reward. Our state (Information State) has to have the Markov property: future is independent of the past given the present. If the environment is fully observable (observation = environment state = agent state), the decision process is a MDP. MDPs formally describe an environment for RL. Almost all RL problems can be formalized as MDPs. It has been popular since 1960's, constructing many fascinating applications over the years, in particular in games and in machine learning. But a rising took place in 2010 when researchers demonstrated a machine that could play just about any Atari game from scratch defeating humans in most of them using only raw pixels as inputs and without any prior knowledge of rules. They applied power of Deep Learning to the field of Reinforcement Learning and it went beyond their dreams.

In Q Learning part of Reinforcement Learning, an agent makes observations and takes actions within an environment, and in return it receives rewards as shown in figure 9. The objective of a Q Learning agent is to take action in a way such that current and future rewards are maximized and the penalty is minimized.

(i)   States: States are defined by taking location and velocity of vehicle at an intersection into consideration. From the intersection, vehicle's coordinates and velocity are fetched. The intersection is considered as a square matrix. The length of the matrix makes sure that no two vehicles can come in the same box of the matrix and a single vehicle can be set into a box so that the computation is minimized. In each box of the matrix, the state can be considered as a set < location, velocity > of the vehicle found inside the box. The location value denotes a 0 or 1 value, which tells if there is a vehicle in the box. Value 1 in the box means that a vehicle is present and 0 tells that vehicle is not present. The velocity part is a numerical value, depicting the vehicle's present velocity.

Figure 9. Simple Q-Learning Algorithm

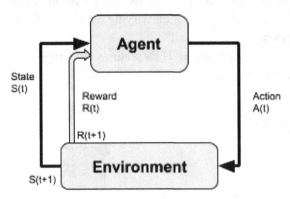

Figure 10 (b) shows how state values are calculated using the location and velocity matrices. This figure 10 (b) is showing that how an intersection to can be visualized for constructing a matrix. The intersection is represented as a matrix. One cell represents one grid. In case of vehicle is not there, it is considered as zero, while if vehicles are there, it is represented with 1. Similar technique is used for velocity matrix formation.

(ii) Action Space: The traffic signal is responsible for choosing an action based on the current state. For this work, choosing every lane's time span in the subsequent cycle specifies the action part. Although, if time span varies between two consecutive cycles, project may become precarious. Thus, the valid lane's time span at the present state should evenly vary. In the depiction, the traffic signal only alters one lane's time span.

Figure 10. Composition of Matrix with a view of Intersection

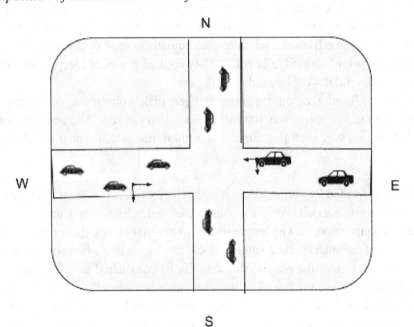

Let's take the intersection in figure 10 (a) as an example. There are four lanes, N-S, E-N and W-S, E-W, and E-S and W-N green. The other lanes are red by default. Let's not consider the yellow light as of now, which will be presented later. In the cycle, four chosen tuple < t1, t2, t3, t4 > shows the time duration at four lanes. Possible action is shown in figure 11 for the next cycle.

Figure 11. Traffic Light Scenario representation using Markov decision Process

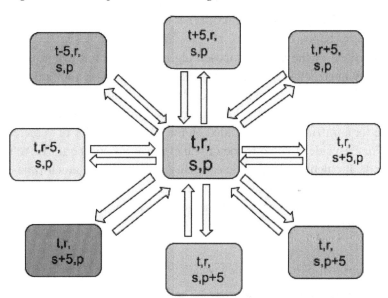

The tuple in circle of figure 11 represents the timings of four sides in a single cycle. The four dimension of a tuple represents the number of sides at an intersection. All sides' traffic timings would be changed cyclically in a sequence. Present state gets transited to the next state after 5 seconds. Out of all the four phases' timings, only one side timings would be added or subtracted by 5 seconds in the next cycle. After selecting the phases' timings in the next cycle, the chosen one becomes the present timings. Additionally the valid maximum and minimum values of a side is taken as 60 and 0 seconds respectively.

(iii) Reward: The differentiating factor which makes Reinforcement learning stand on a higher rank from other learning algorithms is Reward. Reward provides a way to communicate the feedback on previous actions. Thus, defining reward correctly is an instrumental task to navigate the learning, which helps in taking the appropriate action. The main goal is to augment the performance of the agent, which is an intersection. The metric considered, as the efficiency is vehicle's average waiting time. Rewards/ punishment have to be given to agent at each time step. If agent reduces the waiting time, it reduces congestion. Two different observations have been recorded during each time step, once at beginning of the time step ($r1$) and another at end ($r2$). By calculating the difference between them i.e. ($r1 - r2$), it would be decided that this is a reward or punishment. We punish the agent if its actions result in the increment of the waiting time and reward if waiting time is decreased.

The following section discusses the implementation details and results of the proposed algorithms.

IMPLEMENTATION DETAILS AND RESULTS

The following section discusses the details for testing the performance of proposed algorithms. Both the proposed algorithms DLTS and QLTS have been compared with fixed traffic light signaling approach. For fixed timing approach, 23 sec of green light time has been set. This value has been taken in reference to the article by Abdoos (Abdoos, 2011).

To test the performance of the above proposed algorithms, the following assumptions have been considered. A four way intersection with traffic signal installed on all four sides is considered. Each road leading to the intersection is a three lane road. Rightmost lane is used for vehicles going towards right direction. Leftmost lane is used for vehicles going towards left and middle one is going towards straight. Green time for a traffic signal is decided on the basis of density of vehicles currently waiting at a traffic signal. For each side, a video frame of vehicles waiting for the traffic to turn green is given to the neural network. It calculates the vehicle density score and the green time is generated using DLTS algorithm. Figure 12 (a) and (b) shows the vehicle detection in a single lane at an intersection and emergency vehicle detection respectively. Emergency vehicles are detected using HAAR cascades as explained in above sections.

Figure 12. (a) Vehicle detection (b) Emergency vehicle detection

Figure 13 shows the GUI of implemented DLTS algorithm. It can be visualized from the figure 13; there is a four way junction with traffic signals on each side and vehicles gets detected. Based on the density or presence of emergency vehicle, timings of traffic signals becoming red, yellow or green gets changed.

Figure 13. GUI of Implemented DLTS Algorithm

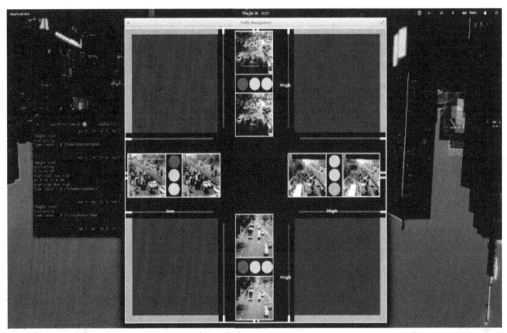

For QLTS algorithm, the input to neural networks is of the format (P, V, and L) which is depicted in figure 14. The convolution filter, first layer consists of 16 filters of 4*4 sizes with stride as 2. Second layer has 32 filters of size 2*2 with stride as 1. ReLU activation function has been applied in both the layers. The third layer is fully connected layer of size 128 and fourth layer is having size 62. For possible actions from agent, final linear layer gives Q values.

Figure 14. Workflow Diagram of Neural Network

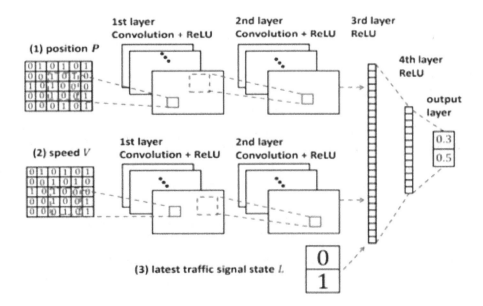

To test the results, SUMO (Simulation of Urban Mobility) simulator (SUMO, 2019) has been used. SUMO is an open source road simulation package that simulates traffic behavior, allows for road network construction, traffic light policy implementation, and traffic data collection. Traci (Traffic Control Interface) Library helps in fetching the exact position and velocity of vehicles and interaction with the simulator. Total waiting time per episode at an intersection would be calculated. Figure 15 shows the simulation of QLTS algorithm.

Figure 15. Simulation of QLTS algorithm

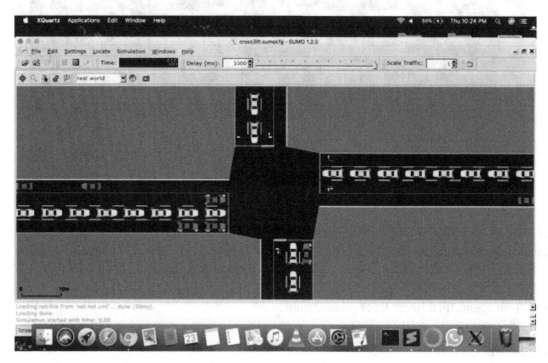

For testing of results, two scenarios with respect to different timings of the day have been considered, rush hours and normal hours. Generally, due to office hours, there is more traffic in the morning and evening hours. Rush hours is actually depicting the morning and evening hours. Thus, in simulation, numbers of vehicles were significantly higher in first scenario in comparison to the second scenario. As the main aim of the proposed algorithms to reduce the waiting time of the vehicles at the traffic light, thus, DLTS and QLTS algorithms has been compared with fixed traffic light signaling approach on the metric, average waiting time. During each simulation run, to represent a heavy traffic, 1200 vehicles have been taken into account for simulation. The chosen time interval is of 1.5 hour. A learning rate of value .0002 for the agent has been decided and size of memory is picked up as 200. Simulation has been run for more than 1000 episodes.

It can be visualized from figures 16 and 17 that average waiting time of vehicles is more in fixed traffic signaling approach in comparison to DLTS and QLTS algorithm. Average waiting time in scenario 1 is more in comparison to scenario 2 which is obvious because of more number of vehicles on the roads during rush hours of the day. As number of episodes is increasing, the QLTS performance becomes better.

Figure 16. Average Waiting Time in Scenario 1

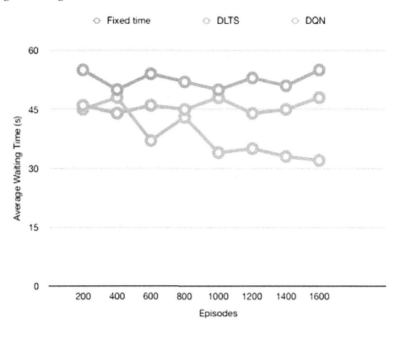

Figure 17. Average Waiting Time in Scenario 2

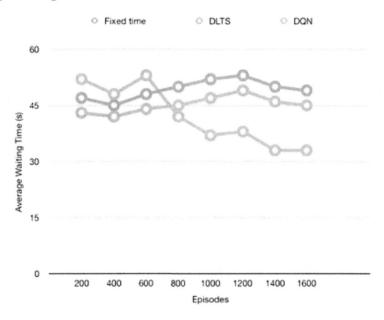

In SUMO, traffic arrival process is probabilistic. It has been observed in the simulation that generated traffic from E-W side is comparatively higher than N-S side. So, green light is required to be turn on more for E-W by an ideal agent. Thus, in this situation, fixed time traffic signaling does not perform well. Total average waiting time in fixed time traffic signaling is approximately 330 seconds, where with DLTS, we achieved the minimum average waiting time as 44 seconds. QLTS performs better than the other two as its minimum average waiting time is 31 seconds, which is about 79% better.

CONCLUSION AND FUTURE WORK

Nowadays, traffic congestion is a critical issue. To handle this issue, the concept of dynamic traffic light signaling using deep learning and Q learning has been proposed. The proposed algorithms signal each side of the traffic light according to the amount of traffic density. This allows a reduced waiting time for the vehicles at the traffic signals. If there is an emergency vehicle at the traffic light, it would be detected and priority would be given to that side of the traffic light. Superiority of QLTS and DLTS algorithms over traditional method of traffic signaling has been illustrated with the results. To get the results, extensive set of experiments has been done using SUMO traffic simulator. Average waiting time of DLTS is less in comparison to fixed time traffic signaling. Even QLTS average waiting time is much lesser in comparison to the other two.

DLTS and QLTS perform better in comparison to traditional traffic signaling algorithm and it has been implemented for a four way intersection. The work can be extended to synchronize traffic signals across multiple intersections. As a future work, it would be interesting to know the performance of these algorithms for a three way intersection.

REFERENCES

Abdoos, M., Mozayani, N., & Bazzan, A. L. (2011, October). Traffic light control in non-stationary environments based on multi agent Q-learning. In *2011 14th International IEEE conference on intelligent transportation systems (ITSC)* (pp. 1580-1585). IEEE.

Adu-Gyamfi, Y. O., Asare, S. K., Sharma, A., & Titus, T. (2017). Automated vehicle recognition with deep convolutional neural networks. *Transportation Research Record: Journal of the Transportation Research Board, 2645*(1), 113–122. doi:10.3141/2645-13

Araghi, S., Khosravi, A., & Creighton, D. (2014, July). Optimal design of traffic signal controller using neural networks and fuzzy logic systems. In *2014 International Joint Conference on Neural Networks (IJCNN)* (pp. 42-47). IEEE. 10.1109/IJCNN.2014.6889477

Araghi, S., Khosravi, A., Johnstone, M., & Creighton, D. (2013, October). Intelligent traffic light control of isolated intersections using machine learning methods. In *2013 IEEE International Conference on Systems, Man, and Cybernetics* (pp. 3621-3626). IEEE. 10.1109/SMC.2013.617

Bui, K. H. N., Lee, O. J., Jung, J. J., & Camacho, D. (2016, June). Dynamic Traffic Light Control System Based on Process Synchronization Among Connected Vehicles. In *International Symposium on Ambient Intelligence* (pp. 77-85). Springer. 10.1007/978-3-319-40114-0_9

Chao, K. H., Lee, R. H., & Wang, M. H. (2008, September). An intelligent traffic light control based on extension neural network. In *International Conference on Knowledge-Based and Intelligent Information and Engineering Systems* (pp. 17-24). Springer. 10.1007/978-3-540-85563-7_8

Chen, Y. R., Chen, K. P., & Hsiungy, P. A. (2016, November). Dynamic traffic light optimization and Control System using model-predictive control method. In *2016 IEEE 19th International Conference on Intelligent Transportation Systems (ITSC)* (pp. 2366-2371). IEEE 10.1109/ITSC.2016.7795937

Driving Tests. (2019, July). *How do traffic jams form*. Retrieved from: https://www.drivingtests.co.nz/resources/how-do-traffic-jams-form/

Face Detection Using OpenCV With Haar Cascade Classifiers. (2019, August). Retrieved from https://becominghuman.ai/face-detection-using-opencv-with-haar-cascade-classifiers-941dbb25177

Features of Smart Cities. (2019, July). Retrieved from: https://www.bestcurrentaffairs.com/features-of-smart-cities/

Hawi, R., Okeyo, G., & Kimwele, M. (2017, July). Smart traffic light control using fuzzy logic and wireless sensor network. In *2017 Computing Conference* (pp. 450-460). IEEE. 10.1109/SAI.2017.8252137

Hindustan Times. (2019, July). Retrieved from: https://www.hindustantimes.com/india-news/20-smart-cities-may-be-ready-only-by-2021/story-g3WNnnHEj8VSDROkTKYWjJ.html

ITS Research Fact Sheets - Benefits of Intelligent Transportation Systems. (2019, July). Retrieved from: https://www.its.dot.gov/factsheets/benefits_factsheet.htm

Lee, J. H., Hancock, M. G., & Hu, M. C. (2014). Towards an effective framework for building smart cities: Lessons from Seoul and San Francisco. *Technological Forecasting and Social Change*, *89*, 80–99. doi:10.1016/j.techfore.2013.08.033

Liang, X., Du, X., Wang, G., & Han, Z. (2019). A Deep Reinforcement Learning Network for Traffic Light Cycle Control. *IEEE Transactions on Vehicular Technology*, *68*(2), 1243–1253. doi:10.1109/TVT.2018.2890726

Maheshwari, P., Suneja, D., Singh, P., & Mutneja, Y. (2015, October). Smart traffic optimization using image processing. In *2015 IEEE 3rd International Conference on MOOCs, Innovation and Technology in Education (MITE)* (pp. 1-4). IEEE. 10.1109/MITE.2015.7375276

Mehta, S., & Kumar, A. (2019). *Towards Inclusive and Sustainable Smart Cities: The Case of Ranchi*. ORF Special Report No. 81. Observer Research Foundation.

Moghaddam, M. J., Hosseini, M., & Safabakhsh, R. (2015, March). Traffic light control based on fuzzy Q-leaming. In *2015 The International Symposium on Artificial Intelligence and Signal Processing (AISP)* (pp. 124-128). IEEE. 10.1109/AISP.2015.7123500

Neural Network Tutorial. (2019, August). Retrieved from https://www.simplilearn.com/neural-networks-tutorial-article

News. (2019, February). Retrieved from: https://www.news18.com/news/india/the-single-statistic-that-shows-why-indian-roads-are-getting-more-congested-each-passing-month-2031835.html

Rana, N. P., Luthra, S., Mangla, S. K., Islam, R., Roderick, S., & Dwivedi, Y. K. (2018). Barriers to the development of smart cities in Indian context. *Information Systems Frontiers*, 1–23.

Rodrigo, A., & Edirisinghe, L. (2015, May). A Study on electronic toll collection systems in expressways in Sri Lanka. In *Proceedings of 8th International Research Conference*. KDU.

Royani, T., Haddadnia, J., & Alipoor, M. (2013). Control of traffic light in isolated intersections using fuzzy neural network and genetic algorithm. *International Journal of Computer and Electrical Engineering, 5*(1), 142–146. doi:10.7763/IJCEE.2013.V5.682

Shamsher, R., & Abdullah, M. N. (2015). Traffic congestion in Bangladesh-causes and solutions: A study of Chittagong metropolitan city. *Asian Business Review, 2*(1), 13–18. doi:10.18034/abr.v2i1.309

Sitting & fuming: traffic congestion statistics. (2019, July). https://static.nationwide.com/static/road-congestion-infographic.pdf?r=52

Smart Cities Definition. (2019, August). Retrieved from https://www.techopedia.com/definition/31494/smart-city

Smart Cities Mission. (2016, August). *Ministry of Urban Development, Government of India.* Retrieved from http://smartcities.gov.in/

Smart City. (2019, August). Retrieved from https://en.wikipedia.org/wiki/Smart_city

Smart City Mission. (2019, July), Retrieved from https://en.wikipedia.org/wiki/Smart_Cities_Mission

Soh, A. C., Rahman, R. Z. A., Rhung, L. G., & Sarkan, H. M. (2011, September). Traffic signal control based on adaptive neural-fuzzy inference system applied to intersection. In *2011 IEEE Conference on Open Systems* (pp. 231-236). IEEE. 10.1109/ICOS.2011.6079251

SUMO Traffic Simulator. (2019, August). Retrieved from http://sumo.sourceforge.net/

Traffic Congestion. (2015, Sept.). Retrieved from: https://www.mapsofindia.com/my-india/society/traffic-congestion-in-delhi-causes-outcomes-and-solutions

Traffic Congestion Costs. (2018, April). Retrieved from: https://timesofindia.indiatimes.com/india/traffic-congestion-costs-four-major-indian-cities-rs-1-5-lakh-crore-a-year/articleshow/63918040.cms

UN Report. (2019, July). Retrieved from https://www.un.org/development/desa/en/news/population/2018-world-urbanization-prospects.html

VDOT. (2019, July). Retrieved from http://www.virginiadot.org/infoservice/smart-default.asp

Viola, P., & Jones, M. (2001). Rapid object detection using a boosted cascade of simple features. *CVPR, 1*(511-518), 3.

Yin, C., Xiong, Z., Chen, H., Wang, J., Cooper, D., & David, B. (2015). A literature survey on smart cities. *Science China. Information Sciences, 58*(10), 1–18. doi:10.100711432-015-5397-4

Zang, L., Jia, L., & Luo, Y. (2006, June). An intelligent control method for urban traffic signal based on fuzzy neural network. In *2006 6th World Congress on Intelligent Control and Automation* (Vol. 1, pp. 3430-3434). IEEE.

Chapter 2
Geocast Routing Protocols for Ad-Hoc Networks:
Comparative Analysis and Open Issues

Indrani Das
Assam University, India

Sanjoy Das
iD https://orcid.org/0000-0001-8018-0870
Indira Gandhi National Tribal University, India

ABSTRACT

Geocasting is a subset of conventional multicasting problem. Geocasting means to deliver a message or data to a specific geographical area. Routing refers to the activities necessary to route a message in its travel from source to the destination node. The routing of a message is very important and relatively difficult problems in the context of Ad-hoc Networks because nodes are moving very fast, network load or traffic patterns, and topology of the network is dynamical changes with time. In this chapter, different geocast routing mechanisms used in both Mobile Ad-hoc Networks and Vehicular Ad-hoc Networks. The authors have shown a strong and in-depth analysis of the strengths and weaknesses of each protocol. For delivering geocast message, both the source and destination nodes use location information. The nodes determine their locations by using the Global Positioning System (GPS). They have presented a comprehensive comparative analysis of existing geocast routing protocols and proposed future direction in designing a new routing protocol addressing the problem.

1. INTRODUCTION

In Ad-hoc networks routing protocols primarily face difficulty in finding an appropriate route from a source node to the destination node. A node in this network frequently changes their locations because of their high mobility. This causes frequent link or connectivity breakage and fragmentation in the network. Therefore, message passing to a particular destination region becomes very difficult and chal-

DOI: 10.4018/978-1-7998-2764-1.ch002

lenging task. In both, Mobile and Vehicular Ad-hoc Networks (VANETs) nodes moves very fast. The node movement depends on the terrain structure. In geocast routing a message or data is delivered to a particular predefined geographical area is known as *geocast region*. The method of message delivery from a particular location i.e. from source to geocast region is known as Geocasting. The main aim of geocasting is to deliver a message within reasonable time, low end-to-end delay, high accuracy i.e., high delivery success ratio, low overheads, and total number of hops be minimum. In this chapter discussed several existing routing protocols for VANETs. These protocols are Geographic Distance Routing (GEDIR)(Ruhil, LOBIYAL, & Stojmenovic, 2005), Voronoi Diagram (Stojmenovic, Ruhil, & Lobiyal, 2003),(Stojmenovic et al., 2003), Voronoi Diagram- Geographic Distance Routing (VD-GEDIR)(Ruhil et al., 2005), Most Forward Progress within Radius (MFR)(Ruhil et al., 2005), Convex Hull (Ruhil et al., 2005)(Stojmenovic et al., 2003)[10,16],Convex Hull Most Forwarding Progress Radius (CH-MFR)(Ruhil et al., 2005), Range Directional (R-DIR)(Ruhil et al., 2005), Location Aided Routing (LAR) (Y. Ko & Vaidya, 1998), Location Based Multicast (LBM) (Y. B. Ko & Vaidya, 2002), Geo Temporally Ordered Routing Algorithm (GeoTORA) (Y. B. Ko & Vaidya, 2000), Geocast Adaptive Environment Routing (GAMER) (Camp, 2003), Adaptive Handshaking- Based Geocasting protocol (AHBG) (Chen, Tseng, & Hu, 2006), GeoGRID (W. Liao, Tseng, Lo, & Sheu, 2000), Geometry Driven Geocasting protocol (GGP)(Lee & Ko, 2006). All of the above protocols may follow flooding, route based or cluster based mechanisms. These protocols are used in MANETs. In VANETs rather than these protocols the following protocols are used-Abiding Geocast (Maihoefer & Leinmueller, 2005), Stored Geocast (Maihöfer, Franz, & Eberhardt, 2003), Cached Greedy Geocast (Maihöfer, Eberhardt, & Schoch, 2004), Probabilistic methods(Yu & Heijenk, 2008), Distributed and Robust Geocast (DRG) (Joshi, 2007), Geocast Routing in Urban Vehicular Ad hoc Networks (GRUV)(Zhang et al., 2009), Intersection Area based Geocast protocol (Das & Lobiyal, 2012; Das & LOBIYAL, 2012). The performance analysis, evaluation, comparisons, reviews and surveys on various geocast protocols for MANET and VANET can be found in (Jiang & Camp, 2002; Maihöfer, 2004; Maihöfer, Cseh, Franz, & Eberhardt, 2003; Ruhil et al., 2005; Schwingenschlogl & Kosch, 2002; Yao, 2004; Yao, Krohne, & Camp, 2004). A comprehensive classification of routing protocols used in VANET is discussed in (Allal & Boudjit, 2012).

The VANETs have some distinguishable characteristics from MANETs. In VANET node have higher mobility and restricted network topology are two main characteristics of that distinguish VANETs from MANETs. The node mobility is fully depends on the terrain structure in the case of VANET.

The main focus of the chapter is the geocast routing protocol exist for MANET as well as VANETs. This chapter includes descriptions of various protocols along with their weaknesses and strengths. Also, focused on various open issues and future directions, which will greatly helpful for research community, new researcher to explore geocast area for both MANET and VANET.

In section 2, discussed the criteria for a geocast routing protocol and existing geocast routing for MANETs and VANETs. In section 3, shown comparison of among various protocols. In section 4, described important characteristics for a future geocast routing protocol. Finally, in section 5 the chapter is summarized.

2. GEOCASTING IN AD-HOC NETWORK

A routing protocol is called geocast routing protocol, if messages from a source nodedelivered to the nodes present in a predefined geographic region known as geocast region in the network. To deliver a geocast message, intermediate nodes present between source and geocast region helps in routing messages to reach to the intended destination. The followings are few basic characteristics of a geocast routing protocol.

a)   A source node generates geocast message and be delivered to all nodes present in the geocast region
b)   A predefined geographic region known as geocast region.
c)   It uses minimum cost forwarding.
d)   Timely dissemination of message to the geocast region.

Figure 1. Classification Geocast Protocols for MANET

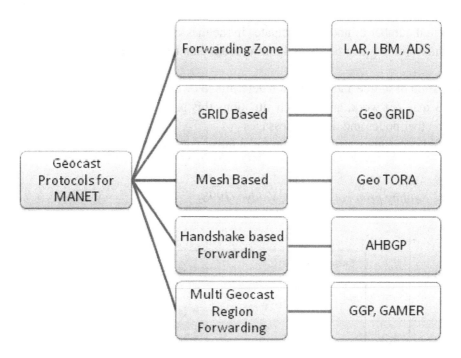

2.1. Geocast Protocols for MANETS

There are various protocols proposed by researchers and academicians in the context of geocasting in Mobile Ad Hoc Networks. We have classified these protocols based on the mechanism they adhere in protocol design. We have identified that geocast protocols proposed for MANET follows forwarding zone, GRID structure and Mesh based techniques for delivery of data to the geocast region. The classifications of these protocols are shown in the figure 1. In the forwarding zone based mechanism, an area between source and geocast region is defined, to minimize the number of messages during communication. The main purpose of this mechanism is to reduce the numbers of participating node. In GRID based mechanism, helps in reducing the number of node participation while messages forwards between source and geocast region. Only one node from each grid participates in message transmission. The Mesh based techniques provides several paths between source and geocast region for better delivery of messages.

2.1.1. Location Aided Routing (LAR)

Y.B.Ko. et al. in (Y. Ko & Vaidya, 1998) proposed two different schemes LAR scheme-1 and LAR scheme-2 shown in figure 2. The location information used between source and destination node to reduce the routing overheads. The locations of nodes are obtained by using GPS receiver attached with every node. In LAR scheme-1, an expected zone is defined for the destination node. The expected zone is a circular area covering last known location of the destination node. The request zone is defined as rectangular area, whose opposite corners are expected zone and source node. In the scheme-2, transmission range of a source determines the request zone. The source node forwards a message to its neighbours that are closer to the destination rather than the source node.

Strength
- ○ Limited number of nodes participates in the message transmission.
- ○ Reduces routing overheads by limiting redundant transmissions.

Weakness
- ○ Location of source and destination determined by GPS receiver. In some geographical region GPS may not work, and in such situations this protocol may not establish communication with other nodes and deliver messages.
- ○ If void occur in expected zone protocol fails to deliver messages.

Figure 2. LAR1 Routing protocol (Y. Ko & Vaidya, 1998)

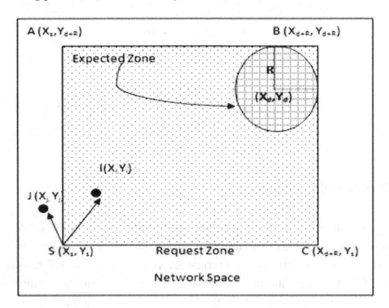

2.1.2. Location-Based Multicast (LBM)

The Location Based Multicast (Y. B. Ko & Vaidya, 2002) and (Y. B. Ko & Vaidya, 2002) protocol uses on restricted flooding mechanism. In this protocol, messages are restricted to a forwarding zone. Any node which does not belong to the forwarding zone shown in figure 3 simply discards the received packets. Two different schemes of LBM namely LBM scheme-1 and LBM scheme-2 are used to forward the geocast packets. In scheme-1, the forwarding zone is the smallest rectangle is drawn between the sender and multicast zone. The area of forwarding zone fully depends on the location of the source node and size of the multicast region. Nodes present within the forwarding zone further transmit packets to its neighbour nodes. Further, the size of forwarding zone is controlled by a parameter δ. If needed forwarding zone is expanded in both X and Y directions by δ. In scheme-2, rather than specifying a forwarding zone, it maintains the following information i) multicast region, ii) center of the multicast region, and iii) coordinate of the sender. Intermediate nodes are receiving multicast packets from the sender, first checks whether it belongs to the multicast region or not. If it belongs to multicast region it accepts the packet otherwise it discard the packet. Further, the intermediate nodes calculate their distance from the center of multicast region, and all transmissions of data are forwarded to the nodes closer to the center of the geocast region.

Strength
- It reduces routing overheads by limiting participating nodes and packet retransmissions.

Weakness
- If no node is present inside the forwarding zone, data transmission to multicast region is not possible.

Figure 3. Forwarding zones in LBM(Y. B. Ko & Vaidya, 2002)

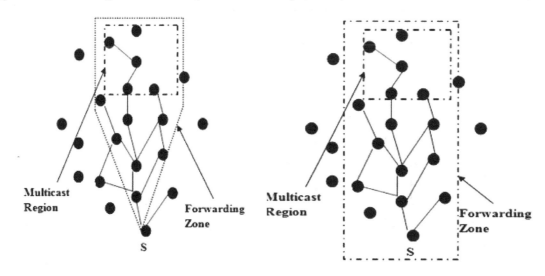

2.1.3. Geo GRID

The Geographical GRID (GeoGRID) routing protocol(Y. B. Ko & Vaidya, 2000) is an extension of GRID (W. H. Liao, Sheu, & Tseng, 2001). Here, network area is partitioned into non overlapping squares called GRID. GeoGRID partitions the network into square of size d × d units 2D logical grids. One node is elected as a gateway node from each grid. Its responsibility to forward the geocast message to its neighbour gateway nodes. The geocast message is only forwarded by the gateway nodes. This method reduces the overheads in the network because except gateway nodes, other nodes are not participating in the transmission of geocast messages. In figure-4 and figure-5 two methods for sending geocast message; Flooding based GeoGRID, Ticket Based GeoGRID is shown respectively. The construction of grid is very important; one value of d (side length of grid) is selected from 2r, r, $r/\sqrt{10}$, $\sqrt{2}r/3$, $r/2\sqrt{2}$, r/10, where *r* is the transmission range of radio signal. In flooding based GeoGRID, only gateway node of each grid participates in transmitting of geocast packets that fall within the forwarding zone. To avoid unnecessary flooding a sequence number is assigned to each transmitted geocast packet. In Ticket Based GeoGRID, source node creates tickets depending on the dimensions of geocast region. If the geocast region having (m×n) grids then source node creates (m+n) tickets. Tickets are evenly distributed among the neighbouring grids of the source node and closer to the geocast region. The forwarding of a message fully depends on the gateway node. The gateway node is elected among nodes in a grid whose physical position is closer to the center of that grid. Once the gateway node is elected, no further election is possible till the elected node does not leave the grid. The problem arises in this gateway election method is when another node comes closer to the center of the grid. To overcome this problem authors suggested multiple gateway nodes should reside temporally in the grid. Both the methods eliminate redundant retransmission of geocast messages, and also maintains high arrival rate of geocast message and lower delivery cost.

Figure 4. Flooding based GeoGRID Protocol (W. Liao et al., 2000)

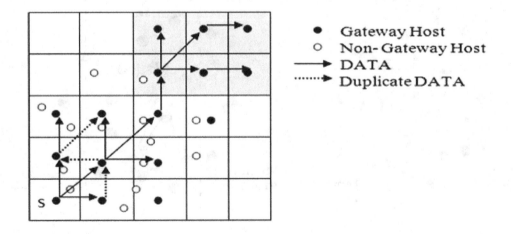

Strength

○ It reduces the redundant retransmissions of messages because only selected gateway nodes from each grid transmit the message.

○ Lesser number of nodes participates in message transmission.

Weakness

○ More than one gateway node present in a grid. No robust mechanism is available to resolve this issue.

○ Performance of the ticket based method is poor.

2.1.4. GeoTORA

The GeoTORA protocol (Y. B. Ko & Vaidya, 2000)is a unicast protocol designed based on Temporally Ordered Routing Algorithm (TORA)(Park & Corson, 2001). Due to the mobility of nodespartitioning among nodes arises, and sometimes no node present inside the geocast region. These problems are addressed in this protocol. In this scheme each geocast group (i.e. set of nodes inside a geocast region) maintains a single directed acyclic graph. The protocol maintains height of each node in the networks as mentioned in(Park & Corson, 2001) and also follows the same link reversal mechanism (Park & Corson, 2001) in case no route is available to the geocast region. GeoTORA is basically the combination of anycast routing and flooding. Anycast routing is used to deliver geocast messages to one of the nodes inside the geocast region by using flooding inside the geocast region. The flooding used here is limited flooding, i.e. it is confined to the members of geocast region only and node outside the region discards the received messages. A sequence number is maintained by nodes inside geocast region to avoid duplicate transmissions. Message delivery is done in three phases- Route Creation, Route Maintenance, and Delivery of geocast message.

Figure 5. Ticket based GeoGRID Protocol (W. Liao et al., 2000)

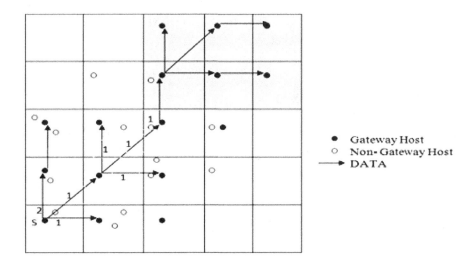

Route creation mechanism is invoked when there is no outgoing link from the forwarding node to geocast region. The route maintenance mechanism is invoked when link failure occurs due to node mobility since nodes join and leave the geocast region. Finally, delivery of geocast message mechanism is invoked to deliver the message and it follows anycast routing and flooding.

Strength
- ○ It combines unicast routing algorithm TORA with flooding.
- ○ Resolves the fragmentation problem arising inside the geocast region due to node mobility.
- ○ It reduces overheads of geocast message delivery, and maintains reasonably high accuracy in data delivery.

Weakness
- ○ In this protocol, sometimes outgoing links from the source are not available for next forwarding nodes. To get rid of this problem route creation and maintenance methods are invoked to find outgoing links. Invoking this method frequently results in increased network overhead and average end-to-end delay.

2.1.5. GAMER

The Geocast Adaptive Mesh Environment for Routing protocol (GAMER)(Camp, 2003) is a mesh based geocast protocol whose primary task is to establish redundant routes from a source node to geocast region. Future data is delivered through these identified routes. The protocol follows source routing, forwarding zones mechanism, and meshes for message delivery. There are two different scheme of GAMER- Passive GAMER and Active GAMER. These methods use two types of packets JOIN-DEMAND and JOIN-TABLE, before transmitting data packets to geocast region. A JOIN-DEMAND packet is forwarded within forwarding zone periodically stillnot reached to the geocast region. The node receives the message within the geocast region sends back a JOIN-TABLE packet through the same path. After receiving the first JOIN-TABLE packet source starts sending geocast packets through the created mesh. It considers different forwarding zones CONE, CORRIDOR, and FLOOD to maintain its performance in dense and sparse network topology. In case of Passive GAMER method JOIN-DEMAND packets are transmitted with a fixed frequency and in Active GAMER, the JOIN-DEMAND packets are periodically sent regardless of receiving a JOIN-TABLE packet.

Strength
- ○ Easily deals with node mobility.
- ○ Data transmission accuracy is good without increasing extra load on the network.
- ○ Data is delivered through one of forwarding zones (CONE, CORRIDOR, and FLOOD) dynamically. When node mobility is high a dense mesh created and in low mobility a sparse mesh is created.

Weakness
- ○ In low mobility Active GAMER introduces high control overheads as compared to Passive GAMER.

2.1.6. AHBG (Adaptive Handshaking- Based Geocasting protocol)

The AHBG (Chen et al., 2006) is a handshaking-based forwarding method. This protocol follows two different modes for data delivery are table driven and handshaking-based to delivery data to a node within the geocast region. Initially, table driven mode is followed for forwarding data to all the nodes. Nodes switch to handshaking mode to find a new route if they fail to find the information of next hop in the table. This information is missed in the table since the record becomes obsolete or the nodes moves away from the sender. A geocast packet sent by a source reaches geocast region with the help of many handshaking forwarding. In figure 6, a data packet is delivered from the source to geocast region by five handshaking-based forwarding techniques. This protocol uses the following control packets for communication are REQUEST, REPLY and ERROR packets. The geocast_id is added in the header of each packet along with source_addr (address of source) and pkt_uid (unique id of packet). For the design and implementation of this protocol following things are considered i) IEEE 802.11 (PHY and MAC), ii) enabled mobile nodes equipped with a wireless based radio and a GPS receiver, iii) source node has the location information of geocast region, and iv) at least one node should be present within the geocast region. In the handshaking mode, a source node first broadcasts REQUEST packet. Nodes present within the radio range of the source node receive the REQUEST message. Further, nodes within the forwarding zone, receiving the message send back a REPLY packet to the source. Once source node receives the REPLY packet, it unicasts DATA packet to the sender of REPLY packet and updates its routing table accordingly. Each node receiving DATA packet continues to forward the packet until it reaches the geocast region. The reliable transmission of DATA packets are done through unicast method. The selection of next node is done on the basis of First REPLY First Select (FRFS) for unicast. But the next hop selection on the basis of FRFS is not always good. Here every replier waits for an interval (defer time + extra time). To compute the interval time, the distance and location of a node is considered. An adaptive forwarding zone is introduced for broadcasting the REQUEST packets. For broadcasting of a REQUEST packet, the protocol chooses different forwarding zones according to the switch timer. The forwarding zones defined in different quadrants are I, II, III and IV. If a sender receives REPLY packet before switch timer expires, it switches gradually from one quadrant to another quadrant.

Strength
- ◦ Packet delivery is high nearly 100% with negligible network overheads.
- ◦ Performance is satisfactory in a densely populated topology with high mobility of nodes.
- ◦ Frequent change in the network topology is easily handled.
- ◦ Highreliability in packet transmission.
- ◦ The '*dead end* 'problem means further communication is not possible is addressed and source node use a control packet, named ERROR.

Weakness
- ◦ Overall performance of the protocol degrades in sparse network.

Figure 6. Adaptive Handshaking-Based Geocast Protocol(Chen et al., 2006)

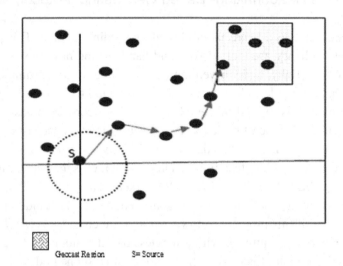

Geocast Region   S= Source

2.1.7. GGP (Geometry Driven Geocasting Protocol)

Geometry Driven Geocasting Protocol (GGP)(Lee & Ko, 2006) is a novel geocast routing scheme, where multiple geocast regions are considered. The protocols discussed above are delivering the messages to a single geocast region only. But, this is the first protocol where message is delivered to multiple geocast regions. The protocol maintains high reliability while deliver a same message to the multiple geocast regions. This protocol follow a tree based structure, and with the fermat point technique shared paths between multiple geocast region are created as shown in figure 7. The Fermat point(Weisstein, 2019) is defined as point inside a triangle for which the sum of its distance from allthe vertices of the triangle is always minimum. The distance from this point to the multiple geocast regions is always optimal. The protocol is able to deliver messages to multiple geocast regions at the same time where as other protocols fail to do the same task.

Strength
  ◦   Message is delivered to the multiple geocast regions.
  ◦   It computes an optimal junction point between source node and all the geocast regions, which significantly reduces the delivery time of geocast messages.
  ◦   Overheads in communication is less..
  ◦   High message delivery ratio.
  ◦   Overall routing cost is minimum.

Weakness
  ◦   The protocol fully depends on computation of Fermat Point. If optimal Fermat point is not decided, the protocol is a total failure.
  ◦   Computation of Fermat Point becomes difficult with increasing number of geocast regions.

Figure 7. Construction of Shared path (Number of geocast region is 2)based on Fermat Point (Lee & Ko, 2006)

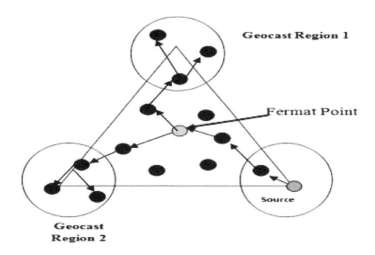

2.1.8 Angular Displacement Scheme (ADS)

Angular Displacement Scheme (ADS)(Onifade, Oju, & Akande, 2008) basically enhances the performance of the protocol proposed in (Y. Ko & Vaidya, 1998) by modifying the forwarding zone. This method reduces the delay introduced in (Y. Ko & Vaidya, 1998) while delivering messages to a geocast region. In this protocol, all the neighbours of a source node rebroadcast the geocast message. Initially for rebroadcasting the geocast message, a source node sets a sequence number i.e.1 for all its neighbours. The packet transmission is limited within the forwarding zone. A source node compares its position with respect to multicast region by calculating the angular displacement. Further, the forwarding zone is computed dynamically based on the calculation of angular displacement occurring for every participating node in the network.

Strength
- ◦ It reduces the message delivery area within forwarding zone.
- ◦ There are lower message delivery overheads.
- ◦ It gives high accuracy in delivery of packets.

Weakness
- ◦ In highly dynamic environment, the performance of the protocol is degrades.

2.2. Geocast routing protocols for VANETs

Geocast routing in VANET is playing many roles. Recent development in the technology and desire of human beings make applications of Geocast protocols more attractive. Here we have identified various mechanism and techniques used by different protocols for forwarding message to geocast region. The various techniques used are storing and caching of messages, time bounded message delivery, forwarding zone, probabilistic method and mesh based. A comprehensive and brief classification is shown in (Allal & Boudjit, 2012). The classification of routing protocols used in VANET shown in figure 8.

Figure 8. Classification Geocast Protocols for VANET

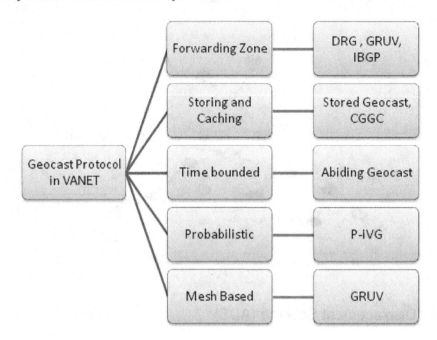

2.2.1 Stored Geocast

Stored Geocast (Maihöfer, Franz, et al., 2003) is a time stable protocol. The message delivery is time dependent and delivered to all nodes present inside the geocast region within a certain period of time. This time period starts with propagation delay, message transmission time. There are three different methodologies are used to deliver messages (i) First method is Infrastructure based approach, server is used to store the messages. The message is first stored in the server and afterward delivered to the geocast region. The message delivery is done either through notification or periodically. Sometimes in the network, communication failure occurs due to frequent fragmentation because of high mobility of nodes. This method guarantees that no message is get lost and delivered to all the nodes present in the intended destination region. In case of long communication distance between a server and the destination region, the messages first stored in the distributed geocast servers closer to destination region. Later on, messages are delivered to the destination region. (ii) Second method is the election approach, a node wihin the geocast region initiate election process to dynamically elect temporarily server. Its responsibility is to store and deliver geocast messages in future either periodically or by notification. Whenever, a server node is moving out from the destination region it hands over the message to the next server node. (iii) Third method is the neighbour approach, where every node stored geocast packets destined for its location. Also, maintains a table about location information of neighbour nodes. When a new node joins the destination region, it immediately receives the message.

Strength
- ○ Message delivery to any node in the geocast region is guaranteed.
- ○ It efficiently manages the network fragmentation.

Weakness

○   Infrastructure based approach introduces high overheads, and low robustness. The successful delivery of messages incorporates too many hops.

○   The network partitioning is not permissible inside the geocast region, otherwise messages are lost. The number of elected nodes increases to store the message and deal with the problem of network partition.

2.2.2 Caching and Transmission Range Control

In this protocol (Maihöfer & Eberhardt, 2004), a high mobile scenario is considered and two schemes for message delivery to geocast region are suggested. These schemes are cached geocast and distance aware neighbour selection. A geocast message traverses in hop by hop manner to reach the geocast region. A caching mechanism is used for the nodes that are unable to forward the messages immediately after receiving due to *local maximum or dead end* problem. The local maximum occur in the network, when a particular node have no neighbouring node is closer to the destination region. To overcome the problem it need to keep closer look over neighbouring nodes. To discover neighbouring nodes, beaconing system is used and a table is maintained to keep records of neighbour nodes. As soon as a new node is discovered handover of message is done. Due to high mobility of nodes, neighbour node information becomes outdated. This leads to retransmission and finding of other neighbours because the earlier nodes may have moved outside the transmission range. Sometimes a node selected as the next forwarding node may moves away from source range before receiving the message. This causes an extra delay, overheads or loss of packets. If no acknowledgement is received, retransmission scheme is used.

Strength

○   Message delivery success ratio is high.

○   It easily deals with network partitioning, by using caching mechanism to store the messages that cannot be forwarded.

Weakness

○   The end to end delay is high because of caching mechanism.

2.2.3. Cached Greedy Geocast (CGGC)

The CGGC is also a cache based geocast protocol designed for highly dynamic network with enhanced forwarding techniques (Maihöfer et al., 2004). In this protocol neighbour nodes change their location frequently and introduce unstable routing paths in a sparse networks topology. There are two geographic forwarding techniques known as hop to multi-hop and hop to hop respectively. In hop to multi-hop technique, one packet is transmitted to multiple next hop nodes, due to this duplicate packet reach to the destination more than once. In hop to hop method, packet is sent to only one next hop. The caching mechanism is used here to store the messages due to local maximum (Maihöfer & Eberhardt, 2004) problem. In the sparse topology to maintain the proper information of neighbour nodes, to find the current position of a node a periodic beaconing system is used.. The caching mechanism operates on demand basis to minimize network overheads. There are two types of caching methods that are used in this protocol. One is size oriented and the other is time restricted cache. In size oriented cache, it maintains a queue for storing the messages resulting limited number of packets is stored. In time restricted cache method, no limitation of size of a packet but for a restricted time period messages are stored. This CCGC method improves the simple greedy forwarding technique. The time restricted and size restricted caching mechanisms increases the success rate of message delivery to a geocast region.

Strength
- ○ It is designed for high node mobility and low node density.
- ○ It improves simple greedy forwarding technique.

Weakness
- ○ Duplicate packets reach the geocast region.
- ○ The end–to–end delay is high due to caching of geocast message.

2.2.4. Abiding Geocast

The abiding geocast method is a time abiding geocast protocol (Maihoefer & Leinmueller, 2005). The geocast messages are delivered by a specific time period within the region. It allows senders to define a lifetime for the geocast message. In this method geocast message delivery is done in four different phases. The phases are geocast routing protocol, storage of messages within their lifetime, handover of abiding geocast messages to other nodes, and delivery of geocast messages. In the phase -1, routing protocol is needed to deliver the first message to the destination region. The storage of messages is needed for future use. The handover of messages is required when the initial storage node (i.e. who earlier store the geocast message) leaves the geocast region. In this case the storage node must handover the geocast message to any other node inside the region before leaving it. The last phase of geocast message is the delivery phase. The messages are delivered through blind periodical resending or notification or on demand schemes. There are three abiding geocast message delivery approaches are Server, Election, and Neighbour Approach. In server approach, geocast message is sent to the server by unicast method, where the message is initially stored. Further, the server delivers message to the destination region with the help of any geocast routing protocol. After the first geocast message is delivered, the rest of the messages are delivered either periodically or by notification. The periodical delivery depends on the velocity of node movement. In this method the lifetime of geocast message is checked on the server side. If the geocast message is expired, no further retransmission is done by the server. To identify such messages, either the actual sender or server itself assigns a unique sequence number to the messages. This way abiding geocast protocol achieves robustness. In the Election Approach, a node from the geocast region is dynamically selected to store and handover the messages to any other node in the geocast region when it leaves that region. The criteria to elect a node are low velocity and closer to the center of geocast region to avoid unnecessary handovers of the messages. In the Neighbour approach, each node stores all the geocast messages sent for its location. Each node maintains a routing table having information of all its neighbour nodes and their location information. Whenever a node discovers that a new node has entered in that region, it immediately delivers the geocast message to that node. However, the messages are delivered periodically or by notification within the one hop distance.

Strength
- ○ It reduces blind periodical retransmissions of messages because delivery of geocast is done within a bounded time.
- ○ It saves bandwidth.

Weakness
- ○   In a dense network with longer distance between source and destination the packet delivery ratio is degraded.

2.2.5. Distributed Robust Geocast (DRG)

Distributed and Robust Geocast (DRG) (Joshi, 2007) protocol is designed for inter vehicle communication in different network scenarios i.e. city and highway scenarios with varying vehicles density. The protocol is designed to overcome the frequent topology changes and fragmentations in the network. The geocast area is divided into Zone of Relevance (ZOR) and Zone of Forwarding (ZOF). ZOR and ZOF both have some geographical conditions which should be satisfied for geocasting. ZOR represents significance of a message to a particular node and ZOF conditions should be satisfied by a node before forwarding a geocast message. The number of hops needed for the geocast message transmission has been reduced with the help of the distance based back-off technique in the forwarding algorithm. To cope with the network fragmentation periodic retransmission and burst retransmission is used. Burst retransmission with short interval is done to overcome the communication losses and periodic retransmission is done after long intervals. To reduce the redundant broadcasting, time persistence technique is used, where a persistence timer is fixed upon receiving a new geocast message. If a timer expires, only the nodes broadcast the message that have not received the recent transmission of messages, broadcast the message. The protocol is easily adapted to different network scenarios.

Strength
- ○   It is distributed in nature.
- ○   It is less sensitive to node density.
- ○   It easily deals with frequent fragmentations occurring in the network.
- ○   It uses distance based back off algorithm resulting in reduction of number of hops and redundant broadcast.

Weakness
- ○   It introduces high overheads in sparse and disconnected network.

2.2.6. Probabilistic Inter Vehicle Geocast (p-IVG)

The P-IVG (Ibrahim, Weigle, & Abuelela, 2009) protocol deals with the spatial broadcast problem occurred due to rebroadcasting of messages to the multiple vehicles at the same time in a densely populated network. Due to this channel contention and collision of messages become very high. The rebroadcasting of message is done by probabilistic approach. This is decided by traffic density surrounding the vehicles. This protocol significantly improves the receptions rate of packets, minimizes the channel contention and faster dissemination of messages to the distant vehicles. In (Hu, Hong, & Hou, 2003; Tonguz, Wisitpongphan, Bai, Mudalige, & Sadekar, 2007; Tseng, Ni, Chen, & Sheu, 2002; Tseng, Ni, & Shih, 2003; Wisitpongphan et al., 2007) different solutions for mitigating broadcast storm problem are proposed. But none of the solutions is fit to solve the spatial broadcast problem as the topology of VANET is different from MANET and also the vehicles movement in VANET is faster.

Strength

- ◦ Minimizes the channel contention.
- ◦ It improves the reception rate.
- ◦ It has faster dissemination of message to distant vehicles.
- ◦ It follows a probabilistic approach for data transmission, so the lesser number of vehicles participates in rebroadcasting of messages.

Weakness

- ◦ The performance is degraded in a sparsely populated network.

2.2.8. Geocast Routing in Urban Vehicular Ad hoc Networks (GRUV)

Geocast Routing in Urban Vehicular Ad hoc Networks (GRUV)(Zhang et al., 2009) is designed for urban scenarios. Geocasting in VANETs is very challenging task as frequent link breaks occur, nodes move faster and signal attenuates due to obstacles in the urban area. This method is very dynamic in nature and as it dynamically switches among different forwarding zone. Further, vehicles are classified in two groups are crossroad and inroad node based on their current location. The working of this protocol uses source routing, concept of forwarding zones and meshes as proposed in (Camp, 2003). Three different forwarding zones are used - BOX, Extended Box (E-Box), and FLOOD. A source node sends a RREQ (Route REQuest) packet to the geocast region before sending messages. Source node also fixes a FA_TIMER for each RREQ before sending RREQ to find a path between source and nodes within the geocast region. If the FA_TIMER expires it destroys the RREQ packet. The node within the geocast region receives the RREQ packet reply with RREP (Route REPly) packet. During message transmission forwarding zones are dynamically selected and BOX FA is selected initially to transmit RREQ packets. In case, FA_TIMER expire then, RREQ further sent through E-BOX. The RREQ is transmitted via FLOOD if both the method is failed. The path between source and geocast region discovered through any of the forwarding zone willcontinue until it encounters a failure. Further, crossroad node selection and inroad node selection algorithm is used to select the next hop based on its location. It is able to find a robust path for data delivery due to next hop selection algorithms according to category of nodes.

Strength

- ◦ It provides two different dynamic next hop selection algorithms.
- ◦ It can easily adapt to the changes in the network.
- ◦ It uses different forwarding zones.
- ◦ It reduces network overheads.

Weakness

- ◦ Its performance is degraded with high mobility of nodes.

2.2.9 Intersection area based Geocast protocol (IBGP)

Intersection are based geocast routing protocol(Das & Lobiyal, 2012; Das & LOBIYAL, 2012) is designed and analysed for highway scenario. In this protocol, highway is divided into equal sizes cell shown in figure 9. Further, radian forwarding zones are used for data delivery from one cell to another. Specially, in this protocol network connectivity is analysed with different node densities and transmission ranges. The intersection area is defined between two successive cells is shown in figure 10. This area gives the number of common nodes (Das & Lobiyal, 2012; Das & LOBIYAL, 2012) exist in that area. Through numerically number of node present and chances of void occurrence is discussed. The node density is varies and accordingly number of node present and void occurrence in the different radian forwarding zones are analysed. This determines the successful delivery of data and connectivity among nodes in the network. If, network is densely populated than data transmitted with lower radio transmission range. The forwarding zones are dynamically switches based on the node density.

Strength
- It provides flexibility of choosing forwarding zone for data delivery.
- It can easily adapt to the changes in the network and switches among different forwarding zones.
- It optimized the network area.

Figure 9. Geocasting on Highway Scenario (Das & Lobiyal, 2012)

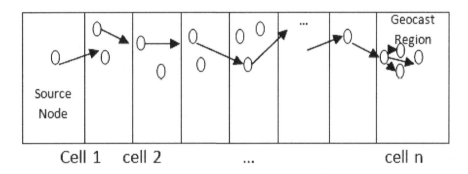

Figure 10. Intersection area between two successive cells (Das & Lobiyal, 2012)

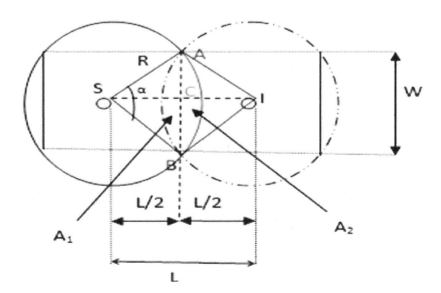

Weakness

- ○ Protocol is only designed for highway scenario, where only linear road structure is considered. So, the applicability of the protocol is limited.

3. COMPARISON OF GEOCAST ROUTING PROTOCOLS

In the Table 1and Table 2, various features of geocast routing protocols for Ad Hoc network is shown. The above discussed protocols are compared based on these essential features.

Table 1.Gecoast routing protocols comparison used in MANET

Features	Routing Protocols								ADS
	LAR	LBM	GeoGRID	GeoTORA	GAMER	GGP	AHBG	ADS
Forwarding Techniques	Restricted flooding	Restricted Flooding	Flooding & Restricted flooding	Any cast routing & Restricted Flooding	Restricted flooding	Flooding	Handshake based	Restricted Flooding
No. of Forwarding Zone	Single	Single but adaptive	Single	Nil	Multiple	Nil	Nil	single
Routing Overhead	Medium	Medium	Medium	Medium	High	Low	Low	Low
Guaranteed Delivery	No	No	No	No	No	Yes	Yes	Yes
GPS required	Yes	Yes	Yes	Yes	Yes	No	Yes	No
Route Caching	No	No	No	No	No	No	No	No
Store and forwarding	No	No	No	No	No	No	No	No
Resilient with changing Network topology	No	No	Yes	Yes	Yes	No	Yes	No
Network topology	Random	Random	GRID	Random	Random	Random	Random	Random
Number of target area	Single	Single	Single	Single	Single	Multiple	Single	Single
Loop Free	Yes	Yes	Yes	Yes	Yes	Yes	Yes	Yes
Type of Forwarding Zone	Static	Dynamic	Static	nil	Dynamic	Nil	Nil	Static
Participation of nodes	All	All	selected	Selected	Selected	Selected	selected	Selected
Types of nodes	Homog eneous	Homogeneous	Homog eneous	Homog eneous	Homog -eneous	Homog Eneous	Homog eneous	Homog eneous
Path between source and geocast region	Single	Single	Multiple	Single	Mesh	Single	single	Single
Mobility Model	RWP[2]	RWP[2]	RWP[2]	RWP[2]	RWP[2]	RWP[2]	RWP[2]	RWP[2]
Simulator used	MaRS[3]	NS-2	NS-2	NS-2	NS-2	NS-2	NS-2	OMNeT++

Table 2. Geocast routing protocols comparison used in VANETs

Features	Routing Protocols						
	Stored Geocast	**CGGC**	**Abiding Geocast**	**DRG**	**p-IVG**	**GRUV**	**IBGP**
Forwarding Techniques	Election and server based	Hop to hop and hop to multi-hop	unicast	distance based back-off mechanism	Probabilistic method	restricted flooding	Restricted flooding
No. of Forwarding Zone	Nil	Nil	Nil	Nil	Nil	Multiple	Multiple
Routing Overhead	High	High	Low	High	Low	Low	Low
GPS required	Yes	Yes	Yes	Yes	Yes	Yes	Yes
Guaranteed Delivery	Yes	Yes	Yes	No	No	NO	Yea
Route Caching	Yes	Yes	Yes	No	No	No	No
Store and forwarding	YES	Yes	Yes	No	No	NO	No
Resilient with changing Network topology	No	Yes	No	Yes	No	Yes	Yes
Network topology	Random	Random	Random	City / highway	random	GRID/ Random	Highway
Number of target area	Single	Single	Single	Single	Single	Single	Single
Loop Free	Yes	Yes	Yes	Yes	Yes	Yes	Yes
Type of Forwarding Zone	Nil	Nil	Nil	Nil	Nil	Dynamic	Dynamic
Participation of nodes	All	All	selected	All	all	selected	Selected
Types of nodes	Homog eneous	Homog eneous	Homog eneous	Homog eneous	Homog eneous	Homog eneous	Homogeneous
Path between source and geocast region	Single	Single	Single	Single	Single	Mesh	Single
Mobility Model	-	RWP[2]	-	STRAW[4]	ASH[1]	-	-
Simulator used	-	NS-2	-	JiST[5] /SWANS	SWANS	NS-2	Matlab

[1]Application-aware SWANS with Highway mobility.

[2]Random way point.

[3]Maryland Routing Simulator.

[4]STreet RAndom Waypoint

[5]scalable wireless network simulator

4. FUTURE DIRECTIONS IN DESIGN A NEW PROTOCOL

Thorough analysis and comparison of all the geocast protocols alludes above, we observed that in future to design a new routing protocol for MANET as well as for VANET, advantages of existing protocols should be utilized since none of the protocol can work for all network conditions. However, none of the existing protocols consider heterogeneous environment. This may be one of the key research directions in future. Further, we have summarized below some of the key parameters which should be incorporated in designing new routing protocols for MANET and VANETs in future:

a) Number of geocast region should be more than one.
b) Node movement should be trajectory based i.e. road, city, and highway scenarios.
c) Both ways traffic flow model.
d) Driver behaviours in designing mobility models.
e) Radio signal obstacles.
f) Data delivery with less number of nodes.
g) Optimum forwarding zone for data delivery.
h) Handling network fragmentation.
i) Varying node mobility and density.
j) Caching mechanism of messages.
k) Heterogeneous nodes.

Further, following network QoS parameters should also be considered for high acceptability and reliability analysis of a routing protocol.

a) High accuracy in message delivery
   Geocast routing protocols main aim is to deliver message to a specific geographical region. Some times in battle ground scenario accurate and exact information delivery plays vital role. Otherwise; it may lead to disaster.
b) Highly scalable and stable
   The analysis of various routing protocols in MANET and VANET context but only few protocols are scalable enough to cope with the changes in the networks. But it is always desirable that protocol must be adhere changes in the network without losing its performance.
c) Minimum average end to end delay
   This is also an important QoS parameter because timely dissemination of messages is very important when time is associated with message delivery.
d) Minimum number of hops
   This parameter is also an important factor because delivery of data through large number of nodes increases the delay in message delivery. Generally, it is observed that minimum number of nodes participating in message delivery reduces the delay and increases the chances to achieve higher throughput.
e) High reliability
   New protocols designed for geocast must be incorporates all the above discussed parameters carefully. Overall acceptability of any protocol depends on its reliability factor. When any protocol achieve high throughput, lower delay and cope with the dynamics of network without degrading the network performances called to be reliable protocol.

5. CONCLUSION

In this chapter, gives broad review of geocast routing protocols for Mobile Ad hoc Networks and Vehicular Ad hoc Networks is presented. The routing protocols for geocast explicitly use the location information of nodes which is achieved by using GPS receivers. The protocols differ from each other based on forwarding zone, forwarding methods, expected zone and flooding mechanism, etc. used for delivers geocast messages. Few protocols used in VANET have adapted store and caching mechanisms of message and have been evaluated for different network topologies. Further, VANET, DRG and GRUV protocols are developed for city highway scenarios and their performance evaluation have been carried out for different traffic density. To improve the network performance different types of forwarding zones have been used i.e., cone shaped, rectangular, triangle etc. Some protocols consider spatial broadcast storm problem occurring during inter-vehicle geocasting in a dense traffic condition and to mitigate the effect of probabilistic rebroadcasting, geocast message is used. Through, this comprehensive analysis of various protocols have shown future directions for designing of a new routing protocol which should include the key features from all existing protocols for high acceptability of the protocol.

REFERENCES

Allal, S., & Boudjit, S. (2012). Geocast Routing Protocols for VANETs: Survey and Guidelines. *2012 Sixth International Conference on Innovative Mobile and Internet Services in Ubiquitous Computing*, 323–328. 10.1109/IMIS.2012.133

Camp, T., & Liu, Y. (2003). An Adaptive Mesh-based Protocol for Geocast Routing. *Journal of Parallel and Distributed Computing: Special Issue on Mobile Ad-Hoc Networking and Computing*, *63*(2), 196–213. doi:10.1016/S0743-7315(02)00064-3

Chen, H. L., Tseng, C. C., & Hu, S. H. (2006). An adaptive handshaking-based geocasting protocol in MANETs. *IWCMC 2006 - Proceedings of the 2006 International Wireless Communications and Mobile Computing Conference, 2006*, 413–418. 10.1145/1143549.1143632

Das, S. (2012). Analysis of neighbour and isolated node of intersection area based geocasting protocol (IBGP) in VANET. *International Journal of Wireless & Mobile Networks*, *1*(1), 7–15. doi:10.5121/ijwmn.2012.4120

Das, S., & Lobiyal, D. K. (2012). *Intersection area based geocasting protocol (IBGP) for Vehicular Ad hoc networks. Lecture Notes of the Institute for Computer Sciences, Social-Informatics and Telecommunications Engineering*. doi:10.1007/978-3-642-27317-9_40

Hu, C., Hong, Y., & Hou, J. (2003). On mitigating the broadcast storm problem with directional antennas. *IEEE International Conference on Communications*, *1*, 104–110. 10.1109/icc.2003.1204151

Ibrahim, K., Weigle, M. C., & Abuelela, M. (2009). P-IVG: Probabilistic inter-vehicle geocast for dense vehicular networks. *IEEE Vehicular Technology Conference*. 10.1109/VETECS.2009.5073804

Jiang, X., & Camp, T. (2002). A Review of Geocasting Protocols for a Mobile Ad Hoc Network. *Proceedings of the Grace Hopper Celebration (GHC)*.

Joshi, H. P. (2007). *Distributed Robust Geocast: A Multicast Protocol for Inter-vehicle Communication*. Dept. of Computer Networking and Electrical Engineering, Master's T.

Ko, Y., & Vaidya, N. H. (1998). Location-aided routing (LAR) in mobile ad hoc networks. *Proceedings of the ACM/IEEE International Conference on Mobile Computing and Networking (MOBICOM'98)*, *3112*, 1–16. 10.1145/288235.288252

Ko, Y. B., & Vaidya, N. H. (2000). GeoTORA: a protocol for geocasting in mobile ad hoc networks. *International Conference on Network Protocols*, 240–250. 10.1109/icnp.2000.896308

Ko, Y. B., & Vaidya, N. H. (2002). Flooding-Based Geocasting Protocols for Mobile Ad Hoc Networks. *Mobile Networks and Applications*, 7(6), 471–480. doi:10.1023/A:1020712802004

Lee, S.-H., & Ko, Y.-B. (2006). Geometry driven Scheme for Geocast Routing in Mobile Ad hoc Networks. *IEEE 63rd Vehicular Technology Conference*, 638–642. 10.1109/VETECS.2006.1682902

Liao, W., Tseng, Y., Lo, K., & Sheu, J. (2000). GeoGRID: A Geocasting Protocol for Mobile Ad Hoc Networks Based on GRID. *Journal of Internet Technology*, 1(2), 23–32. http://www.citeulike.org/user/sfujii/article/2246138

Liao, W. H., Sheu, J. P., & Tseng, Y. C. (2001). GRID: A fully location-aware routing protocol for mobile ad hoc networks. *Telecommunication Systems*, 18(1–3), 37–60. doi:10.1023/A:1016735301732

Maihoefer, C., & Leinmueller, T. (2005). *Abiding Geocast : Time – stable Geocast for Ad Hoc Networks*. Academic Press.

Maihöfer, C. (2004). A survey of geocast routing protocols. *IEEE COMMUNICATIONS SURVEYS*, 6(2), 32–42. doi:10.1109/COMST.2004.5342238

Maihöfer, C., Cseh, C., Franz, W., & Eberhardt, R. (2003). Performance evaluation of stored geocast. *IEEE Vehicular Technology Conference*, 58(5), 2901–2905. 10.1109/vetecf.2003.1286151

Maihöfer, C., & Eberhardt, R. (2004). Geocast in vehicular environments: Caching and transmission range control for improved efficiency. *IEEE Intelligent Vehicles Symposium, Proceedings*, 951–956. 10.1109/IVS.2004.1336514

Maihöfer, C., Eberhardt, R., & Schoch, E. (2004). CGGC: Cached greedy geocast. Lecture Notes in Computer Science (Including Subseries Lecture Notes in Artificial Intelligence and Lecture Notes in Bioinformatics), 2957, 13–25. doi:10.1007/978-3-540-24643-5_2

Maihöfer, C., Franz, W., & Eberhardt, R. (2003). Stored Geocast. *Proceedings of Kommunikation in Verteilten Systemen (KiVS)*, 257–268. doi:10.1007/978-3-642-55569-5_21

Onifade, F. W., Ojo, K., & Akande, O. (2008). Angular Displacement Scheme (ADS): Providing Reliable Geocast Transmission for Mobile Ad-Hoc Networks (MANETs). *IJCSNS International Journal of Computer Science and Network Security*, 8(8), 334–339.

Park, V., & Corson, S. (2001). Temporally-ordered routing algorithm (TORA). In Internet Draft: draft-ietf-manet-tora-spec-04.txt.

Ruhil, A. P., Lobiyal, D. K., & Stojmenovic, I. (2005). Performance Evaluation of Geocasting Protocols in Mobile Ad Hoc Networks. *11th National Conference on Communication (NCC-2005)*, 46–50. Retrieved from http://www.tjprc.org/view-archives.php

Schwingenschlogl, C., & Kosch, T. (2002). Geocast enhancements of AODV for vehicular networks. *Mobile Computing and Communications Review*, 6(3), 96–97. doi:10.1145/581291.581307

Stojmenovic, I., Ruhil, A. P., & Lobiyal, D. K. (2003). Voronoi diagram and convex hull based geocasting and routing in wireless networks. *Proceedings - IEEE Symposium on Computers and Communications*, 51–56. 10.1109/ISCC.2003.1214100

Tonguz, O., Wisitpongphan, N., Bai, F., Mudalige, P., & Sadekar, V. (2007). Broadcasting in VANET. *2007 Mobile Networking for Vehicular Environments, MOVE*, 7–12. doi:10.1109/MOVE.2007.4300825

Tseng, Y. C., Ni, S. Y., Chen, Y. S., & Sheu, J. P. (2002). The broadcast storm problem in a mobile ad hoc network. *Wireless Networks*, *8*(2–3), 153–167. doi:10.1023/A:1013763825347

Tseng, Y. C., Ni, S. Y., & Shih, E. Y. (2003). Adaptive approaches to relieving broadcast storms in a wireless multihop mobile ad hoc network. *IEEE Transactions on Computers*, *52*(5), 545–557. doi:10.1109/TC.2003.1197122

Weisstein, E. W. (2019). *Fermat Points*. Retrieved December 12, 2019, from https://mathworld.wolfram.com/FermatPoints.html

Wisitpongphan, N., Tonguz, O. K., Parikh, J. S., Mudalige, P., Bai, F., & Sadekar, V. (2007). Broadcast storm mitigation techniques in vehicular ad hoc networks. *IEEE Wireless Communications*, *14*(6), 84–94. doi:10.1109/MWC.2007.4407231

Yao, P. (2004). Evaluation of Three Geocasting Protocols for a MANET. *Grace Hopper Celebration of Women in Computing*, 1–6.

Yao, P., Krohne, E., & Camp, T. (2004). Performance comparison of geocast routing protocols for a MANET. *Proceedings - International Conference on Computer Communications and Networks, ICCCN*, 213–220. 10.1109/icccn.2004.1401631

Yu, Q., & Heijenk, G. (2008). Abiding geocast for warning message dissemination in vehicular ad hoc networks. *IEEE International Conference on Communications*, 400–404. 10.1109/ICCW.2008.81

Zhang, G., Chen, W., Xu, Z., Liang, H., Mu, D., & Gao, L. (2009). Geocast routing in urban vehicular ad hoc networks. *Studies in Computational Intelligence*, *208*, 23–31. doi:10.1007/978-3-642-01209-9_3

Chapter 3
Evaluation of Topology–Based Routing Protocols for Dissemination of Emergency Messages in Urban Vehicular Traffic Scenarios in India

Pawan Singh
Indira Gandhi National Tribal University, Amarkantak, India

Suhel Ahmad Khan
Indira Gandhi National Tribal University, Amarkantak, India

Pramod Kumar Goyal
ⓘD https://orcid.org/0000-0002-8390-9273
Department of Training and Technical Education, Aryabhatt Institute of Technology, India

ABSTRACT

VANET is a subclass of MANET that makes the dream of intelligent transportation systems come true. As per the report of the Ministry of Road Transport and Highways, India, 1.5 million people were killed in road accidents in 2015. To reduce casualty and provide some kind of comfort during the journey, India must also implement VANETs. Applicability of VANET in Indian roads must be tested before implementation in reality. In this chapter, the real maps of Connaught Place, New Delhi from Open Street maps websites is considered. The SUMO for traffic and flow modeling is used. Many scenarios have been used to reflect real Indian road conditions to measure the performance of AODV, DSDV, and DSR routing protocols. The CBR traffic is used for the dissemination of emergency messages in urban vehicular traffic scenarios. The throughput, packet delivery ratio, and end-to-end delay are considered for performance analysis through the NS-2.35 network simulator.

DOI: 10.4018/978-1-7998-2764-1.ch003

INTRODUCTION

Due to the lack of adequate public transport in large countries like India and giving importance to private vehicle use by the people, the Indian transport system faces a serious problem. Increasing vehicle density has increased the frequency of the accidents caused by which the rate of death in the accident has also increased alarmingly. As per the Ministry of Road Transport and Highways report 4, 64,910 road accidents reported in which 1, 47,913 people died during 2017("Ministry Of Road Transport And Highways", 2018). In the road accident, the first hour for the injured person is very critical, if the injured persons get the right treatment during the time, then many of them can be saved. Due to tremendous enhancements in wireless and sensor technologies, the dream of an intelligent transportation system can come to be true.

Wireless communication technology has made a lot of progress which allows us to exchange data efficiently over the network regardless of positions and time. If it is possible that vital signs like Body temperature, Pulse rate, Respiration rate, and Blood pressure, etc can be captured by some sensors that are already implanted into the patient body or are in the form of a wearable jacket and accessing overall patient's overall health condition by capturing images and video by vehicle inbuilt camera and sending this information to the nearby server of ambulance/hospital or doctor in real-time then So many lives of people can be protected. By analyzing patient health information related doctors can take a faster decision about the best feasible treatment at an accident spot. If We could know the exact location of an accident site then ambulance from the nearest hospital with the life-supporting system, equipment, and medicines required as per the accessed patient health information can reach the accident site within the time. It would decrease the rate of casualty in accidents.

Vehicular Ad-hoc Network (VANET) may be a very useful technology in reducing the deaths of roadside accidents. Many VANET related research projects are completed and going on around the world such as CarTALK 2000(Reichardt et al., 2002), FleetNet(Franz et al., 2005), NoW (Network on Wheels) (Festag & Andreas, 2008) and CarNet(Morris et al., 2000).

VANET is an emerging research area which uses cluster of vehicles on the road to establish and maintains a wireless communication among them without using any fixed infrastructure. VANETs can be a very handy tool in passing patient's health information to the nearest hospital in absence of fixed infrastructure in emergencies where there is no infrastructure while it is significant and necessary to passing on the health information for saving many lives. VANET is a subclass of a mobile ad-hoc network (MANET) in which moving vehicles like cars, trucks, etc. work as nodes and communicate with each other wirelessly by using 802.11p standard if they are within the range of 100 to 1000 meters. VANET uses smart vehicles that are equipped with Global Positioning System (GPS), application Unit (AU), On-Board Unit (OBU) devices (Moustafa & Zhang, 2009). VANET may be used to improve vehicle wellbeing, upgrade traffic productivity, and giving infotainment by sending priority-based or periodic messages to others within the range vehicles. These messages can be categories into three types. The first kind of message is periodic and broadcasted messages which give information about the vehicles' direction, speed and position. The second kind of message is high priority messages which are delivered in an emergency i.e. messages related to passenger safety. These types of messages are event-driven and very time-critical so they required a higher transmission rate. The third type of message is informational and non-safety application messages and they required prioritized access (Biswas et al., 2006).VANET has a few distinctive qualities that separate it from MANET. The network topology in VANET is highly dynamic because of vehicle mobility at a high speed whereas the mobility of vehicles is regular and predictable and there is no power constraint. In VANET Vehicles have high processing capabilities and enough storage capacity, unlike MANET (Corson & Macker,1999).

Background and Related Work

Authors overview VANET architecture, namely V2V, V2I, and V2P. Authors then outline various VANET communication models, namely Pure Cellular Networks, Pure Ad-Hoc Networks, and Hybrid Networks. Authors then overview various wireless access methods in vehicular environments, namely DSRC/WAVE, Cellular, Wi-Fi, WiMAX, etc. The authors then review various routing protocols designed for vehicular networks. Authors have classified routing protocols in five different categories as Position-Based Routing Protocol, Topology Based Routing Protocol, Broadcast Based Routing Protocol, Cluster-Based Routing Protocol and Geo Cast Based Routing Protocol on the basis of their data dissemination, route update method, and most suitable applications. Finally, Authors present evaluation of topology-based routing protocols namely, Ad hoc On-Demand Distance Vector (AODV)(Perkins & Royer, 1999), Dynamic Source Routing (DSR)(David et al., 2004) and Destination-Sequenced Distance-Vector (DSDV) (Charles et al., 1994) for dissemination of emergency messages in Urban Vehicular Traffic Scenarios.

Many researches have been performed previously related to the performance analysis of different routing protocols for dissemination of real-time data. In (Imane Zaimi et al., 2017) authors have demonstrated the comparative study of different protocols for MPEG-4 video quality on the basis of QoS merits. Authors (Mimoza Durresi et al., 2005) have developed an emergency broadcast protocol designed for sensor inter-vehicle communications and based on geographical routing. In (Jose Grimaldo et al., 2018) authors have analyzed the impact of black hole attacks on VANETs performance in Panama City scenario by using four AODV, DSDV, DSR and OLSR routing protocols. Authors (Pooja Rani et al., 2011) have compared the performance of three routing protocols, namely AODV, DSDV and DSR for different parameters. (Manyi Qian et al., 2018) also, have analyzed and compared typical proactive and reactive routing protocols by using NS2 simulations. Another comprehensive study on the performance and behavior of AODV), DSDV) and ZRP routing protocol in VANETs was performed by authors (Abhishek Singh et al., 2013).

VANET'S ARCHITECTURE

VANET architecture mainly consists of Road Side Unit (RSU) and running vehicles (V). These Moving vehicles can communicate with other moving vehicles in the following ways:

A. Vehicle to Vehicle Communication (V2V)
B. Vehicle to Infrastructure Communication (V2I)
C. Vehicle to Pedestrian Communication (V2P)

The V2V communications can be used in transferring emergency messages, real-time information such as an accident or road traffic congestion information so that other vehicles can take other routes to avoid traffic jam and increasing GPS accuracy. Moving vehicles can also communicate wirelessly (by IEEE 802.11p standards) with fixed infrastructure units installed at roadside generally called RSU to access internet facilities.

Figure 1. VANET's Architecture

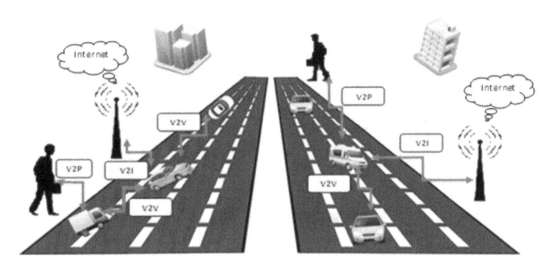

RSU uses cellular technologies like 2G/3G/4G/Volet etc. to access internet services. RSU acts like a gateway/router for providing coverage to within range vehicles. RSU has a higher coverage range than the vehicle range. VANET uses smart vehicle that's having On-Board Units (OBUs), which consist of processors, sensors, Omnidirectional antennas, Global Positioning System (GPS), to perceive its own accurate position and other vehicles, and Electronic license plate (ELP) for vehicle identification to conduct vehicle to vehicle communication (V2V)(Bhoi et al., 2014).

Vehicle to Infrastructure Communication (V2I) can be used in toll collection, getting entertainment facilities and localized traffic information, etc. Vehicles can also exchange information with the people walking on the footpath to access local information that is called Vehicle to Pedestrian Communication (V2P).

VANET'S COMMUNICATION MODELS

VANET uses moving vehicles as a router to create ad-hoc networks. VANET uses the Institute of Electrical and Electronics Engineers (IEEE) Wireless Access in Vehicular Environment (WAVE) protocol and stranded to supports Intelligent Transportation Systems (ITS).

VANET does not depend on fixed network infrastructure. It may use three kinds of network architecture as follows:

1. Pure Cellular Networks
2. Pure Ad-Hoc Networks
3. Hybrid Networks

VANET may use cellular networks and WLAN provided by installed Road Side Unit at traffic intersections to get Internet Facilities and collect traffic information like road congestion, road accidents or routing information.

Figure 2. VANET Communication Models

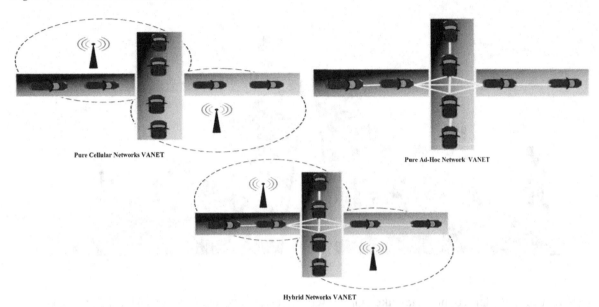

VANET may also use Pure Ad-Hoc Networks in absence of Cellular Networks or WLAN. In this network, moving vehicles use their wireless access capabilities to make Ad-Hoc networks and to perform vehicle to vehicle communication to achieve blind crossing, etc.

VANET may also use a hybrid network as shown in the figure 2. It is a mixture of cellular networks, WLAN and ad hoc networks. In hybrid architecture, VANET uses those vehicles as router or gateway which have WLAN capability and are under the range of cellular networks. Vehicles with WLAN capability can communicate with others through multi-hop topological links to stay connected to the world (Li & Wang, 2007).

WIRELESS ACCESS STANDARDS FOR VANET

VANET uses many wireless access technologies to perform inter-vehicle communications (V2V), or to communicate with fixed infrastructures (RSU) and to communicate with people nearby the road (V2P). The basic motives of these technologies are to improve road safety by minimizing roadside accidents by sending alert messages to the drivers as well as the passenger in a vehicle or nearby road. These technologies can provide traffic management facilities to the concerned authority and can also provide entertainment facilities. On the basis of data transmission range, wireless access protocols can be categorized into three categories as shown in the figure below.

Some of the prime wireless access standards are described below:

Cellular Networks

The cellular network is a radio network that uses electromagnetic waves or radio waves to transmit data over a geographical area. The cellular network uses a "limited frequency reuse" theory to greater area

Figure 3. Wireless communication technologies based on range

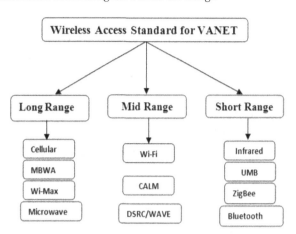

coverage and multiple transmissions together. Today's Mobile phone networks are based on the cellular network. Cellular technology has many small interconnected transmitters called cells to provide larger coverage (multiple data/ voice connections into a single radio channel).Popular cellular technologies are 1G, 2G, Global System for Mobile Communication(GSM), General Packet Radio Service(GPRS) / 2.5G, Enhance data rate for GSM(EDGE) / 2.75G,Code Division Multiple Access(CDMA),3G,4G, HSPA (HIGH SPEED PACKET ACCESS), 4G LTE, VOLTE.

Analog signals were used to transmit in the first generation system (1G). GSM is a 2G standard that was launched in the year 1991. It supports data encryption to send data securely and it has more than 90% of market share and access into nearby 220 countries. GSM can provide data rates up to 9.6kps and it uses FDMA and TDMA technologies (Anwer & Guy, 2014).

General Packet Radio Service (GPRS) is considered 2.5G standard and it is an extended version of GSM. GPRS supports packet oriented mobile data facility speed and it was being used for internet access. It has data transfer speed up to 170kbps and it uses 1710-1785 MHz band for uploading and 1805-1800 MHz band for downloading.

3G Technologies offer faster data transfer rates and enable video calls. This is more suitable for modern Smartphone which required high-speed internet connection. 3G UMTS (Universal Mobile Telecommunications System) uses 1.8GHz to the 2.5GHz frequency band and it can provide up to 2Mbps data transfer rate. 3G HSPA (HIGH-SPEED PACKET ACCESS) provides a 14Mbps data rate for downloading and 5.74 Mbps for uploading. 3G HSPA+ (Evolved high-speed packet access) provides a 42Mbps data rate for downloading and 11 Mbps for uploading.

4G (fourth generation) is a successor of 3G Technologies and provides ultra-broadband internet access for mobile devices such as laptops, Smartphone, and wireless modems, etc. It offers voice, data and multimedia services at data rates of up to 100 Mbps. LTE (Long Term Evolution) and LTE Advanced are the two standards of 4G technologies presently.4G LTE uses 2 - 8 GHz Frequency Band, 5-20 MHz Bandwidth and Up to 20 Mbps data transfer rate.

WiMax

WiMax (Worldwide Interoperability for Microwave Access) is a wireless access standard based on the IEEE 802.16, for long-range (up to 50km) wireless networking for both mobile devices as well as for fixed infrastructure networks. Due to amendment in IEEE 802.16 standard WiMax technology were divided into two standard one is called Fixed WiMax (IEEE 802.16-2004) and another is called Mobile WiMax (IEEE 802.16e). Fixed WiMax works in 2.5 GHz and 3.5 GHz frequency bands and having up to 75 Mbps data rate and covers up to 10 km geographical area whereas Mobile WiMax works in 2-6 GHz frequency band having up to 30 Mbps data rate and having up to 3.5 km range.

WiMax provides high-speed Internet facilities to such areas where normal wired technologies like DSL, Cable or Dedicate T1 line do not cover. It provides reliable communication with higher Quality of Service supports for Video, Multimedia and VoIP (voice over internet protocol) requiring applications ("WiMAX- 802.16").

DSRC

DSRC (Dedicated short-range communication) is a mid range wireless access standard specially designed for inter-vehicle communication for an intelligent transportation system (ITS). DSRC technology works on the 5.9 GHz band radio frequency band and having 75 MHz bandwidth. DSRC technology provides high reliability because of very low interference that's makes it the best technology for VANET.

The main drive of DSRC development is to build collision prevention applications that have required frequent data exchanges between vehicles and vehicles to RSUs. When vehicles are equipped with DSRC device then they can broadcast their position information, current speed and acceleration data to other within few hundred-meter ranges vehicles and RSUs. A receiving vehicle may use this information

for computation of path between itself and neighboring vehicles and later on this information can be used for determination of accident risk posed by any neighbor vehicle. DSRC technology can be used in both vehicle-to-vehicle (V2V) communications through onboard unit (OBU) for safety applications and vehicle-to-infrastructure (V2I) communication by roadside unit (RSU) for non-safety applications like electronic payments(tolls, fuel, parking payments, entertainment facilities (listing music, watching movies, playing online games)(Kenney, 2011).

WAVE

WAVE stands for Wireless Access in Vehicular Environments standard. It is IEEE 1609 family standard that defines the architecture, services, and interfaces for wireless communication with 27 MB/s data rate over 1000 meter range and up to 200km velocities. Its enables low latency wireless communication in the vehicular environment (John & Kenney, 2011).Its aims to support interoperability and robust safety communications in a vehicular environment. The IEEE 1609 standard family consists of six standards as follows:

- IEEE P1609.0
- IEEE 1609.1-2006
- IEEE 1609.2 -2006
- IEEE 1609.3 -2007

- IEEE 1609.4 -2006
- IEEE P1609.11

VANET'S APPLICATIONS

The VANET application can be divided into five major categories (Cunha et al., 2016): 1. Safety 2. Efficiency 3. Comfort 4. Entertainment and 5. Urban Sensing

Safety Applications

These applications are delay-sensitive applications with the motive to avoid and decrease the number of road accidents. These applications use vehicle-to-vehicle communication. Examples of such applications are collision alert, pedestrian crossing warning and other vehicles lane changing.

Efficiency Applications

These applications are used to improve vehicle mobility on the roads, controlling the traffic circle and intersections and prevent traffic jams. In such applications, communication occurs between the vehicles and from vehicles to RSUs.

Comfort Applications

These applications are used to provide comfort and pleasure during the journey. These applications required communication between vehicles and roadside units. Examples of such applications are the information about free parking space, weather information, nearby petrol pump or gas station information, restaurant location, tourist point information, toll tax collection services (Anwer & Guy, 2014).

Entertainment Providing Applications

These applications provide entertainment-related services to drivers and as well as to passengers during the journey. Here communications occur among vehicles or between vehicles and RSUs. Internet access, web browsing, online video games, social networking, chats, music downloads, and file sharing are some examples of applications in this category.

Urban Sensing Applications

VANET with wireless sensor networks can be used for environmental monitoring, surveillance and mobile social networking in a geographical area (Lee & Gerla, 2010).

VANET'S ROUTING PROTOCOLS

VANET uses a multi-hop wireless communication system for data transmission from the sender to the designated node. There may be many paths to reach from sender to receiver in multi-hop communication. Routing is the process of finding an optimal path from available paths to reach the destination node. Routing protocols gather the required information to find a path, control information for connection maintenance and maintain this information into routing tables. Routing algorithms are being used to find the optimal path with minimum congestion. In VANET, routing protocols are classified in Topology Based Routing Protocol, Broadcast Based Routing Protocol, Position-Based Routing Protocol Cluster-Based Routing Protocol and Geo Cast Based Routing Protocol, five major categories according to their data dissemination, route update method and most suitable applications(Wang et al., 2007)(Syal et al., 2014)(Altayeb et al., 2013)(Dhankhar et al., 2014)(Dua et al., 2014)(Paul et al., 2012)(Rana et al., 2014) (Paul et al., 2011)(Kumar et al., 2012)(Jindal et al., 2016).

Figure 4. VANET Routing Protocols

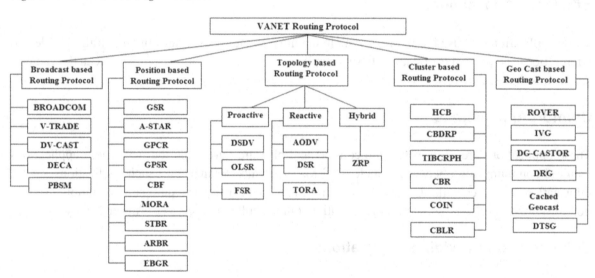

Broadcast Based Routing Protocols

VANET uses broadcast-based routing protocol for the dissemination of safety-related messages, weather conditions, road conditions, and advertisements. Broadcasting is achieved by multi-hop flooding in which each node rebroadcast messages to other nearby nodes. Flooding can cause more data packets collisions, which cause more bandwidth consumption and performance degradation. The further Broadcast based routing protocol can be classified into two main categories as Single-hop broadcasting protocol and Multi-hop broadcasting protocol(Kumar et al., 2012). The various broadcast-based routing protocols are BROADCOM (Durresi et al., 2005) Vector-Based Tracing Detection(V-TRADE)(Sun et al., 2000), Distributed vehicular broadcast protocol (DV-CAST)(Tonguz et al., 2007), Density aware reliable broadcasting protocol (DECA)(Nakorn et al., 2010), Parameter less broadcasting in static to highly mobile wireless ad -hoc (PBSM) (khan et al., 2008).

Position Based Routing Protocols

These routing protocols are also called Geographical protocols. In such protocols, mobile nodes are assumed to have inbuilt GPS devices that provide geographical information of its position as well as the position of its neighbors. These protocols don't use the routing table because routing decisions are made on the position of neighbor hop and packet's destination. These protocols are categorized into the categories of Delay Tolerant Network (DTN), non-Delay Tolerant Network (non-DTN) and Hybrid protocols.

DTN uses to store and carry technique for packet dissemination in frequently disconnected VANET. Non-DTN protocols use a greedy forwarding technique to send the packet to its nearest neighbor. non-Delay Tolerant Network position-based routing protocols can further be classified into Non-Beacon protocols, Beacon protocols and Non-Overlay protocols(Karimi et al., 2011, November) (Karimi et al., 2011, September). Hybrid protocols use the quality of both DTN and non-DTN protocols. Some of the position based routing protocols are Geographical Source Routing (GSR)(Iwata et al., 1999), Anchor-Based Street and Traffic-Aware Routing (A-STAR) (Seet et al., 2004), Greedy Perimeter Coordinator Routing(GPCR)(Lochert et al., 2003), Greedy Perimeter Stateless Routing (GPSR)(Karp et al., 2000), Contention-Based Forwarding (CBF)(Fubler et al., 2004), Movement-Based Routing Algorithm (MORA) (Granelli et al. 2006), Street Topology Based Routing (STBR) (Forderer, 2005), Adaptive Road-Based Routing (ARBR)(Ahmadi et al., 2010), Edge Node Based Greedy Routing (EGBR)(Kumar, 2012).

Cluster-Based Routing Protocols

Cluster-based routing focuses on creating a network of a small group of nearby nodes called cluster () Lin & Gerla, 1997),(Luo et al., 2010),(Rawashdeh & Mahmud, 2012). This is a small group of nodes identifies themselves to be a part of the cluster. The size of a cluster is determined by specific routing algorithms based on locations of nodes and the number of nodes. Each cluster has one cluster-head that is responsible for within-cluster and outside cluster nodes communication. Cluster-Based Routing (CBR) (Luo et al., 2010), Hierarchical Cluster-Based Routing (HCB)(Yang et al., 2009), Cluster-Based Directional Routing Protocol (CBDRP)(Song et al. 2010), TIBCRPH(Wang & Wang, 2010), Clustering for Open IVC (Inter-vehicle communication) Network (COIN)(Blum et al., 2003), Cluster-Based Location Routing (CBLR)(Santns et al., 2004) are few examples of Cluster-based routing protocols.

Geo Cast Based Routing Protocols

Protocols under this category are location-based multicasting protocols. In Geo Cast based routing protocol data packet is being forwarded from a sender node to all other nodes which are inside a particular region. This region is called the zone of relevance (ZOR). These protocols use zone of forwarding (ZOF) techniques to send the packet to the other ZORs. The nodes inside a particular ZOF forward the data packet to the other ZORs (Chen et al., 2009). The various Geo Cast based routing protocols are Robust Vehicular Routing Protocol (ROVER)(Kihl et al., 2007), Inter-Vehicle Geo-cast Routing Protocol (IVG) (Allal et al., 2013), Direction-Based Geo-cast Routing Protocol for Query Dissemination (DG-CASTOR) (Atéchian et al., 2008),Distributed Robust Geo-cast Routing Protocol (DRG) (Joshi et al., 2007),Cached Geocast(Maihöfer et al., 2004), Dynamic Time–Stable Geo-cast Routing Protocol (DTSG) (Rahbar et al., 2010).

TOPOLOGY BASED ROUTING PROTOCOLS

These protocols use network topology and connection information to perform routing. Due to nodes mobility, these protocols can be categories into three major categories as proactive routing protocols, reactive routing protocols and hybrid routing protocols.

These protocols maintain route information of all the nodes all the time whether currently, they are participating in the network or not. A control message is sent periodically to update network topological information so whenever a node wants to send data packets to other nodes, routes are already known to it. If the network size increased then overheads of maintaining topology information are also increased (Venkatesh & Murali, 2014).Destination-Sequenced Distance-Vector (DSDV) (Charles et al., 1994), Optimized Link State Routing (OLSR) (Clausen & Jacquet, 2003), Fisheye State Routing (FSR)(Guangyu et al., 2000) are few examples of proactive routing protocols.

Reactive routing protocol, sometimes called on-demand routing protocols works on a demand basis. They discover a route for sending any information from sender to destination whenever it is required. Further reactive routing protocols can be categorized into source routing protocol and hop-to-hop routing protocol (Venkatesh & Murali, 2014). Source routing protocols use a mechanism to store whole route information in data packets. Hop-to-hop routing protocol utilizes only the next-hop address and destination address. Ad hoc On-Demand Distance Vector (AODV)(Perkins & Royer, 1999), Dynamic Source Routing (DSR)(David et al., 2004), Temporally Ordered Routing Algorithm (TORA)(Park & Corson, 1997) is few examples of Reactive routing protocol.

Hybrid routing protocols utilize the good qualities of proactive routing protocols as well as reactive routing protocols. These kinds of protocols are much suitable for the huge sized network which can be divided into many zones. Inside a zone proactive routing is being used zone whereas reactive routing is used in Intra Zone communications. Zone Routing Protocol (ZRP)(Zygmunt, et al., 2002) is one of the hybrid routing protocols examples.

Figure 4 list some examples of routing protocols from each category. Authors have chosen AODV, DSR as reactive routing protocols and DSDV as the proactive routing protocols for their performance evaluation on Indian city scenarios. DSDV, AODV and DSR are explained in the next subsections.

Destination-Sequenced Distance-Vector Routing Protocol

DSDV is a popular proactive routing protocol developed by C. Perkins in 1994. It based on a modified Bellman-Ford routing algorithm. DSDV uses this algorithm to avoid routing loops. Every mobile node maintains its own routing table. Here routing table contains an entry for all available destinations, the number of hops to reach the destination. Every routing table entry contains a sequence number that is generated by the destination. The formation of routing loops is avoided by a sequence number that is used to differentiate fusty routes from new ones.

Each mobile node broadcasts its routing tables periodically or occasionally when network topology changed, to their immediate neighbors, for updating the routing information of the other nodes. If any node movements happen then routing information must be sent immediately and maintaining consistency routing updated must be sent after a fixed interval. Thus routing information is updating on time and event basis (Rahbar, 2010).

The main advantage of this protocol is a lower delay because of no requirement of route discovery mechanism. The problem arises when the size of network increases and topology changed frequently then it will consume more bandwidth because of maintaining available routing information even though they are not used(Bai et al., 2017).

Dynamic Source Routing Protocol

DSR is a popular reactive routing protocol that is designed to use source routing, in which the sender has information of the entire hop- to- hop route to the destination. This route information is stored in the route cache. Whenever a source wants to send some data packets to other nodes, it will look into route cache for a route existence. Route absence from route cache will prompt the sender to start a new route discovery process which dynamically determines new routes. The main feature of DSR is the restricted network bandwidth consumptions by control packets by reducing the periodic table-update messages requirement in the proactive routing approach (Jhnson, et al., 2004).

In the DSR route recovery process, the source node constructs route request (RREQ) packets and broadcast it to neighbor nodes. Each RREQ packet has a sender's and destination's address, and a unique Request ID. When a node forwards RREQ packets then it appends it's identifier to this packet. Receiving nodes check their route cache for rout availability. If route is absent then these nodes will further broadcast the RREQ packet to the nearby nodes by adding their own address to route record of the packet. This process will continue unless the RREQ packet reaches its destination or the intermediate node has a route to the destination in its route cache (Grimaldo & Mart, 2018).

Once the destination node received the RREQ packet, it will construct a Route Reply Packet (RREP) and send RREP back to the source node. RREP reaches to the original source by traversing backward. Route information in RREP is stored in route cache for further use. Due to the dynamic topology route maintenance process is required and it is activated in case any link is broken. It informs the source node by using a route error (RERR) packet. If the route is still missing and required then the source will start a new route discovery process. Thus DSR protocol uses source routing and route caching aggressively (Bai et al., 2017). The drawback of the DSR routing protocol is its route maintenance mechanism which cannot repair broken links locally. Cache information of the Stale route can cause inconsistencies in the route reconstruction phase. Time taken in connection establishment is higher than in proactive routing protocols.

Ad Hoc On Demand Distance Vector (AODV) Routing Protocol

AODV (Perkins & Royer, 1999) is a reactive routing protocol which is a mixture of DSR and DSDV routing protocol. Here route discovery and its maintenance process are the same as in DSR but for maintaining routing information it uses the table-driven approach as in DSDV. It allows faster route discovery for new destinations and doesn't maintain routing information of such nodes who are inactive during that communication. AODV works in a time-bound fashion in link breakages and topology change situations. AODV provides a loop-free mechanism for route recovery.

AODV uses RREQ message for searching a new route, RREP message when a route is discovered and RERR message when a route is broken or link failure. When the source node wants to send some data to the destination then the route discovery process starts with the broadcasting of RREQ message, in which receiving nodes adds a destination sequence number in its routing table. This sequence number is the basis for loop-free operations. Basically routing table contains next-hop information for the destination, hop count, timeout value and destination sequence number. This entry in the routing table will be automatically deleted after reaching the time limit if that route is not being used anymore for sending data. The destination sequence number is auto-incremented whenever a node starts route discovery or replies to route requests. In the situation of more than one route to reach the destination, the route which has uppermost sequence number is selected for routing. Finally, when the destination receives the RREQ packets, it delivers it to the source backwardly in the RREP packet. RREP packet has full path information and it is unicasted to the source node. The source node uses this route for sending of information.

Here nodes examine the link status of next hops in current routes. AODV sends HELLO message periodically for having the information of link failures. When a link failure is detected, a RERR message is constructed and sent to a neighboring node for notification of link failure. The RERR message receptors have to update their routing table accordingly (Perkins & Royer, 1999).

TRAFFIC AGENT CBR

CBR stands for Constant Bit Rate which is an application traffic agent. It is an application layer protocol that imports the data from UDP (User Datagram Protocol) and transmits the data at a constant bit rate over a limited bandwidth channel. CBR has an expected kind of transmission. The problem with CBR is that it provides a unidirectional and unreliable type of communication. In UDP/CBR traffic moves only in one direction from source to destination without any acknowledgments from the destination. Lack of acknowledgment causes the no assurity of successfully data delivery (Sharma & Gupta, 2012). CBR provides support for timing sensitive applications with guaranteed Quality of Services (QOS) in ad-hoc networks. CBR used in many applications like video streaming, interactive audio/video, video conferencing, the transmission of MP3 files

Network traffic monitoring and traffic modeling etc.CBR can be used in the dissemination of emergency messages in a fixed time interval. Therefore authors have used CBR for the performance evaluation of topology-based protocol as a traffic agent for emergency message dissemination in VANET.

RESEARCH METHODOLOGY USED

For evaluating the performance of any routing protocol an efficient research methodology is required in VANETs. Due to budget constraints and technical complexity in actual experimentation of VANET, simulation is considered as a better choice in the validation and performance assessment of VANETs protocols. In this chapter to evaluate the routing protocol, simulation is carried out by using open-source Network Simulator NS2.35 ("The Network Simulator – ns-2"). For pragmatic simulation firstly Authors required a real map of Indian metro cities for network scenarios, for which Authors have used OSM (www.openstreetmap.org/.)("OpenStreetMap"). Authors have used Traffic simulator SUMO (Simulation for urban mobility) (Hilbrich) for realistic traffic scenarios.

Realistic Road Network is creating by OSM files which are used by Traffic simulator SUMO. SUMO generates vehicle mobility on that road network. Traffic files generated by SUMO are inputted to NS2.35 Network Simulator. NS2.35 processes these files and generates a trace file. Finally, awk scripts are used to generate some results and further evaluations.

Figure 5. Research Methodology Used

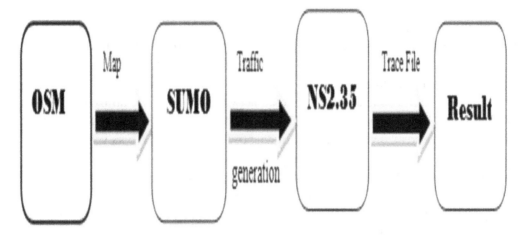

Simulations tools utilization, simulation environment and parameters, performance metrics used for making different comparisons and evaluation are discussed in this section.

Tools Utilization

OSM

OpenStreetMap (OSM) ("OpenStreetMap") is the project that creates and distributes free geographic data for the world. OSM is created by Steve Coast in 2004. It is absolutely free to use. OSM users can collect data using physical survey, GPS devices and aerial photography. It provides the xml based .osm file for any geographic location in the world through it website www.openstreetmap.org/.

SUMO

Simulation for urban mobility (SUMO) (Hilbrich) is a widely used, cross platform, microscopic and open source traffic simulator developed by Institute of Transportation Systems, Berlin. SUMO offers many features like Microscopic simulation, online interaction, Simulation of multimodal traffic, Scheduling of traffic lights, unlimited network size and support to OpenStreetMap, VISUM, VISSIM, NavTeq.

NS-2.35

Network Simulator 2.35 is the most popular and widely used network simulator for research purpose. NS-2 was developed by the US DARPA (Defense Advanced Research Projects Agency). it is open source and it's code is written C++ and TCL programming and interpreted by OTCL interpreter, that's generating an output file for NAM (Network animator). NS-2 has freeway model and the Manhattan model that may be used in VANET simulation. Due to more CPU cycle and memory consumption, limited scalability and complexity to implement VANET mobility model NS-2 project had been closed in 2010 ("The Network Simulator – ns-2").

Simulation Environment

For evaluating the performance of emergency message dissemination, authors have chosen Connaught Place, New Delhi from Indian city because of its overcrowded nature and high traffic level (Figure 6.). Making more realistic simulation, a real map of Connaught Place has been imported from Open Street Map for creating urban city scenarios. Simulation Area of 19983 m × 8415 m is selected from available map (Figure 7.). For Traffic simulation on this road network, authors have utilized a python script on osmWebWizard.py utility which is available under SUMO/tools directory of SUMO -0.32.0 traffic simulator. Here authors have created vehicle density of 25, 50, 100,150 and 200 cars vehicle type by altering count per hour per kilometer and Through Traffic factor (5 constant) options available in osmWebWizard. py. Random trips is created by executing another python script on randomTrips.py utility(under sumo/ tools directory). Authors have taken 500 seconds as total simulation time for traffic simulations. SUMO converts this configuration file (.sumocfg) in to a trace file in xml file format which have the information about the car's positions in every moment. Finally this SUMO trace file is imported to NS2.35 by traceExporter.py utility to simulate VANET. It generates three .tcl files named by activity.tcl, mobility.tcl and NS2config.tcl. The generated NS2config.tcl have to be modified as per the networking parameters like Routing protocol, Mac layer, CBR packet size etc. mentioned in Table 1. Authors have used UDP connection and data traffic of CBR between sender and receiver nodes. Our scenarios use CBR traffic flows with a packet size of 1000,2000,3000,4000 and 5000 bytes and data rate 2 Mbps.

Figure 6. OpenStreetMap of Connaught Place New Delhi

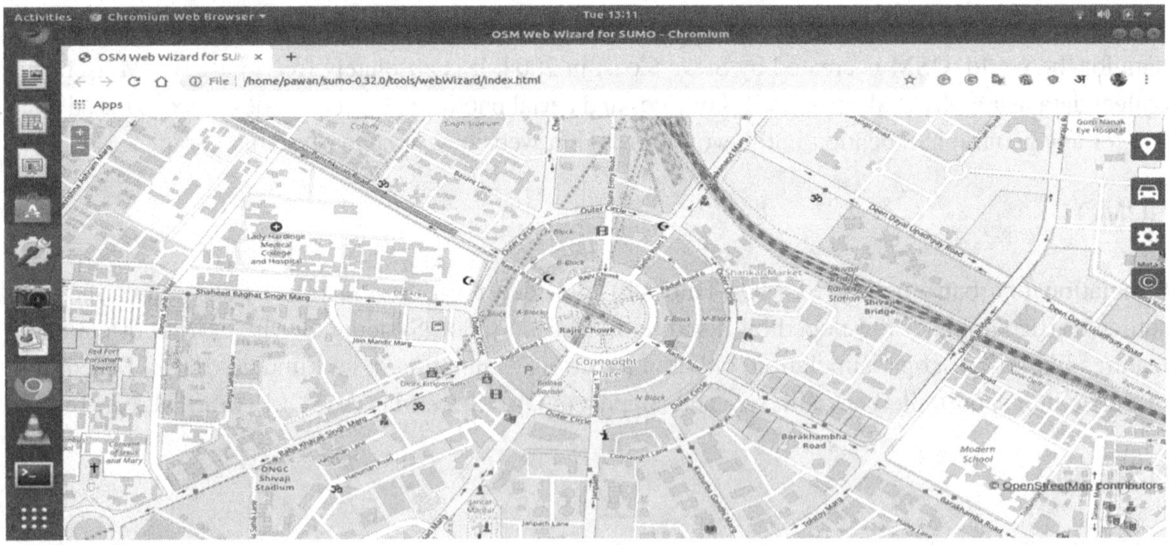

7.3. Simulation Setup

The following table summarizes the simulation setup/network parameters used to evaluate the performance.

Figure 7. SUMO screenshot

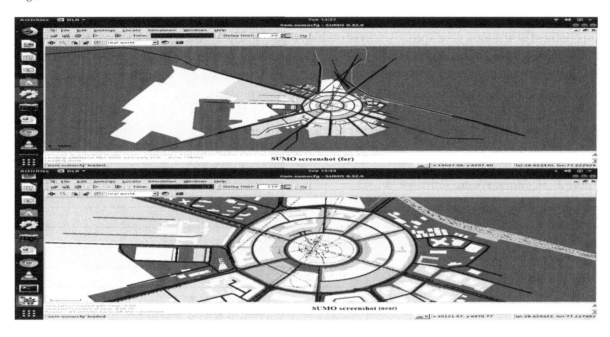

Performance Metrics

Many network simulator metrics can be used as performance metrics for the evaluation of a routing protocol under different network setups. In our study authors have used the following metrics for the performance analysis of AODV, DSDV and DSR routing protocols in highly mobile VANET environment:

Throughput

Throughput defined as the ratio of successfully delivered bits to total simulation time. It also indicates the bandwidth of the route. It is measured in Kbps. A protocol which gives high throughput is assumed a better one (Bhadoria & Jaiswal, 2016) (Dhaka et al., 2014).

Throughput = (Packet Received × Packet Size)/ Simulation End Time

Packet Delivery Ratio (PDR)

PDR is defined as the ratio of received data packets at the destination node to data packets sent by all the sources nodes. Higher PDR indicates the better is the routing protocol.

PDR = (Total number of packets sent by all source node / Total number of packets received by destination node) × 100

Average End to End Delay (AED)

It is defined as the total time spent to deliver each data packet. Delay includes delay in route discovery, delay in packet dissemination, and delay in sending time and the time spent by the packets in the queue. It is the ratio of total delivery time to the total number of packets received by the destination node. Lower Average End to End Delay indicates the better is the routing protocol.

AED = Total Delivery Time / Total number of Packets Received

Table 1. Simulation Setup Parameters

Parameters	Values
Platform	Linux, Ubuntu 18.04 LTS
Network Simulator	ns-allinone-2.35
Traffic Simulator	SUMO -0.32.0
Map Used	Open Street map (www.openstreetmap.org)
Scenario	Connaught Place, New Delhi, India
Channel Type	Wireless Channel
Radio Propagation Model	Two Ray Ground
Network Interface Type	Phy/WirelessPhy
MAC Type	IEEE 802.11
Link Layer Type	LL
Antenna Model	Omni-directional Antenna
Interface Queue Type	Drop Tail Priority Queue
Maximum Packet in Queue	50 Packets
Routing Protocol	AODV,DSDV,DSR (NS2 default)
Traffic type	UDP/CBR (Constant Bit Rate)
Node Type	Car
No. of Vehicles	25,50,100,150,200
Speed of Vehicle	10-40 km/hr
UDP Packet Size	2000 Bytes
CBR Packet Size	1000,2000,3000,4000,5000 Bytes
Road Traffic Direction	Multidirectional
No. of Road lanes	2
Simulation Area	19983 m × 8415 m
Through Traffic Factor	5
Trip Type	Random Trips
Performance Metrics	Throughput, Packet Delivery Ratio, End-to-End Delay, Jitter
Simulation Time	500 sec

Jitter

It is also called packet delay variance. It is the difference between expected time and the actual arrival time of data packets. It is the variation of latency or variance in the time delay between data packets at the received side. It is measured in milliseconds (ms). It causes packet loss and network congestion.

SIMULATION RESULTS ANALYSIS

After executing .tcl as per the traffic simulation parameters and network simulation parameters mentioned in Table 1. Simulation Setup Parameters, a trace file (with .tr extension) and an Network Animator file(with .nam extension) file are generated (Figure. 8).

Figure 8. Network Animator (NAM) View

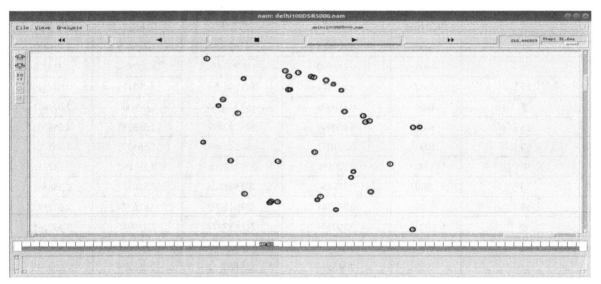

Here authors have used Perl script on trace files for analyzing of network metrics like throughput, Packet Delivery Ratio, Jitter and End to End delay. Table 2(given below) contains the result of AODV protocol on different CBR packet size obtained by Perl script.

Here Table 3.(given below) contains the result of DSDV protocol on different CBR packet size obtained by the same Perl script.

Finally Table 4.(given below) contains the result of DSR protocol on different CBR packet size obtained by the same Perl script.

Throughput

As authors have already mentioned that throughput is a measure of the protocol performance in terms of successful transmission rate. Any network performance depends on many factors such as packet size, node mobility, and connection duration. In figure 9, throughputs graph are plotted at a different number of nodes with different CBR packet size.

From figure 9, it is observed that the AODV protocol provides the highest throughput in all network scenarios made by alterations in the CBR packet size. As being reactive routing protocols, DSR also provides an equal amount of throughputs as of AODV. Therefore the performance of AODV and DSR are almost the same. Being on-demand AODV and DSR try to make a connection when there is a need to send data from source to destination. So routing overhead is very less here.

Throughput under different CBR packet size of DSDV is low as compared to AODV and DSR. DSDV is a table-oriented routing protocol that has to maintain routing information of all nodes even though there is not participating in the communications. An out of date routing table entry can cause the forwarding of data packets over a broken path.

Table 2: Performance Analysis of AODV Protocol with different Constant Bit Rates

No. of Vehicles	Constant Bit Rate (in Bytes)	Packet Delivery Ration	Throughput (in Kbps)	Average End to End Delay (in ms)	Jitter (in ms)
25	1000	0.129484	135.525967	1.416305	1.416477
25	2000	0.134890	139.798956	2.237596	2.238122
25	3000	0.122814	141.986290	2.042115	2.042510
25	4000	0.150003	155.510390	2.099008	2.099451
25	5000	0.120000	136.133493	2.368285	2.368808
50	1000	0.201042	200.261405	1.565075	1.565197
50	2000	0.229518	226.407106	2.581862	2.582217
50	3000	0.178454	202.981406	2.586197	2.586541
50	4000	0.211944	209.058803	2.676774	2.677173
50	5000	0.200244	221.617374	2.439945	2.440265
100	1000	0.299472	298.321172	1.406886	1.406956
100	2000	0.343346	338.680812	2.253535	2.253735
100	3000	0.284223	328.691433	2.051983	2.052146
100	4000	0.341996	337.336016	2.178910	2.179103
100	5000	0.293360	331.694461	2.169023	2.169210
150	1000	0.099263	98.888950	2.716768	2.717125
150	2000	0.106808	105.358917	2.872295	2.872840
150	3000	0.086570	90.172579	3.009144	3.009763
150	4000	0.097041	95.750154	3.732566	3.733462
150	5000	0.094667	99.305399	3.206667	3.207335
200	1000	0.295129	293.996989	1.390275	1.390345
200	2000	0.325648	321.201294	2.383080	2.383304
200	3000	0.267154	317.482810	2.241888	2.242080
200	4000	0.331319	326.825333	2.464031	2.464258
200	5000	0.262503	298.170634	2.608480	2.608734

Table 3: Performance Analysis of DSDV Protocol with different Constant Bit Rates

Vehicles	CBR	PDR	Throughput	AED	Jitter
25	1000	0.092292	98.352248	0.835642	0.835776
25	2000	0.105012	110.018547	1.400163	1.400562
25	3000	0.087059	122.314699	1.250208	1.250550
25	4000	0.098674	102.273243	1.402363	1.402783
25	5000	0.102177	128.532460	1.585596	1.585992
50	1000	0.109875	109.453344	1.094377	1.094530
50	2000	0.130155	128.386683	2.046875	2.047368
50	3000	0.107508	121.094361	1.636505	1.636861
50	4000	0.115457	115.394813	1.760440	1.760917
50	5000	0.114721	126.288491	1.737802	1.738193
100	1000	0.199491	198.717114	1.338764	1.338868
100	2000	0.222204	219.173590	2.351259	2.351590
100	3000	0.162070	188.501958	2.237510	2.237820
100	4000	0.219356	216.399515	2.459021	2.459375
100	5000	0.178721	201.666035	2.232187	2.232518
150	1000	0.041648	41.665800	3.556577	3.557754
150	2000	0.048849	50.295563	4.478204	4.480993
150	3000	0.039501	45.893420	5.576360	5.579690
150	4000	0.038007	37.517260	4.869767	4.873704
150	5000	0.038694	44.519932	5.302290	5.305785
200	1000	0.132879	132.366952	1.914740	1.914968
200	2000	0.156180	155.401315	3.400609	3.401302
200	3000	0.140667	160.963211	2.841054	2.841534
200	4000	0.172272	181.160025	3.402212	3.402837
200	5000	0.154857	174.037749	3.035979	3.036504

Packet Delivery Ratio

The Packet Delivery Ratio (PDR) is the ratio of packets received to the number of packets sent by the source generated by CBR. PDR become significant in identifying problems that might lead to reduced throughput. In the figure 10, PDR are plotted at different number of nodes and different CBR packet size to analysis how the PDR varies for different network scenarios.

From figure 10, it is observed that the AODV protocol provides the best packet delivery ratio, around 35% in all network scenarios, followed closely by DSR, around 30%. DSDV performs worst as compared to AODV and DSR, providing a maximum packet delivery ratio of around 25%.

Table 4: Performance Analysis of DSR Protocol with different Constant Bit Rates

Vehicles	CBR	PDR	Throughput	AED	Jitter
25	1000	0.116537	119.974110	2.449902	2.450206
25	2000	0.139298	143.545960	3.681274	3.682061
25	3000	0.099084	115.424270	4.258728	4.259739
25	4000	0.114706	118.168255	3.045568	3.046384
25	5000	0.117687	133.364009	3.925775	3.926641
50	1000	0.142643	139.643212	3.483509	3.483865
50	2000	0.152620	149.318842	4.840427	4.841399
50	3000	0.096905	108.410445	4.608341	4.609320
50	4000	0.137693	135.441984	5.435627	5.436828
50	5000	0.127211	139.979734	4.532665	4.533597
100	1000	0.250494	244.640773	1.554094	1.554153
100	2000	0.301584	294.539263	2.888267	2.888424
100	3000	0.220258	259.238365	3.153908	3.154204
100	4000	0.179782	181.070309	4.596340	4.596982
100	5000	0.274014	313.212519	2.520652	2.520886
150	1000	0.032342	50.227165	9.091231	9.094680
150	2000	0.043788	49.336077	9.555962	9.562368
150	3000	0.031248	40.317975	8.144920	8.146191
150	4000	0.046529	104.289603	9.668570	9.674514
150	5000	0.010966	12.769147	18.62245	18.65690
200	1000	0.216567	220.780939	1.518790	1.518891
200	2000	0.289502	282.776203	3.107152	3.107480
200	3000	0.206641	247.352292	3.347945	3.348283
200	4000	0.292463	290.406184	2.522708	2.522968
200	5000	0.203265	234.658627	3.073958	3.074270

End to End Delay

End to end delay is determined by time taken by a packet to reach from source node to destination node. Higher end to end delay time indicates the hectic channel, in which packets are being delayed and consuming more time to reach to the destination. End to end delay caused by network load, buffering during the route discovery process and retransmission delay. In figure 11, end to end delay graph are plotted at the different number of nodes and different CBR packet size.

From figure 11, it is observed that, except for a few inconsistencies, DSDV shows the lowest end-to-end packet delay on 25, 50 and 100 nodes for CBR transmission. On more than 100 nodes AODV outperforms DSR and DSDV protocols. DSDV performs better in terms of end to end delay on low node density because rout information already exists in the routing table whereas AODV and DSR have to start a new route discovery process that increases the end to end delay. It is also analyzed that AODV has a lesser amount of end-to-end delay than DSR on different node density.

Figure 9. Throughputs with different CBR Packet Size Byte

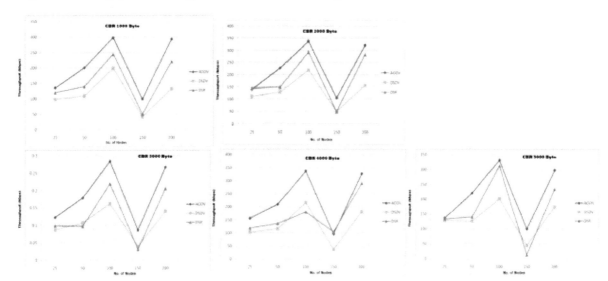

Figure 10. Packet Delivery Ratio with different CBR Packet Size 1000 Byte

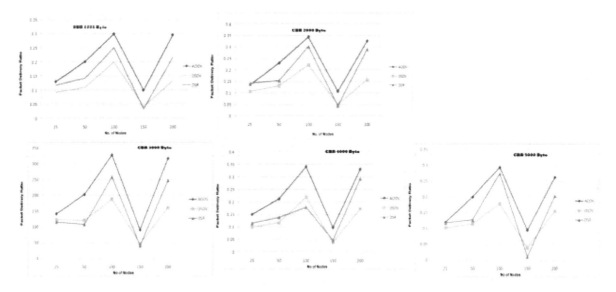

Jitter

"Jitter is the delay between two consecutive packet deliveries at a node. Quality of Service of the network is measured by Average Jitter Rate" (Rani et al., 2011). In figure 28-32, Jitter graph is plotted with 25, 50,100,150 & 200 number of nodes and different CBR packet size to analysis how jitter varies for different network scenarios.

Figure 11. End to End Delay with different CBR Packet Size

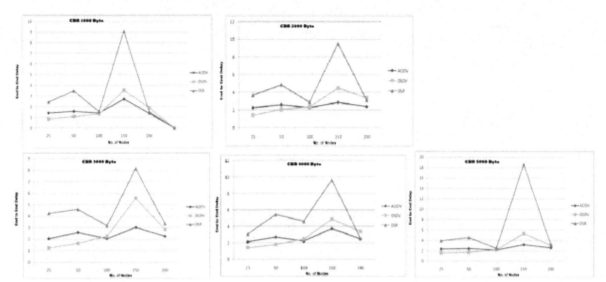

Figure 12. Jitter with different CBR Packet Size

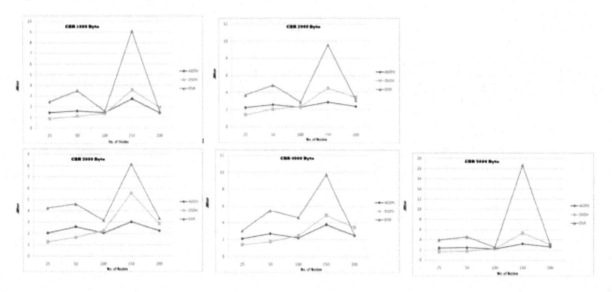

From the figure 12, it is observed that DSDV shows the lowest jitter on 25, 50 and 100 nodes for CBR transmission. On more than 100 nodes AODV outperforms DSR and DSDV protocols. DSDV performs better in terms of jitter in a sparse network. It is also observed that AODV has less jitter than DSR on different node density.

CONCLUSION

In this work, the authors have summarized the VANET architecture, communication models, application areas and VANET routing protocols. The authors have also summarized the topology based VANET routing protocols. Authors have analyzed the performance of AODV, DSDV and DSR topology-based routing protocols in Connaught Place, New Delhi, Indian metro cities environments. Authors have used OSM, SUMO, and NS2 for performance comparison. Our evaluation shows that AODV performs better in terms of throughput and packet delivery ratio than DSDV and DSR. DSDV performs better than AODV and DSR in terms of end to end delay and jitter on low node density.

REFERENCES

Allal & Boudjit. (2013, February). Geocast Routing Protocols for VANETs: Survey and Geometry-Driven Scheme Proposal. *Journal of Internet Services and Information Security, 3*(1-2), 20-36.

Altayeb & Mahgoub. (2013, July). A Survey of Vehicular Ad hoc Networks Routing Protocols. *International Journal of Innovation and Applied Studies, 3*(3), 829-846.

Answer & Guy. (2014). A Survey of VANET Technologies. *Journal of Emerging Trends in Computing and Information Sciences.*

Anwer, S., & Guy, C. (2014). A Survey of Vehicular technologies. *Journal of Emerging Trends in Computing and Information Science, 5*(9).

Arzil, S., Hosseinpour, M., & Jabraeil Jamali, M. (2010). *Adaptive routing protocol for VANETs in city environments using real-time traffic information.* Academic Press.

Atéchian, T., & Brunie, L. (2008). *DG-Castor: Direction-Based Geocast Routing Protocol for Query Dissemination in Vanet. IADIS International Telecommunications. Networks and Systems.*

Bai, Y., Mai, Y., & Wang, N. (2017). Performance comparison and evaluation of the proactive and reactive routing protocols for MANETs. *IEEE Wireless Telecommunications Symposium (WTS).* 10.1109/WTS.2017.7943538

Bhadoria & Jaiswal. (2016). Performance Analysis of Traffic Type and Routing Protocols in VANET for City Scenario. *International Journal of Urban Design for Ubiquitous Computing, 4*(1).

Bhoi, S. K., & Khilar, P. M. (2014). Vehicular communication: A survey. *IET Network, 3*(3), 204–217. doi:10.1049/iet-net.2013.0065

Biswas, S., Tatchikou, R., & Dion, F. (2006). Vehicle-to-vehicle wireless communication protocols for enhancing highway traffic safety. *IEEE Communications Magazine, 44*(1), 74–82. doi:10.1109/MCOM.2006.1580935

Blum, J., Eskandarian, A., & Hoffman, L. (2003, June). Mobility management in IVC networks. *Proceedings of IEEE Intelligent Vehicles Symposium.* 10.1109/IVS.2003.1212900

Chen, Lin, & Ling. (2009). A Mobicast Routing Protocol in Vehicular Ad-Hoc Networks. *GLOBECOM, IEEE Global Telecommunications Conference.*

Clausen, T., & Jacquet, P. (2003). *RFC 3626 - Optimized Link State Routing Protocol.* OLSR.

Corson & Macker. (1999, January). *Mobile Ad hoc Networking (MANET): Routing Protocol Performance Issues and Evaluation Considerations.* RFC 2501.

Dhaka, Poonia, & Raja. (2014, April). The realistic mobility evaluation of vehicular ad-hoc network for indian automotive networks. *International Journal of Ad hoc, Sensor & Ubiquitous Computing, 5*(2).

Dhankhar & Agrawal. (2014, June). VANETs: A Survey on Routing Protocols and Issues. *International Journal of Innovative Research in Science, Engineering and Technology, 3*(6).

Domingos da Cunha, F., Villas, L., Boukerche, A., Maia, G., Viana, A. C., & ... . (2016). Data Communication in VANETs: Survey, Applications and Challenges. *Ad Hoc Networks, Elsevier, 44*(C), 90–103. doi:10.1016/j.adhoc.2016.02.017

Dua, A., Kumar, N., & Bawa, S. (2014). A systematic review on routing protocols for Vehicular Ad Hoc Networks. *Vehicular Communications, 1*(1), 33–52. doi:10.1016/j.vehcom.2014.01.001

Durresi, M., & Durresi, A. (2005). Emergency Broadcast Protocol for Inter-Vehicle Communications. *IEEE International Conference on Parallel and Distributed Systems (ICPADS'05).* 10.1109/ICPADS.2005.147

Durresi, M., Durresi, A., & Barolli, L. (2005). Emergency Broadcast Protocol for Inter-Vehicle Communications. *11th International Conference on Parallel and Distributed Systems (ICPADS'05).* 10.1109/ICPADS.2005.147

Festag, A. (2008). NoW - Network on wheels: Project objectives, technology and achievements. *5th International Workshop on Intelligent Transportation (WIT)*, 211-216.

Forderer, D. (2005, May). *Street-Topology Based Routing* (Master's thesis). University of Mannheim.

Franz, W., Hartenstein, H., & Mauve, M. (Eds.). (2005, November). *Inter-Vehicle-Communications Based on Ad Hoc Networking Principles-The Fleet Net Project.* Universitatverlag Karlsuhe.

Fubler, H., Hartenstein, H., Mauve, M., Effelsberg, W., & Widmer, J. (2004). Contention-based forwarding for street scenarios. In *1st International workshop in intelligent transportation (WIT 2004)* (No. LCA-CONF-2004-005). Academic Press.

Granelli, F., Boato, G., & Kliazovich, D. (2006). MORA: A movement-based routing algorithm for vehicle ad hoc networks. *Proceeding in 1st IEEE Workshop AutoNet.*

Grimaldo, J., & Mart, R. (2018). Performance comparison of routing protocols in VANETs under black hole attack in Panama City. *IEEE International Conference on Electronics, Communications and Computers (CONIELECOMP).* 10.1109/CONIELECOMP.2018.8327187

Haas, Pearlman, & Samar. (2002, July). *The Zone Routing Protocol (ZRP) for Ad Hoc Networks.* Internet Draft.

Hilbrich, R. (n.d.). *Eclipse SUMO–Simulation of Urban Mobility*. Retrieved August 3, 2019 from https://www.dlr.de/ts/en/desktopdefault.aspx/tabid-9883/16931_read-41000

IEEE 1609 - Family of Standards for Wireless Access in Vehicular Environments (WAVE). (n.d.). Retrieved July 25, 2019 from https://www.standards.its.dot.gov/factsheets/factsheet/80

Iwata, Chiang, Pei, Gerla, & Chen. (1999, August). Scalable Routing Strategies for Ad Hoc Wireless Networks. *IEEE Journal on Selected Areas in Communications*, 1369-79.

Jindal & Bedi. (2016, March). Vehicular Ad-Hoc Networks: Introduction, Standards, Routing Protocols and Challenges. *IJCSI International Journal of Computer Science Issues, 13*(2).

Johnson, Maltz, & Hu. (2004, July). *The Dynamic Source Routing Protocol for Mobile Ad Hoc Networks (DSR)*. draft-ietf-manetdsr-10.txt.

Joshi, H., Sichitiu, M., & Kihl, M. (2007). Distributed Robust Geocast Multicast Routing for Inter-Vehicle Communication. *Proceedings of WEIRD Workshop on WiMax, Wireless and Mobility*.

Karimi, Ithnin, Razak, & Najafzadeh. (2011a, November). DTN Routing Protocols for VANETs: Issues and Approaches. *International Journal of Computer Science Issues, 8*(6), 89-93.

Karimi, Ithnin, Razak, & Najafzadeh (2011b, September). Non DTN Geographic Routing Protocols for Vehicular Ad Hoc Networks. *International Journal of Computer Science Issues, 8*(5), 86-91.

Karp, B., & Kung, H. T. (2000, August). GPSR: Greedy perimeter stateless routing for wireless networks, In *Proceedings of the 6th annual international conference on mobile computing and networking* (pp. 243–254). ACM. 10.1145/345910.345953

Kenney, J. B. (2011, July). Dedicated short-range communications (DSRC) standards in the United States. *Proceedings of the IEEE, 99*(7), 1162–1182. doi:10.1109/JPROC.2011.2132790

Khan, A. A., Stojmenovic, I., & Zaguia, N. (2008). Parameterless broadcasting in static to highly mobile wireless ad hoc, sensor and actuator networks. *Proceeding of 22nd International Conference on Advanced Information Networking and Applications(AINA -2008)*.

Kihl, M., Sichitiu, M., Ekeroth, T., & Rozenberg, M. (2007). Reliable Geographical Multicast Routing in Vehicular Ad-hoc Networks. *Proceeding in WWIC '07 Proceedings of the 5th international conference on Wired/Wireless Internet Communications*, 315 – 325. 10.1007/978-3-540-72697-5_27

Kumar, A. (2012). *Enhanced Routing in Delay Tolerant Enabled Vehicular Ad Hoc Networks. International Journal of Scientific and Research Publications* , 2.

Kumar, R., & Dave, M. (2012). A Review of Various VANET Data Dissemination Protocols. International Journal of u- and e- Service, Science and Technology, 5(3).

Lee, U., & Gerla, M. (2010). A survey of urban vehicular sensing platforms. *Computer Networks*, *54*(4), 527–544. doi:10.1016/j.comnet.2009.07.011

Li, F., & Wang, Y. (2007, June). Routing in Vehicular Ad Hoc Networks: A Survey. *IEEE Vehicular Technology Magazine*, *2*(2), 12–22. doi:10.1109/MVT.2007.912927

Li, F., & Wang, Y. (2007). Routing in vehicular ad hoc networks: A survey. *IEEE Vehicular Technology Magazine, 2*(2), 12–22. doi:10.1109/MVT.2007.912927

Lin, C., & Gerla, M. (1997). Adaptive clustering for mobile wireless networks. *IEEE Journal on Selected Areas in Communications, 15*(7), 1265–1275. doi:10.1109/49.622910

Lochert, C., Hartenstein, H., Tian, J., Fussler, H., Hermann, D., & Mauve, M. (2003, June). A routing strategy for vehicular ad hoc networks in city environments. In *Intelligent vehicles symposium, 2003, proceedings IEEE* (pp. 156–161). IEEE. doi:10.1109/IVS.2003.1212901

Luo, Y., Zhang, W., & Hu, Y. (2010). A new cluster based routing protocol for vanet. *IEEE Second International Conference on Networks Security Wireless Communications and Trusted Computing (NSWCTC)*. 10.1109/NSWCTC.2010.48

Maihöfer, C., Eberhardt, R., & Schoch, E. (2004). *CGGC: cached greedy geocast.* . doi:0.1007/978-3-540-24643-5_2

Ministry of Road Transport and Highways. (2018, October 1). *Road accidents in India – 2017.* Retrieved July 10, 2019 from http://www.indiaenvironmentportal.org.in/content/459084/road-accidents-in-india-2017

Morris, R., Jannotti, J., Kaashoek, F., Li, J., & Decouto, D. (2000, September). CarNet: A scalable ad hoc wireless network system. *9th ACM SIGOPS European Workshop*, Kolding, Denmark. 10.1145/566726.566741

Moustafa, H., & Yan, Z. (2009). *Vehicular networks: Techniques, Standards, and Applications.* CRC Press. doi:10.1201/9781420085723

Nakorn & Rojviboonchai. (2010). *DECA: Density-Aware Reliable Broadcasting in Vehicular Ad Hoc Networks.* In International Conference on Electrical Engineering/Electronics, Computer, Telecommunications and Information Technology (ECTI-CON2010), Chiang Mai, Thailand.

OpenStreetMap. (n.d.). Retrieved August 5, 2019 from https://en.wikipedia.org/wiki/OpenStreetMap

Park, V. D., & Corson, M. S. (1997). A highly adaptive distributed routing algorithm for mobile wireless networks. *Proceedings of the INFOCOM '97.* 10.1109/INFCOM.1997.631180

Paul & Islam. (2012). Survey over VANET Routing Protocols for Vehicle to Vehicle Communication. *IOSR Journal of Computer Engineering, 7*(5), 1-9.

Paul, Paul, & Bikas. (2011, April). VANET Routing Protocols: Pros and Cons. *International Journal of Computer Applications, 20*(3).

Pei, G., Gerla, M., & Chen, T.-W. (2000). Fisheye state routing: a routing scheme for ad hoc wireless networks. *IEEE International Conference on Communications.*

Perkins, C. E., & Royer, E. M. (1999). Ad-hoc On-Demand Distance Vector Routing. In *Proceedings of WMCSA '99. Second IEEE Workshop on Mobile Computer Systems and Applications.* Washington, DC: IEEE Computer Society.

Perkins & Bhagwat. (1994). Highly Dynamic Destination Sequenced Distance-Vector Routing (DSDV) for Mobile Computers. *ACM Conference on SIGCOMM.*

Rahbar, H., & Naik, K. (2010). *DTSG: Dynamic time-stable geocast routing in vehicular ad hoc networks.* doi:10.1109/MEDHOCNET.2010.5546872

Rana, Rana, & Purohit. (2014, June). A Review of Various Routing Protocols in VANET. *International Journal of Computer Applications, 96*(18).

Rani, P., Sharma, N., & Singh, P. K. (2011). Performance Comparison of VANET Routing Protocols. *7th International Conference on Wireless Communications, Networking and Mobile Computing*, Wuhan, China.

Rani, P., Sharma, N., & Singh, P. K. (2011). *Performance Comparison of VANET Routing Protocols.* IEEE. doi:10.1109/wicom.2011.6040428

Rawashdeh & Mahmud. (2012). A novel algorithm to form stable clusters in vehicular ad hoc networks on highways. *EURASIP Journal on Wireless Communications and Networking*, (1), 1–13.

Reichardt, D., Miglietta, M., Moretti, L., Morsink, P., & Schulz, W. (2002). CarTALK 2000 – safe and comfortable driving based upon inter-vehicle-communication. In *Intelligent Vehicle Symposium*. IEEE.

Santns, R. A., Edwards, R. M., Edwards, A., & Belis, D. (2004). A novel cluster-based location routing algorithm for intervehicular communication. *IEEE 15th International Symposium on Personal, Indoor and Mobile Radio Communications.*

Seet, B. C., Liu, G., Lee, B. S., Foh, C. H., Wong, K. J., & Lee, K. K. (2004). A-STAR: A mobile ad hoc routing strategy for metropolis vehicular communications. In *NETWORKING 2004, networking technologies, services, and protocols; performance of computer and communication networks; mobile and wireless communications* (pp. 989–999). Springer. doi:10.1007/978-3-540-24693-0_81

Sharma & Gupta. (2012, October). Comparison based Performance Analysis of UDP/CBR and TCP/FTP Traffic under AODV Routing Protocol in MANET. *International Journal of Computer Applications, 56*(15).

Singh & Verma. (2013, September). Simulation and analysis of AODV, DSDV, ZRP in VANET. *International Journal in Foundations of Computer Science & Technology, 3*(5).

Song, T., Xia, W., Song, T., & Shen, L. (2010). *A Cluster-Based Directional Routing Protocol in VANET.* IEEE 12th International Conference on Communication Technology, Nanjing, China.

Sun, M.-T., & Feng, W.-C. (2000). GPS-based message broadcast for adaptive inter-vehicle communications. *52nd Vehicular Technology Conference Fall (IEEE VTS Fall VTC).*

Syal & Kaur. (2014). A Study of Routing Protocols for Vehicular Ad-Hoc Networks. *International Journal of Engineering Trends and Technology, 15*(1).

The Network Simulator – ns-2. (n.d.). Retrieved July 30, 2019 from https://www.isi.edu/nsnam/ns/

Tonguz, O. K., Wisitpongphan, N., Bai, F., Mudalige, P., & Sadekar, V. (2007,May). Broadcasting in VANET. *Proc. IEEE INFOCOM MOVE Workshop 2007.*

Venkatesh, A., & Indra, M. (2014, January). Routing Protocols for Vehicular Adhoc Networks (VANETs): A Review. *Journal of Emerging Trends in Computing and Information Sciences, 5*(1).

Wang, T., & Wang, G. (2010). *TIBCRPH: Traffic Infrastructure Based Cluster Routing Protocol with Handoff in VANET.* IEEE The 19th Annual Wireless and Optical Communications Conference (WOCC 2010), Shanghai, China.

WiMAX - 802.16 - Worldwide Interoperability for Microwave Access. (n.d.). Retrieved July 28, 2019 from https://ccm.net/contents/808-wimax-802-16-worldwide-interoperability-for-microwave-access

Xia, Y., Yeo, C. K., & Lee, B. S. (2009). *Hierarchical Cluster Based Routing for Highly Mobile Heterogeneous MANET. IEEE International Conference on Network and Service Security*, Paris, France.

Zaimi, Houssaini, Boushaba, Oumsis, & Aboutajdine. (2017, August). *An Evaluation of Routing Protocols for Vehicular Ad-Hoc Network Considering the Video Stream.* Springer.

Chapter 4
Survey on VANET and Various Applications of Internet of Things

Nithiavathy R.
Arjun College of Technology, Coimbatore, India

Udayakumar E.
https://orcid.org/0000-0002-4456-5391
Kalaignarkarunanidhi Institute of Technology, Coimbatore, India

Srihari K.
Department of CSE, SNS College of Engineering, India

ABSTRACT

The user of the cloud storage can store an enormous amount of the data without any worries of the local maintenances of hardware and software. The user outsources the data and takes security control in order to maintain the reliability of the data. The data deposited in the cloud server is under frequent audit to the user to check the correctness of the service provider using wireless networks. The user can service a third-party checker to do the security audit on behalf of them for managing time constraints. The confidentiality of the data outsourced is preserved as of the third-party checker also. The system should be more efficient build for securing the data from various vulnerabilities. The proposed audit mechanism satisfies the user by providing integrity of the data stored simultaneously effectively and efficiently using VANET.

INTRODUCTION

The greater profits of the cloud computing is immense for a large user of the internet and information technology enterprises. The objective of the paper is application of VANET in big data, IoT and cloud. The scarcity of the resources is eradicated as cloud computing can employ any hardware or software

DOI: 10.4018/978-1-7998-2764-1.ch004

without maintaining locally. They can pay as the uses for resources that they use for the time. The cloud computing prime service is provided for low cost, flexible to access the data. There is security issues when the data are outsourced remotely are exposed to internal and external threats. The verification process should be more simple and effective as the retrieving data, performing many operations to verify the data integrity. Beside many users access the same cloud loading provided by the common service provider in a frame setting using wireless networks. It is vital to enable public checking services for the data storage in each cloud. Either the user can audit the storage system with enhanced techniques or hire a resource person like TPA (third-party auditors) without violating security measures.

The data leak to the TPA may lead to new security vulnerabilities, so the TPA has only authorization to verify the data with resources given not aware of the data stored in cloud security. To overcome these issue the proposed techniques uses IoT based homomorphic properties along with the public key is employed where the TPA could not hold a local copy using VANET.

The remote servers stores the data from various location, Schwarz and Miller *et al.*(2006) model verifies the data in distributed servers for correctness by employing erasure code.

The public auditing using the PDP(Provable data Possession) model is explained in the Atenies*et al.*(2007) for data files which resides in the un-trusted storage server where cloud service provider itself vulnerable.

Spot checking and error correction codes are used in this PoR(Proof of Retrievability) model in Juels *et al.* (2007) for ensuring the retrievability and data storage on the remote archives .

The online storage is maintained by the TPA by encryption using symmetric key hash function is proposed by the Shah *et al.*(2008).the TPA verifies only with the decryption key which as previously committed.

The design by Shacham and Waters *et al.* (2008) is improvised PoR model with BLS signature along with the security proof, public audit using homomorphic authenticator for integrity check.The erasure –correcting code on the remote stored data is extended POR model for distributed data assurance and availability is proposed byBowers *et al.*(2008).The verification is not limited which also satisfies the remote data control is described in Sebe*et al.*(2008).The trade-off between running time of the technique and local storage is preset for the user.The replicas are stored across the servers which are distributed across the geographical locations. The extension of the PDP is described in Curtmola *et al.*(2009) to handle the multiple replicas without encoding each copy of it.The data dynamics which enable provable data control based on the skip list is explained by Erway *et al.*(2009).the protocols requires linear combination for blocks and does not maintain privacy of the data outsourced. Both public audit and data dynamics are combined by Wang *et al.*(2011) with BLS,HLA along with MHT, but it does not meet the necessities privacy preserving in cloud computing.

RELATED WORK

The various factors involved in cloud security like data authentication, correctness, data dynamics and privacy preservation. There are different approaches which have pro and cons make applicable to application. The next are several methods handled in cloud security services. Vanet is applied in all real time system and it can be used for more specific applications

PROOF OF RETRIEVABILITY

The PoR model works with concepts like spot checking and error correction which is described by Juels *et al.* (2007) .it ensures the possession of the data stored and data retrievability on remote servers system. Only very small portion of data file is accessed for integrity check. The scheme encrypts the data and embeds the random values blocks called Sentinels. By specifying the position of sentinels, the challenge is issued to cloud server, where it returns the associated sentinel's values are sent back to the challenger as the proof of data integrity. If there are deletions in the portion of the sentinels then there is high probability of suppressed sentinels using wireless networks.

MAC (MESSAGE AUTHENTICATION CODE)

The data integrity is preserved by using MAC in the cloud storing. The data holder embeds MAC before outsourcing data into the cloud and the Mac is maintained locally. The verification of the data is processed by recalculate the Mac values of the established data file which the owner desire to retrieve, and then it is compared to the pre-computed values using VANET. The disadvantage is that MAC cannot be used on large data files. If the owner employs TPA, then a secret key is generated and given to them for verification process. The TPA retrieves the data blocks and MAC randomly for integrity check.

PDP (PROVABLE DATA POSSESSION)

The public adaptability is considered in PDP method by Ateniese *et al.* (2011) which protects the data files from the unfaithful storage servers. The method uses RSA-based authenticators for checking the cloud storing. Samples of files are retrieved randomly for integrity check. With the linear combination of the blocks the public auditability is carried out. The probabilistic proof of the data possessed is achieved along with the identification of misbehaving servers, loss of data in the cloud storage.

DYNAMIC SECURITY SYSTEM

The scheme consist of a) IoT based servers: which provides the storage services to the users b)user: who is the owner of the data files which are outsourced to the IoT based service providers c) IoT based services provider: who owns the cloud servers and provides the service and computation to the users for money, the third-party checker who to minimize the time and computations burden for them without violating the privacy preservation. The data owner outsources the data to the IoT based servers along with pre-computed token for security measures. The owner verifies the data integrity, availability and confidentiality at frequently time interval for data assurance. The server calculates the response and sent it as proof using VANET. The values are compared if they are equal, then the data integrity is maintained, otherwise data is corrupted, error correction and find the misbehaving server is found by using erasure codes. Using homomorphic properties along with erasure code enhance the security of the dynamic data like add, erase, append etc.

The advantage of the system is the public auditing for maintaining data correctness without local copy at TPA. Storage correctness is maintained by identifying the threats and privacy preservation. Batch auditing is one of the maintain advantage as it is capability to delegate multiple different users simultaneously. The process of auditing is less complex in both time and computational aspects; hence it is light weight process.

IOT

IoT in reality, may bring assortment of preferences inside the administration and improvement of antiquated open administrations, similar to move and stopping, lighting, police examination and upkeep of open territories, conservation of social legacy, junk gathering, salubriousness of emergency clinics, and workforce udayakumar and krishnaveni(2019), The developing advancement inside the field of correspondence and computerized innovation. The possibility of reasonable town on the possibility of IoT gadgets is changing into more intelligent than previously. In light of the fast ascension the framework and administrations region unit expected to supply the needs of the town occupants. the various increment for computerized gadgets, for example sensors, actuators, and reasonable telephones that drive to enormous business possibilities for the IoT, since all gadgets will interconnect and speak with each other through net. The reviews of administrations which will be arrangement in urban IoT territory unit of potential enthusiasm for reasonable town. The instance of quickening the standard and upgrading the administrations offered to the voters while conveyance a shabby bit of leeway for the town organization as far as decrease of the operational costs. In thought of reasonable town there region unit various structure obstructs that region unit recorded beneath, anyway the principal vital four Pillars of reasonable town vision using wireless networks, Mahmood Hussain Mir and Dr. D. Ravindran (2017).

In the analysts join broadly RFIDs for labeling and ID as a piece of the strong waste variety foundation. In particular, the creators have anticipated partner RFID-based continuous reasonable waste collection framework. The paper displays the usage of RFID and weight detecting component innovation as a piece of waste variety. The IoT configuration is well-attempted to diminish squander combination operational costs and allows computerizing and streamlining waste recognizable proof for exercise and any procedure of waste. what is more weight measure forms territory unit fused inside the anticipated continuous waste variety system using VANET Mahmood Hussain Mir and Ravindran (2017). The paper finishes up with partner application that adventures RFID related weight detecting component learning in order to plot a programmed Waste Identity, Weight, and taken Bins Identification System (WIWSBIS). A dark Level Aura Matrix (GLAM) approach is utilized in order to remove the canister picture surface. Glitz neighboring framework parameters territory unit blocked to work out their ideal qualities. The framework is assessed by instructing and testing the extricated picture with Multi-Layer Perceptions (MLPs) and K-closest neighbor (KNN) classifiers. The paper demonstrates that the anticipated framework execution is amazing and might be connected to very surprising types of waste and receptacle level location underneath various conditions. The creators have anticipated a totally special unique programming and steering model fusing GIS, that cut back the task costs and waste material discharges of MSW grouping, Swati K. Rajput and Madhavi Patil, (2018).

IOT IS A BROADBAND NETWORK

IoT is a broadband system that utilizations standard correspondence conventions while its union point is the Internet. The genuine idea of IoT in reality is through incorporating a few advancements. Radio Frequency Identification (RFID) frameworks are contained a few labels. RFID labels can be exploited to display protests continuously; there is no need of viewable pathway. From a connected to radio wire going about as both sending and accepting gadget. Remote Sensor Network is another innovation that additionally assumes a significant job in IoT. Clearly it can coordinate (participate) with RFID in monitoring things for example area, temperature, developments and so on. In short sensors are acting like as extensions among physical and computerized world. The following best innovation is the mix of both RFID and sensor that is known as RFID Sensor Networks (RSN). It has both detecting, figuring and just as RFID per a user which includes more power for system task.

SENSORY STRUCTURE OF THE "KEEN CITY"

At present the essential sensor edifices actualized in explicit physical articles or various cell phones of the city occupants and visitors assuming the job of socio-open portable sensors, are the educational mechanical establishments of IOT advancements bunch in the "shrewd urban areas". Sensors executed in frameworks and area components of the "brilliant city" idea are the fundamental wellsprings of producing heterogeneous data sets. Data from sensors is gathered due to IoT gadgets associated with the correspondence systems. Cell phones associated with versatile systems GSM/3G/4G are utilized for determination and transmission of socially situated urban information using VANET. The information gathered in such a way are prepared and broke down in the "savvy city" investigative information handling focus which virtual model is sensibly to send on the cloud stage utilizing cloud information stores. The mix and solidification of information got from the sensors in buildings of the spaces of various kinds make it conceivable to improve altogether the parameters of administrations and data innovation administrations given by the "savvy" urban program-algorithmic applications using wireless networks, Udayakumar and Krishnaveni (2019). The advantages: vanet is applied in space research, military application and vanet devices are cost effective. The disadvantages: vanet cannot be used for certain application where the device range is not used.

A creative system that automates concentrated and periodic modification of the sent sensors. This sensor change organization is performed out and out at our backend establishment, and prevents any modifications in the sent DCUs gear or programming using VANET. On a very basic level, data from sent sensors is differentiated. ETSI M2M master, which can be accessed using a M2M Network Application. All bar sub streams can in like manner be addressed with GET techniques. The pro association and director of the BusNet vehicular framework gives a REST API to getting to the BusNet dataflows that can be gotten.

The citywide data arrangement of incorporated checking and investigation of installments for devoured assets alongside the support of generation business capacities can fill in as a powerful instructive methodological device in instructive procedures expanding the urban network "learning potential" managing the issues of affordable utilization and the proficient utilization of the wide scope of assets and administrations . The preparing and investigation of Big Data from sensors, meters and stream meters enables us to create proposals for customers with respect to ideal time profiles, working methods of family unit gear and anticipated volumes of important assets. Simultaneously, this framework can be utilized as the preparation research facility stand model for directing classes with understudies of various strengths, execution of genuine course tasks and reproduction of numerous procedures requiring the examination and investigation in the "keen urban communities" incorporated data frameworks dependent on data innovative IoT, Udayakumar and Krishnaveni (2019).

VANET MODEL OVERVIEW

Impromptu Networks VANETs are a subset of MANETs (Mobile Adhoc Networks) in which correspondence hubs are fundamentally vehicles. All things considered, this sort of system should manage an incredible number of exceptionally portable hubs, in the long run scattered in various streets. In VANETs, vehicles can impart one another (V2V, Vehicl eto-Vehicle interchanges). In addition, they can interface with a foundation (V2I, Vehicle-to Infrastructure) to get some assistance. This foundation is thought to be situated along the streets.

There are numerous substances associated with a VANET settlement and sending. Despite the fact that by far most of VANET hubs are vehicles, there are different substances that perform fundamental activities in these systems. It is mostly made by those substances that deal with the traffic or offer an outer assistance. Vehicle enrollment and offense revealing are two significant errands. Specially appointed condition From the VANET perspective, they are outfitted with three distinct gadgets. Right off the bat, they are furnished with a correspondence unit (OBU, On-Board Unit) that empowers Vehicle-to-Vehicle (V2V) and Vehicle-to Infrastructure (V2I, I2V) interchanges. Then again, they have a lot of sensors to quantify their very own status (for example fuel utilization) and its condition (for example elusive street, wellbeing separation). These sensorial information can be imparted to different vehicles to build their mindfulness and improve street security. At last, a Trusted Platform Module (TPM) is regularly mounted on vehicles.

A FRAMEWORK

To mimic VANET situations with SUMO situation utilizing sensible vehicular versatility models. This structure utilizes the open source programming called "Reenactment of Urban Mobility" (SUMO) and the "input direction documents" highlight of OPNET. Irregular versatility and direction portability is good. The last-referenced is setting with one direction document for every hub. This strategy permits expounding complex hub developments. Tragically, communications between hubs are not considered, so reasonable versatility is constrained. plan to confine the quantity of parcel sent. T contrarily relative to the good ways from past sender: T = tmax. (1-d/R) With tmax the greatest dispute time, d the good ways from past sender, R the radio run. At the point when the clocks arriving at zero the hub forward the parcel. Other holding up hubs get this bundle and drop their clock. In this manner, we lessen the quantity of bundle sent in the system. Correspondence with SUMO enabling us to characterize increasingly complex recreation situations in OPNET modeler.

MODEL GPS SATELLITE

In this module we have contemplated the insights regarding GPS satellite and we have executed the model of GPS satellite for getting the position subtleties. There are 2 sorts of synthetic satellites in the sky over: One sort of satellite ORBITS the earth more than once per day, and the other kind is known as a correspondences satellite and it is PARKED in a STATIONARY position 22,300 miles (35,900 km) over the equator of the STATIONARY earth. The most conspicuous satellites in medium earth circle (MEO) are the satellites which contain the GLOBAL POSITIONING SYSTEM or GPS as it is called. GPS satellites fly in medium Earth circle (MEO) at a height of around 20,200 km (12,550 miles). Expandable 24-Slot satellite group of stars, as characterized in the SPS Performance Standard. The satellites in the GPS heavenly body are orchestrated into six similarly divided orbital planes encompassing the Earth. Each plane contains four "spaces" involved by benchmark satellites. This 24-opening game plan guarantees clients can see in any event four satellites from for all intents and purposes any point on the planet. The Air Force ordinarily flies in excess of 24 GPS satellites to keep up inclusion at whatever point the gauge satellites are adjusted or decommissioned. The additional satellites may expand GPS execution however are not viewed as a component of the center star grouping.

VANET SECURITY AND SAFETY

Security is increasingly fundamental in VANETs, VANET must be satisfy various exacting necessities earlier they can be conveyed. These necessities incorporate client and information verification, protection, obligation and secure communicate transmission. Fulfilling these necessities in profoundly powerful and versatile VANETs is an extreme errand yet one that is explicitly significant due to traded off VANET could bring about the loss of human life . Security in VANET framework is a difficult issue for researchers in the hour of digital dangers. The data which is going starting with one vehicle then onto the next vehicle might be gotten or hacked by a programmer who makes helplessness in the framework execution. In vehicular correspondence a few sorts of assault happen on the system framework, for instance, position hood winking, ID deceiving, GPS information hacking, message change and so forth. Malevolent drivers cause issues in the action which prompts car influx and mishap. Consequently, the vehicles must use wellbeing and security segments to contradict these perils circumstances. Around there we look at about the realities of VANETs security and wellbeing applications.

SECURITY ISSUES IN VANETS

Security verification is an imperative property for the VANET engineering. Different dangers are available with respect to accessibility highlight to influence the presentation criteria of vehicular framework. There are most more often than not experienced dangers on openness are talked about as pursues: Denial Attacks: The Denial of administration assaults can be executing by inside or outside vehicles to the VANET. For these conditions, the aggressors break and isolated the essential correspondence among vehicles and subsequently upset administrations. Nonetheless, the administration couldn't access by the affirmed customers. Sticking Attacks: In this assault, the aggressors hinder with the radio wave base trades diverts in the vehicular framework utilizing an over controlled sign in the equal recurrence extend. This chops down the message signal characteristics until the recurrence band gets precarious or isolated to the customers. Malware Attacks: The malware (infection) assault can be invaded into the vehicular framework by means of programming segments acquainted with use actualize the RSUs and OBU. Malware may lead the hinder of general value of the vehicular framework. Communicate Altering Attacks: In this assault, the authentic clients may work in as insider assaults and send wrong security ready messages in the VANET. This may cover the correct security messages to endorsed customers, which can manual for exacting mishaps. Also, it furthermore impacts in general aftereffect of the VANET framework. Blackhole Attacks: The Blackhole assault for the most part happens by means of certifiable VANET customer being coordinated by external hotspots for some reasons. Vanet is applicable for all devices and it is not domain specific. The assailants assault the usefulness of the MAC layer of IEEE 802.11. The malevolent vehicles intentionally misuse the MAC convention to grow the information transmission at the expense of different vehicles.

The principle explanation for these assaults is to restrict different vehicles from the activity of help and administrations of the VANET. In the covetous nature, the malevolent drivers also attempt to abbreviate its sitting tight time for brisk access. This may cause crash issue in the remote medium, which add to postpone in the genuine client's administrations. . Spamming Attacks: This kind of assault is imbues the bothersome spam messages. For instance, plugs in the VANET framework and uses the data transfer capacity pointlessly to achieve deliberate accidents. Development Analysis Attacks: In VANET plan, the traffic investigation assault is definitely not a unique assault. In this assault the assailants can listens the information communicate data and afterward break down the recurrence and timeframe of message being transmitted. From the examination, the undesirable clients can perceive the idea of correspondence and take a stab at aggregating the vast majority of the significant information for its own points of interest. Social Attacks: The aggressors send corrupt and unmoral messages to vehicle drivers with the goal that drivers get confounded and bother. The basic goal of the assailant is to achieve the correct vehicle customers react in an upset way in the wake of having such sort of messages and henceforth impact the driving execution of the vehicle in the VANET framework. Burrowing Attack: The burrowing assault is a wormhole type assault, Juels and et.al (2017).

In this assault the outside wormhole aggressors' joint two far-away pieces of the vehicular framework by using an extra correspondence channel called as a passage. Thus, the customers from far-away of the framework can pass on as near ones. Worldwide Position System (GPS) Issues: GPS satellite keeps up the area table; it contains the geographic area information about each vehicle on the VANET. An assailant can make false readings about its situation rather than exhorting its correct position using GPS satellite test framework to hoodwink the vehicle to believe that it is availability in a substitute district. Replay Attacks: Replay assault is furthermore called as a playback assault in which right data is perniciously or erroneously retransmitted or deferred to convey an unapproved sway. To avoid replay assault, the VANET needs a period source with a reserve memory to contrast the as of late got messages and the at present got messages. Key as well as Certificate Replication: For this circumstance, the assailants use duplicate keys and supports of various vehicles as an approval affirmation to make question anyway which makes hard to TAs for recognizing a vehicle. These assaults are to bewilder TAs and cautions affirmation of vehicle customers in attempt at manslaughter occasions Santos et al.,(2018). Message Altering: In this assault, the aggressors are modifying the messages traded in vehicle to vehicle or vehicle to foundation correspondence so as to phony trade application demands or to counterfeit reactions.

SECURITY BASED CHALLENGE IN VANET

The significant test while executing wellbeing and security frameworks in Vehicular Ad-hoc system are referenced underneath: Validation: There must be an affirmation of the impressive number of messages discussed beginning with one dissent then onto the following. Each vehicle in the framework is to be affirmed by the focal position. High Mobility: As the vehicle moves quicker, various issues happened because of high versatility, for instance, aggravation issue and handshaking is lost. Thus, the vehicles are not prepared to work together and develop secure correspondence between them. Zone Based Schemes: Beacon messages help us to know the region of interchange vehicles. In any case, by taking care of, sensors, GPS and Laser, perceive the accurate area of the vehicles. Ongoing System: High versatility zone avoids the advancement of constant framework. Along these lines, it is troublesome assignment to transmit ready message to different gadgets in right time earlier the cutoff time.

In a conventional SDN sort out, each OpenFlow-drew in Switch (OF-Switch) accomplices with other OF-Switches and possibly to end-client contraptions that are the sources and destinations of traffic streams in the structure. All OF-Switch has different tables acknowledged in equipment or firmware that it uses to process (i.e., planning) the got gatherings. Specifically, the controller alters the substance of the table called sending table. Ceaseless stockpile of a bundle, the OF-Switch plays out a request in its sending table to discover the territory which chooses the relating activity for the got gathering. A table-miss happens when there is no arranging section found for the pack, and it is dealt with according to the activities (e.g., send it to the controller through the southbound API or drop the group) conveyed in the table-miss (or default) region. The controller basically deals with the structure direct by sending stream mod bundles that changes the substance of sending table at OF-Switches. The point by point talk on SDN structure and its headways are out of the level of this paper, for an absolute report on SDN, if it's not too much issue propose, Bharathi sharma and et al. (2019). 1) Benefits and Challenges: The SDN absolute unwinds sort out the heap up by performing beneficial assets use with the assistance of the general structure data, and it in addition support the utilization of the systems association associations for SDN applications by abstracting the information plane from the applications and engaging them to affirm their dynamic necessities on information plane substances through dependably bound together controller(s). Despite the manner in which that SDN brings different focal points, the unavoidable attributes (e.g., programmable SDN-based switches, the restricted trade speed of the southbound channel, and obliged assets at SDN controllers) of SDN arrangement additionally raises new security concerns. Vanet execution in square chain will be clarified for future book part. Underneath, we quickly graph both the significant good conditions and inconveniences in the use of SDN progressions Curtmola and et al. (2008).

Sponsorship for heterogeneity and improved resource use: With the use of its standard programmable interface, for instance, openflow, SDN building fortifies the device heterogeneity, i.e., managing contraptions starting from different merchants can associate with each other and with the control plane parts as long as they are composed with the open correspondence interfaces (e.g., OF show). The controller attempts to reliably keep a present as a rule point of view on the vital structures affiliation establishment. In this way, past what one real applications can share, through virtualization philosophies, the proportionate physical framework to have a reasonably free structure. This makes the SDN re-usable correspondingly as multi-reason, i.e., it could be shared among different applications at the family member or explicit motivation driving occasions. In particular, the controller can dispatch unmistakable social affairs of keen OF-attracted switches over a lone physical framework with the target that each physical substance could reliably work for different applications, while each application will get a vibe like the part is working just for it. Such dispatch of data plane substances pushes toward the most extraordinary use of structure resources by guaranteeing each application a changed introduction which relies on their given rudiments. Improved framework security: The controller can accumulate key information about the structure by talking with the OF-Switches. These switches can total the central information by performing structure traffic appraisal and using obvious unpredictability district instruments. Starting there, the controller detaches and relates the response from the data plane parts to make or enable its general framework see.

In setting on the examination results, new structures and ways to deal with oversee keep up a vital good ways from the evident or foreseen security threats can be presented in the whole framework. Thusly, these measures could improve the framework execution and help in speedier control and rule of clear security vulnerabilities. Single reason behind disillusionments: The gathered SDN controller, low transmission limit correspondence channel between the controller and OF-Switch and stream table size confinement on OF-Switches makes the SDN slight against a blend of DDoS attacks, Swati K. Rajput and Madhavi Patil, (2018). Also, the nonattendance of (I) trust between data plane substances on account of structures support for open programmability, and (ii) best practices unequivocal to purposes of control and bits of SDN; remain basic bottlenecks in the brilliant and bona fide choice of SDN. Slow spread of horrendous information: At OF-Switch, when a pack having a spot with a particular traffic stream finds a match in the sending table, the switch perceives how to treat the remainder of the social occasions of a relative stream. As needs be, it doesn't require any further correspondences with the SDN controller. As it manufactures the traffic sending sufficiently of the switch, yet it similarly makes issues in light of adaptability, which makes the sending table principles clashing with the present framework conditions. As such, the confuse between the physical topology and overall topology at controller causes package hardships (due to wrong sending information at OF-Switches) until the controller invigorates the sending table areas with new standards.

To expand the security gauges and techniques open in P2P correspondence to VANETs BC. A bit of the huge security challenges in VANET are bogus information, ID disclosure, and Sybil attacks. There are different courses of action open for these security perils in the composition, for instance, For any situation, one standard test in the composing is that it is overwhelmingly based on P2P convenient extemporaneous frameworks. In order to fuse these security remembers for VANET BC, we have mastermind these segment into three social events: Authentication, Anonymity and Availability of advantages, which is excited by work put forth in. Affirmation is a system of favoring both sender and related message by getting vehicle, Sebe, et al (2008). The endorsement technique requires sender recognizing evidence, which is portrayed by different properties, for instance, territory, bearing, speed, and owner of the vehicle. The confirmation part sets up the trustworthiness of the sender's information, which finally gives the framework empowering balancing activity of Sybil ambushes in VANETs. Besides, the system of mystery coordinates hiding sender information similarly as encoding this information to make it mistook for unintended customers. Sender vehicles that are either source or move vehicles may be glad to share information given a framework to avoid following of vehicles or sharing genuine vehicle information. Of course, a secured structure is moreover required to merge inadequacy tolerant arrangement, adaptable to attacks similarly as continuance shows so to remain available and operational inside seeing issues or harmful ambushes.

These three specific social events of security perils are furthermore explored with respect to P2P and BC systems in the going with sections: Security in Point-to-Point (P2P) Communication A Point-to-Point (P2P) correspondence incorporates in any event two vehicles, specifically source and objective.

Source vehicle transmits information proposed for an objective vehicle, which uses a trust segment to set up the validness of the got information. In Mahmood Hussain Mir and Dr. D. Ravindran (2017), trust relies upon a method considered approval that assistants in adequately perceiving source vehicle. This approval method contains three particular sorts, to be explicit ID check, property affirmation, and territory confirmation. ID approval uses uncommon IDs, which are either license number or chaises number of a vehicle, for recognizing evidence of a vehicle. The property affirmation energizes in recognizing the sort of sources, for instance, a vehicle or a traffic signal, of course, region confirmation perceives the region of a source allowing getting vehicles to favor got information. Affirmation is an amazing methodology of separating the source similarly as endorsing transmitted information. Nevertheless, this would deal the lack of clarity of a source vehicle giving a supportive strategy for following similarly as perceiving the vehicle and its explorers. In a united system is executed with the help of RSUs giving encryption part to all of the vehicles that are enlisted with the structure. A confirmation strategy is used by the joined system to favor similarly as offering affirmations to selected vehicles. Source vehicles are given encoded presentations during the transmission of information, while, these supports are decoded by giving an open key to objective vehicles.

In the pseudonym, a vehicle is administered a moniker from a pool of pen names using a substitute estimation to achieve vehicle anonymity. On the other hand in k-mystery approach, vehicle information qualities are either smothered or summarized to avoid conspicuous evidence and following of a vehicle and its voyagers.

ACOUSTIC SENSOR SIGNAL PROCESSING

Around there we give particular bits of knowledge in regards to the execution of our structure Santos et al.,(2018) distinguish the thickness of vehicles inside urban conditions. The system utilizes engine sounds to choose the occasion of three improvement events: A single vehicle passing, a stationary vehicle, and a movement of automobiles moving along the street. For the most part, the system is involved four modules: Filtering, signal imperativeness figuring, event recognizable proof, and vehicle counting, Santhi and et.al, (2019) Our experimentation technique sought after a progressive approach; along these lines, in order to achieve consistency of the structure module's lead; we finished the preliminary's starters on a conservative PC with a collector associated; we accumulated engine traces of the vehicle advancement events as of late referenced and recorded them onto the PC hard drive. In order to process the sign sounds with sign taking care of counts at different objectives degrees, we accumulated the sound sign at the best rates permitted by the PC hardware. The sound annals were ten seconds, the models were 16-bits, and the sounds were acquired at a data pace of 44100 models for each second. We started the test by continuing the filtering stage with the recorded sound sign; yield was passed to the sign essentialness module. A brief timeframe later, we adjusted the parameters of the event area module, whose yield supported into the vehicle checking module.

TRAFFIC SIMULATION AND DENSITY EXTRAPOLATION

There are two essential sorts of traffic propagation: Microscopic and distinguishable, which are related to the significance of assessment to be performed. The little amusement is the improvement of each vehicle independently, requiring a ton of data and computational resources, for instance, memory, enrolling power, accumulating units of data, and so forth. This sort of proliferation gives results that give Wang, et.al (2011) a point by point image of framework execution and affectability of the structure to unequivocal changes in busy time gridlock. While a normally noticeable multiplication relies upon traffic examination from an overall perspective, where traffic is seen as endless and its application is essentially in urban orchestrating. In order to create the entertainment circumstance (guide) and the vehicular adaptability structures we used the Mobility model generator for Vehicular frameworks (MOVE), which utilizes an open-source scaled down scale traffic test framework called SUMO (Simulation of Urban MObility) for mirroring our traffic circumstance. Thusly, we have had the choice to reenact reasonable vehicular advancements, for instance, car over-burdens and stops at intersection focuses. We masterminded the circumstance subject to the five paths picked in Xalapa city, México, and we considered unmistakable traffic densities to improve the SUMO multiplication. SUMO makes a yield record with vehicular adaptability follows. This report was put into the framework test framework NS-2 to get the last reenactment results. We structured the most extraordinary speed of the vehicles as obliged to 50 km/h. The transmission extend was fixed at 150 meters.

OVERVIEW OF VANET RESEARCH IN THE LAST DECADE

Starting from the overview of the most outstanding investigate subjects in VANETs (isolated and merged from a couple 'require papers' of PC sorting out gatherings and journals), we described a get-together of eight ask about regions (top-level classes), covering a wide extent of focuses related to vehicular trades (Table 1). For example, if a paper bases on any point of view related to the association or physical layers, for instance, a MAC estimation, channel showing, compose coding, or flexible transmit power control, the paper is named as MAC-PHY. At the furthest edge there is the APP class, containing all papers keeping an eye on customer applications (e.g., union accident avoiding, road blockage notice, and intelligent media spilling). As in other PC sorting out districts, there are various papers concerning execution appraisal of shows. A paper is assumed as having a position with the PERF class if and just if its guideline responsibility is on the introduction evaluation itself. Thusly, if another MAC or controlling show was proposed, trailed by its introduction appraisal, by then the paper was set apart as MAC-PHY, or ROUT, as opposed to PERF. Papers delineating another device, stage, structure, or building were set apart as TOOL. For ease, each and every exploratory assessment, by and large concerning association and field testing, were moreover included into that class. The ROUT class speaks to papers proposing another directing show while the MOB class relates to adaptability issues, for instance, movability showing and packing estimations. We end our course of action with the DATA and SERV names.

The past was used for works focusing on data aggregation/dispersing plans, while the latter is for what we call 'correlative organizations, for instance, Quality of Service (QoS), security, and control. Figure 2 depicts the substance and transient apportionment for the dispersed papers. Practically a fourth of them was on MAC-PHY issues (23%). During the latest decade, both insightful world and industry have worked to engage suitable and successful remote correspondence in vehicular circumstances. The IEEE 802.11p amendment similarly as the IEEE 1609 Wireless Access in Vehicular Environments (WAVE) models result from such an effort. What's more, our results suggest a slight augmentation on such issues. The congruity of framework coding plans in VANETs may be considered as one critical clarification behind this trend.4 At the ensuing spot, we got the SERV class, which consolidates papers as to vital organizations, whether or not it be Quality of Service (QoS), security approaches, or territory based organizations. In the consequent period, we saw more assessments identified with the mix between vehicular frameworks and ordinary establishment frameworks (e.g., cell). There is a craving for VANETs to be facilitated with 5G compact advancement by 2020 23. Udayakumar and et.al, (2019) Directing (ROUT name) is up 'til now a huge purpose of research. Directly off the bat, regular MANET controlling shows were found not sensible for the huge essentials, and stand-out characteristics of VANETs' circumstances and applications. A few coordinating shows have been proposed during the latest decade, including diverse logical orders for organizing them. Curtmola, Khan, and et.al (2008). Rather than the customary MANETs' coordinating shows, which are topology-based (proactive, responsive, or hybrid), the most promising VANETs' choices are the geographic and the deferment tolerant strategies. The past is progressively fitting for vehicular correspondence while the last incorporates the carryand-forward framework which is used to beat sporadic accessibility, a normal condition in vehicular circumstances. We saw a basic augmentation on the amount of works related to dissipating frameworks and broadcasting figurings (DATA mark).

Believe it or not, it was the one subject with the most raised improvement among all (38%). As confirmed by Lee and et.al (2008) most application shows rely upon varieties of the pandemic data dispersing approach so the best possible information causes to centers in a zone where the information is begun. The standard test around there is on keeping an eye on redundancy and capability all together. In the meantime, creations in the PERF class dropped from 20 to only 8 papers between the double cross casings. This result suggests that less effort has been put just on show execution assessment and examination. As the investigation in VANETs grows, more thought is given to novel shows, organizations, and applications rather than perceiving how existing developments would carry on in new conditions. Along these lines, one could take this result somehow envisioned.

This likely could be because of the way that, during the primary long stretches of research, there is an enormous requirement for devices and structures for setting out the foundations for viable research. For example, Table 2 shows a rundown of understood reproduction devices for VANETs, and it is observable that every one of them were created during the main time frame or much prior. By and by, with the reception of vehicular correspondence innovation via vehicle producers in the next years, it is conceivable that numerous new devices and systems will be presented. Ultimately, two research classifications had indicated a slight reduction throughout the most recent decade: versatility displaying and examination, and application layer conventions and administrations. With respect to the previous, as there are as of now sensible two-dimensional traffic-based vehicular versatility models, Mell and T. Grance (2009) we foresee future research to be progressively express, covering subjects like geo-social transportability showing, and three-dimensional accessibility examination. Of course, concerning the last topic (i.e., APP class), we were somehow surprised by the decrease on considers concerning the application layer, regardless, it's legitimate that, after a basic period exhibiting the lead of existing applications in the new VANETs circumstances, organize has moved to progressively viable research focuses.

CONCLUSION

The users of the IoT based increases in large numbers year by year and it vital to find feasible solution for the storage security for maintaining data integrity for both static and dynamic data .The auditing methods are enhanced by using many techniques to achieve the data integrity and data availability without data leakage. This paper brings out the various methods and techniques which used to maintain the data security and finding the misbehaving servers using public auditing. For the data which keep on changing frequently in real-time applications like, weather, share market data integrity is still on research for the better solution with minimum overhead.

REFERENCES

Ateniese, G. (2007). Proble Data Posseon.atUntrued and Store. *Proc. 14th ACM Conf. Computer and Comm. Security (CCS '07)*, 598-609.

Bowers, K. D. (2009). A High Availabe& Integrity based Layers for Cloud Storage. *Proc. ACM Conf. Comput& Comm. Security (CCS '09)*, 187-198.

Curtmola, R., Khan, O., & Burns, R. (2008). Robust Remote Data Checking. *Proc. Fourth ACM Int. Worksp Storage Security systems & Survivability*, 63-68.

Curtmolaand. (2008). MR-PDP: MultileReplicationProvale Data Posssion. *Proc. IEEE Int. Conf. Distrtd Computing Systs (ICDCS '08)*, 411-420.

Erway, C. (2009). Dynic Proable Data Possson. *Proc. ACM Conf. Computer and Comm. Security (CCS '09)*, 213-222.

Juels. (2007). Pors: Proofs of Retrievability for Large Files. *Proc. 14th ACM Conf. Comptr & Comm. Security*, 584-597.

Juels. (2017). PORs: Proof of Retrievability of Large File. *Proc. ACM Conf. Computer and Comm. Security (CCS '07)*, 584-597.

Mell, P., & Grance, T. (2009). *Above clouds: A review of cloud comptg.* Univ. of California, Berkeley, Technology. Rep. UCBEECS-2009-28.

Mir & Ravindran. (2017). Role of IoT in Smart City Applipn: A Review. *Int. Jornl of Advd Research in Comptr Engg. & Tech*, 6(7), 1099–1104.

Rajput, S. K., & Patil, M. (2018). Waste Mangnt in IoT- Facilitated Smart Cities- A Suvery. *Internl Journal of Computer Apps*, 182(24), 21–26.

Reyes. (2014). Vehicle density in VANET application. *Journal of Ambient Intelligence and Smart Environments*, 6, 469-481.

Santhi, S. (2019). *SoS Emergency Ad-Hoc Wireless Network, Computational Intelligence and Sustainable Systems (CISS)*. EAI/Springer Innovations in Comm and Computing.

Santos, P. M. (2018). Porto Living Lab: An IoT-Based Sensing Platform for Smart Cities. IEEE Internet of Things Journal, 5(2), 523-532.

Schwarz, T., & Miller, E. L. (2006). Store, Forget & Check: using Algbric Signtres to Chck Remtel Admnied Storge. *Proc. IEEE Int Conf. Distribtd Comptng Sytms*, 1-6.

Sebe, F. (2008). Efficnt Remote Data Possen Checkg in Critical Inf. Infrastes. *Trans. Knowledge and Data Eng*, *20*(8), 1034–1038. doi:10.1109/TKDE.2007.190647

Shah, M. A. (2008). Privacy-Preserving Audit & Extracting of Digital Content. Cryptology based Print of the Report.

Sharma. (2019). A survey: issues and challenges of vehicular ad hoc networks (VANETs). *International conf on sustainable computing in science, technology and management (SUSCOM-2019)*, 2491-2503.

Shrinivas. (2011). Privacy-Preserving Public Auditing in Cloud Storage security. *Intl Jornl of Computer Science and Information Technology*, *2*(6), 2691-2693.

Sivaganesan, S. (2020). An Event based Neural Network Architecture with Content Addressable Memory. *International Journal of Embedded and Real-Time Communication Systems, IGI Global*, *11*(1), 23–40. doi:10.4018/IJERTCS.2020010102

Srihari. (2015). Automatic Battery Replacement of Robot. *Advances in Natural and Applied Sciences*, *9*(7), 33-38.

Udayakumar, E., & Krishnaveni, V. (2019). Analysis of various Interference in Millimeter- Wave Communication Systems: A Survey. *Proceedings of IEEE International Conference on Computing, Communication and Networking Technologies (ICCCNT 2019)*, 1-6. 10.1109/ICCCNT45670.2019.8944417

Udayakumar, E., & Krishnaveni, V. (2019). A Review on Interference management in Millimeter-Wave MIMO Systems for future 5G Networks. *Proceedings of International Conference on Innovations in Electrical and Electronics Engineering (ICIEEE 2019)*, 1-6.

Vats. (2017). Vanet. A future technology. *International Journal of Science and Research Publications*, *7*(2), 378-389.

Vetrivelan, P. (2015). PAPR Reduction for OQAM/OFDM Signals using Optimized Iterative Clipping and Filtering Technique. *Proceedings of IEEE International Conference on Soft-Computing and Network Security (ICSNS'15)*, 72.

Vetrivelan, P. (2015). PAPR Reduction for OQAM/OFDM Signals by using Neural Networks. *International Journal of Applied Engineering Research*, *10*(41), 30292–30297.

Vetrivelan, P (2019). *A Neural Network based Automatic Crop Monitoring Robot for Agriculture. In The IoT and the Next Revolutions Automating the World*. IGI Global.

Wang, C., Chow, S. S. M., Wang, Q., Ren, K., & Lou, W. (2013). Privacy_preserving Public Auditing for Secure Cloud Storage. *IEEE Transactions on Computers*, *62*(2), 362–375. doi:10.1109/TC.2011.245

Wang, Q., & Wang, C. (2011). Enabling Public Audita & Data Dynamic for Storage in the Cloud Comptg. *IEEE Transactions on Parallel and Distributed Systems*, *22*, 847–859. doi:10.1109/TPDS.2010.183

Wang, C. (2012). Towards the Secure& Dependable Storage Service in the Cloud Comptng. *IEEE Trans. Service Computing*, *5*(2), 220-232.

Watersand, B. (2008). Compact the Proofs of the Retrievability. *Proc. Int. Conf. Theory &Applicn of Cryptology &Infn Security: Advan of Cryptology*, *5350*, 90-107.

Chapter 5
Two–Stage Non–Cooperative Game Model for Vertical Handoffs in Heterogeneous Wireless Networks

Pramod Kumar Goyal

https://orcid.org/0000-0002-8390-9273

Department of Training and Technical Education, Government of Delhi, India

Pawan Singh

Indira Gandhi National Tribal University, Amarkantak, India

ABSTRACT

In a heterogeneous wireless network (HWN) environment, performing an efficient vertical handoff requires the efficient qualitative evaluation of all stakeholders like wireless networks (WN) and mobile users (MU) and mutual selection of best WN-MU. In the literature, most of the work deals with both these requirements jointly in the techniques proposed by them for the vertical handoffs (VHO) in HWNs, leaving very little scope to manipulate the above requirements independently. This may result in inefficient vertical handoffs. Hence, this chapter proposed a generalized two-stage two players, iterative non-cooperative game model. This model presents a modular framework that separates the quantitative evaluation of WNs and MUs (at Stage 1) from the game formulation and solution (at Stage 2) for mutual selection of best WN-MU pair for VHO. The simulation results show a substantial reduction in the number of vertical handoffs with the proposed game theory-based two-stage model as compared to a single-stage non-game theory method like multiple attribute decision making.

DOI: 10.4018/978-1-7998-2764-1.ch005

1. INTRODUCTION

Heterogeneous Wireless Networks (HWN)(Pramod Goyal, Lobiyal, & Katti, 2018c) comprises of different types of Wireless Networks (WN) having a hierarchical structure. The difference in the constituent WNs are generally in terms of Network Technologies, Network Architecture & Protocols and Network Operators in the market (Trestian, Ormond, & Muntean, 2012). Fig.1 shows an HWN consisting three wireless networks; Wi-Fi, CDMA and Wi-Max overlapping each other. When a Mobile User (MU) or group of mobile users sitting in a car or a train wish to roam in an HWN environment, they may need to change the current network and connect to another network. This event is termed as Handoff. The handoff is mainly classified between two types as Horizontal Handoff (HHO) and Vertical Handoff (VHO). The HHO occurs between the same type of networks while VHO occurs between two different. In today's fast changing world, the next generation networks like 4G and 5G will all be HWNs. Even the Vehicular Ad-Hoc networks will have to be part of these networks so as to provide cloud based seamless data roaming services to the mobile users.

Like different constituent WNs in a HWN, the participating MUs may also be different. The MUs may be differentiated in terms of the service requests as real-time (e.g. voice/video call) or non- real time service (e.g. emails). Now days, the communicating devices like mobile phone or laptop are equipped with the capability to work as multi-mode or multi-home terminals. A MU with such communicating devices (Wang & Kuo, 2013) can connect with more than one different WNs at any point in time. At the same time, a WN may experience different service requests from multiple MUs. In such situations where multiple mobile nodes are competing with multiple WNs, the selection of mutually best WN – MU pair to perform the seamless and efficient Vertical Handoff (Pramod Goyal, Lobiyal, & Katti, 2017) becomes a challenging task.

Describing a WN as best in HWNs from MU's perspective depends on multiple decision factors which are termed in literature as network selection attributes or Handoff Decision Attributes (HDA) like Received signal strength (RSS), Offered Bandwidth, Delay, Jitter, Bit Error rate (BER), Velocity, Power Consumption, Distance and network usage cost etc. The HDAs may be conflicting in nature to each other like bandwidth and cost. A MU may prefer one HDA over another. Such relative preferences of users are termed in literature as User Preferences. The user preferences may be Static or Dynamic. However, the Dynamic User Preferences (Pramod Goyal, Lobiyal, & Katti, 2018b) are more useful in accommodating the changes in the values of HDAs on real time basis when a MU roam within a HWN which may result in higher user satisfaction.

Similarly, describing a MU as best from the network's perspective is depends on multiple factors like typeof service requested by the MU, requested bandwidth and expected revenue receivable from MU's etc. A WN operator generally charge different network usage cost for different type of service requests from a user. The network usage charges for voice and data services are based on per unit time (e.g. Rs / minute) and per unit data (Rs /Mb) respectively. The differential network usage cost policy force a WN to prefer one type of service request over another and prioritise the competing MU's accordingly in order to maximise its expected revenue.

The Multiple Attribute Decision Methods (MADM) (Pramod Goyal et al., 2017) based on utility theory (Zanakis, Solomon, Wishart, & Dublish, 1998) like "Simple Additive Weighting (SAW), Multiplicative Exponential Weighting (MEW), Analytical Hierarchical Process (AHP), Grey Relational Analysis (GRE) and Technique of Order Preference Similarity to Ideal Solution (TOPSIS)" are commonly used techniques to rank the available WNs. These methods can incorporate multiple & conflicting HDAs along with their

Figure 1. Heterogeneous Wireless Networks

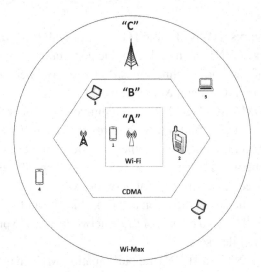

"User Preference Weights". These MADM techniques work well when a network has sufficient resources to serve one or all users at all times. However, when multiple MUs compete with multiple WNs having limited resources, the MADM techniques failed to serve efficiently. Game Theory(Pramod Goyal et al., 2018c) presents good mathematical solutions to model such multi MU – multi WN competition to find an optimum solution.

In a HWNs environment, as shown in fig.1, the selection of mutually best WN – MU pair to perform the seamless and efficient Vertical Handoff (VHO) required two important steps-

1. an efficient qualitative evaluation of different WNs & MUs, and
2. an efficient mutual selection of best WN-MU pair

in order to minimise the number of Vertical Handoffs (VHO) while maximising the profit & satisfaction of WNs & MUs respectively.

In the literature most of the work, as per my best knowledge, deals with both the above steps jointly in the techniques proposed by them for the vertical handoffs in HWNs leaving a very little scope to manipulate the above requirements independently. This may result in inefficient vertical handoffs. Therefore, in this chapter, the authors propose a generalised two stage two player non-cooperative game formulation to represent the competition among multiple MUs and multiple WNs. The network efficiency is expressed in terms of *User Payoff* receivable to a MU from a WN with all the considered handoff decision attributes. The novelty of the proposed two stage non-cooperative game model is in four ways –

1. It utilises multiple HDAs and the respective user preferences to assess the Quality of Experience (QoE) from a WN. QoE is used to assess service quality of a network from user's perspective and is a subjective measure.
2. It utilises the concept of dynamic user preferences(Pramod Goyal et al., 2018b)

3. It utilises the concept of using the WNs as game strategies for MUs and the MUs as game strategies for WNs (Pramod Goyal, Lobiyal, & Katti, 2018a) which is further explained pictorially here using a special diagram.

4. It separates the game formulation and solution (at stage 2) from qualitative evaluation of WNs and MUs (at stage 1).

The solution of the game gives a pair of WN-MU which are best for each other to perform an efficient vertical handoff. The proposed model provides a modular framework to solve the VHO decision problems using game theory. The simulations, carried out to analyse the effect of user preferences on the vertical handoffs, shows substantial reduction in number of vertical handoffs with the proposed game theory based method as compared to non-game theory methods like MADM using utility theory.

The rest of the chapter is organized as follows: Related work in section 2, Vertical Handoff overview in section 3, important concepts of Game Theory Section 4, proposed Non Cooperative Game Model for VHO in section 5, simulation and result analysis in Section 6, and section 7 states the conclusion.

2. RELATED WORK

The key challenges for an efficient network resource management in heterogeneous wireless networks are presented in (Piamrat, Ksentini, Bonnin, & Viho, 2011) along with an overview of recent solutions for vertical handoff decision making. In HWNs, The network selection is an important step for performing vertical handoff decisions which needs to consider a large number of complex and conflicting HDAs. The handoff decision factors can be static and/or dynamic (P Goyal & Saxena, 2008). The "Multi-Criteria Decision Making (MCDM)" or "Multi-Attribute Decision Making (MADM)" techniques (Obayiuwana & Falowo, 2016) are generally used to evaluate and ranked the available wireless networks for network selection in HWNs. The MADM methods are efficient and sufficient only to evaluate the various alternatives WNs for ranking by a MU while the available resources are unlimited but failed otherwise. In such situations game theory is proving an efficient tool to model and solve the VHO Decision problems in HWNs.

The SAW, MEW, TOPSIS, and GRA are prominent MADM techniques. A comparative analysis of these techniques with "SAW with Elimination Factor" method is presented in (Pramod Goyal et al., 2017). It shows that the "SAW with Elimination Factor" for the selection of best networks is more efficient among other MADM techniques as it results in less number of vertical handoffs to be occurring in a particular roaming duration of a mobile user.

A concept of Dynamic User Preferences is proposed in (Pramod Goyal et al., 2018b). The predefined "static user preferences" for the considered HDAs are moderated to accommodate the changes in current value of respective HDAs on real time basis. Such user preferences are termed as "Dynamic User Preferences". The use of Dynamic user preferences always results in less number of VHOs.

A comparative study of various types of games is presented in (Pramod Goyal et al., 2018c). There may be three types of competitions between the stakeholders of HWNs to claim the resources that is- i) competition between mobile users ii) competition between wireless networks and iii) competition between mobile users and wireless networks. It presents three non-cooperative game models to represent these three types of competitions. The researchers may use these game models as ready reference in the area of wireless networks.

A non-cooperative game between competing access network is proposed in (Antoniou & Pitsillides, 2007) to distribute a set of service requests from a set of users among a set of networks. Later a cooperative game based network selection scheme proposed in (Chang, Tsai, & Chen, 2009) to maximize number of call admissions, minimize handoff occurrence frequency, and fulfil quality of service (QoS) requirements. A user efficiency–cost ratio (PCR) based unified quantification model is proposed in (Chen, Zhou, Chai, & Tang, 2011) for evaluating the access services in HWNs. Similarly a non-cooperative game between networks to minimize energy consumption by a terminal while maintaining the desired link QoS is proposed in (Bendaoud, Abdennebi, & Didi, 2015). It considers expected QoS and expected remaining battery life time as two important handoff decision factors. A three stage non-cooperative game-theoretic framework is presented in (Dusit Niyato & Hossain, 2008) for bandwidth allocation and admission control between networks. All these papers considers only the competition between access networks to select a MU or service request and considers mostly the network aspects of the problem of network selection for vertical handoffs. A user-centric game based on user preferences for network selection (Salih, See, & Ibrahim, 2015) based on user preferences for the selection of the best heterogeneous wireless network considers only the user preferences but does not consider the network preferences for a user.

To consider the competition between users for a network, a non-cooperative game between competing users based on actual data rate of users to select the networks is presented in (Cui Yang, Xu Yubin, Xu Rongqing, & Sha Xuejun, 2011). A dynamic evolutionary game between the competing groups of users in different service areas is formulated in (D. Niyato & Hossain, 2009) to share the limited amount of bandwidth available in wireless access networks.

To consider the competition between MUs and WNs, non-cooperative games between selfishly acting users and access networks are formulated in (Cesana, Malanchini, & Capone, 2008)(Xu, Fang, & Liu, 2010)(Radhika, 2011) in order to maximize their profit while satisfying QoS for all users as well as load for networks. A matching game between users and networks (Meirong Chen, Fan Li, & Junqing Wang, 2011) consider synthetically the different requirements and targets of users and networks which guarantee the profit of both sides through obtaining stable matching. An N-person cooperative game is proposed in (Liu, Tian, Wang, & Fan, 2014) for network selection based on bankruptcy game with the combination of analytic hierarchy process (AHP). In a repeated game based scheme for vertical handoff (Fu, Li, Li, & Ji, 2014), each game is formulated as a non- cooperative strategic game between a mobile node (MU) and an access point (AP) to optimize the utility function of a network by finding a NASH equilibrium point. The payoff or utility function is defined in terms of the allocated bandwidth of a MU by an AP.

A Group Vertical Handoff decision model based on non-cooperative game is proposed in (Pramod Goyal et al., 2018a). It utilizes the concept of "Dynamic User Preferences" along with multiple handoff decision attributes. The MUs and WNs are used as game strategies against each other to reach at NASH equilibrium in order to select the best available WNs by group MUs for vertical handoffs.

All the above work, as per my best knowledge, does not separate the network evaluation with network selection and perform both the operations combined which lack the modularity in vertical handoff management. Thus this chapter proposed a novel idea of separating the analysis of worthiness of MUs & WNs from the network selection for performing the VHO. In this endeavour, the author extend the concept of dynamic user preferences and their application as game strategies developed by him earlier and published in (Pramod Goyal et al., 2018b)(Pramod Goyal et al., 2018c)(Pramod Goyal et al., 2018a).

3. VERTICAL HANDOFF

Handoff (or Handover) alludes to an occasion when a MU changes its place of connection starting with one passageway then onto the next of an equivalent or diverse wireless network. The handoffs in HWN systems can be delegated

1. Horizontal handoff (Intra-Network handoff)
2. Vertical handoff (Inter-Network handoff)
   a. Upward VHO
   b. Downward VHO

Horizontal handoff (HHO) happens when an MU moves starting with one cell then onto the next cell inside a similar wireless network. The HHOs [6] in wireless networks can be additionally delegated Intra-BSC handoff, Inter-BSC handoff and Inter-MSC handoff. The primary reasons/criteria for HHOs are: Poor Signal Quality (RSS) or Loss of Signal, Bandwidth, Traffic Load Balancing and Velocity of MU. The HHO involves three principle steps: Handoff initiation, Channel assignment, and Connection transfer / handoff execution.

Vertical handoff happens when a MU moves starting with one wireless network then onto the next various wireless network for example from Wi-Fi cell to a GSM/UMTS cell. Vertical handoffs are additionally named upward VHO and downward VHO (Pramod Goyal et al., 2017). The Upward VHO is from a lower size cell of a wireless network with higher Bandwidth to a higher size cell of various wireless network with lower data transfer capacity for example from Wi-Fi to Wi-Max. The Downward VHO is from higher size cell of a wireless network with lower transmission capacity to a lower size cell of a wireless network with higher data transfer capacity for example From Wi-Fi to Bluetooth.

The choice that for what reason to and when to perform vertical handoff in HWN is reliant on different parameters called as Handoff Decision criteria/Attributes. The handoff choice properties are principally arranged into three gatherings.

Network Related Attributes: To depict accessibility and condition of neighbouring network links for example data transfer capacity (bandwidth), coverage, use cost, delay, jitter, packet loss ratio, received signal strength (RSS), security, throughput, Signal to Noise Ratio (SNR), Carrier to Interference Ratio (CIR), Signal to Interference Ratio (SIR), Bit Error Ratio (BER) and so forth.

Terminal/User Related Attributes: To depict the cell phones/mobile device's state for example Remaining Battery Power, Speed of Mobile Terminal, and requested service type

User Preferences: To depict relative user inclinations for the different considered parameters to implement the Quality of Experience (QoE) for a mobile user. The user inclinations are expressed in terms of relative user inclination loads/weights.

The vertical Handoff Decision Process is basically comprise of three stages-

1. Handoff data gathering,
2. Network Selection and
3. Handoff execution.

1. *Handoff Data Gathering*
   This stage is otherwise called System Discovery or Network disclosure as it gathers data about the different handoff decision parameters related to user as well as networks
2. *Network Selection*
   This stage chooses when and Where to trigger the handoff by investigating the data accumulated in before stage according to different Handoff Decision Algorithms. The Handoff Decision Algorithms for the VHO are primarily classified [7] as Received Signal Strength (RSS) Based, Bandwidth Based, Multi Attribute Decision Methods (MADM) utilizing Cost/Utility capacities, and Combination calculation dependent on Neural Network, Fuzzy Logic and Game Theory.
3. *Handoff execution*
   This stage is the execution/implementation stage. It does the real connection transition from current wireless network to the chosen wireless network.

The network selection stage is the centre of any VHO process. The performance of every VHO Process is evaluated based on Handoff Delay, Number of Handoffs, Handoff Failure Probability, and Throughput. In light of who control the handoff decision process, the handoff control approaches are named as -

- Network Controlled Handoff (NCHO) (In First Generation Networks)
- Network-controlled, Mobile Assisted Handoff (MAHO) (In Second Generation & Third Generation Networks)
- Mobile Controlled Handoff (MCHO) (In Fourth Generation/ Fifth Generation/Next Generation Networks/HWN)

4. GAME THEORY

4.1 Essential Elements of a Game

Game theory is an analytical tool to model the circumstances where explicit actions of decision makers lead to commonly clashing outcomes to one another (Charilas & Panagopoulos, 2010; Trestian et al., 2012). Such a model is called Game. The fundamental components of a game are:

Player: The individual partners who performs the strategic moves/choices. The objective of each player is to maximize his/her own payoff/profit by a choice of strategy. The players can be of two kinds Rational and Irrational. A player who consistently endeavours to augment its result is named as rational player.

Strategy: A strategy is an activity by a player which brings about a relating result to the player. The strategies can be arranged into three kinds Pure, Mixed and Dominant Strategy. The dominant strategy can be strictly dominated or weakly dominated.

Payoff: The utility that a player can get by taking certain strategy when the strategies of all the other players are fixed.

Equilibrium: An answer of the game gives the best blend of strategies of all the players which brings about the best result to every player of the game.

The games can be arranged in any of four different ways-

1. Non-Cooperative Games versus Cooperative Game
2. Static versus Dynamic Games
3. Complete Information Games versus Incomplete Information Games
4. Perfect Information Games versus Imperfect Information Games

In Non-Cooperative games, the strategies/moves/actions of players are autonomous while in Cooperative games, the technique/move of one player relies upon move of different players. In Cooperative games, the players share the data to choose their moves with the goal that all players can get best results. Here, the authors are giving the proposed model with non-cooperative game. Nonetheless, this might be stretched out to other sort of games also.

4.2 Game Representation and Important Concepts

The Non-Cooperative games (Cesana et al., 2008) are consistently of unique enthusiasm for HWNs, since the distinctive WNs constrained by various network administrators consistently attempt to augment their income without helping out some other WN, until and except if it turns out to be exceptionally important to do as such. Henceforth the authors present the idea of a game theory through non-cooperative games. The following is the proper brief portrayal of a non-cooperative game and its related significant concepts which are utilized in this paper. A Non-Cooperative Game in strategic form (or Normal Form), is a triplet-

$$G = \left(P, \left(S_i \right)_{i \in P}, \left(U_i \right)_{i \in P} \right) \tag{1}$$

Where-
  P: A finite set of rational player's i.e. $P = \{1,2,3,\ldots,n\}$
  S_i: Strategy Set for player *i*

U_i: $S \rightarrow R$, utility (Payoff) function for player *i* $\tag{2}$

$$S = S_1 \times S_2 \times \ldots \times S_i \times \ldots \times S_n . \tag{3}$$

Here, S is the strategy space characterized as the Cartesian product of the individual strategy set of all the players.

Let, $S_{-i} = \{S_j\}_{j \in N, j \neq i}$ the set of "strategy sets" of all players except player *i* then $s = \left(s_i, s_{-i} \right) \in S$ will represents a *strategy profile* of player *i*. When a player $i \in P$ selects a strategy $s_i \in S_i$ in a deterministic manner i.e. with probability 1, this strategy is known as *Pure Strategy*. A strategy $s_i \in S_i$ is said to be *Dominant Strategy* for player *i* if-

$$U_i \left(s_i, s_{-i} \right) \geq U_i \left(s_i', s_{-i} \right), \forall s_i' \in S_i \ and \ \forall s_{-i} \in S_{-i} \tag{4}$$

Here, s_i' is any strategy other than s_i, belongs to strategy set S_i of player i, called as *Dominated Strategy*.

However, if

$$U_i\left(s_i, s_{-i}\right) > U_i\left(s_i', s_{-i}\right), \forall s_i' \in S_i \text{ and } \forall s_{-i} \in S_{-i} \tag{5}$$

Then s_i' will be a strictly dominated strategy, otherwise a weakly dominated strategy.

4.3 Game Solutions

Nash Equilibrium(Nash, 1951) gives the best solution of a Non-Cooperative game. A pure strategy *Nash Equilibrium (NE)* of a non- cooperative game $G = \left(P, \left(S_i\right)_{i \in P}, \left(U_i\right)_{i \in P}\right)$ is a strategy profile $s* \in S$ such that-

$$U_i\left(s_i^*, s_{-i}^*\right) \geq U_i\left(s_i, s_{-i}^*\right), \forall s_i \in S_i, \forall i \in P \tag{6}$$

However, if

$$U_i\left(s_i^*, s_{-i}^*\right) > U_i\left(s_i, s_{-i}^*\right), \forall s_i \in S_i \tag{7}$$

Then the NE will be strict NE.

At the end of the day, in NE, no player has a motivator to singularly go amiss to another strategy profile given that the strategy of other player's remains fixed. Two methodologies used to discover the NE in a game are – Iterative Elimination of Dominant Strategies and Best Response Function.

The *Best Response* $br_i\left(s_{-i}\right)$ of player *i* to the profile of strategies s_{-i} of opponents is a strategy s_i such that

$$br_i\left(s_{-i}\right) = argmax_{s_i \in S_i} U_i\left(s_i, s_{-i}\right) \tag{8}$$

There are two execution issues related with the game arrangement utilizing Nash Equilibrium-

1. Existence and Multiplicity of NE: a non-cooperative game can have zero, one or various NE
2. Efficiency: a NE isn't really the best outcome from the result point of view. Additionally if there is an occurrence of multiple NE, the selection of ideal NE is significant.

To take care of the above issues related with NE, the idea of Pareto Optimality is given. The Pareto optimality is a proportion of effectiveness to choose an ideal NE among different NE's, if exists. A strategy profile $s \in S$ is pareto-superior to another strategy profile $s' \in S$ if for every player $i \in N$ there exist $U_i\left(s_i, s_{-i}\right) \geq U_i\left(s_i', s_{-i}'\right)$ with strict inequality for at least one player. A pareto-optimal result can't be enhanced without harming at least one player for example one can't improve the result for one player without diminishing the result for at least one other player.

5. PROPOSED TWO STAGE NON COOPERATIVE GAME MODEL FOR VERTICAL HANDOFFS

The proposed non cooperative game model for VHO is a two stage model as shown in fig.2. Stage-1 is about Handoff Information Gathering and System Evaluation. The efficiency of a WN for a MU is expressed in terms of *User Payoff* receivable from a WN. Similarly, the usefulness of a MU for a WN is expressed in terms of *Network Payoff* receivable from a MU. Stage-2 is about formulating a non-cooperative iterative game. It models the competition between multiple WNs and multiple MUs to select a mutually best WN-MU pair based on game solution using NASH Equilibrium. The *User Payoff* is calculated using Simple Additive Weighting (SAW) method in Section 3.1. Similarly, the *Network Payoff* from a MU is calculated in section 3.2. The proposed non cooperative game formulation and its solution is described in section 3.3. The proposed non cooperative game may leads to convergence only if either *MUs* or *WNs* have at least one dominant strategy. The important notations and symbols which are used in explaining the proposed game model are summarised in Table1.

The proposed algorithm comprises the following important steps-

Stage-1

> **Step1:** System Identification
> **Step2:** Handoff Information Gathering
> **Step3:** Payoffs Calculation

Stage-2

> **Step4:** Check whether (*No. of MU=0* or *No. of WN=0*)
> > If yes go to step5 else go to step10
> **Step5:** Formulate a Non-Cooperative game between Mus and WNs (mxn)
> **Step6:** Find NASH equilibrium
> **Step7:** is NASH exist
> > If yes go to step 8 else go to step 9
> **Step8:** Remove the optimal MU-WN pair and go to step 4
> **Step9:** Find the suboptimal solution and go to step4
> **Step10:** stop

5.1 User Payoff

The efficiency of a WN is expressed in terms of *User Payoff (UP)*. We have proposed to utilize the individual utility of a handoff decision attribute rather than direct utilization of the attribute's value in order to make the User Payoff unit free inside the scope of 0 and 1. This also ensures the participation of both upward and downward handoff decision attributes on same scale. The User Payoff from WN *i* to the MU *j* is calculated as below-

Figure 2. Iterative Non-Cooperative Game Model for Vertical Handoffs

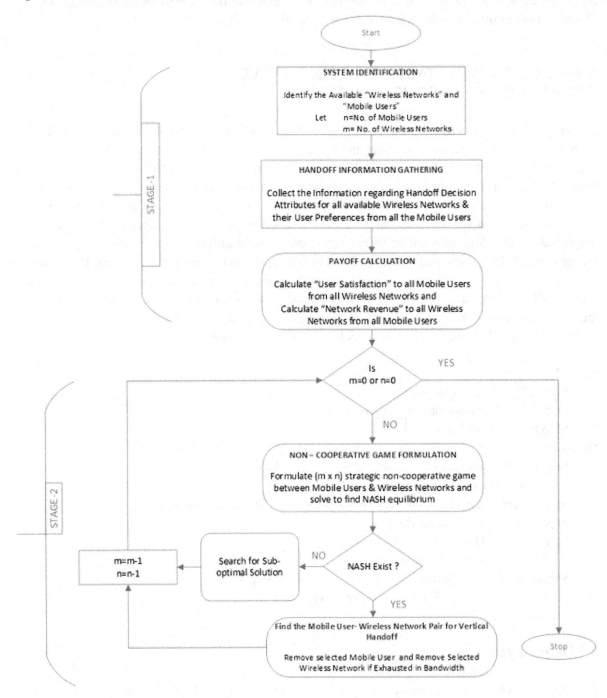

$$UP_{ij} = \sum_{l=1}^{p} \left(w_{ij,l}^{k} * u_{ij,l}^{k} \right)$$

(9)

Table 1. Symbols and Notations with Description

Notations	Description
m	Number of Wireless Network (WN)
n	Number of Mobile User (MU)
p	Number of Handoff Decision Attributes
k = {1, 2}	Service Type k=1 Real-Time Services k=2 Non-Real-Time Services like email
$w_{ij,l}^k$	Dynamic User Preference Weight of Handoff Decision Attribute *l* of WN *i* for MU *j* for service type *k*
$u_{ij,l}^k$	Normalized Utility of HDA *l* of WN *i* for MU *j* for service type *k*
$A_{ij,l}^k$	Current value of HDA *l* of WN *i* for MU *j* for service type *k*
$A_{thij,l}^k$	Threshold value of a HDA *l* of WN *i* for MU *j* for service type *k*
UP_{ij}	The *User Payoff* from WN *i* to MU *j*
NP_{ij}	Network Payoff receivable by the WN *i* *from* MU *j* for service type *k*
C_i^k	Price of using a WN *i* for service type *k*
B_j^r	Bandwidth Requested by MU *j*
G	Represents a Non Cooperative Game
U	Set of MUs
N	Set of WNs
S_U	Set of MU's strategies
S_N	Set of WN's strategies
n_i	ith WN
u_j	jth MU
πU	Payoff MUs
πN	Payoff WNs
π	Combined Payoff matrix for both MUs and WNs

Where- $\sum_{l=1}^{p} w_{ij,l}^k = 1$

Here, the utility $u_{ij,l}^k$ is given as

$$u_{ij,l}^k = sigmf\left(x,[a,c]\right) \tag{10}$$

Where- $x = A_{ij,l}^k$, $c = \dfrac{A_{thij,l}^k}{2}$ and a is curve steepness (positive for upward and negative for downward attributes)

5.2 Network Payoff

The Network Payoff NP_{ij} is defined as the price payable by the user j to the network i for service type k, and is given as

$$NP_{ij} = C_i^k * UP_{ij} * B_j^r, \; i=1...m, j=1...n, k = \{1, 2\} \tag{11}$$

Here, C_i^k is the price per unit time for voice or price per unit data for data services, receivable by i^{th} WN from j^{th} MU for service type k when the network efficiency is 100% or US_{ij} is 1.

The bandwidth requested by j^{th} MU is B_j^r. Here for the sake of simplicity, it is assumed that the MU gets the 100% of the requested bandwidth from the selected WN.

5.3 Non-Cooperative Game Formulation for VHO

It is proposed to model the competition between n MUs and m WNs as Two Player Non-Cooperative game. The Non-Cooperative game in strategic form for VHO developed in (Pramod Goyal et al., 2018c) is further expressed here pictorially using a specially designed diagram by author which is shown in Fig.3. This pictorial representation will give better understanding of the concept of using the MUs and WNs as the game strategies for the each other.

Figure 3. Representation of Non- Cooperative game between n Mobile Users and m Wireless Networks in strategic form

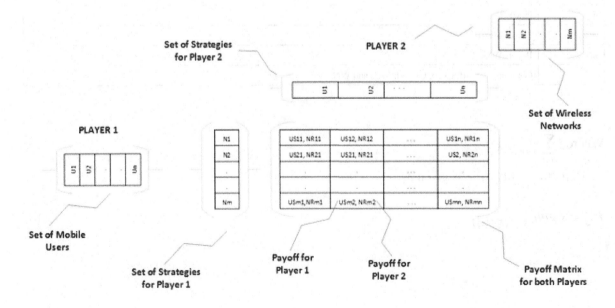

The first Player (Player 1) is the set of MUs. The second player (Player 2) is the set of available WNs. The players are assumed to be rational. Player 1 considers all available WNs as their strategy set while player 2 considers all available MUs as their strategy set for the game. A WN is represented by a set of multiple handoff attributes while A MU is represented by their respective dynamic user preferences. It is assumed that at a time one WN can select one MU only and the algorithm runs till every MU selects a suitable WN.

The Non-Cooperative game between mobile users and wireless networks is defined as -

$$G = \left(\{U, N\}, \{S_U, S_N\}, \{\pi_U, \pi_N\} \right) \tag{12}$$

Where-

$U = \{U_1, U_2, ..., U_n\}$ The Player 1
$N = \{N_1, N_2, ..., N_m\}$ The Player 2
$S_U = \{n_1, n_2, ..., n_m\}$ Strategy set for Player 1
$S_N = \{u_1, u_2, ..., u_n\}$ Strategy set for Player 2
π_U: S→R, Payoff for Player 1
π_N: S→R, Payoff for Player 2

The strategy space S of size (m x n) is defined as

$$S = S_U \times S_N \tag{13}$$

A strategy n_i for Player 1 corresponding to i^{th} *WN* is given as-

$$n_i = \{\{ ((A)_{i,l}^k, (A_{th})_{i,l}^k) \mid l=1,2,..p\}\}, i=1..m, k=\{1,2\} \tag{14}$$

Here, $(A)_{i,l}^k$ **and** $(A_{th})_{i,l}^k$ is the considered Handoff Decision Attribute and its threshold value respectively and p is the total number of network selection attributes.

Similarly, a strategy u_j for player 2 corresponding to j^{th} MU is given as-

$$u_j = \{ w_{j,l}^k \mid l=1..p ; k=\{1,2\}\}, j=1..n \tag{15}$$

Such that $\sum_{l=1}^{p} w_{j,l}^k = 1$ and $w_{j,l}^k \geq 0$

Here, $w_{j,l}^k$ is the dynamic user preference weight of lth handoff decision attribute

The payoff of Player 1 for a strategy combination (n_i, u_j) where player 1 select strategy n_i and player 2 select strategy u_j is given as

$$\pi U_{(ni, uj)} = UP_{i_j} \mid i=1, 2... m; j=1, 2... n \tag{16}$$

The User Payoff UP_{ij} is calculated as specified above in eq. (9) - (10)

The payoff of Player 1 for a strategy combination (n_i, u_j) where player 1 select strategy n_i and player 2 select strategy u_j is given as

$$\pi N_{(ni, uj)} = NPi_{j|} \quad i=1, 2\dots m;\ j=1, 2\dots n \tag{17}$$

The Network Payoff NP_{ij} is calculated as specified above in eq. (11)

5.4 Game Solution

Nash Equilibrium gives an optimal solution point for any non-cooperative game where no player has a motivating force to singularly go amiss to another strategy profile given that the strategy of other player's remains fixed. The Lemke-Howson algorithm (Lemke and Howson, 1964) for discovering NE in a 2-player game is the state of art even after passing of more than 50 years. The NASH equilibrium for the proposed 2-player game is characterized as beneath

Let i and j are the index values of strategies of Player 1 (n_i) and Player 2 (u_j) respectively, and i^* and j^* are the index values of the strategies at the NASH equilibrium (Buttler & Akchurina, 2013). Then the pure strategy pair $\left(n_{i^*}, u_{j^*}\right)$ will be in NASH equilibrium if

$$\pi_U\left(n_{i^*}, u_{j^*}\right) \geq \pi_U\left(n_{i'}, u_{j^*}\right), \ \forall i' \neq i^* \tag{18}$$

And

$$\pi_N\left(n_{i^*}, u_{j^*}\right) \geq \pi_N\left(n_{i^*}, u_{j'}\right), \ \forall j' \neq j^* \tag{19}$$

The n_{i^*} and u_{j^*} are the dominant strategies of player 1 and player 2 respectively which can be obtained using Best Response (BR) function also as given below-

$$\left(n_{i^*}\right) = BR_U\left(u_{j^*}\right) = argmax_{n_i}\, \pi_U\left(n_i, u_j\right), \forall i = 1\dots m\, and\ \forall j = 1\dots n \tag{20}$$

And

$$\left(u_{j^*}\right) = BR_N\left(n_{i^*}\right) = argmax_{u_j}\, \pi_N\left(n_i, u_j\right), \forall i = 1\dots m\, and\ \forall j = 1\dots n \tag{21}$$

Here $\pi U_{(ni, uj)}$ and $\pi N_{(ni, uj)}$ are the payoff matrix for player 1 and player 2 respectively.

The payoff matrix for Player 1 for total strategy space S can be specified as-

$$\grave{A}_U = \left(US_{ij} \right)_{mxn} = \begin{bmatrix} US_{11} & \cdots & US_{1n} \\ \vdots & \ddots & \vdots \\ US_{m1} & \cdots & US_{mn} \end{bmatrix} \tag{22}$$

And the payoff matrix for Player 2 for total strategy space S can be specified as-

$$\grave{A}_N = \left(NR_{ij} \right)_{mxn} = \begin{bmatrix} NR_{11} & \cdots & NR_{1n} \\ \vdots & \ddots & \vdots \\ NR_{m1} & \cdots & NR_{mn} \end{bmatrix} \tag{23}$$

Then the combined payoff matrix for both the Players for total strategy space S can be given as-

$$\pi = \left(US_{ij}, NR_{ij} \right)_{mxn} = \begin{bmatrix} \left(US_{11}, NR_{11} \right) & \cdots & \left(US_{1n}, NR_{1n} \right) \\ \vdots & \ddots & \vdots \\ \left(US_{m1}, NR_{m1} \right) & \cdots & \left(US_{mn}, NR_{mn} \right) \end{bmatrix} \tag{24}$$

In case NASH equilibrium does not exist then a suboptimal solution comprising a pure strategy pair $\left(n_{i^{\wedge}}, u_{j^{\wedge}} \right)$ is obtained such that

$$\left(n_{i^{\wedge}}, u_{j^{\wedge}} \right): \text{Max } \{ US_{ij} / NR_{ij} \mid i=1\ldots m; j=1\ldots n\}$$

Subject to: $US_{ij} > 0, NR_{ij} > 0$ (25)

NASH equilibrium, if exists, gives the pair of strategies ($\boldsymbol{n}_{i^*}, \boldsymbol{u}_{j^*}$) in terms of a MU and an available WN which can select each other. This MU-WN pair is expelled from further thought in next emphasis and the game is rehashed with the rest of the MU and WN till all MUs get an accessible WN. In case NASH equilibrium does not exist at all, the same set of user and networks is allowed to search for a sub optimal solution $\left(n_{i^{\wedge}}, u_{j^{\wedge}} \right)$ as shown in equation (25).

6. SIMULATION AND RESULT ANALYSIS

The proposed two stage non cooperative game model for VHO is implemented in MATLAB and simulations are carried out to analyse the results. Two modules are developed to implement the Stage-1 and Stage -2 separately. The results of stage-1 are used as input to stage-2. The Stage-1 is about handoff information gathering and evaluation of MUs & WNs. The evaluation is carried out with Summative Additive Weighting (SAW). In stage-2, the Non cooperative game is formulated as two player strategic game as detailed in section 3.3 above. The game will leads to an optimal solution when at least one dominant strategy is available of either player. The simulation setup developed in (Pramod Goyal et al., 2018a) is reused here which is detailed as below.

An HWN comprising three overlapping WNs: Wi-Fi, CDMA and Wi-Max are considered for simulations as shown above in fig.1 in Section 1. The author considered the following five handoff decisions attributes –

i)   Network *Bandwidth (B)*, ii) *Distance (D)* of a MU from an Access Point (AP) or Base Station Controller (BSC) of a WN, iii) Velocity (V) of Mobile Terminal, iv) *Power Consumption (P)* by a network interface, and v) Network *Usage Charges (C)*. The threshold values of the considered handoff decision attributes for all the three networks are reuse as given in *Table 2*. It is assume that all the MUs are requesting for only single service type (k=1) of voice communication.

The efficiency of the proposed game theory based method for vertical handoff is compared with non-game theory methods SAW using utility theory. Here, the authors are considering the considering the user initiated handoffs where the important consideration is always on reducing the number of handoff initiations while maximising the overall *User Payoff* as well as *Network Payoff*. The efficiency of the system is expressed in terms of total number of VHOs required to be performed by a MU for an application to be completed, since the authors are The *User Payoff* is the overall Quality of Experience (QoE) receivable from a WN by the MU while the *Network Payoff* is the total revenue receivable from a selected MU by the WN.

Table 2. Handoff Decision Attributes and their Threshold values

Network →	Wi-Fi	CDMA	Wi-Max
Network Selection Attributes ↓			
Bandwidth	54 Mbps	2Mbps	30Mbps
Velocity	1Km/Hrs	150Km/Hrs	60km/hrs
Distance	50mtr	20Km	50Km
Power Consumption	100mw	50mw	20mw
Usage Charges	10p/bps	100p/bps	50p/bps

Table 3. User Preference Weight Factors and Their Values

Static Weights	Round Number				
	1	2	3	4	5
W_B: For Bandwidth	**0.6**	0.1	0.1	0.1	0.1
W_V: For Velocity	0.1	**0.6**	0.1	0.1	0.1
W_D: For Distance	0.1	0.1	**0.6**	0.1	0.1
W_P: For Power	0.1	0.1	0.1	**0.6**	0.1
W_C: For Cost	0.1	0.1	0.1	0.1	**0.6**

The simulations are carried out to find the following-

1. The impact of initial connectivity of all the MUs in a particular area during the course of simulation on the system efficiency. For this, the Simulations are conducted for the following three scenarios of the MUs, when initially all the MUs are in:
    I.   region 'A' having connectivity with Net-1 (Wi-Fi) (Fig.4)
    II.   region 'B' having connectivity with Net-2 (CDMA) (Fig.5)
    III. region 'C' having connectivity with Net-3 (Wi-Max) (Fig.6)
2. The impact of a particular Handoff Decision Attribute on the *"Number of VHOs"* observed by a user, in comparison to other attributes. For this, in each simulation run, there are five rounds corresponding to five handoff attributes. In each round, the authors set the user preference weight of one particular handoff decision attribute as highest and the user preference weights of other attributes equal and lower as shown in Table *3*.

Figure 4. Initially All MUs are in region 'A' & connected to Wi-Fi

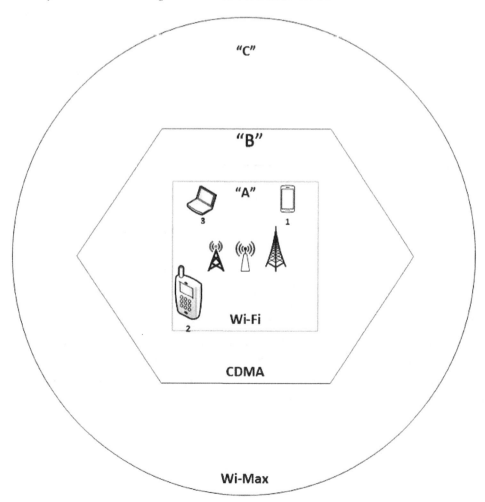

Figure 5. Initially All MUs are in region 'B' & connected to CDMA

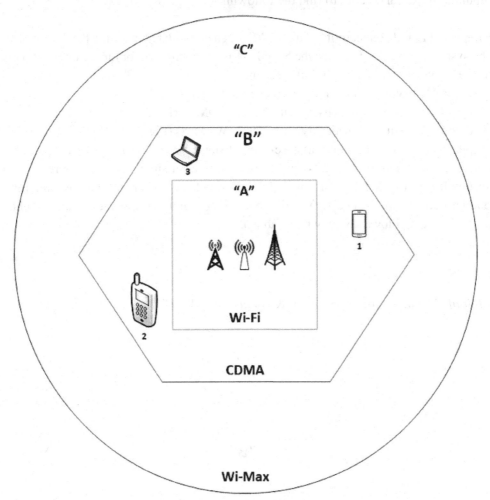

The impact of Mobile User population in a particular duration within a considered hotspot area on the *"Number of VHOs"* to be observed by the Mobile Users.

The simulation results for finding the effect of a particular HDA on the *"Number of VHOs"* observed by a user, in comparison to other attributes are presented in fig. 7, fig.8 and fig.9. Fig.10 presents the simulation results for finding the effect of mobile user population on number of VHOs.

Fig.7, 8 & 9 consider the fixed populace of three mobile users and three wireless networks inside the HWN. The simulation results are results are exhibited regarding number of vertical handoffs resulted in one occasion of handoff initiation by all the three MUs considered for the over three situations separately. The X-Axis represents the user preference weight for a handoff decision factor which is considered as highest among others as per Table 3 in each round.

Figure 6. Initially All MUs are in region 'C' & connected to Wi-Max

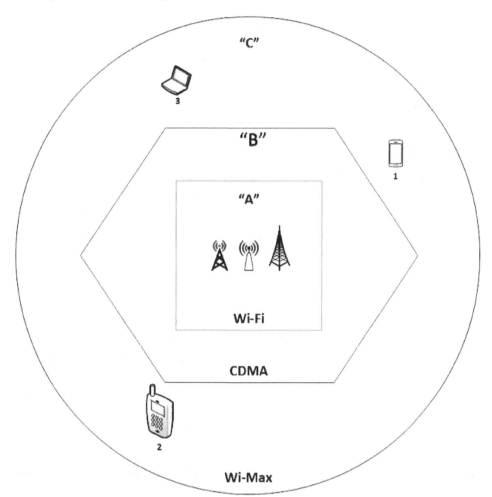

Figure 7. Initially All MUs in Net-1 (Wi-Fi)

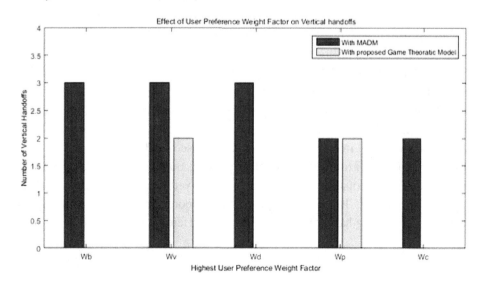

Figure 8. Initially All MUs in Net-2 (CDMA)

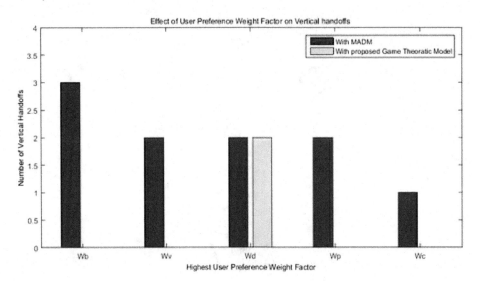

As it can be seen from Table 2 that Wi-Fi ought to be favoured network for Bandwidth and Network utilization cost, CDMA ought to be favoured network for Velocity and Wi-Max ought to be favoured network for Distance and Power Consumption as vertical handoff Decision factors. At the end of the day, if most elevated inclination is given for either data transfer capacity (bandwidth) or Network utilization cost and at first every one of the MUs are associated with Wi-Fi network, at that point they ought to be stay associated with Wi-Fi and number of vertical handoffs ought to be least in these cases. The results presented in Fig.7 prove the same more appropriately with our proposed game theoretic model in comparison to MADM based methods.

Similarly the results presented in fig.8 and fig.9 proves that the "Number of VHOs" are substantially less with the proposed game theoretic model in comparison to MADM based methods in case of highest user preference for velocity when all MUs are initially connected with CDMA and in case of highest user preference for distance when all MUs are initially connected with Wi-Max respectively. Further, it can be seen from fig. 7, 8 & 9, that the number of vertical handoffs performed by all the three MUs are always less for all the user preference weights in all situations with the proposed game theoretic model in comparison to MADM based utility methods like SAW.

Fig.10 presents the number of VHOs observed by all the MUs in a group of 3, 6, 9, 12 and 15 in one instance of handoff initiation for the three scenarios considered in fig.4-6. The user preferences of MUs for WNs are considered as predefined and fixed. The results shows that even in the situation when the competing MUs are more than the available WNs, the number of VHOs is substantially less with the proposed game theoretic model in comparison to MADM based methods.

The results presented in fig.7 to fig.10 above clearly proves that the proposed two stage non cooperative game based method does not allows all the user initiated vertical handoffs in order to maximise the User Payoff and Network Payoff. Hence the proposed game theoretic model performs better, by reducing the "Number of VHOs", during handoff decision process in Heterogeneous Wireless Networks.

Figure 9. Initially All MUs in Net-3 (Wi-Max)

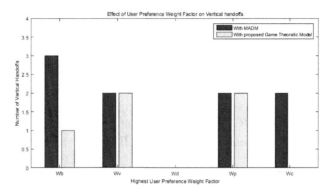

Figure 10. Effect of Mobile User Population on Vertical Handoffs

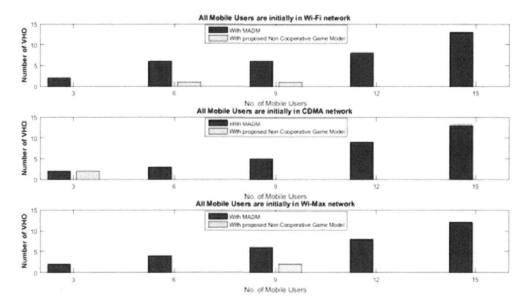

7. CONCLUSION

This chapter proposes a two stage Non-Cooperative Game model for Vertical Handoffs. This is a 2-stage modular framework. Stage-1 is used to evaluate the "Mobile Users" and "Wireless Networks". Stage-2 is used to model the competition between multiple MUs and multiple WNs using a Non Cooperative Game to select the mutually best MU-WN pair for performing VHO. The results shows that the network selection using the proposed approach in non-cooperative game model substantially reduces the "Number of vertical handoffs" in comparison to the network selection based on classical MADM based methods like SAW.

In order to effectively communicate the concept of proposed model, the authors have briefly introduced the concept of Vertical handoff and Game theory also in this chapter. This model separates the quantitative evaluation of Mobile Users and Wireless Networks from the optimal selection of the best available Wireless Networks by a Mobile User. This model can be extended successfully to apply any technique at Stage -1 while applying any other technique at Stage-2.

REFERENCES

Antoniou, J., & Pitsillides, A. (2007). *4G converged environment: Modeling network selection as a game. In 16th IST Mobile and Wireless Communications Summit.* IEEE. doi:10.1109/ISTMWC.2007.4299242

Bendaoud, F., Abdennebi, M., & Didi, F. (2015). Network selection using game theory. In *3rd International Conference on Control, Engineering & Information Technology (CEIT)* (pp. 1–6). IEEE. 10.1109/CEIT.2015.7233014

Buttler, J., & Akchurina, N. (2013). Nash Equilibria in Normal Games via Optimization Methods. *2013 European Control Conference (ECC).* 10.23919/ECC.2013.6669658

Cesana, M., Malanchini, I., & Capone, A. (2008). Modelling network selection and resource allocation in wireless access networks with non-cooperative games. In *5th IEEE International Conference on Mobile Ad Hoc and Sensor Systems* (pp. 404–409). IEEE. 10.1109/MAHSS.2008.4660055

Chang, C.-J., Tsai, T.-L., & Chen, Y.-H. (2009). *Utility and Game-Theory Based Network Selection Scheme in Heterogeneous Wireless Networks. In 2009 IEEE Wireless Communications and Networking Conference.* IEEE. doi:10.1109/WCNC.2009.4918016

Charilas, D. E., & Panagopoulos, A. D. (2010). A survey on game theory applications in wireless networks. *Computer Networks*, *54*(18), 3421–3430. doi:10.1016/j.comnet.2010.06.020

Chen, M., Li, F., & Wang, J. (2011). A game theoretical approach of network selection algorithm in heterogeneous wireless networks. In *IET International Communication Conference on Wireless Mobile and Computing (CCWMC 2011)* (pp. 148–153). IET. 10.1049/cp.2011.0865

Chen, Q.-B., Zhou, W.-G., Chai, R., & Tang, L. (2011). Game-theoretic approach for pricing strategy and network selection in heterogeneous wireless networks. *IET Communications*, *5*(5), 676–682. doi:10.1049/iet-com.2010.0249

Fu, S., Li, J., Li, R., & Ji, Y. (2014). A Game Theory Based Vertical Handoff Scheme for Wireless Heterogeneous Networks. In *10th International Conference on Mobile Ad-hoc and Sensor Networks* (pp. 220–227). 10.1109/MSN.2014.37

Goyal, P., Lobiyal, D. K., & Katti, C. P. (2017). Vertical handoff in heterogeneous wireless networks: A tutorial. In *2017 International Conference on Computing, Communication and Automation (ICCCA)* (pp. 551–566). IEEE. 10.1109/CCAA.2017.8229862

Goyal, P., Lobiyal, D. K., & Katti, C. P. (2018c). Game Theory for Vertical Handoff Decisions in Heterogeneous Wireless Networks: A Tutorial. In S. Bhattacharyya, T. Gandhi, K. Sharma, & P. Dutta (Eds.), Advanced Computational and Communication Paradigms (1st ed., Vol. 475). Singapore: Springer Singapore. doi:10.1007/978-981-10-8240-5

Goyal, P., Lobiyal, D. K., & Katti, C. P. (2018a). Dynamic user preference based group vertical handoffs in heterogeneous wireless networks: A non-cooperative game approach. *Wireless Networks*. Advance online publication. doi:10.100711276-018-1826-9

Goyal, P., Lobiyal, D. K., & Katti, C. P. (2018b). Dynamic User Preference Based Network Selection for Vertical Handoff in Heterogeneous Wireless Networks. *Wireless Personal Communications*, *98*(1), 725–742. doi:10.100711277-017-4892-x

Goyal, P., & Saxena, S. (2008). A dynamic decision model for vertical handoffs across heterogeneous wireless networks. In *World academy of science, engineering and Technology* (Vol. 31, pp. 677–682). Retrieved from http://citeseerx.ist.psu.edu/viewdoc/download?doi=10.1.1.306.7734&rep=rep1&type=pdf

Lemke, C. E., & Howson, J. T. Jr. (1964). Equilibrium Points of Bimatrix Games. *Journal of the Society for Industrial and Applied Mathematics*, *12*(2), 413–423. doi:10.1137/0112033

Liu, B., Tian, H., Wang, B., & Fan, B. (2014). AHP and Game Theory based Approach for Network Selection in Heterogeneous Wireless Networks. *Consumer Communications and Networking Conf. (CCNC)*, 973–978. 10.1109/CCNC.2014.6866617

Nash, J. (1951). Non-Cooperative Games. *Annals of Mathematics*, *54*(2), 286. Advance online publication. doi:10.2307/1969529

Niyato, D., & Hossain, E. (2008). A Noncooperative Game-Theoretic Framework for Radio Resource Management in 4G Heterogeneous Wireless Access Networks. *IEEE Transactions on Mobile Computing*, *7*(3), 332–345. doi:10.1109/TMC.2007.70727

Niyato, D., & Hossain, E. (2009). Dynamics of Network Selection in Heterogeneous Wireless Networks: An Evolutionary Game Approach. *IEEE Transactions on Vehicular Technology*, *58*(4), 2008–2017. doi:10.1109/TVT.2008.2004588

Obayiuwana, E., & Falowo, O. E. (2016). Network selection in heterogeneous wireless networks using multi-criteria decision-making algorithms: A review. *Wireless Networks*, 1–33. doi:10.100711276-016-1301-4

Piamrat, K., Ksentini, A., Bonnin, J.-M., & Viho, C. (2011). Radio resource management in emerging heterogeneous wireless networks. *Computer Communications*, *34*(9), 1066–1076. doi:10.1016/j.comcom.2010.02.015

Radhika, K. (2011). Vertical Handoff Decision using Game Theory Approach for Multi-mode Mobile Terminals in Next Generation Wireless Networks. *International Journal of Computers and Applications*, *36*(11), 31–37. doi:10.5120/4535-6451

Salih, Y. K., See, O. H., Ibrahim, R. W., Yussof, S., & Iqbal, A. (2015). A user-centric game selection model based on user preferences for the selection of the best heterogeneous wireless network. *Annales des Télécommunications*, *70*(5-6), 239–248. doi:10.100712243-014-0443-6

Trestian, R., Ormond, O., & Muntean, G. M. (2012). Game theory-based network selection: Solutions and challenges. *IEEE Communications Surveys and Tutorials*, *14*(4), 1212–1231. doi:10.1109/SURV.2012.010912.00081

Wang, L., & Kuo, G.-S. G. S. (2013). Mathematical Modeling for Network Selection in Heterogeneous Wireless Networks— A Tutorial. *IEEE Communications Surveys and Tutorials, 15*(1), 271–292. doi:10.1109/SURV.2012.010912.00044

Xu, P., Fang, X., & Liu, X. (2010). A Non-cooperative Pairwise Matrices Game Model for Heterogeneous Network Selection. In *International Conference on Communications and Mobile Computing* (Vol. 3, pp. 387–391). IEEE. 10.1109/CMC.2010.29

Yang, C., Xu, Y., Xu, R., & Sha, X. (2011). A heterogeneous wireless network selection algorithm based on non-cooperative game theory. In *6th International ICST Conference on Communications and Networking in China (CHINACOM)* (pp. 720–724). IEEE. 10.1109/ChinaCom.2011.6158248

Zanakis, S. H., Solomon, A., Wishart, N., & Dublish, S. (1998). Multi-attribute decision making: A simulation comparison of select methods. *European Journal of Operational Research, 107*(3), 507–529. doi:10.1016/S0377-2217(97)00147-1

Chapter 6
A Fuzzy Multi-Criteria Decision-Making Method for Managing Network Security Risk Perspective

Suhel Ahmad Khan

Indira Gandhi National Tribal University, Amarkantak, India

Waris Khan

Babasaheb Bhimrao Ambedkar University, Lucknow, India

Dhirendra Pandey

Babasaheb Bhimrao Ambedkar University, Lucknow, India

ABSTRACT

Security threats evaluation accepts a pivotal part in network security management. In this chapter, the author has depicted the significant measures and parameters with respect to huge industry/organizational prerequisites for building up a secure network. The existing fuzzy model is a combination of fuzzy techniques and expert's opinions. The work aims to manage network security risks during D2D data communication through the network to optimize security assurance. The idea is to provide a means of security risk assessment during D2D data communication through the network. Security risks are those that prevent the accomplishment of the objectives specified by developers as well as organizations. The basic idea of the proposed work is to identify and prioritize the security risks methods, which is used to find the problems and fix them only to minimize cost, rework, and time. The work examines the effect of multi-criteria decision analysis methods for security risk assessment.

DOI: 10.4018/978-1-7998-2764-1.ch006

INTRODUCTION

The modern world is critically reliant on a broad range of network communication. Dependency on networking is so high that life cannot be imagined without them. With all the advantages of networking and the web applications running on them, there is fear too. News headlines are scaring us over data and information theft nowadays. In April 2011, data theft has been reported in Sony Play Station, where hackers have stolen about 77 million subscriber's personal data. This was due to the privacy breach in Sony's Play Station Network. According to security experts, this breach of privacy was among the biggest recorded. It took the $171 million cost to restore its systems and provide its customers with credit protection services (Agrafiotis et al., 2018; Dark Reading, 2011; Wilton, 2017). These incidents raise questions about the security status of stored data, processed by networking that is shared via the Internet. Security is characterized as the set of laws, rules, and practices that govern an organization's management, security, and dissemination of sensitive information. This applies to maintaining confidentiality, integrity, authenticity, availability and non-repudiation etc. (Khan et al., 2018a; Khan et al., 2018b; Punter et al., 2016).

Focusing on network security during data sharing could protect the network against unauthorized use, access, disclosure and modification. The attackers can not be blamed exclusively for the incidences discussed; the same responsibility lies with designers and developers. Attackers do not create security holes on their own; they just exploit vulnerabilities present in the network. Vulnerabilities are the defects that are introduced during D2D communication. The presence of even a single vulnerability may cause irreparable loss to the organization in terms of money and reputation (Abomhara & Køien, 2015; Charles & Pñeeger, 2012; Kizza, 2013; Roozbahani & Azad, 2015). Even after so many life-threatening security incidents, when interacting D2D network, it is still viewed as an afterthought (Nitti et al., 2015). Security features are often sprayed onto the fully developed structure of the network. The drawback is that the security professionals can never be sure of identifying and patching all the security holes. Consequently, security has become a major challenge. Today practitioners will think not only of consumers but also of adversaries to succeed in this competitive era. Addressing security at each data communication process is called network protection (Ahmad & Habib, 2010; Awodele et al., 2012; Berner, 2011; Daya, 2010; Kizza, 2005; Krishnan, 2004; Stallings, 2011).

For successful project control, information about the project should be objective and quantitative, ranging from the development process to the management process. The need for the process to have quantitative data requires the use of methods. It is a valuable tool that helps security professionals to incorporate security features in the network. In addition, optimization models are prevalent in the quantification and assessment of security risks. They have become the basic foundation for informed security risk-related decision making. An optimization model based on classic set theory, however, may not be able to describe some security risks in a meaningful and practical manner. Lack of knowledge data intertwined with cause-and-effect relationships and imprecise data makes it difficult to determine the presentation level of some security risk model using only traditional optimisation models. Sometimes the origin of the security risk and its characteristics may be incompletely understood, even with a robust quantitative security risk model tailored to data experience (Birge et al., 2018; Chen et al., 2018; Viduto et al., 2012).

Certain models of optimization, such as fuzzy logic, implicit Markov and decision tree models, and artificial neural and Bayesian networks, specifically understand the underlying cause-and-effect relationships and identify the unknown complexity (Liu & Liu, 2016; Meng et al., 2011). Such new models could do a better job of identifying and assessing other risks, including operational risk. Interestingly, while well-accepted and sophisticated quantitative models are available for market, credit, and insurance risks, these various security risks are usually beyond business managers control. On the other hand, with appropriate risk detection and risk management in place, operational risk can be greatly mitigated, despite lacking agreement on which quantitative models should be used. Construction and implementation of increasingly suitable organizational risk models using a newer approach, such as fuzzy logic, could be worthwhile in this way (OWASP, 2017).

The aim of the proposed work is to manage network security risks during D2D data communication through the network in order to optimize security assurance. The idea is to provide a means of security risk assessment during D2D data communication through the network. The measures can be used by organizations to get them insight into the security risk under development (Aldosari & Taeib, 2015; Hamoud et al., 2017). Security risks are those that prevent accomplishment of the objectives specified by developers as well as organizations. The basic idea of the proposed work is to identify and prioritize the security risks methods, which is used to find the problems and fix them only to minimize cost, rework and time. Combination of fuzzy techniques and expert's opinions are the basis for the existing fuzzy model. It takes help of mastery and data from prior exercises conveyed for security estimation during network communication. The paperwork examinations the effect of multi-criteria decision analysis methods for security risk assessment. The outcome shows that this strategy with accessible task information and assessment technique provides enhanced outputs than existing technique.

RELATED WORK

In 2009, the author Flauzac et al., has introduced a methodology for the execution of distributed security planning in a controlled society oriented manner, called framework of security, which guarantees that device is dependable and correspondences among devices can be leveled out of the framework approaches (Flauzac et al., 2009). In 2005, the author Marin characterized the center pragmatic network administration parts of security including computer intrution detection, traffic examination, and network monitoring aspects of network security (Marin, 2005). In 2009, the author Wu Kehe et. al., discuss information security in three major sections including protection of data, network system security, and network business security model (Wu et al., 2009). A conceptual explanation for the protection of security for a programmed generation system for big business has also been developed. In 2009, Wuzheng described a Public Key Infrastructure (PKI)— based remote system security structure (Tan et al., 2009). Various authors have discussed about the benefits, strategies, methodologies, actions and different tools which are helpful for cryptography and charectrazing the essential propertirs of network security (Brenton & Hunt, n.d.; CISCO Systems, 2001; Farrow, n.d.; McClure et al., 2009; Murray, 2004; Stallings, 2006; Stallings, 2007). The significant issues realted with network security and their applications are 'Advance Encryption Standard (AES), CMAC for validation and the CCM for encryption guidelines' must be discussed in an elaborative manner. Also, different hacking pactices and their recognition, remedial must be discussd with extremely productive mode. There are various factors and sub-factors are discussed in this paper which affects the network security risk.

Today, data / information transmission over a network in a safer and secure way is the most challenging task for the industry. The intruders and the network security efforts characterize how the use of network security tools, a superior, safe and sound network for an association/industry can be deliberated and maintained. This research caters the issues around network security, which needs urgent attention for organizational use. Moreover the Security strategies and a contextual analysis is very much helpful to understand the controlling of network-security in an organization. Security threats are expanding progressively and making rapid wired/remote systems and internet providers, uncertain and problematic. Security measures at Present scenario are working all the more effectively to meet the front-line demands of the present emerging projects. The need is also acted upon in regions such as defence, where secure and verified access to information is a major issues linked with data security.

NETWORK SECURITY

Network security begins with authentication, usually by a client's username and his password. When it confirms, the firewall authorizes access control policies that what services are legalized to be accessed by the network clients. Despite the fact that compelling to avoid unauthorized entry, this potrion may fail to ensure potentially destructive content, for example, trojans and worms over the networks. The operation of such malware is detected and repressed by an intrusion prevention system (IPS) or anti-virus software. It is very importat to track the wires traffic of networks, high level analysis, logged and audit record with the help of anomaly-based intrusion detection devices. To preserve anonymity, contact between two hosts that use a network could be encrypted. An advancement of huge open networks, large numbers of security threats have expanded essentially in the last 20 years. Therefore, threats preventions is the primary concer related to security. Nevertheless as opposed to closed the network from outer world few alternative options to protect from these network attacks.

Network Security requires courses of action to avoid and control 'unauthorized access, misuse, alteration or denial of a services' and available resources over the network. Network gadgets, endeavor servers, and PCs are a portion of the objectives of these assaults (Awodele et al., 2012; Canavan, 2000; Daya, 2013; Hamedani, 2010). So security issues assume a noteworthy job. There are various existing approaches which are used in network security like Firewalls, Intrusion Detection Systems, Virtual Private Networks. Firewall is designed to provide security by protecting the issues of data integrity, traffic authentication and privacy of inward network. Firewalls can be compelling methods for ensuring over the local network from network-based security threats while simultaneously controlling access to the outer world through broad areas network and the internet (Chopra, 2016; Dong & Peng, 2012; Prabhakar, 2017; Yan et al., 2015). But Firewalls can't prevent inner clients from accessing websites with malignant code.

Intrusion Detection is another issue of recognizing the illigal use and maltreatment of computer systems. Outside attacks are the not just issue, the risk of approved clients abusing and manhandling their benefits is similarly squeezing concern. Intrusion Detection System (IDS) may turn into the objective of an attack itself (Sekar et al., 2002; Singh & Silakari, 2009). An attacker may use the strategies to lessen the capacity of IDS to distinguish an attack inorder to enable the attacker to slip their traffic undetected (Analoui et al., 2005).

Denial of Service attack has the essential objective of keeping the defrauded framework to perform genuine action or reacting to authentic traffic as appeared in figure-1. Two essential sorts of DoS attack is discussed. The primary structure exploits a shortcoming to make a system to hang, freeze, etc. The final product is that the defrauded PC can't process any genuine errands (Elleithy et al., 2006). The subsequent structure form the unfortunate casualty's correspondence pipeline with trash system traffic. The final product is that the defrauded PC can't send or get real arrange correspondences. The unfortunate casualty has been denied the capacity to execute typical activities.

Denial of Service is certainly not a solitary attack but instead a entire class of attacks. Few are capable to harm the operating system software, while others are targeting the intalled software applications, running services and protocols including *"Internet Protocol (IP), Transmission Control Protocol (TCP), Internet Control Message Protocol(ICMP) and User Datagram Protocol (UDP)"*. Denial of service attacks arise among one attacker and one victim on a regular basis. Be that as it may, they don't need to be pursued in such straightforward way. DoS attacks utilize same type of mediator structure (generally a reluctant and unconscious member) so as to conceal the attacker from the person in question.

Figure 1. Denial of Service (DoS) Attack

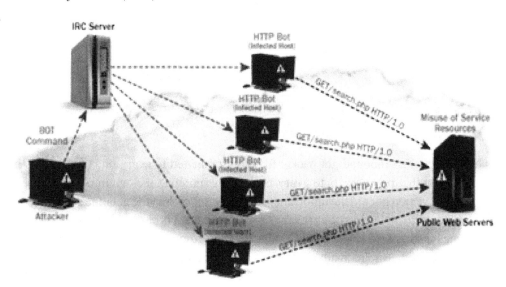

For instance, in the event that an aggressor sends attack packet straightforwardly to an unfortunate casualty, at that point it's workable for the victim to find who the attacker is. This is made progressively troublesome, despite the fact that certainly feasible, using spoofing. Numerous DoS attack are pursued by first trading off or penetrating at least few mediator systems that fill in as dispatch focuses, or attack stages. The attacker introduces the remote control tools, frequently called bots, zombies, or specialists, onto these systems (Mahjabin et al., 2017; Malik & Singh, 2015). As such, the victim might have the option to find the one or numerous zombied systems which are the real cause of DoS attack however likely won't have the option to find the genuine attacker. The Distributed Denial of Service attack (DDoS), as appeared in Figure 2 uses such types of of attack including zombied systems.

The third degree of DoS: Denial of Service known as Distributed Reflective Denial of Service (DRDoS). Such types of attack utilizes an enhancement or ricochet network which is a reluctant and unconscious member however that has lamentably left on its capacity to get communicate messages and make message reactions, echoes, or ricochets. Basically spoofed messages packets were send by attackers to enhnce network's broadcast address (Behal & Kumar, 2016; Izaddoost et al., 2007; Mahjabin et al., 2017; Malik & Singh, 2015).

Figure 2. An example of DDoS: Distributed Denial of Service Attack

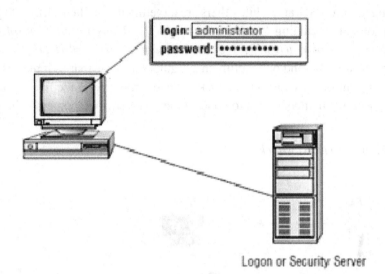

It effcts every particular inbound got packet to be disseminated to every one of the hosts inside the network. Each host at that point reacts to every packet, except since the origin of the first packet was misrepresented, the reaction goes to the unfortunate casualty rather than the genuine sender (the attacker). Consequently, what originateted by the attacker as a solitary packet is changed into various packets leaving the enhancement network and eventually flooding the unfortunate victim's correspondence interface. Plantey of tools and techniares are available for DoS, DDoS, and DRDoS.

Virtual Private Networks (VPN) cross-sectionally expands a private network over an open network such as the internet. This allows consumers to transmit and collect information through public or open networks as if their processing devices were linked to the private network (Sharma & Yadav, 2015; Zhiyong et al., 2011). A VPN is created through the establishment of a virtual point-to-point association using committed associations, traffic encryption vitual tunneling conventions. A VPN's one impediment is the way the organization requires a high level of knowledge and understanding of such factors as open network security. Security of VPN requires encryption of secret key information. Network addresses can also be encrypted, and for included security To stay away from security and sending issues, planning is fundamental and legitimate safeguards ought to be taken.

Security Risks in Network Communication

The security of the network is possibly the basic problem that IT administrators have long faced. However, even when security threats and problems come up every day, there are some vectors of attacks that cyber criminals typically leverage to penetrate corporate networks, according to several cybersecurity reports. To address such kind of problems, it becomes necessary to identifying access contol and authentication method of network security.

The system by which clients are allowed or denied the capacity to associate through and utilize assets is acknowledged as access control. The term authorization is regulary allowed or associated with access control. Authorization characterizes the sort of access to assets clients are allowed or what clients are approved to do. Authorization is frequently viewed as the following coherent advance following authentication. Authentication is the demonstrating of your personality to a framework or the demonstration of signing on. With legitimate authentication, a framework will appropriately control access to assets so as to forestall illegal or unautorize access. There are some primary regular access control techniques:

a) "Mandatory Access Control (MAC)"
b) "Discretionary Access Control (DAC)"
c) "Role-Based Access Control (RBAC)"
d) "Rule-based Access Control (RuBAC)"
e) "Attribute-based Access Control (ABAC)"

a) Mandatory Access Control (MAC): Mandatory access control is a type of access control ordinarily utilized by military and government sectors. It determines that access is conceded dependent on a lot of principles as opposed to at the circumspection of a client. The principles which administer mandatory access control are hierarchical in nature and are regularly identifyed affectability labels and security domains (Bays et al., 2015; Henricksen et al., 2007). Mandatory access control conditions characterize a couple of explicit secure areas or affectability levels and after that utilization of related labels from the realm to inflict access control on subjects and objects. Various sectors of government incliding military are practicing MAC on regular basis incorporates at five levels:

i)   "Unclassified"
ii)   "Sensitive yet unclassified"
iii) "Confidential"
iv)   "Secret"
v)   "Top secret"

Objects or assets are appointed affectability labels comparing to one of these security areas. Every particular security area characterizes the security systems and confinements must be forced so as to give insurance to items inside the domain. Normally four degrees of security spaces are included which are "*public, sensitive, priveate and confidential*".

The main role of a mandatory access control domain is to avert divulgence: the infringement of the security priciple of confidentiality. At the point when an unauthorized client accesses a verified asset, this behaviour is security infringement. Items are appointed for the particular affectability level, dependent on damage that would be reason if exposure happened (Bays et al., 2015; Franco et al., 2008; Henricksen et al., 2007). For instance, if a high secured asset was unveiled, it could case critical destruction.

MAC is named as it is on the grounds that the access control it enforces on a domain is required. It is doled out categorization and the subsequent allowing and confinement of access can not be modified by clients. Rather, principles which characterize nature and review the task of control authorization of affectability labels and clearance levels (Chandramouli, 2001; Sailer et al., 2005). MAC is certifiably not a security environment controlled in granular form. The update to MAC introduces the utilzation of the requirement to be familiar with: a security limitation with few objects (assets or information) are limited except the issue needs to be acquainted with them. Objects requiring detailed information are given an affectability label, but are compartmentalized from the rest of the items with a separate mark of affectability (in a similar security domain). The need to learn is a requirement all by itself, which communicates that only subjects who have been allocated job errands are granted access to the cordoned-off object.

b) Discretionary Access Control (DAC): Discretionary access control is like the access control or authorization that utilizes in mainly business and home situations. DAC is client coordinated or, all the added explicitly, constrained by the proprietor and makers of the assets in the environment. It is identify based. Access is allowed or limited by an object's proprietor dependent on client identification and the caution of the item proprietor. Subsequently, proprietor of an entity be able to choose whom to deny or allow to access the object (Chandramouli, 2001; Wang et al., 2019). It uses the access control list (ACL), which is capable to join the assest and items in the environment with the help of security logical devices. It characterizes which clients are allowed or prevented the different kinds from claiming access accessible dependent on the object. Separate client records or combined group records may be included to an object's ACL and conceded or denied get to. In the event that your client record is not conceded admission throughout an object's ACL, at that point it denied access by default. In the event that your client record is explicitly conceded access through an object's ACL, at that point it will allowed the particular stage or sort of access characterized.

Generally, a Denied background in an ACL abrogates every single setting. Table 1 (Cumulative Access Based on Group Memberships) demonstrates an access matrix for client that can successsivily access the folders on network server and also the memeber of three groups. It overrides the seeting of any other access authorized from another group with denied presence. In this way the participation in first client set awards to compose admittance above an item, yet other group explicitly refuse to compose access to a similar item, at that point it will denied compose access to the item.

Table 1. Cummulitive access based on group membership

S. No.	Sales Group	User Group	Research Group	Resulting Access
1	Change	Read	None specified	Change
2	Read	Read	Change	Change
3	None specified	Read	Read	Denied
4	Full control	Denied	None specified	denied

c) Role-Based Access Control (RBAC): RBAC is an additional type of rules-based access control. It might be assembled with the nondiscretionary access control strategies alongside MAC. The rules utilized for RBAC are fundamentally sets of descriptions: Clients are allocated a particular job in a domain, and access to objects is conceded dependent on the important work assignments of that job (Bennett et al., 2006; Ferraiolo et al., 1999; Ferraiolo et al., 2003; Reid et al., 2003). For instance, job of reinforcement administrator might conceded the capability to sustain each records on a system drives. The client prearranged the reinforcement administrator job that have the option to play out that work. RBAC is primarily appropriate for situations with a good pace of representative yield. It permits the sets of roles or jobs to stay static notwithstanding as the client playing out that job modify frequently.

d) Rule-based Access Control (RuBAC): A Security model where administrator of system characterizes the standards for administering access to asset objects. Those rules often depend on certain conditions whose focus on mainly on time or location. Sometimes to enforce access policies and procedures is not extraordinary while using the forms of rule-based access control and role-based access control (Kizza, 2005).

e) Attribute-based Access Control (ABAC): A procedure which oversees access rights by assessing a lot of principles, strategies and associations utilizing the properties of clients, systems and environmental circumstances (Hu et al., 2014). ABAC requires comprehension of the essential standards of logical access control. The reason for logical access control is to ensure objects like information, services, network devices, executable applications, or some other sort of data/information from unauthorized tasks. These tasks may incorporate finding, reading, making, altering, erasing, and executing objects. These articles are claimed by an individual or association and have some natural worth that persuades those owners to protect them. As owners of the items, they have the position to set up a strategy that portrays what activities might be performed upon those objects, by whom, and in what context those subjects may play out those tasks. On the off chance that the subject fulfills the access control policy built up by the object owner, at that point the subject is approved to play out the ideal activity on that object—otherwise called being conceded access to the object. In the event that the subject doesn't satisfied the policy, at that point it is denied access to the object.

The possiblittes of threat for unauthorized access to physical and logical systems is optimized through access control. Access control plays a vital role to secure systems and maintain security infrastructure, and access control measures that are put in to protect private data including information about clients. Many organizations, for example, have establishment and suggestive measures that limits access to networks, computer systems, software, documents and highly sensitive personalized information, and items under intellectual property. Access control systems are more complex for monitoring in diverse information technology environments which include on-site services and cloud services. Software providers have switched to centralized access management after some notable attacks, and includes access controls for on-site and cloud environments.

Acoording to network security risk the second and the most important factor is authentication. Authentication is the component by which an individual demonstrates their uniqueness to a system. Username and a password are the regular souces of authentication. However, other progressively composite authentication factors or credential-assurance mechanism are engaged with request to give solid security to the logon and account-verification process. Authentication is minimal more than the way toward demonstrating that a subject is the valid client of an account. The authentification procedure necessitates that the subject give an identity and afterward evidence of that identity. To prrof identity commonly appears as at least one of the accompanying three factors: (a) Knowing by password (b) Knowing by smart card (c) Knowing by fingerprint

USERNAME/PASSWORD

The combination of a client's username and his password is the most well-known type of authenification as showm in figure 3 (Logon process by using a username/password). If the used password is equivalent to the password stored in a system's records database for the predefined client, at that point that client is validated by the system. Validation of authenticated records must be verified on the basis of the predefined password with respect to the passwords stroed in system's database. The true value indicates the authenticated client means client is validated to the system. Nonetheless, in light of the fact that utilization password protection system is widely accepted medium for authentication mechanism but it is not the well established medium for maximum security. Unexpectedly, it's commonly viewed as the least secure type of authentication.

Figure 3. Logon Process by Using a Username/Password

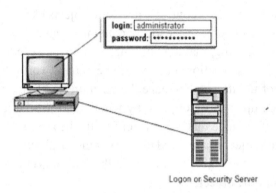

Logon or Security Server

Different goals have been produced to enhance the basic username / password combination. First is storing passwords in quite a while database in an encrypted form. The values from one way hash function is an example of such type. Secondly, the exercise of an authentication protocol that avoid password transmission over a network, or especially the Internet, in an effectively coherent manner. Second, there is regular implementation of strong (complex) passwords at various application programming level (Dinesha & Agrawal, 2012a). It will provide a guarantee that the program will only require passwords that are hard to discover for a password-cracking device.

The strength of any password is commonly estimated with the measure of time and exertion. These measures can be estimated as responsible effort associated for cracking the password through different types of cryptographic hits. These efforts are known as password cracking or password speculating. A weak password perpetually utilizes just alphanumeric characters; regularly utilizes dictionary or other basic words; and may incorporate client profile–related information, for example, birthdates, pet names, etc.

Strong passwords comprise of various characters (at least 8); incorporate at any rate three kinds of characters (capitalized, lowercase, numerals, and console images); are changed all the time (at regular intervals); do exclude any word list or normal words and do exclude a few piece of the subject's genuine name, client name, or email address. Passwords ought to be sufficiently able to oppose revelation through attack yet simply adequate for the individual to recall.

Tokens

A special type of authentication factor is sometimes explained through tokens. A hardware device with well implemented software codes to produce transitory single-use passwords to make more grounded authentication. Thus, a client account is not attached to a solitary static password. Rather, the client should be in physical ownership of the password generating devices. There are a few types of tokens. Some produce passwords dependent on schedule, though others create passwords dependent on challenges from the authentication server. The client can utilize the created password only once before they should either hang tight for whenever window or solicitation another challenge. Passwords that must be utilized single time are acknowledged as one-time or single time passwords. It is one of the most secured type of password, since in spite of its utilization brings about an effective log-on, that one-time use password is never legitimate once more for reprocess. One-time passwords must be utilized when a token device is utilized, because of the unpredictability and regularly varying environment of the passwords (Dinesha & Agrawal, 2012a; Sumathi et al., 2013). A token might be a gadget similar to a little calculation machine with or without a keypad. It might likewise be a top of the line smartcard as depicted in figure 4 (Authentication process through smartcard). At the point when appropriately conveyed, a token-based authetication scheme is much safer than a password scheme.

Figure 4. Authentication Process through Smartcard

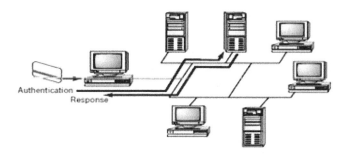

Multi-Factor Authentication

In multi factor authentication client is required to produce more than one or atleat two authentication factor to reveal his identity. These requirements are the basic prerquisite for the same. The three perceived categories of authentication factors are generally mentioned below:

- Knowledge about user, (for example, a password)
- Knowledge what user have, (for example, a token)
- Knowledge who is user, (for example, a biometric)

When two distinctive authentication factors are utilized, this is recognized as two-factor authentication or multi factor authentication as shown in figure 5. If two of a same authentication components are utilized, this is known as hard or strong authentication.

At whatever point various factorss are utilized, that is constantly an extra protected arrangement than some number of a similar authentification factors (Dinesha & Agrawal, 2012a; Dinesha & Agrawal, 2012b; Sumathi et al., 2013). This is because of the way that with at least two unique factors, at least two distinct kinds of attacks must occur so as to take or catch the authentication factor itself. With strong authentification, regardless of whether ten passwords are essential, just a single sort of password-stealing attack should be pursued to get through the authentication security.

Figure 5. Multi-factor Authentication

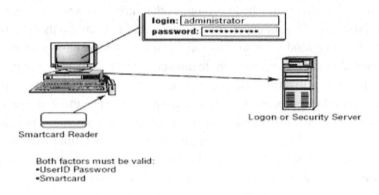

Mutual Authentication

Another important two way authentication mechanism is also known as Mutual authentication. In this case two way authentication is being executed where client validates the autheitcity of servers and other end server validates the authenticity of clients. Thusly, at the both ends communications have proof of the identity of the other accomplice (Dinesha & Agrawal, 2012a). Figure 6 explains about the mutual authentication process.

Figure 6. Mutual Authentication Process

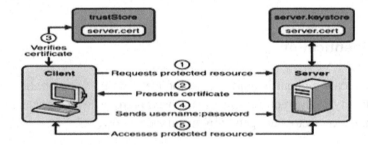

Authentication Via Biometrics

Biometrics is the advance terminology for authentication purpose depict the accumulation of physical characteristic of the human being with the aim of authenication aspect. Authtication through biometrics appear into the authentification factor class of "something you will be": 'Human', has the component of recognition proof as a component of his physical apperance. Biometrics facility may be used through fingerprints, palm checks (utilization of the whole palm as though it were a unique mark), hand geometry, scanning veins at the back of the eye: retinal scans, scanning coloured region of the eye around the pupil: iris scans, face recognition, voice recognition, signature dynamics, and keyboard dynamics (Clancy et al., 2003; Podio & Jeffrey, 2002; Reid, 2003; Soutar et al., 1998) as illustrated in figure 7 (biometric identification).

Figure 7. Biometric Identification

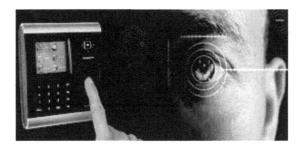

In spite of the fact that biometrics are a more grounded type of authentication than passwords alone, biometrics all by themselves are not the top arrangement. Definitely, even with implementing biometrics, the more secure and satisfactory results are achieved through multi-factor authentication.

Methodology

The main aim is to determine goals supported on weight and classification of the security risk factor of the network by means of a multi-criteria decision building process in which the exercise of analytical hierarchy is demonstrated, in order to establish a secure and reliable network. Because no attempts have been made to quantitatively classify and rate the network security risk factor, the fuzzy AHP can therefore be used to prioritize the factor. Fuzzy AHP provides more accurate results compared to traditional AHP because it is beneficial in the decision-making process to eliminate the problem of confusion and ambiguity. This will enhance the protection and early detection of vulnerabilities that will directly benefit users / organization by improving secure network capacity and durability. Study of network security risk factor prioritization using the Multi-Criteria Decision Making System i.e., Analytic Hierarchy Process (Chang, 2012; Kumar et al., 2016). MCDM is a sub-discipline of operations research which is very helpful in the decision-making process in carrying out different assessments of competing criteria (Chung & Seo, 2015).

Therefore AHP is a superior technique to measure the subjective and objective values of the factors compared to other MCDA strategies. Be that as it may, AHP is unable to determine the inherent vagueness and ambiguity identified by mapping the consciousness of correct numbers of a decision maker. Author found that Fuzzy theory was consolidated with AHP by practitioners as the real world is exceptionally questionable for investigating uncertain real issues (Chang, 2008 and Lious, 1992). This exercise receives the Buckley technique and the own vector technique is used to assess the weights in order to analyze the safety risks of a network by examining data and reaching an agreement between specialists. Furthermore, the AHP uses the matrix for pair-wise comparisons to assess uncertainty in *"Multi critera decision analysis MCDA"* problems as in equation (1.0).

$$A = [J_{ij}] = \begin{array}{c} \\ C_1 \\ C_2 \\ \vdots \\ C_n \end{array} \begin{array}{cccc} C_1 & C_2 & \cdots & C_n \\ \begin{bmatrix} 1 & a_{12} & \cdots & a_{1n} \\ 1/a_{12} & 1 & \cdots & a_{2n} \\ \vdots & \vdots & \ddots & \vdots \\ 1/a_{1n} & 1/a_{2n} & \cdots & 1 \end{bmatrix} \end{array} \text{n*n} \qquad (1.0)$$

Here $a_{ij} = 1$ and $a_{ij} = 1/a_{ij}$, i, j = 1, 2,..., n.

A n-by-n matrix, A can be articulated as appeared in equation (1.0). Let C_1, C_2,..., C_n signify the arrangement of feature while a_{ij} stand for an evaluated decision on a couple of features C_i, C_j. The relative consequences of the two attributes is appraised utilizing a scale (Buckley, 1985 and Saaty, 1980). The Fuzzy AHP strategy involves four noteworthy strides as talked about underneath.

Next, the issue is aligned into a hierarchical graded framework to address using Fuzzy AHP. It should be evidently expressed and an organizational level framework is defined for organization in figure 8 (Network security factors hierarchy diagram). The goal of this analysis is to provide a hybrid model of MCDM network security methods. The figure shows the network protection factor structure. This hierarchy can be achieved using the opinions and reactions of experts in questionnaires or by using brainstorms and others. The hierarchy is then defined by the triangular fluzzynumbers (TFN).

First of all, the issue is partitioned into a hierarchical leveled arrangement to tackle it utilizing Fuzzy-AHP. It ought to be expressed very clerarly and a hierarchical leveled arrangement is made for arrangement appeared in figure 8 (Hierarchy diagram of network security factors). The objective of this study is to have resource towards a hybrid model of MCDM methods for network security. The figure shows the structure of network security factors. This hierarchy is made by utilizing expert's opinions and reactions in questionnaire/openion poll or utilizing brainstorming and another available technique. Afterwards, the triangular fuzzynumbers (TFN) is established from the hierarchy are recognized.

Figure 8. Hierarchy Diagram of Network Security Factors

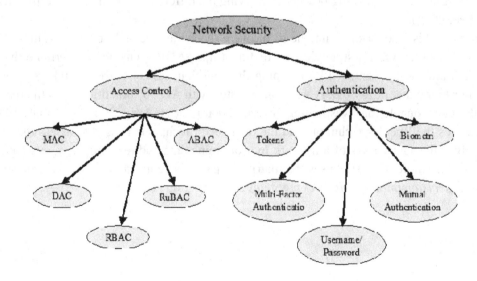

Fuzzy set theory is packed with ambiguous details. A fuzzy collection is a grouping of artifacts of membership ranges. Such an attribute is defined by a membership function, which gives every entity a membership grade somewhere lies between zero (0) and one (1). Figure 9 illustrates a fluffy triangular figure

Figure 9. An example of triangular fuzzy numbers

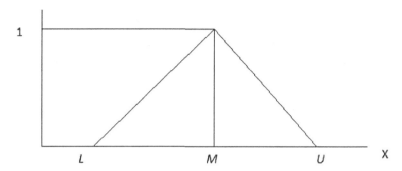

"*Triangular fuzzy numbers (TFN)*" is indicated basically as (Lo, Mi, Up). The equations (2-4) are used to convert the numeric values into "*Triangular Fuzzy Number (TFN)*" (Cherdantseva et al., 2016) and signified as "(Lo_{ij}, Mi_{ij}, Up_{ij}) where, Lo_{ij} is lower value, Mi_{ij} is middle value and Up_{ij} is highest level events". Further, TFN [η_{ij}] is set up as the accompanying:

$$"\eta_{ij} = [Lo_{ij}, Mi_{ij}, Up_{ij}]" \text{ Here } Lo_{ij} \leq Mi_{ij} \leq Up_{ij} \tag{2.0}$$

$$Lo_{ij} = min(J_{ijk}) \tag{3.0}$$

$$Mi_{ij} = (J_{ij1}, J_{ij2} \ldots \ldots J_{ijk})^{1/k} \tag{4.0}$$

$$Up_{ij} = max(J_{ijk}) \tag{5.0}$$

In the above calculations, Jijk demonstrates the comparative value between two parameters provided by the expert z. Where I and j represent parameters that experts evaluate. This value is determined by the geometric mean for a defined assocoations. The GM will correctly sum and depict stakeholder consensus, which reflects the lowest and highest scores for the relative value between the two parameters. Upon acquiring the TFN value for each pair of reference, a fuzzy matrix is set as nxn matrix. This study includes analysts and engineers with experience in network management and security risks. Reliable AHP analysis is ensured totally based on chosen participants. "*Triangular fuzzy numbers (TFN)*" membership function and pair-wise comparisons are determined to produce the ambiguous decision matrix in the third stage after qualitative assessment.

Therefore, defuzzification is done after the matrix is developed to produce a quantifiable value dependent on calculated TFN values. Defuzzification is reverse fuzzification. The defuzzification approach implemented in this study was extracted from ("Buckley, 1985; Deng, 1999 and Saaty, 1980") as developed in equation (5-7), commonly called alpha cutting.

$$\rho\alpha\beta\ (\tilde{A})= [\beta.\ \tilde{A}_{\alpha}(Lo_{ij})+ (1\text{-}\beta).\ \tilde{A}_{\alpha}(Up_{ij})] \qquad (6.0)$$

where $0 \le \alpha \le 1$ and $0 \le \beta \le 1$

Such that,

$$\tilde{A}_{\alpha}(Lo_{ij}) = (Mi_{ij}\text{-}\ Lo_{ij}).\alpha\text{+}Lo_{ij} \qquad (7.0)$$

$$\tilde{A}_{\alpha}(Up_{ij}) = Up_{ij}\text{-}\ (Up_{ij}\text{-}\ Mi_{ij}).\alpha \qquad (8.0)$$

Where these calculations use α and β for professional tastes. Those two values range 0-1. A fuzzy set's alpha cut is all-element package. The alpha-threshold is any number from 0 to 1. It has an alpha threshold value superior than or equal to the α-defined membership value. $\tilde{A}\alpha(Loij)$ and $\tilde{A}\alpha(Upij)$ indicate lower and upper defused values. Equation (8) displays the matrix prepared after assessment of participants ' decisions.

$$\rho\alpha\beta\ (\tilde{A}) = {\acute{A}\pm,^2}\ [\tilde{a}ij] = \begin{array}{c} \\ C_1 \\ C_2 \\ \vdots \\ C_n \end{array} \begin{matrix} C_1 & C_2 & \cdots & C_n \\ \left[\begin{matrix} 1 & \acute{A}\pm,^2\ (\tilde{a}11) & \cdots & \acute{A}\pm,^2\ (\tilde{a}1i) \\ 1/\acute{A}\pm,^2\ (\tilde{a}21) & 1 & \cdots & \acute{A}\pm,^2\ (\tilde{a}2i) \\ \vdots & \vdots & \ddots & \vdots \\ 1/\acute{A}\pm,^2\ (\tilde{a}j1) & 1/\acute{A}\pm,^2\ (\tilde{a}j2) & \cdots & 1 \end{matrix}\right] \end{matrix} \qquad (9.0)$$

Where[ãij] denotes the relative importance of two C1 parameters for a Fuzzy number. Alpha cut often helps one to view a blurry package as a series of flat sets. Crisp sets $\pi\alpha,\beta(a)$ basically represent whether or not an entity is a part of the group. Single pair matrix in equation (8) ("M. Alenezi et al., 2019"). Therefore, the another action in this approach is to evaluate the peer-to-peer reference matrix. The use behind own vector computing is to decide the aggregated weight of specific criteria. Expect that $\pi\alpha,\beta$ signifies the own vector, while π denotes the peculiar attribute of aij[89-94].

$$[\rho_{\alpha,\beta}(\tilde{A})\text{-}\ \lambda I].\rho=0 \qquad (10.0)$$

Equation (9) relies on linear vector transformation, where I describe unit matrix. Through adding equations (1-9), weights with specific criteria could be produced for all other possile criteria. Test the Consistency Ratio (CR) (Chang, 2008 and Lious, 1992). If the CR meaning is less than 0.1, then the AHP measurement is correctly evaluated again[95-100].

ASSESSMENT OF NETWORK SECURITY RISK FACTORS

Network security factors are multidimensional and typically qualitative in nature. Consequently, it turn into a challenging assignment to assess the network security factors quantitatively. Hence, respective weightages and ranks of network security factors demonstrate an important responsibility for highly secure design of network. Constructed aggregated fuzzy pair-wise comparison matrix shows the priorities obtained from various pair wise comparisons at level 1 is shown in table 2. The fuzzified aggregated pair wise comparison matrix at level 2 for sub-factors is prepared by analyzing experts opinions by using geometric average approach. The prepared matrix Fuzzy Aggregated Pair-wise Comparison Matrix at level 1 & 3 are shown in table 2 and table 3. Where [*"C11→Mandatory Access Control (MAC), C12→Discretionary Access Control (DAC), C13→Role-Based Access Control (RBAC), C14→ Rule-based Access Control (RuBAC), C15→Attribute-based access control (ABAC)"*]Where [*"C21→ Username/Password, C22→ Tokens, C23→ Multi-Factor Authentication, C24→ Mutual Authentication, C25→ Biometrics"*]

Table 2. Fuzzy Aggregated Pair-wise Comparison Matrix at Level 1

	Access Control (C1)	Authentication (C2)
Access Control (C1)	1,1,1	0.230, 0.280, 0.360
Authentication (C2)	-	1,1,1

Table 3. Fuzzy Aggregated Pair-wise Comparison Matrix at Level 2

	C11	C12	C13	C14	C15
C11	1,1,1	0.690, 0.890, 1.100	0.230, 0.280, 0.360	0.700, 0.950, 1.350	0.300, 0.440, 0.800
C12	-	1,1,1	0.490, 0.640, 1.000	0.270, 0.350, 0.520	0.170, 0.200, 0.250
C13	-	-	1,1,1	1.000, 1.320, 1.550	0.660, 1.170, 1.690
C14	-	-	-	1,1,1	1.150, 1.440, 1.700
C15	-	-	-	-	1,1,1

According to hierarchy, Table 1, 2 and 3 depict the fuzzy aggregated pair-wise comparison matrix at level 1 and level 2). This paper used α cut method of defuzzification with the help of equation 5 to 8. Further, CR values are also less than 0.1. The independent weights of risk attributes of network security and CR values are shown in table 4 to table 6.

As per the hierarchy order, Table 5 demonstrates about "defuzzified aggregated pair-wise comparison matrix and local weights of level 1 attributes".

As per the hierarchy order, table 6 demonstrates about "defuzzified aggregated pair-wise comparison matrix and local weights of level 2 attributes".

As per the hierarchy, table 6 shows the defuzzified aggregated pair-wise comparison matrix and local weights of level 2 attributes. Table 7 shows the dependent or overall weights and overall ranking of the hierarchy. Final or global weights is stated in Table 8.

Table 4. Fuzzy Aggregated Pair-wise Comparison Matrix at Level 2

	C21	C22	C23	C24	C25
C21	1,1,1	0.660, 1.170, 1.690	1.150, 1.440, 1.700	1.190, 1.580, 2.150	0.220, 0.290, 0.420
C22	-	1,1,1	1.000, 1.520, 1.930	0.490, 0.640, 1.000	0.270, 0.350, 0.520
C23	-	-	1,1,1	1.000, 1.320, 1.550	1.000, 1.520, 1.930
C24	-	-	-	1,1,1	0.310, 0.390, 0.560
C25	-	-	-	-	1,1,1

Table 5. Aggregated Pair-wise Comparison Matrix at level 1

	C1	C2	Weights
C1	1	1.173	0.5398
C2	0.853	1	0.4602
			C.R.=0.0004

Table 6. Aggregated Pair-wise Comparison Matrix at level 2

	C11	C12	C13	C14	C15	Weights
C11	1	0.892	1.173	0.994	0.494	0.1647
C12	1.121	1	0.691	0.372	0.203	0.1092
C13	0.853	1.447	1	1.298	1.172	0.2134
C14	1.006	2.688	0.770	1	1.363	0.2315
C15	2.024	4.926	0.853	0.734	1	0.2812
						CR=0.08775

As per the hierarchy order, table 6 demonstrates the defuzzified aggregated pair-wise comparison matrix and local weights of level 2 attributes. Table 8 demonstrates the dependent or overall weights and overall ranking of the hierarchy. Final or global weights is expressed in Table 8. The evaluative criteria are weighted as given in table 8 that are most important risks for network security.

Table 7. Aggregated Pair-wise Comparison Matrix at level 2

	C21	C22	C23	C24	C25	Weights
C21	1	1.172	1.363	1.633	0.303	**0.1762**
C22	0.853	1	1.491	0.691	0.372	**0.1514**
C23	0.734	0.671	1	1.298	1.491	**0.2034**
C24	0.612	1.447	0.770	1	0.411	**0.1394**
C25	3.300	2.688	0.671	2.433	1	**0.3296**
						C.R.=0.0102

Table 8. Summary of the Results

First Level Attributes	Local Weights of First Level	Second Level Attributes	Local Weights of Second Level	Overall Weights	Overall Ranks
C1	0.5398	C11	0.1647	**0.0889**	6
		C12	0.1092	**0.0589**	10
		C13	0.2134	**0.1152**	4
		C14	0.2315	**0.1250**	3
		C15	0.2812	**0.1518**	1
C2	0.4602	C21	0.1762	**0.0811**	7
		C22	0.1514	**0.0697**	8
		C23	0.2034	**0.0936**	5
		C24	0.1394	**0.0642**	9
		C25	0.3296	**0.1517**	2

CONCLUSION

Network security risk is a booming area for research in this era. Factors contributing in the field of network security plays a vital role for the determination of security risk. Subsequently choosing the significant factor among a rundown of attributes is critical for effective network security risk. This paper represented views on the direct associated factors and sub-factors based on network security. As indicated by the exploration, the directed dependency on Fuzzy ANP, ecological instance of validation and trustworthiness are observed to be the most organized variables among all. Subsequently for successull execution of Fuzzy AHP the global values has been determined. This priority wise listing of factors is helpful for deciding the most significant factors among the horde of factors in network security. Further, the priotization will be helpful for designing guidelines to network engineers to know the productive usage of network security risk in explicit experiments and their mitigation mechanism.

REFERENCES

Abomhara, M., & Køien, G. M. (2015). Cyber Security and the Internet of Things: Vulnerabilities, Threats, Intruders and Attacks. *Journal of Cyber Security*, *4*, 65–88. doi:10.13052/jcsm2245-1439.414

Agrafiotis, I., Nurse, J. R. C., Goldsmith, M., Creese, S., & Upton, D. (2018). A taxonomy of cyber-harms: Defining the impacts of cyber-attacks and understanding how they propagate. *Journal of Cybersecurity*, *4*(1), 1–15. doi:10.1093/cybsec/tyy006

Agrawal, A., Alenezi, M., Pandey, D., Kumar, R., & Khan, R. A. (2019). Usable-Security Assessment through a Decision Making Procedure. *ICIC Express Letters*, *10*(8), 665–672.

Agrawal, A., Zarour, M., Alenezi, M., Kumar, R., & Khan, R. A. (2019). Security durability assessment through fuzzy analytic hierarchy process. *Peer J. Computer Science*, *5*, 1–44. doi:10.7717/peerj-cs.215

Ahmad, N., & Habib, K. (2010). *Analysis of Network Security Threats and Vulnerabilities by Development & Implementation of a Security Network Monitoring Solution*. Blekinge Institute of Technology.

Aldosari, W., & Taeib, T. E. (2015). Secure Key Establishment for Device-To-Device Communications among Mobile Devices. *International Journal of Engineering Research and Reviews*, *3*(2), 43–47.

Alenezi, M., Kumar, R., Agrawal, A., & Khan, R. A. (2019). Usable-security attribute evaluation using fuzzy analytic hierarchy process. *ICIC Express Letter-An International Journal of Research and Survey.*, *13*(6), 1–17.

Analoui, M., Mirzaei, A., & Kabiri, P. (2005). Intrusion detection using multivariate analysis of variance algorithm. *Third International Conference on Systems, Signals & Devices SSD*, 3.

Awodele, O., Onuiri, E. E., & Okolie, S. (2012). Vulnerabilities in Network Infrastructures and Prevention/Containment Measures. Informing Science & IT Education Conference (InSITE), 53-67.

Bays, L. R., Oliveira, R. R., Barcellos, M. P., Gaspary, L. P., & Madeira, E. R. M. (2015). Virtual network security: Threats, countermeasures, and challenges. *Journal of Internet Services and Applications*, *6*(1), 1–19. doi:10.118613174-014-0015-z

Behal, S., & Kumar, K. (2016). Trends in Validation of DDoS Research. *Procedia Computer Science*, *85*, 7–15. doi:10.1016/j.procs.2016.05.170

Bennett, K., Rigby, M., & Budgen, D. (2006). Role Based Access Control – a Solution with Its Own Challenges. *IEEE Proceedings - Software*, *153*(1), 1-3.

Berner, B. (2011). Seven unforgivable errors in network security. *Binesh Magazine*, 53-55.

Birge, J. R., Khabazian, A., & Peng, J. (2018). Optimization Modeling and Techniques for Systemic Risk Assessment and Control in Financial Networks. *Tutorials in Operations Research (INFORMS)*, 64-84.

Brenton, C., & Hunt, C. (n.d.). *Mastering Network Security* (2nd ed.). Wiley.

Buckley, J. J. (1985). Fuzzy hierarchical analysis. *Fuzzy Sets and Systems, 17*(3), 233–247. doi:10.1016/0165-0114(85)90090-9

Canavan, J. E. (2000). *Fundamentals of Network Security*. Artech House Telecommunications Library.

Chandramouli, R. (2001). A framework for multiple authorization types in a healthcare application system. *17th Annual Computer Security Applications Conference*. 10.1109/ACSAC.2001.991530

Chang, C., Wu, C., & Lin, H. (2008). Integrating fuzzy theory and hierarchy concepts to evaluate software quality. *Springer Software Qual. J., 16*(2), 263–276. doi:10.100711219-007-9035-2

Chang, S. H. (2012). *Fuzzy Multi-Criteria Evaluation and Statistics*. Wunan Books.

Charles, P., & Pñeeger, S. L. (2012). *Analyzing Computer Security: A Threat / Vulnerability / Countermeasure Approach*. Prentice Hall.

Chen, X., Zhao, P., Peng, Y., Liu, B., Li, W., Xie, Y., Chen, X., & Yuan, M. (2018). Risk analysis and optimization for communication transmission link interruption in Smart Grid cyberphysical system. *International Journal of Distributed Sensor Networks, 14*(2), 1–12. doi:10.1177/1550147718756035

Cherdantseva, Y., Burnap, P., Blyth, A., Eden, P., Jones, K., Soulsby, H., & Stoddart, K. (2016). A review of cyber security risk assessment methods for SCADA systems. *Computers & Security, 56*, 1–27. doi:10.1016/j.cose.2015.09.009

Chopra, A. (2016). Security Issues of Firewall. *International Journal of P2P Network Trends and Technology, 6*(1).

Chung, B. D., & Seo, K. K. (2015). A Cloud Service Selection Model Based On Analytic Network Process. *Indian Journal of Science andTechnology, 8*(18), 1-5.

CISCO Systems. (2001). *A beginner's guide to network security*. http://www.cisco.com/ warp/public/cc/so/neso/sqso/ beggu_pl.pdf

Clancy, T. C., Kiyavash, N., & Lin, D. J. (2003). Secure smartcard-based fingerprint authentication. *Proceedings of the ACM SIGMM 2003 Multimedia, Biometrics Methods and Workshop*, 45–52.

Dark Reading. (2011). *Sony data breach cleanup to cost $171million*. http:// www.darkreading.com/attacks-and-breaches/sony-data-breach-cleanupto-cost-\$171-million/d/d-id/1097898

Daya, B. (2010). *Network Security: History, Importance, and Future*. University of Florida Department of Electrical and Computer Engineering.

Daya, B. (2013). *Network Security: History, Importance, and Future*. University of Florida Department of Electrical and Computer Engineering. http://web.mit.edu/~bdaya/www/Network%20 Security.pdf

Deng, H. (1999). Multi criteria analysis with fuzzy pair wise comparisons. *International Journal of Approximate Reasoning, 21*(3), 215–231. doi:10.1016/S0888-613X(99)00025-0

Dinesha, H. A., & Agrawal, V. K. (2012a). Formal Modeling for Multi-Level Authentication in Sensor-Cloud Integration System. *International Journal of Applied Information Systems, 2*(1), 16–21.

Dinesha, H. A., & Agrawal, V. K. (2012b). Multi-dimensional Password Generation Technique for accessing cloud services. Special Issue on: Cloud Computing and Web Services. *International Journal on Cloud Computing: Services and Architecture, 2*(3), 31–39.

Dong, L., & Peng, Y. (2012). Network Security and Firewall Technology. *Proceedings of 2010 3rd International Conference on Computer and Electrical Engineering (ICCEE2010no.2).*

Elleithy, K. M., Blagovic, D., Cheng, W., & Sideleau, P. (2006). Denial of Service Attack Techniques: Analysis, Implementation and Comparison. *Systemics, Cybernetics and Informatics, 3*(1), 66–71.

Farrow, R. (n.d.). *Network Security Tools.* http://sageweb.sage.org/pubs/whitepapers/ farrow.pdf

Ferraiolo, D. F., Cugini, J. A., & Kuhn, D. R. (1999). *Role-Based Access Control (RBAC): Features and Motivations.* National Institute of Standards and Technology.

Ferraiolo, D. F., Kuhn, D. R., & Chandramouli, R. (2003). *Role-Based Access Control.* Artech House.

Flauzac, O., Nolot, F., Rabat, C., & Steffenel, L. A. (2009). Grid of Security: A New Approach of the Network Security. *Proc. of Int. Conf. on Network and System Security, NSS '09,* 67-72. 10.1109/NSS.2009.53

Franco, L., Sahama, T., & Croll, P. (2008). Security Enhanced Linux to Enforce Mandatory Access Control in Health Information Systems. *Australasian Workshop on Health Data and Knowledge Management, the Australian Computer Science Week, Conference in Research and Practice in Information Technology Series, 327,* 27-33.

Goli, D. (2013). Group fuzzy TOPSIS methodology in computer security software selection. *International Journal of Fuzzy Logic Systems, 3*(2), 29–48. doi:10.5121/ijfls.2013.3203

Gray, D., Allen, J., Cois, C., Connell, A., Ebel, E., Gulley, W., & Wisniewski, B. D. (2015). *Improving federal cyber security governance through data driven decision making and execution.* Technical report–CMU/SEI-2015-TR-011, Software Engineering Institute, Carnegie Mellon University United States.

Hahn, W. J., Seaman, S. L., & Bikel, R. (2012). Making decisions with multiple attributes: A case in sustainability planning. *Graziadio Business Review, 15*(2), 365–381.

Hamedani, A. R. F. (2010). *Network Security Issues, Tools for Testing.* School of Information Science, Halmstad University.

Hamoud, O. N., Kenaza, T., & Challal, Y. (2017). Security in Device-to-Device communications (D2D): A survey. IET Networks, 1-10.

Henricksen, H., Caelli, W., & Croll, P. R. (2007). Securing Grid Data Using Mandatory Access Controls. *Proceedings of the fifth Australasian symposium on ACSW, ACM Intnl. Conf., 68,* 25-32.

Hu, V. C., Kahn, D. R., & Ferraiolo, D. (2014). *Guide to Attribute Based Access Control (ABAC) Definition and Considerations.* NIST Special Publication 800-162, Nat'l Institute of Standards and Technology.

Hua, J. (2009). The Application of Artificial Neural Networks in Risk Assessment on High-tech Project Investment. *International Conference on Business Intelligence and Financial Engineering,* 17-20.

Izaddoost, A., Othman, M., & Rasid, M. F. A. (2007). Accurate ICMP traceback model under DoS/ DDoS attack. *Proceedings of the international conference on advanced computing and communications, (ADCOM 2007)*, 441–446.

Karabey, B., & Baykal, N. (2013). Attack Tree Based Information Security Risk Assessment Method Integrating Enterprise Objectives with Vulnerabilities. *The International Arab Journal of Information Technology*, *10*(3), 297–304.

Kelly, D., & Smith, C. (2011). *Bayesian Inference for Probabilistic Risk Assessment: A Practitioner's Guidebook*. Springer. doi:10.1007/978-1-84996-187-5

Khan, M. W., Pandey, D., & Khan, S. A. (2018a). Measuring the Security Testing Attributes through Fuzzy Analytic Network Process: A Design Perspective. *Journal of Advance Research in Dynamical & Control Systems*, *10*(12), 1514–1523.

Khan, M. W., Pandey, D., & Khan, S. A. (2018b). Test Plan Specification using Security Attributes: A Design Perspective. *ICIC Express Letters*, *12*(10), 1061–1069.

Kizza, J. M. (2005). Computer Network Security. New York: Springer Science+Business Media, Inc.

Kizza, J. M. (2013). Guide to Computer Network Security. Springer.

Koçak, S. A., Alptekin, G. I., & Bener, A. B. (2014). Evaluation of Software Product Quality Attributes and Environmental Attributes using ANP Decision Framework. *3rd International Workshop on Requirements Engineering for Sustainable Systems*. 1-8.

Krishnan, K. (2004). *Computer Networks and Computer Security*. North Carolina State University.

Kumar, R., Khan, S. A., & Khan, R. A. (2016). Analytical Network Process for Software Security: A Design Perspective. CSI Transactions on ICT1-4.

Kumar, R., Khan, S. A., & Khan, R. A. (2017). Fuzzy Analytic Hierarchy Process for Software Durability: Security Risks Perspective. Advances in Intelligent Systems and Computing (Originally Published with the Title: Advances in Intelligent and Soft Computing), 469-478.

Kumar, R., Zarour, M., Alenezi, M., Agrawal, A., & Khan, R. A. (2019). Measuring Security Durability of Software through Fuzzy-Based Decision-Making Process. *International Journal of Computational Intelligence Systems*, *12*(2), 627–642. doi:10.2991/ijcis.d.190513.001

Lious, T. S., & Wang, M. J. J. (1992). Ranking fuzzy numbers with integral value. *Fuzzy Sets and Systems*, *50*(3), 247–255. doi:10.1016/0165-0114(92)90223-Q

Liu, S., & Liu, Y. (2016). Network security risk assessment method based on HMM and attack graph model. *17th IEEE/ACIS, International Conference on Software Engineering, Artificial Intelligence, Networking and Parallel/Distributed Computing (SNPD)*, 1-6.

Mahjabin, T., Xiao, Y., Sun, G., & Jiang, W. (2017). A survey of distributed denial-of-service attack, prevention, and mitigation techniques. *International Journal of Distributed Sensor Networks*, *13*(12), 1–33. doi:10.1177/1550147717741463

Malik, M., & Singh, Y. (2015). A Review: DoS and DDoS Attacks. *International Journal of Computer Science and Mobile Computing, 4*(6), 260–265.

Marin, G. A. (2005). Network security basics. *In Security & Privacy, IEEE, 3*(6), 68-72.

McClure, S., Scambray, J., & Kurtz, G. (2009). *Hacking Exposed: Network Security Secrets & Solutions* (6th ed.). TMH.

Meng, S., Wang, P., & Wang, J. (2011). Application of Fuzzy Logic in the Network Security Risk Evaluation. *Advanced Materials Research, 282*(283), 359–362. doi:10.4028/www.scientific.net/AMR.282-283.359

Mikhailov, L. (2003). Deriving priorities from fuzzy pairwise comparison judgments. *Fuzzy Sets and Systems, 134*(3), 365–385. doi:10.1016/S0165-0114(02)00383-4

Mohammed, O. S., & Taha, D. B. (2016). Conducting multi-class security metrics from enterprise architect class diagram. *International Journal of Computer Science and Information Security, 14*(4), 56–61.

Mougouei, D. (2017). PAPS: A scalable framework for prioritization and partial selection of security requirements. *ArXiv*, 1–12.

Mu~noz-Gonz'alez, L., & Lupu, E. C. (2017). Bayesian Attack Graphs for Security Risk Assessment. *IST-153 Workshop on Cyber Resilience*, 1-5.

Murray, P. (2004). *Network Security*. http://www.pandc.org/peter/presentations/ohio-tech-2004/Ohio-tech-security-handout.pdf

Nitti, M., Stelea, G. A., Popescu, V., & Fadda, M. (2015). When Social Networks Meet D2D Communications: A Survey. *International Journal of Advanced Networking and Applications, 7*(1), 2576–2581.

OWASP. (2017). *OWASP Top 10. The Ten Most Critical Web Application Security Risks*. https://www.owasp.org/images/7/72/OWASP Top 102017%28en%29.pdf.pdf

Podio, L., & Jeffrey, S. D. (2002). *Biometric Authentication Technology: From the Movies to Your Desktop. National Institute of Standards and Technology (NIST)*. Information Technology Laboratory.

Prabhakar, S. (2017). Network Security In Digitalization: Attacks And Defence. *International Journal of Research in Computer Applications and Robotics, 5*(5), 46–52.

Punter, A., Coburn, A., & Ralph, D. (2016). *Evolving risk frameworks: modelling resilient business systems as interconnected networks*. Centre for Risk Studies, University of Cambridge. http://cambridgeriskframework.com/ page/17

Reid, J., Cheong, I., Henricksen, M., & Smith, J. (2003). A novel use of RBAC to protect privacy in distributed health care information systems. *8th Australasian Conference on Information Security and Privacy*, 403-415. 10.1007/3-540-45067-X_35

Reid, P. (2003). *Biometrics for Network Security*. Prentice Hall PTR.

Roozbahani, F. S., & Azad, R. (2015). Security Solutions against Computer Networks Threats. *International Journal of Advanced Networking and Applications, 7*(1), 2576–2581.

Saaty, T. L. (1980). *The Analytic Hierarchy Process*. McGraw Hill.

Saaty, T. L. (1996). *Decision Making with Dependence and Feedback the Analytic Network Process.* RWS Publications.

Sailer, R., Jaeger, T., Valdez, E., C'aceres, R., Perez, R., Berger, S., Grifðn, J., & van Doorn, L. (2005). Building a MAC based security architecture for the Xen opensource hypervisor. *Proceedings of the Annual Computer Security Applications Conference*, 1-10.

Sekar, R., Gupta, A., Frullo, J., Shanbhag, T., Tiwari, A., Yang, H., & Zhou, S. (2002). Specification-based anomaly detection: a new approach for detecting network intrusions. *Proceedings of the 9th ACM conference on Computer and communication security*, 265– 274.

Sharma, T., & Yadav, R. (2015). Security in Virtual private network. *International Journal of Innovations & Advancement in Computer Science*, *4*, 669–675.

Singh, S., & Silakari, S. (2009). A Survey of Cyber Attack Detection Systems. *International Journal of Computer Science and Network Security*, *9*(5), 1–10.

Sodiya, A. S., & Onashoga, A. S. (2009). Components-Based Access Control Architecture. *Issues in Informing Science and Information Technology*, *6*, 699–706. doi:10.28945/1090

Soutar, C., Roberge, D., Stojanov, S. A., Gilroy, R., & Kumar, B. V. (1998). Biometric encryption using image processing *Proceedings of the SPIE - Optical Security and Counterfeit Deterrence Techniques II*, *3314*, 178–188.

Stallings, W. (2006). *Cryptography and Network Security* (4th ed.). Prentice Hall.

Stallings, W. (2007). *Network security essentials: applications and standards* (3rd ed.). Prentice Hall.

Stallings, W. (2011). *Network Security Essentials: Applications And Standards.* Pearson Education *Inc.*

Sumathi, M., Sharvani, G. S., & Dinesha, H. A. (2013). Implementation of Multifactor Authentication System for Accessing Cloud Service. *International Journal of Scientific and Research Publications*, *3*(6), 1–8.

Tan, W., Yang, M., Feng, Y., & Wei, R. (2009). A security framework for wireless network based on public key infrastructure. *Proc. of Computing, Communication, Control, and Management. CCCM*, *9*(2), 567–570.

Viduto, V., Maple, C., Huang, W., & López-Peréz, D. (2012). A novel risk assessment and optimisation model for a multi-objective network security countermeasure selection problem. *Decision Support Systems*, *53*(3), 599–610. doi:10.1016/j.dss.2012.04.001

Wang, Y., Tian, L., & Chen, Z. (2019). Game Analysis of Access Control Based on User Behavior Trust. *Information'19*, *10*(132), 1-13.

Wilton, C. (2017). Sony, Cyber Security, and Free Speech. *Preserving the First Amendment in the Modern World.*, *7*(1), 1–43.

Wu, K., Tong, Z., Li, W., & Ma, G. (2009). Security Model Based on Network Business Security. *Proc. of Int. Conf. on Computer Technology and Development, ICCTD '09*, *1*, 577-580.

Yan, F., & Yang, J. YLin, C. (2015). Computer Network Security and Technology Research. *Seventh International Conference on Measuring Technology and Mechatronics Automation*, 293-296. 10.1109/ ICMTMA.2015.77

Zhiyong, L., Zhihua, D., & Peili, Q. (2011). Formal Description of IPSec Security Policy in VPN Networks. *Journal of Hua Zhong University of Science and Technology,* 14-16.

Chapter 7
Software–Defined Vehicular Adhoc Network:
A Theoretical Approach

Ram S. Raw

Ambedkar Institute of Advanced Communication Technologies and Research, India

Manish Kumar

Ambedkar Institute of Advanced Communication Technologies and Research, India

Nanahay Singh

Ambedkar Institute of Advanced Communication Technologies and Research, India

ABSTRACT

Vehicular adhoc networks (VANETs) and software-defined networking (SDN) are the key enablers of 5G technology in developing intelligent vehicle networks and applications for the next generation. In recent years, many studies have been concentrated on SDN and VANET incorporation, and many researchers worked at various architecture-related issues along with the advantages of software-defined VANET services and features to adapt them. This chapter discusses the current state of the art of SD-VANET with the directions of future research work. This chapter presents a theoretical approach of architectures of software-defined VANET for its networking infrastructure design, functionalities, benefits, and challenges of future generation networks.

The evolving of the fast-cellular network such as LTE, 5G, WiMax, etc. makes networks more readily available for new network applications and business models. The application of IoT with conventional Vehicular Ad-hoc Network (VANET) using these cutting-edge technologies give a promising paradigm for future automobiles in the form of IoV (Internet of Vehicles). The tremendous market demands in IoV motivates the researchers to develop more generalized IoT. Many efforts have been taken in recent years to acknowledge different challenges like performance analysis, data dissemination, mobility, routing, etc. Despite these efforts, there still exist many challenges which must be tackled like handling the

DOI: 10.4018/978-1-7998-2764-1.ch007

heterogeneous network, diverse requirements of QoS (low latency and high reliability for safety-related services, High-speed connection for streaming services, bandwidth consumption, etc.).

Software Defined Networking (SDN) is an emerging technique which has the capability to separation of data and control plane. Control Plane performs the processes of Routing protocols. Data Plane performs the processes like Layer 2 switching, Layer 3 (IPv4 | IPv6) switching, MPLS forwarding, VRF Forwarding, QOS (Quality of Service) Marking, Classification, Policing, Netflow flow collection, Security Access Control Lists.

Vehicular Adhoc Networks (VANETs) and Software Defined Networking (SDN) are the key enablers of 5G technology in developing intelligent vehicle networks and applications for the next generation. In recent years, many studies have been concentrated on SDN and VANET incorporation and many researchers worked at various architecture-related issues along with the advantages of software-defined VANET services and features, to adapt them. This chapter discusses the current state of art of SD-VANET with the directions of future research work. This chapter presents a theoretical approach of architectures of Software Defined VANET for its networking infrastructure design, functionalities, benefits, and challenges of future generation networks.

1. INTRODUCTION

In recent years, traffic safety has been major concern. Not even traffic safety, the manufactures are concerning to provide many applications which could make travelling effortlessly and conveniently. In order to achieve these, road safety and other application, it is necessary to have a network which is capable of providing all the data efficiently to the vehicles. A network with the capability of mobile ad-hoc network in vehicles can give the solution of required network such type of network is Vehicular Ad-hoc Network. The nodes in VANET is equipped with the Wireless communication system. The nodes in VANET are fast moving hence, unlike the conventional network, each node has the capability of routing and end system working. To achieve the proper communication among vehicles, all vehicles are equipped with OBU (On Board Unit) by which vehicles can directly communicate with the vehicles. There is another infrastructure, RSU (Road Side Unit), installed along road side to communicate vehicles.

To standardise these communications, IEEE communication society has approved a standard 802.11p for DSRC (Dedicated Short-Range Communication) / WAVE (Wireless Access in Vehicular Environment) Protocol. The 802.11p facilitates the communication between high speed vehicles and between road side infrastructure and vehicles i.e. V2X.

The IEEE defines the architecture and standardizes the services and interface in 1609 family for WAVE Protocol stack, for high speed, short range and low latency wireless communication in the vehicular environment. The WAVE protocol stack along with the standards is given in figure.

1.1 Network Architectures of VANET

The architecture of VANET falls within three categories first a pure wireless ad hoc network where vehicle to vehicle without any support of infrastructure. Second a wired backbone network with wireless hops that give an impression of wireless vehicular network and third is hybrid structure, the communication between the roadside units (RSU), a fixed infrastructure.

Figure 1. DSRC/WAVE Protocol Stack

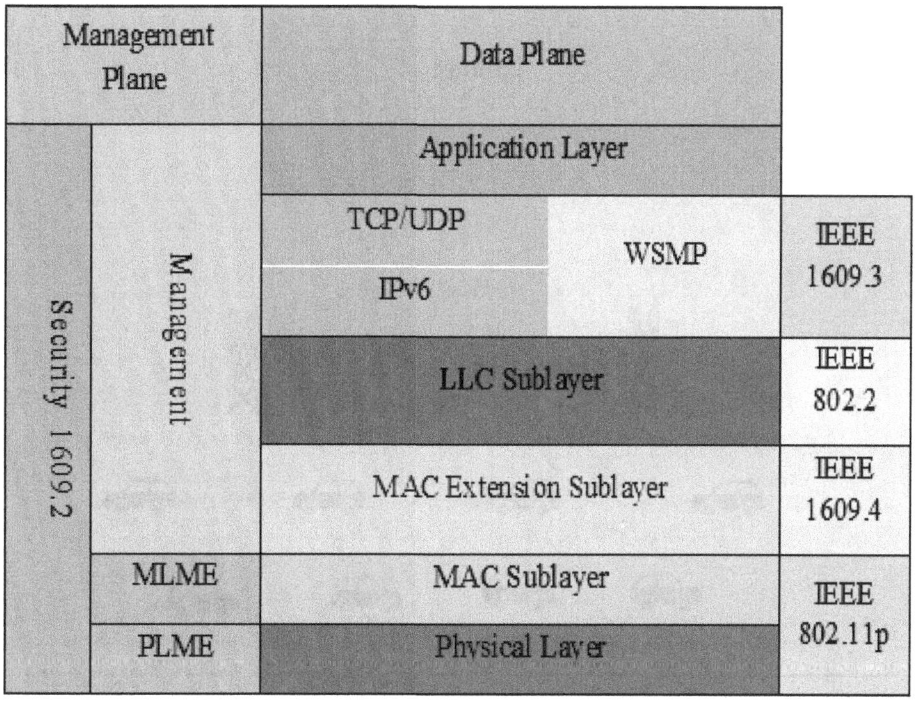

Management Plane		Data Plane	
Security 1609.2	Management	Application Layer	
		TCP/UDP / IPv6 — WSMP	IEEE 1609.3
		LLC Sublayer	IEEE 802.2
		MAC Extension Sublayer	IEEE 1609.4
	MLME	MAC Sublayer	IEEE 802.11p
	PLME	Physical Layer	

1.1.1 Pure Cellular/WLAN

Like the cellular network, Cellular gateways or access point is installed on roadside or traffic intersection. When a vehicle enters into the access point range, it connects to the access point. Vehicle node can communicate through these access point only as the nodes don't have any gateway capabilities.

1.1.2 Pure Ad Hoc

This architecture does not follow the concept of the cellular network. All vehicles along with roadside wireless unit form a mobile ad-hoc network. All moving nodes have the gateway capability. Any moving vehicle can communicate with other moving vehicle using the ad-hoc network.

1.1.3 Hybrid

This network architecture uses the benefit of cellular and ad-hoc network architecture. All moving vehicles have the capability of gateway and network routers by which they are capable of communicating each vehicle inside the ad-hoc network. The roadside unit gives the facility of the cellular network. The roadside unit is connected to the outside world using the internet. Hence, the moving vehicle can be connected to the outside world through a roadside unit.

Figure 2. The C2C -CC reference communications

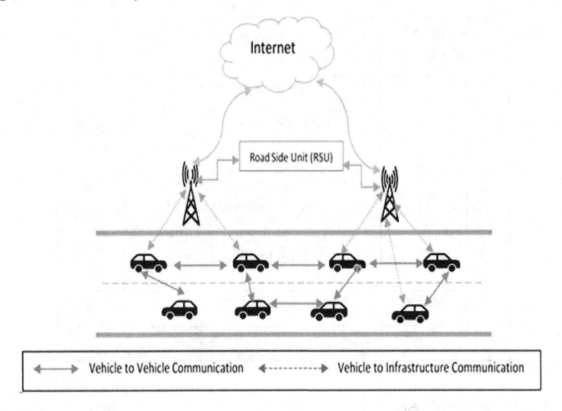

1.2 Applications of VANETs

The services provided by the VANET can be categorised into two broad categories: Safety Related Application and User Application.

1.2.1 Safety Related Application

These applications are used to increase the safety on the roads. These applications basically be used in following way.

a)   Collision Avoidance: According to some studies, "60% accidents can be avoided if a driver were provided a warning half a second before collision" (Raya & Hubaux, 2007). If a driver gets a warning message on time collision can be avoided.

b)   Cooperative Driving: Drivers can receive warnings linked to traffic such as the warning of curve velocity, the warning of Lane change, etc. The driver can collaborate with these signals for uninterrupted and safe driving.

c)   Traffic optimisation: By sending signals such as jams, accidents etc. to the cars, traffic can be optimized so that they can choose their alternative route.

1.2.2 User Based Application

These applications provide the user infotainment. A VANET can be utilised to provide following services for the user apart from safety:

a)   Peer to peer application: These apps are helpful in providing services such as sharing music, films, etc. among the vehicles in the network.

b)   Internet Connectivity: People always want to link all the time to the Internet. Thus, VANET offers users with the Internet's steady connectivity.

c)   Other services: VANET can be used to payment service to collect the tall taxes, find the fuel station, restaurant etc. with other user-based applications.

1.3. Characteristics of VANET

1)   **High Mobility:** Usually the nodes in VANETs move at high velocity. This makes it more difficult to predict the position of a node and protect the privacy of the node.

2)   **Rapidly changing network topology:** The network topology in VANETs tends to change regularly due to high velocity of node mobility.

3)   **Scalability:** VANET networks more scalable than any other network. It can be sparse and dense. It can be implemented in entire City. Hence, the network size is not limited. At any time network size can be increased or decreased because of addition of new vehicle in the network.

4)   **Frequent exchange of information:** VANET has two types of communication, V-V (Vehicle to Vehicle) and V-I (Vehicle to Infrastructure i.e. RSU). Hence, the information exchange between nodes become frequent. Different nodes can communicate to vehicles while others may communicate with infrastructure. The information may be for routing, data dissemination or for other applications.

5)   **Wireless Communication:** VANETs are inherently a Mobile Ad-hoc Network. Therefore, they use wireless communication. The wireless communication may suffer from attenuation, noise, and security challenges.

6)   **Time Critical:** Most application in VANET is related to safety. These messages require timely data packet transmission. So, a node will be able to get the data in time and act accordingly.

7)   **Sufficient Energy:** The VANET nodes have no energy or computing resources problem. This enables VANET to implement complex algorithms such as RSA, application of ECDSA and offers unlimited transmission energy as well.

8)   **Better Physical Protection:** The nodes in VANET are better protected physically. Thus, VANET nodes are more difficult to compromise physically.

1.4 Challenging issue in VANET

The VANET has many special characteristics and features but still, there are many challenges in implementation of VANET. (Raw, Kumar, & Singh, 2013) categorised these challenges in to two categories.

1.4.1 Technical Challenges

The technical challenges involve the issues related to network resource management, the physical channel, protocols management etc. The following are the major technical challenges.

1) **Network Management:** The network topology and channel situation are changing quickly due to high velocity nodes in VANET. Due to these issues, tree-like structures can not be used because these structures can not set up and maintain as fast as topology change. Therefore, finding a suitable mechanism for network management is a big challenge.

2) **Congestion and collision Control**: The unlimited size of the network also poses a technical challenge. Traffic load in rural regions is small and even in metropolitan regions is small at night. Because of this, network partitions often occur while the traffic load is very high in rush hours, resulting in congestion of the network and collision occurring in the network.

3) **Environmental Impact:** For communication, VANETs use electromagnetic waves. The atmosphere affects these waves. The environmental impact must therefore be regarded in order to deploy the VANET.

4) **MAC Design:** Usually, VANET uses the shared medium to interact, so the main problem is the MAC design. There have been many methods such as TDMA, SDMA, and CSMA etc. The CSMA based Mac for VANET was adopted by IEEE 802.11.

5) **Security:** As VANET offers the request for road safety that is life-critical, the security of these texts must therefore be met. An attempt can be made to tamper the messages to mislead the traffic by the malicious node.

2 SOFTWARE-DEFINED NETWORKING

In recent years, advanced computing like cloud computing, Big Data, IoT, etc. have a big impact on the network. Due to these advancements, network traffic demand has been increased. The advancement in transmission technology, like Wi-Fi, 4G, and 5G, etc., has increased the supply of data on the network. The advancements in computing and transmission technology lead the network providers and users to rethink on the traditional approach of the network architecture. The traditional approach of internetworking has many limitations (Open Networking Foundation, 2012).

- Inconsistent Policies
- Static and complex architecture
- Inability to scale
- Vendor Dependencies

To overcome the problem discussed in the previous section, Software Defined Networking (SDN) has been introduced. SDN makes the network more adaptable and scalable. SDN is an approach to designing, building and operating large scale networks based on programming the forwarding decisions in routers and switches through software from a central server. Unlike the conventional network, the SDN is capable to separate the control plane and data plane.

a). Data Plane: The data plane is responsible for forwarding packets. Data planes interact with the SDN Control Layer to support programmability using resource control interfaces. The switch communicates with the controller and the controller manages the switch using OpenFlow protocol. Data plane accepts incoming packets from other network or end systems and forwards them along the data forwarding paths that have been computed and established according to the rules defined by the SDN applications.

b). Control plane: Control panel of SDN provides the solution the shifting traffic patterns, the intelligence in designing routes. The functions of the control panel include shortest path forwarding, Notification Management, Security Management, Topology management, Statistics Management, Device Management, etc. It communicates with Network application layer vis Northbound API and Data plane through Southbound API.

c). Application Plane: This includes the application program that communicates the SDN controllers programmatically about their requirements. It abstracts the network view in order to making internal decisions.

d). Southbound Interface: The interface is used to communicate between network infrastructure and SDN controller. The OpenFlow API is used to exchange the message between controller and forwarding devices.

e). Northbound Interface: This interface is used to communicate between network applications like security application, network virtualisation, topology management, monitoring of network, load balancing etc. There is no standard protocol has been proposed.

The figure 3 illustrates the basic SDN architecture.

Figure 3. SDN Architecture

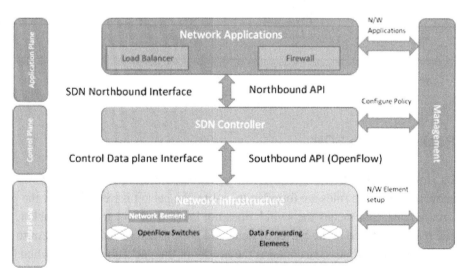

2.1 Standardisation of SDN

Many consortia have been involved in SDN standardization. The Open Networking Foundation (ONF) was intended to encourage the implementation of SDN through the introduction of the OpenFlow protocol as an open standard for communicating control measures to data plane systems.

The Software Defined Networking Research Group (SDNRG) has been created by an associated body that focuses on research aspects for the evolution of the Internet, the Internet Research Task Force (IRTF). This team investigates SDN from different perspectives in order to identify the methods that can be defined, implemented and used in the near future.

The Institute of Electrical and Electronic Engineers (IEEE) has currently undertaken some initiatives to standardize SDN capacities based on IEEE 802 facilities through the P802.1CF to adopt new control interfaces for both wired and wireless systems.

The European Institute for Telecommunications Standards (ETSI) focuses its attempts on Network Function Virtualization (NFV) through a newly established Industry Specification Group (ISG) for the same.(Kreutz et al., 2015). The figure 4 shows a particular OpenFlow Switch.

Figure 4. OpenFlow Switch (Open Networking Foundation, 2013)

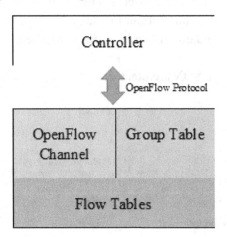

2.2 Basic Packet Flow in SDN

In the common flow control of SDN, a policy/flow table, that contains all the policies, is searched on the arrival of new packet. If the rules are found in the table, the packet is treated as per the policy. If the packet is not in the table, that means the switch does not know how to handle the packet. When table miss occurs, the packet is stored in the buffer of node and policy request message is sent to the controller. Usually, the policy request message contains the header of the packet but in case when buffer of the node is full, the whole packet is sent to the controller. The controller then replies to the switch with new rules, and the switch update its policy/flow table.

There are two approaches to handle flow rules by the controller i.e. proactive approach and reactive approach. In proactive approach, the controller sends all rules to the switches before starting of network flow. In reactive approach, the controller sends the rule as per the requirement. The OpenFlow uses the reactive approach.

2.3 Advantages of Software Defined Network

a). Easier Programming: Programming these systems becomes simpler as it is possible to share the abstractions offered by the control platform and/or the languages of network programming.

b). Consistent and Effective Decisions: All applications can benefit from the same network data (the universal view of the network), leading to more consistent and efficient policy choices while reusing software modules for control planes.

c). Easy actions: These applications can take action from any segment of the network. Therefore, there is no need to devise an accurate approach regarding the place of the new functionality.

d). Effortless application integration: Integrating various applications becomes simpler(Casado, Foster, & Guha, 2014). For example, applications for load balancing and routing can be combined sequentially, having decisions for load balancing preceding routing policies.

3 SOFTWARE DEFINED NETWORKING IN VANET

Implementing the concept of software defined networking in conventional VANET requires many changes. In VANET, nodes move very fast hence, to maintain the global topology and minimising the management overhead and congestion on control-data communication are among big challenges in order to implement SDN in VANET. In this section, the structure of SD-VANET has been discussed followed by the benefit and challenges of SD-VANET.

3.1 Architecture of SD-VANET

The architecture basically defines how things are going to be operational. In recent years, researchers have focused on the integration of SDN and VANET. To use SDN in VANET, the architecture of both has been mixed as per the requirement. The major concern to design an architecture for SD-VANET, is when and where to place the control plane and data plane to accommodate the frequent changing topology and flowless communication. There are three type of architecture broadly found in the literature (Ku et al., 2014).

3.1.1 Centralised Architecture

In this type of architecture, SDN controller is responsible to control all the actions performed by RSU or Node. SDN controller controls all flow rules that provides the guidance of data packet delivery and the strategy to treat traffic. Vehicles to vehicle communication uses data plane communication only. There could be two different communication channels for data plane and control plane. The data plane uses frequent communication of data among nearby nodes, hence, low range but high bandwidth wireless communication like WiFi would be better choice, whereas for control plane communication, where network traffic is less usually and could communicate with RSU, long range wireless communication like LTE/WiMax could be used.

Pros:

    a). Controller has all information about topology and changes in topology.

    b). Path selection is easy.

    c). Good for sparse network

Cons:

    a). Due to high mobility of node, the congestion between data plane and control plane. Hence, this architecture suffers from different kinds of delay.

    b). The processing power of control plane is major concern.

    c). Not suitable for dense network.

3.1.2 Distributed Architecture

This architecture is very similar to the conventional self-organising network. In this mode of architecture, each vehicle controls all the behaviour of each individual node. RSU does not get any flow rules from the controller. However, all packet delivery and traffic management are done by the node itself. The role of RSU is similar to conventional VANET. An RSU can only communicate to the nodes inside the sector. Node is not dependent on RSU for the control plane or flow rules. A node itself is sufficient enough to manage flow rules and data packet delivery by communicating nearby vehicles. A node requests the control information to the RSU only when the flow rules are not available, from its own table or from its neighbours.

Pros:

    a). No dependency on separate control plane

    b). The network is self-organised.

Cons:

    a). Each node must update its routing table

    b). Each node must select the path

    c). End to End delay shall increase

3.1.3 Hybrid Architecture

This architecture uses the advantages of both, centralised and distributed, architecture. In this architecture, the controller does not have full control over flow rules instead it delegates the control to local agents. SDN controller can instruct the local agents directly to apply specific routing protocol with some parameters. There are two types of communication can be observed in this type of architecture. One from SDN controller to the RSU and other is RSU to vehicle. The SDN controller communicates with the RSU, where general policies are installed, and flow rules are exchanged, using control plane. If the node is not able to handle the traffic control request by itself, the node can communicate with the RSU for exchanging the data or to exchange the control information as per requirement. Node communicates with the RSU from which it gets highest link strength.

Pros:

    a). Control plane responsibility is distributed hence, congestion between data plane and control plane is reduced.

b). Each individual node is capable of control plane and data plane.

Cons:

a). Rollback mechanism must available if control plane is lost.

b). Network traffic is increased in network due to simultaneous flow of packets for data plane and control plane among nodes.

c). Network throughput may decrease.

3.1.4 Hierarchical Distributed Architecture

In this architecture, the load of the central control panel is reduced. The control plane responsibility is performed by cluster of SDN controllers. The RSU is also play a role of control plane partially. However, data plane responsibility is performed by individual vehicles. The hierarchy of control plane with distributed architecture benefit, it becomes a very generic architecture used in VANET. The design is described in figure 5.

3.2 State of The Art of Structure of SD-VANET

In (Sudheera, Ma, & Chong, 2019), a hierarchical distributed architecture of SD-VANET has been proposed. In this control panel has been divided into two layers, the top layer has been constituted on the Internet and the bottom layer has been on RSU level. For the data plane, two type of communication channel has been proposed (i) LTE (Long Term Evaluation) to connect top layer (ii) DSRC to connect bottom layer and other data plane elements.

In (Z. He, Cao, & Liu, 2016), a centralised architecture has been proposed. The authors' focus was to develop an abstract model for SD-VANET so that communication among heterogeneous wireless devices can be done using unified interface. The network slicing technology has been used to improve the bandwidth utilisation.

In (Correia, Boukerche, & Meneguette, 2017), A hierarchical structure of SDVN has been proposed to improve performance in connectivity loss. A clustering technique has been used to create independent local SDN domains.

In (Truong, Lee, & Ghamri-Doudane, 2015a), hierarchical structure has been proposed using fog computing to improve location awareness and delay sensitive services for safety and non-safety services. The proposed architecture addresses the two use-cases called Data streaming and Lane-Change assistance services. The researchers have proposed their models for software-defined VANET, but they are requirement specific. (Jaballah, Conti, & Lal, 2019) has proposed a generic model shown in figure 5.

3.3 Software-Defined VANET benefits

The SDN based VANET can be benefitted in the following area:

a) Path Selection: The control panel of SDN keeps the global topology. Hence, it is easy to get the shortest path every time. If a node requires a greater bandwidth to transfer the data, like video dissemination, the route can be modified to reduce the congestion and hence, improved network utility.

Figure 5. Generic Software Defined Vehicular Ad-hoc Network

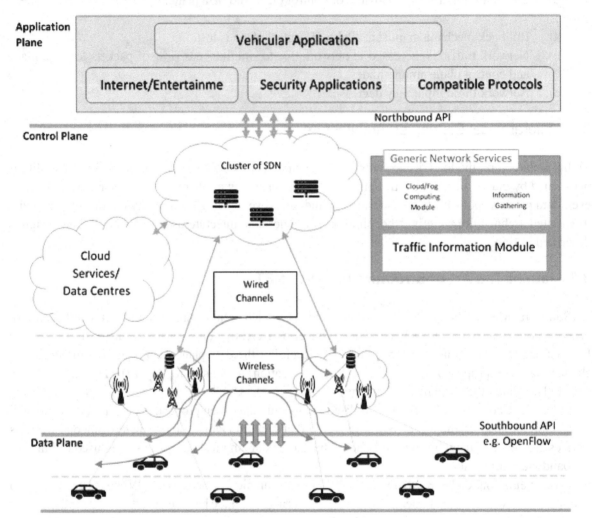

b) *Channel Selection: The network utility can be improved by using thee different wireless channel for different use.* (Sudheera et al., 2019) *used LTE and DSRC to communicate different layers. In this type of scenario, when multiple wireless interfaces or cognitive radio*(Akyildiz, Lee, & Chowdhury, 2009; Khan, 2017) *is used for communication, an SDN controller can better decide which channel should be used at what time.*

c) Power Selection of wireless interface: It is reasonable to adjust the power of wireless interface of nodes to increase or decrease the transmission range according to sparse and dense network, sensed by the controller. If the nodes are sparse then a message can be sent to the nodes to increase the transmission range to increase the packet delivery.

d) Optimized resource utilization: The SDN controller keeps the global view of network. The controller can put logical switches on top of physical network. These switches act as an individual switch for a particular node. Physical resources can be virtually divided into multiple logically separate network using network virtualisation. Hence, the resource can be distributed as per the requirement and priority by which resource utilisation can be optimised.

e) Heterogeneous network integration: The standard programmable interface such as OpenFlow makes the Software Defined Vehicular Ad-hoc Network capable to accommodate the heterogeneity of vendors and architecture of OBU.

4. ROUTING IN SD-VANET

The Vehicular Ad-hoc Network is very different from conventional wireless networking. The high mobility of nodes makes VANET special. The traditional wired network routing protocol cannot be applied directly to the VANET. A variety of routing protocols have been proposed by the researchers in recent years. The conventional ad-hoc routing protocol has been categorised in three category on the basis of Routing Information Update Mechanism (Siva Ram Murthy & Manoj, 2004).

a). Proactive or table-driven routing protocols: In this approach, the routing table is maintained by each node. A node maintains its routing table information by periodically exchanging routing information generally flooded in entire network. Whenever a node wants to send the packet, it just runs the appropriate path finding algorithm on the routing table it maintains. DSDV(Perkins, 1994), wireless routing protocol (WRP)(Murthy & Garcia-Luna-Aceves, 1996), Cluster-Head Gateway Switch Routing Protocol (CGSR)(C. C. Chiang, H. K. Wu, W. Liu, 1997), Source-tree adaptive routing protocol (STAR)(Garcia-Luna-Aceves & Spohn, 1999) are few examples of this type of routing protocol.

b). Reactive or on-demand routing protocols: The problem in table-driven routing protocols was (i) a node must maintain a table whether it has to send a packet or not (ii) every time periodically network topology information packet utilises the network resources. Therefore, a new approach, on-demand routing protocols, was introduced. This type of protocol does not maintain a routing table, rather node finds the path when it is required. Dynamic Source Routing Protocol (DSR) (Johnson & Maltz, 1996), Temporally ordered routing algorithm (TORA)(Park & Corson, 1997), Location-aided routing protocol (LAR)(Ko & Vaidya, 2000), Associativity-based routing (ABR) (Toh, 1997), Signal stability-based adaptive routing protocol (SSA)(Dube, Rais, Wang, & Tripathi, 1996), Flow-oriented routing protocol (FORP)(Su & Gerla, 1999) and Ad hoc on-demand distance vector (AODV)(Marina & Das, 2006) are the some popular examples.

c). Hybrid routing protocols: Hybrid routing protocols combines the best features of table-driven routing and on-demand routing. A node uses the table-driven approach when the destination node is within a certain distance or within a particular geographic region. When the destination node is outside the zone, the reactive or on-demand approach is followed. Core extraction distributed ad hoc routing (CEDAR)(Sivakumar, Sinha, & Bharghavan, 1999), Zone routing protocol (ZRP) (Haas, 1997), Zone-based hierarchical link state (ZHLS)(Joa-Ng, Member, Lu, & Member, 1999) are some examples.

However, the routing in SDN based VANET very similar to conventional VANET but it requires some changes according to architecture of SDN. In recent literature some notable work has been done.

(Sudheera et al., 2019) proposed a novel packet routing scheme for SVDN with a source routing based flow instantiation (FI) operation. The routing problem was converted as an ILP problem. An incremental packet allocation scheme was introduced to solve the routing problem with time complexity.

The proposed framework was designed to send the packets via multiple routes along all possible shortest paths with enough stability. A source routing based FI operation was also introduced to deliver the routing info efficiently to the node.

(M. Zhu, Cao, Pang, & Z. He, 2015) proposed an SDN-based routing framework for message propagation in VANET. The proposed routing protocol calculates globally optimized routing paths to reduce routing overhead. They proposed a new metric to overcome the problem of dynamic network density in VANET. The proposed routing protocol automatically switches between Multihop forwarding model to carry and forward model.

(Ming Zhu, Cai, Cao, & Xu, 2015) proposed a new routing protocol which works on Spray and Prey multiple copy routing. The spray process was used for the elimination process and prey was used for reducing the packet delivery delay.

(Y. C. Liu, Chen, & Chakraborty, 2015) "proposed a GeoBroadcast protocol for Software Defined Network (SDN) architecture in VANETs. In this protocol, the sender node sends the periodic warning message to notify the receiver node. To support efficient transmission and delivery of warning message to receiver area, Floodlight SDN controller was installed with RSU location management and GeoBroadcast components.

(Ghafoor & Koo, 2018) "proposed routing protocol with cognitive radio software-defined vehicular networks. This protocol is two phase protocol i.e. registering and route prediction phase. The RSU was used as local controller for registering phase while the main controller was used for registering phase. A link is formed between two nodes if they both have consensus about a common idle channel. Therefore, spectrum sensing is performed based on a belief propagation algorithm to find common free channels.

(You, Cheng, Wang, Chen, & Chen, 2019) proposed a cross layer routing approach. The routing protocol considers the position and velocity of vehicles as a metric along with channel allocation and link duration. The vehicle registers itself by sending the hello message to the local controller. The local controller registers the vehicle and also sends the vehicle information to the global controller. The route request is sent to the RSU, the local controller, RSU sends the route reply to the source node. The destination node and intermediate node is also informed about the route. The route is stored for some limited time only so that the next route can be calculated to maintain dynamism of topology. The cloud computing has been used for global controller.

(C. Wang et al., 2019) proposed a lifetime-based network state routing protocol. The 4G cellular technology has been used for the communication. The protocol first check whether there is V2V routing path from source to destination? If the path exists, the route information is sent to the vehicles i.e. source and destination along with the validity of route time. Otherwise, the optimised route has been selected from the available route and sent to the vehicles along with intermediate node. The route finding is performed by SDN controller.

5. SECURITY ISSUES IN SD-VANET

As wireless communications are very prone to security breaches, the SD-VANET security becomes the major concern. The threats in SD-VANET includes the threats of SDN and the threats of conventional VANET. Many proposed architectures of SD-VANET have given less priority. In this section, we give the brief of some security issues and attacks in SD-VANET that violates the security services like Integrity,

Availability, Confidentiality and Authentication. (Jaballah et al., 2019) has identified a list of possible attacks possible in SD-VANET.

5.1 Major Attacks in SD-VANET

a). **Control Plane resource exhaustion:** This is the most common attack in SDN structure. The basic flow control of SDN has been discussed in section 2.1. In this attack, the attacker exploits the scenario when a new packet rule is not found in the policy table at SDN switches. To achieve the table, miss at switch, the malicious node sends large number of the malicious packets. The packets are spoofed by filling the random values that have the low probability to be found in the flow/policy table. Therefore, the controller becomes exhausted which ultimately reduces the network throughput significantly.

b). **Impersonation:** The control plane sends the rules to the data plane. It is possible that the rules come from control plane has been sent from malicious one, which impersonates as controller. This type of impersonation attack is possible in SD-VANET. In some cases, the owner of vehicle uses his personal details for authentication. It is easy to find the details and perform malicious activities on the network in the name of another node. Sybil attack is the most famous attack.

c). **DDoS**: Since SD-VANET architectures are divided into three primary functional layers: infrastructure layer (Cars, RSU), control layer (RSU controllers) and application layer, prospective DDoS attacks on one or more of these three layers can be initiated. The DDoS attack can be initiated by sending multiple packets to the target node to stop it to access the services through multiple nodes.

d). **Network Topology Injection:** The network topology information is very crucial for the SDN based networks. A malicious node can inject the false link in the topology like Man-In-The-Middle and Black Hole attack. In block hole attack, the malicious node pretends as a most suitable node by which the legitimate user can initiate transmission of packets. When communication starts through the malicious node, the malicious node either eavesdrop or manipulate messages. Host Location Hijacking attack is another form of network poisoning attack. In this type of attack, malicious node takes advantages of the Host Tracking Services. The malicious node can hijack the network server location to phish the other legitimate nodes. For example, in parking system, a malicious node can hijack the server and can send fabricated messages or can get the crucial security related information from the legitimate node which can be exploited later.

e). **Jamming:** The SD-VANET uses the wireless network, a powerful transmitter can jam the whole network that can lead the network partition without compromising the cryptographic mechanism. Using this attack, a malicious node can block the legitimate node to access the crucial data that ultimately collapse the whole network. However, the RSU can easily detect this type of attack by sensing channel and forwards the information to the controller. The controller sends the list of bad channels to RSU that can be further forwarded to the sensors.

f). **Application based attack:** There are many applications that run on the vehicle by which a node can perform the task like changing lane, accelerating/decelerating vehicles, traffic redirection etc. In SD-VANET, the rules for these applications can also be installed by the controller that can guide the vehicle/node to take decision on lane changing, traffic merging etc. applications according to the condition of traffic. The controller gathers the information from the vehicle to analyse the traffic condition. A malicious node can maliciously send the wrong information to the RSU which can lead a chaos or disastrous moment.

Apart from all above-mentioned major attack, some more attacks e.g. Malware injection attack, Tempering, Forgery could be implanted by the malicious node.

6. EMERGING TECHNOLOGICAL ADVANCEMENT IN SD-VANET

The utilisation of current technological advancement like cloud computing and machine learning could be an edge to solve the challenges of SD-VANET. The new advancement in technology like IoT, 5G etc caused the heavy network load. The traditional VANET is not capable of to handle the heavy traffic loads using single wireless connection. As a result of this, the network latency increases. Hence, Heterogeneous VANET is emerged as a new concept. In this type of VANET, IEEE 802.11p and cellular network has been integrated. To handle the massive amount of traffic data, many technological advancements have been used.

6.1 Cloud Computing

In heterogeneous VANETs, the main challenge is to collect and processing data in time. The additional servers are required to process the large amount of data in distributed areas. The cloud computing may be the appropriate solution. Many researchers have paid their attention on using cloud computing along with SD-VANET.

The (Ammara Khan, Anjum Khan, Abolhasan, & Ni, 2018) proposed a new holistic hierarchical architecture integrating of SDN and Cloud-RAN with 5G communication. To avoid frequent handover, the fog computing has been used.(Salahuddin, Al-Fuqaha, & Guizani, 2015) has proposed an architecture to integrate the flexibility of SDN and RSU cloud to cope of the problem of dynamically reconfigured services and data forwarding information.(Truong, Lee, & Ghamri-Doudane, 2015b) has proposed a new VANET architecture called FSDN. The proposed architecture integrates the SDN and Fog Computing. The proposed architecture optimizes resources utility and reducing latency. Non-safety service like data streaming and safety service are also presented in proposed architecture. (J. Liu et al., 2017) proposed a new approach to cope up with high latency and low reliability using SDN-enabled network along with Mobile Edge Computing (MEC). It meets application-specific requirements and maintains good scalability and responsiveness.

6.2 Machine Learning

In recent years, Machine learning became a major choice of researchers to solve problems related to pattern and interface. The researchers have used this technique in various areas in VANET like security, routing, QoS etc.

(Zhang, Yu, & Yang, 2018) proposed a framework which uses trust-based deep reinforcement learning in Sd-VANET. The framework deploys a deep Q-Learning algorithm in centralised controlled SDN. The SDN controller has been used as an agent. The SDN controller learn routing path trust value using convolution neural network. The trust model evaluates neighbors' behaviour of forwarding packets. (Tang et al., 2019) proposed a mobility prediction based centralised routing scheme. The SDN controller was used to predict mobility using advanced neural network technique. The SDN gathers information from RSU or BS and computes the optimised routing paths based on the global information. (Grover, Prajapati,

Laxmi, & Gaur, 2011) presented an approach to classify multiple misbehaviour using machine learning. The author classified the misbehaviour on the basis of received signal strength (RSS), number of packets delivered, dropped packets, speed-deviation of node etc. (Kim, Jang, Choo, Koo, & Pack, 2017) tried to predict the attacks in advance. They proposed a collaborative security attack detection mechanism with software-defined vehicular networks. The multi-class support vector machine (SVM) was used to detect various types of attacks dynamically.

6.2.1 ML-based Traffic Classification

(Nakao & Du, 2018) has proposed an approach for traffic classification solution. The approach used Deep Neural Network for application aware classification on the basis of packet size, destination address, protocol type etc. (Amaral et al., 2016) proposed an architecture for traffic classification using random forest model of machine learning in SDN. The framework analyses the traffic data gathered using Open-Flow protocol based on the features like packet size, packet time stamp, flow duration.

(Uddin & Nadeem, 2017) used the SDN to policy-driven network management with machine learning. The author used Decision tree, k- NN Learning model for the classification. They designed the architecture, TrafficVision, to deploy the real-time policy for to classify the network traffic flow efficiently. (Yunchun Li & Li, 2015) proposed a solution for application-layer classification. The author combined the conventional approach like Deep Packet Inspection with ML to achieve high speed classification with good accuracy rate.(Xiao, Qu, Qi, Xu, & Li, 2015) proposed the solution for the extremely large flow of traffic over network link i.e. elephant flow. The solution used the Decision tree method as a learning model. The author claims the proposed solution has the high detection rate with low overhead. (Qazi et al., 2013) used the crowdsourcing approach for SDN data. The crowdsourcing is an approach to gather data from less specific, more public group in the network. The proposed approach used the centralised SDN and Decision tree model of machine learning. The top 40 applications was used as a dataset.(P. Wang, Lin, & Luo, 2016) proposed a framework which is capable of classify the QoS traffic for SDN. The classification of network traffic has been performed on the basis of QoS requirement instead of identifying specific application. The proposed framework makes use of semi-supervised learning approach along with Data Packet Inspection.

6.2.2 ML-based Routing Optimization Solutions

(Yanjun Li, Li, & Yoshie, 2014) presented a framework which used Neural Network, supervised learning approach, to cope up with the complexity of dynamic routing problem. The proposed framework builds meta-layer based multiple ML modules. The meta-layer approach is able to provide heuristic like results in reasonable time.

(Azzouni & Pujolle, 2018) proposed a network Traffic Matrix based frame work. Network Traffic Matrix is a two-dimensional matrix which keeps the information about the traffic from source node i to node j. The network Traffic Matrix is essential for network management. The proposed model used Long Short-Term Memory Recurrent Neural Networks (LSTM RNNs), a variation of recurrent neural network architecture, generally used in the field of deep learning. The model predicts the future network traffic from gathered network traffic data.

(Sendra, Rego, Lloret, Jimenez, & Romero, 2017) proposed a model for distributed routing. The model uses the reinforcement learning along with OSPF routing protocol with SDN. The model is capable of avoiding routes where loss rate is high to provide a better QoS.

(Budhraja et al., 2017) proposed a model for the risk-based privacy and compliance preserving routing. The model used the k-means method to classify the packets based on the risk level. The real time decision was made using ACO. The Meta-data and Timestamp are used as a risk parameter. The data packets are processed and classified by the SDN controller using k-means and the real time decision is made.

(Lin, Akyildiz, Wang, & Luo, 2016) proposed a QoS-aware routing model using multilayer hierarchical SDN. The algorithm used reinforcement learning with reward function based on QoS. Markov decision processes is used to model the reinforcement learning. There are two controllers, Super controller and Domain controller, placed hierarchically. When a packet comes, it is analysed whether the packet belongs to the same subnet. If the packet is in same subnet both controllers execute the reinforcement learning method otherwise only domain controller executes the learning module.

6.2.2 Resource Management Solutions using ML

(Y. He, Yu, Zhao, Yin, & Boukerche, 2017) proposed a model that optimises the network resource cache, network and computation jointly. The author also proposed a deep reinforcement learning approach. In this model, a mobile virtual network operator manages the base stations, MEC servers and cache content and gets the status from all these resources collectively. After collecting data, it sends it to the agent, deep Q-network, and gets the response of arranging the resource for the vehicles.

(Cai, Gao, Cheng, Sang, & Yang, 2016) proposed a spectrum allocation mechanism using SDN. The model uses the game theory for the allocation of spectrum i.e. (LTE-U) and WiFi. The controller builds the decision tree based on the data set and it finds the network status of the opponent. To maximise the resource utilisation, repeated game is played.

(M. He, Kalmbach, Blenk, Kellerer, & Schmid, 2017) used neural network, logistic regression and decision tree to model the network optimisation. The proposed model uses controller placement as a case study.

(Haw, Alam, & Hong, 2014) proposed a scheme to for content delivery using SDN and CCN. The reinforcement learning is used in the model. The model assumes two network interfaces, LTE and WiFi. A user can select any one. There are two kind of contents assumed: the non-content services like SMS, e-mail etc. and content services video streaming, large file etc. the service information is gathered by the SDN agent which is further utilised by learning engine.

7. SOFTWARE-DEFINED VANET CHALLENGES

Applying SDN in VANET, SDVN has many obstacles mainly because of highly dynamic network topology. These challenges comprise of the challenges of conventional VANET, challenges of SDN and challenges of other technologies, which can be integrated with SD-VANET. This section provides the challenges, apart from the challenges of VANET discussed in section 1.4.

The key challenge in SDVN are:

a). **Dynamic network topology**: The velocity of node in VANET is very high. The network topology changes frequently. It is a big challenge for SDN control plane to keep the global view of network. It may cause delay in sending command to the nodes. There are few techniques like fog computing and vehicle's future direction prediction, which can handle the problems of high mobility in VANET.

b). **Distribution of flow rule and policies**: The data plane receives the flow rules from the controller and maintains the forwarding table according to that. Due to rapid changing networks, sending of flow rules becomes difficult. The controller would be too busy to handle the all requests. However, the controller can offload its tasks to the RSU by sending general flow rules and policies to minimise the load on controller.

c). **Security and privacy**: In SD-VANET, the controller manages all network resources hence, it is important to protect controller from different cyber-attacks like, DoS and DDoS attack which can paralyse the network. It is also important to investigate whether the flow rules are coming from the real controller or someone impersonates it. The location privacy and Location verification is also a big challenge due to absence of trusted authority.

d). **Interworking of heterogeneous networks**: In future, the diversity of vehicles will increase and so will increase the heterogeneity of the network. For example, different vehicle may use different channels and frequency for communication. The SD-VANET lacks the standardisation, therefore, it is big challenge to incorporate the heterogeneity in SD-VANET.

e). **Management of Networking and Computing Infrastructure:** The SD-VANET is largely depend upon the control plane for forwarding policy. Hence, the deployment of servers and their interconnection is a big issue to provide better Quality of Service.

f). **Message Discrimination:** In VANET, broadly two types of messages are handled, i.e. time critical like security related messages and non-time critical message. The discrimination of these two types of message, required for processing, is a big issue especially in cloud-based implementation.

g). **Misbehaviour of different technology:** The advancement in technology like 5G, Cloud, Information Centric Networking (ICN) etc. and their integration with VANET can increase the vulnerabilities of SD-VANET. The VANET can inherit the vulnerabilities form the advanced technologies.

h). **Scalability:** The scalability has been the issue of conventional VANET also. In case of SD-VANET, it is important to look that how will the network behave when network dynamically grows and shrinks.

8. CONCLUSION

Traditional networks are complicated and difficult to handle. One obvious region is the encapsulation of control and data plane, and they are vendor specific. Another reason is that conventional networking devices are firmly coupled with products and versions. Software Defined networking has emerged as a promising technology in computer networks to cope up traditional network difficulties. However, initially it was limited to the wired network only but, usage of SDN in wireless network attracts the researchers more. It becomes more interesting to implement SDN with VANET. This paper tries to give the overview of SDN and its application in VANET. We studied the VANET first and discuss its feature, challenges and applications. The SDN is discussed next with its application and challenges. The SDN with VANET has been discussed having details of architecture and complexities to implement

SD-VANET. The different architecture of SDN along with routing strategies has been discussed in this paper. Security has been a major concern in conventional VANET, hence, the security issues has been addressed. It would be interesting to see the integration of current technological advancement with the SD-VANET. Therefore, the utilisation of current technological advancement like cloud computing and machine learning to solve the challenges of SD-VANET has been conversed about. This article aims to provide the significant information regarding issues and challenges of SD-VANET.

REFERENCES

Akyildiz, I. F., Lee, W. Y., & Chowdhury, K. R. (2009). CRAHNs: Cognitive radio ad hoc networks. *Ad Hoc Networks*, 7(5), 810–836. doi:10.1016/j.adhoc.2009.01.001

Amaral, P., Dinis, J., Pinto, P., Bernardo, L., Tavares, J., & Mamede, H. S. (2016). Machine learning in software defined networks: Data collection and traffic classification. *Proceedings - International Conference on Network Protocols, ICNP*. 10.1109/ICNP.2016.7785327

Azzouni, A., & Pujolle, G. (2018). NeuTM: A neural network-based framework for traffic matrix prediction in SDN. In *IEEE/IFIP Network Operations and Management Symposium: Cognitive Management in a Cyber World, NOMS 2018* (pp. 1–5). Institute of Electrical and Electronics Engineers Inc. 10.1109/NOMS.2018.8406199

Ben Jaballah, W., Conti, M., & Lal, C. (2019). *A Survey on Software-Defined VANETs: Benefits, Challenges, and Future Directions*. Retrieved from https://arxiv.org/abs/1904.04577

Budhraja, K. K., Malvankar, A., Bahrami, M., Kundu, C., Kundu, A., & Singhal, M. (2017). Risk-Based Packet Routing for Privacy and Compliance-Preserving SDN. In *IEEE International Conference on Cloud Computing, CLOUD* (pp. 761–765). 10.1109/CLOUD.2017.109

Cai, F., Gao, Y., Cheng, L., Sang, L., & Yang, D. (2016). Spectrum sharing for LTE and WiFi coexistence using decision tree and game theory. *IEEE Wireless Communications and Networking Conference, WCNC*. 10.1109/WCNC.2016.7565015

Casado, M., Foster, V. N., & Guha, A. (2014). Abstractions for Software-Defined Networks. *Communications of the ACM*, 57(10), 86–95. doi:10.1145/2661061.2661063

Chiang, C. C., Wu, H. K., & Liu, W. (1997). Routing in Clustered MultiHop Mobile Wireless Networks with Fading Channel. *Proceedings of IEEE SICON*, 197–211.

Correia, S., Boukerche, A., & Meneguette, R. I. (2017). An architecture for hierarchical software-defined vehicular networks. *IEEE Communications Magazine*, 55(7), 80–86. doi:10.1109/MCOM.2017.1601105

Dube, R., Rais, C. D., Wang, K.-Y., & Tripathi, S. K. (1996). *Signal Stability based Adaptive Routing (SSA) for Ad-Hoc Mobile Networks*. Academic Press.

Garcia-Luna-Aceves, J. J., & Spohn, M. (n.d.). *Source-Tree Routing in Wireless Networks £*. Academic Press.

Ghafoor, H., & Koo, I. (2018). CR-SDVN: A Cognitive Routing Protocol for Software-Defined Vehicular Networks. *IEEE Sensors Journal, 18*(4), 1761–1772. doi:10.1109/JSEN.2017.2788014

Grover, J., Prajapati, N. K., Laxmi, V., & Gaur, M. S. (2011). Machine learning approach for multiple misbehavior detection in VANET. In *Communications in Computer and Information Science* (Vol. 192, pp. 644–653). CCIS. doi:10.1007/978-3-642-22720-2_68

Haas, Z. J. (n.d.). *A new routing protocol for the reconfigurable wireless networks.* Retrieved from http://www.ee.cornell.edu/~haas/wnl.html

Haw, R., Alam, M. G. R., & Hong, C. S. (2014). A context-aware content delivery framework for QoS in mobile cloud. In *APNOMS 2014 - 16th Asia-Pacific Network Operations and Management Symposium* (pp. 1–6). 10.1109/APNOMS.2014.6996607

He, M., Kalmbach, P., Blenk, A., Kellerer, W., & Schmid, S. (2017). Algorithm-data driven optimization of adaptive communication networks. In *Proceedings - International Conference on Network Protocols, ICNP* (pp. 1–6). 10.1109/ICNP.2017.8117592

He, Y., Yu, F. R., Zhao, N., Yin, H., & Boukerche, A. (2017). Deep reinforcement learning (DRL)-based resource management in software-defined and virtualized vehicular ad hoc networks. In *DIVANet 2017 - Proceedings of the 6th ACM Symposium on Development and Analysis of Intelligent Vehicular Networks and Applications, Co-located with MSWiM 2017* (Vol. 17, pp. 47–54). 10.1145/3132340.3132355

He, Z., Cao, J., & Liu, X. (2016). SDVN: Enabling rapid network innovation for heterogeneous vehicular communication. *IEEE Network, 30*(4), 10–15. doi:10.1109/MNET.2016.7513858

Joa-Ng, M., Member, S., Lu, I.-T., & Member, S. (1999). A Peer-to-Peer Zone-Based Two-Level Link State Routing for Mobile Ad Hoc Networks. *IEEE Journal on Selected Areas in Communications, 17*(8), 1415–1425. doi:10.1109/49.779923

Johnson, D. B., & Maltz, D. A. (n.d.). Dynamic Source Routing in Ad Hoc Wireless Networks. In *Mobile Computing* (pp. 153–181). Springer US. doi:10.1007/978-0-585-29603-6_5

Khan, A., Khan, A. A., Abolhasan, M., & Ni, W. (2018). *5G Next generation VANETs using SDN and Fog Computing Framework.* Retrieved from https://www.researchgate.net/publication/323570830

Khan, A. A. (n.d.). *Cognitive-radio-based internet of things: Applications, architectures, spectrum related functionalities, and future research directions.* Retrieved from https://ieeexplore.ieee.org/abstract/document/7955907/

Kim, M., Jang, I., Choo, S., Koo, J., & Pack, S. (2017). Collaborative security attack detection in software-defined vehicular networks. In *19th Asia-Pacific Network Operations and Management Symposium: Managing a World of Things, APNOMS 2017* (pp. 19–24). 10.1109/APNOMS.2017.8094172

Ko, Y. B., & Vaidya, N. H. (2000). Location-aided routing (LAR) in mobile ad hoc networks. *Wireless Networks, 6*(4), 307–321. doi:10.1023/A:1019106118419

Kreutz, D., Ramos, F. M. V., Verissimo, P. E., Rothenberg, C. E., Azodolmolky, S., & Uhlig, S. (2015). Software-defined networking: A comprehensive survey. *Proceedings of the IEEE, 103*(1), 14–76. doi:10.1109/JPROC.2014.2371999

Li, Y., Li, X., & Yoshie, O. (2014). Traffic engineering framework with machine learning based meta-layer in software-defined networks. In *Proceedings of 2014 4th IEEE International Conference on Network Infrastructure and Digital Content, IEEE IC-NIDC 2014* (pp. 121–125). 10.1109/ICNIDC.2014.7000278

Li, Y., & Li, J. (2015). MultiClassifier: A combination of DPI and ML for application-layer classification in SDN. In *2014 2nd International Conference on Systems and Informatics, ICSAI 2014* (pp. 682–686). doi:10.1109/ICSAI.2014.7009372

Lin, S. C., Akyildiz, I. F., Wang, P., & Luo, M. (2016). QoS-aware adaptive routing in multi-layer hierarchical software defined networks: A reinforcement learning approach. In *Proceedings - 2016 IEEE International Conference on Services Computing, SCC 2016* (pp. 25–33). 10.1109/SCC.2016.12

Liu, J., Wan, J., Zeng, B., Wang, Q., Song, H., & Qiu, M. (2017). A scalable and quick-response software defined vehicular network assisted by mobile edge computing. *IEEE Communications Magazine*, *55*(7), 94–100. doi:10.1109/MCOM.2017.1601150

Liu, Y. C., Chen, C., & Chakraborty, S. (2015). A Software Defined Network architecture for GeoBroadcast in VANETs. *IEEE International Conference on Communications*, 6559–6564. 10.1109/ICC.2015.7249370

Marina, M. K., & Das, S. R. (2006). Ad hoc on-demand multipath distance vector routing. *Wireless Communications and Mobile Computing*, *6*(7), 969–988. doi:10.1002/wcm.432

Murthy, S., & Garcia-Luna-Aceves, J. J. (1996). An efficient routing protocol for wireless networks. *Mobile Networks and Applications*, *1*(2), 183–197. doi:10.1007/BF01193336

Nakao, A., & Du, P. (2018). Toward in-network deep machine learning for identifying mobile applications and enabling application specific network slicing. *IEICE Transactions on Communications*, *E101B*(7), 1536–1543. doi:10.1587/transcom.2017CQI0002

Open Networking Foundation. (2012). Software-Defined Networking : The New Norm for Networks. *ONF White Paper*, *2*, 2–6. Retrieved from https://www.opennetworking.org/images/stories/downloads/sdn-resources/white-papers/wp-sdn-newnorm.pdf

Open Networking Foundation. (2013). OpenFlow 1.4 Specifications. *Onf*, *0*, 1–36. doi:10.1002/2014GB005021

Park, V. D., & Corson, M. S. (1997). *A Highly Adaptive Distributed Routing Algorithm for Mobile Wireless Networks*. Copyright. doi:10.1109/INFCOM.1997.631180

Perkins, C. E. (n.d.). *Highly Dynamic Destination-Sequenced Distance-Vector Routing (DSDV) for Mobile Computers*. Academic Press.

Qazi, Z. A., Lee, J., Jin, T., Bellala, G., Arndt, M., & Noubir, G. (2013). Application-awareness in SDN. Computer Communication Review, 43, 487–488. doi:10.1145/2486001.2491700

Raw, R. S., Kumar, M., & Singh, N. (2013). Security challenges, issues and their solutions for VANET. *International Journal of Network Security & Its Applications*, *5*(5). Advance online publication. doi:10.5121/ijnsa.2013.5508

Raya, M., & Hubaux, J.-P. (2007). Securing vehicular ad hoc networks. *Journal of Computer Security*, *15*(1), 39–68. doi:10.3233/JCS-2007-15103

Salahuddin, M. A., Al-Fuqaha, A., & Guizani, M. (2015). Software-Defined Networking for RSU Clouds in Support of the Internet of Vehicles. *IEEE Internet of Things Journal*, *2*(2), 133–144. doi:10.1109/JIOT.2014.2368356

Sendra, S., Rego, A., Lloret, J., Jimenez, J. M., & Romero, O. (2017). Including artificial intelligence in a routing protocol using Software Defined Networks. In *2017 IEEE International Conference on Communications Workshops, ICC Workshops 2017* (pp. 670–674). 10.1109/ICCW.2017.7962735

Siva Ram Murthy, C., & Manoj, B. S. (n.d.). *Ad Hoc Wireless Networks Architectures and Protocols C. Siva Ram Murthy B. S. Manoj.*

Sivakumar, R., Sinha, P., & Bharghavan, V. (1999). CEDAR: A Core-Extraction Distributed Ad Hoc Routing Algorithm. *IEEE Journal on Selected Areas in Communications*, *17*(8), 1454–1465. doi:10.1109/49.779926

Su, W., & Gerla, M. (n.d.). IPv6 Flow Handoff In Ad Hoc Wireless Networks Using Mobility Prediction. In *Seamless Interconnection for Universal Services. Global Telecommunications Conference. GLOBECOM'99. (Cat. No. 99CH37042)* (pp. 271–275). Academic Press.

Sudheera, K. L. K., Ma, M., & Chong, P. H. J. (2019). Link Stability Based Optimized Routing Framework for Software Defined Vehicular Networks. *IEEE Transactions on Vehicular Technology*, *68*(3), 2934–2945. doi:10.1109/TVT.2019.2895274

Tang, Y., Cheng, N., Wu, W., Wang, M., Dai, Y., & Shen, X. (2019). Delay-Minimization Routing for Heterogeneous VANETs with Machine Learning Based Mobility Prediction. *IEEE Transactions on Vehicular Technology*, *68*(4), 3967–3979. doi:10.1109/TVT.2019.2899627

Toh, C. K. (1997). Associativity-Based Routing for Ad-Hoc Mobile Networks. *Wireless Personal Communications*, *4*(2), 103–139. doi:10.1023/A:1008812928561

Truong, N. B., Lee, G. M., & Ghamri-Doudane, Y. (2015a). Software defined networking-based vehicular Adhoc Network with Fog Computing. *Proceedings of the 2015 IFIP/IEEE International Symposium on Integrated Network Management, IM 2015*, 1202–1207. 10.1109/INM.2015.7140467

Truong, N. B., Lee, G. M., & Ghamri-Doudane, Y. (2015b). Software defined networking-based vehicular Adhoc Network with Fog Computing. *Proceedings of the 2015 IFIP/IEEE International Symposium on Integrated Network Management, IM 2015*, 1202–1207. 10.1109/INM.2015.7140467

Uddin, M., & Nadeem, T. (2017). Traffic Vision: A Case for Pushing Software Defined Networks to Wireless Edges. In *Proceedings - 2016 IEEE 13th International Conference on Mobile Ad Hoc and Sensor Systems, MASS 2016* (pp. 37–46). 10.1109/MASS.2016.016

Wang, C., Ma, X., Jiang, W., Zhao, L., Lin, N., & Shi, J. (2019). IMCR: Influence maximisation-based cluster routing algorithm for SDVN. In *Proceedings - 21st IEEE International Conference on High Performance Computing and Communications, 17th IEEE International Conference on Smart City and 5th IEEE International Conference on Data Science and Systems, HPCC/SmartCity/DSS 2019* (pp. 2580–2586). 10.1109/HPCC/SmartCity/DSS.2019.00361

Wang, P., Lin, S. C., & Luo, M. (2016). A framework for QoS-aware traffic classification using semi-supervised machine learning in SDNs. In *Proceedings - 2016 IEEE International Conference on Services Computing, SCC 2016* (pp. 760–765). 10.1109/SCC.2016.133

Xiao, P., Qu, W., Qi, H., Xu, Y., & Li, Z. (2015). An efficient elephant flow detection with cost-sensitive in SDN. In *Proceedings of the 2015 1st International Conference on Industrial Networks and Intelligent Systems, INISCom 2015* (pp. 24–28). 10.4108/icst.iniscom.2015.258274

You, Z., Cheng, G., Wang, Y., Chen, P., & Chen, S. (2019). Cross-layer and SDN Based routing scheme for P2P communication in vehicular Ad-hoc networks. *Applied Sciences (Switzerland)*, 9(22), 4734. doi:10.3390/app9224734

Zhang, D., Yu, F. R., & Yang, R. (2018). A Machine Learning Approach for Software-Defined Vehicular Ad Hoc Networks with Trust Management. *2018 IEEE Global Communications Conference, GLOBECOM 2018 - Proceedings*. 10.1109/GLOCOM.2018.8647426

Zhu, M., Cai, Z., Cao, J., & Xu, M. (2015). Efficient multiple-copy routing in software. *Proc. Int. Conf. Inf. Commun. Technol.*, 1–6.

Zhu, M., Cao, J., Pang, D., & He, Z. (2015). SDN-Based Routing for Efficient Message Propagation in VANET Min. *Proc. 10th Int. Conf. Wireless Algorithms, Syst. Appl.*, 788–797. doi:10.1007/978-3-319-21837-3

Chapter 8
Vehicle Monitoring and Surveillance Through Vehicular Sensor Network

Pooja Singh

CSE/IT Department, Amity School of Engineering and Technology, Noida, India

ABSTRACT

There are a lot of prospects of the vehicular network, including the artificial neural networks incorporating a wireless sensor network. Its number comes after the mobile communication network and the internet. The network is characterized by more through measure and sense and exhibits more comfortable operability and intelligence. A wireless sensor network can be simply defined as "a network of wireless devices using sensors to monitors and recording the physical conditions of the environment and organizing the collected data at a central location." WSNs measure environmental conditions like temperature, sound, pollution levels, humidity, wind speed and direction, pressure, etc. Thus, wireless sensor networks are widely used for fulfilling the essential needs of environmental sensing applications. These applications show the broad ranges in precision agriculture, monitoring of the vehicle, and video surveillance.

1. INTRODUCTION

Vehicular sensor network is a novel technology which is very high much needed and demanded technology for new generation digital and technical society. Since the entire material thing can be related to the digital world and the facilities of the material production and service management can be effectively developed and integrated using the internet of things, which is a very broad sector of technology. This internet of things can effectively integrate both the worlds i.e. the physical and the digital world and vehicular sensor network technology can be easily considered the various and wide applications of internet of things and is a thus a growing sector developing technologies of internet of things. The areas which are covered under the vehicular sensor network of internet of things applications are security of public, protection of the environment, urban management, intelligent industry, business services, mod-

DOI: 10.4018/978-1-7998-2764-1.ch008

ern agriculture, construction and infrastructure From seeing the prospects of vehicular technology, the internet of things forms a high level of global information system comprising hundreds and millions of objects which can be identified, sensed and processed which is based on the standard and interoperable communication protocols. The management and decision making control can also be easily provided using this technologies of cloud computing and indulging with broadband vehicular communication and internet of things. They can even manage and co-operate with each other without any intervention of humans. Regarding the global society this internet of things can function as a global infrastructure which provides the advanced services which are enabled by the interconnection of physical and the virtual world. This interconnection is based on the information and the communication technology which are existing and evolving and are interoperable (Vermesan et al., 2012). The definitions of internet of things is that a device of network which directly connects with each other to share and capture the vital data through a secure service layer connecting the central command and control server (Niwolney, 2013).

The wireless sensor networks are gaining impact in our daily lives. In several domains they are exhibiting a wide range of applications and covering several fields like health care, scenarios of assisted and enhanced-living, monitoring of the industrial and production, control networks, and many other such related fields. In near future also, the wireless sensor networks are integrated with the vehicular sensor network as under IoT, for beneficial results to society and environment. There is a dynamic connection of sensor nodes with the internet and theses are further collaborated for the accomplishment of the tasks. When the wireless sensor networks are integrated with the internet the issues regarding their integration should be investigated and analyzed carefully. There are several approaches evaluating the integration of wireless sensor network with the vehicular internet and the challenges are outlined and solved giving this world and society various smart applications (Oniga et al., 2014).

Vehicle detection and tracking applications play an important role in civil and military applications such as highway traffic monitoring control, management and urban traffic planning. The vehicle detection process on the road is used for vehicle tracking, calculation, average speed of each individual vehicle, traffic analysis and vehicle grading purposes and can be applied under various environmental changes. The chapter introduced applications of WSNs that included developing traffic monitoring systems.

2. WIRELESS SENSOR NETWORK IN VEHICLE MONITORING: LITERATURE SURVEY

A wireless sensor network is a sophisticated system used to monitor military, oceans or wildlife (G. Padmavathi et al., 2010), for example. The same concept of mass surveillance and monitoring by wireless sensor networks can be applied to provide enhanced security measures and innovative traffic control techniques. Innovative routing systems have used a wireless sensor network in which sensor nodes are installed in all communicating automobiles and with central monitoring stations and at appropriate points on roads mounted sensor nodes.

The modes installed in the vehicle act as nodes in the network and assist in sending or receiving data to or from the central monitoring station. They can effectively control traffic, report the cause of over speed directly to the traffic police, and alert the medical department immediately to reduce traffic. The sensor node with its advanced chip is embedded in data fusion and neural network technology (formerly known as Advanced Artificial Technology, AI) such as CSM to easily detect the speeding of a particular vehicle and the speeding of the neighboring vehicle with shows the distance between the vehicles.

2.1 Sensor Technology

As the current modern society maximum dependent on the wireless sensor networks, e.g. for entertainment, for smart technology education, for getting real experienced through the simulations, for fast communication, etc. All the needs and demands increased toward as IoT (Internet of things) (L. Atzori et al., 2010) and (Vermesan, O et al., 2012), which are becomes most popular with the different types of embedded sensor chip.

The different types of sensor can be used for their different purpose and application's such as:

i. Speed sensor, ultrasonic and night vision sensor, camera sensors, radars sensor; these type of sensor typically used for the security and safety purposes.
ii. Temperature sensor, airbag sensor, gas composition sensor, these are used for the real time diagnostic events.
iii. Proximity sensor, radars and laser sensor, cameras and ultrasonic sensors used for monitoring the traffic condition.
iv. Humidity sensor, torque sensor, image sensor, rain sensor, fogging prevention sensors and distance sensor are used for the assistance of any application.

2.1.1. Sensors for Vehicle

There are different types of sensors (Juan Guerrero-Iz et al., 2018), which can be used for any car or automobiles sectors to solves the many problems like:

(1) Road congestion information and vehicle parking space,
(2) Travelling and commuting times,
(3) Emissions of CO_2 level and pollution information generated by particular car,
(4) The increase in vehicle accidents is important to improve vehicle performance and improve the driving experience.

3. DATA AGGREGATION AND FUSION FOR VEHICLE WIRELESS TECHNOLOGY

This chapter describes an approach to improving road surveillance in wireless sensor networks: multiple sensors can be distributed on the road to capture the traffic flow, speed, and habitat of the road. Each WSN cluster has a video-based surveillance system that generates information that can be processed independently of the weather to clearly explain road conditions.

Therefore, it is necessary to integrate video surveillance information with parameters measured by other sensors, e.g. Power sensor for traffic detection. The benefits of using WSNs in this area are many.

WSN can automatically and continuously monitor and evaluate paths/roads:

• A WSN can also work with bad weather conditions during the night, when there is presence of fog or dust (pollution, volcanic ash) in the air.
• WSNs are low cost and low power.

Figure1. **Types of sensors used in Vehicle [***Juan Guerrero-Iz et al., 2018***]**

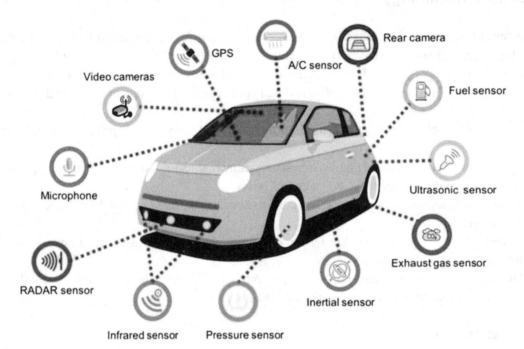

- A WSN allows integration of video surveillance with magnetic or power sensors. In this way, it is possible to get complete and integrated information (video-picture and traffic volume information).

WSNs allow dynamic changes in network topology based on actual needs and reports coming from roadside sensors.

- When needed, the number of cameras that control a particular area may increase to produce more detailed information. However, it can increase the network workload that will be managed properly by the proposed approach.

A system for monitoring road traffic, operating under adverse environmental conditions, involves the coexistence of a large number of devices that, while working together, ensure proper analysis of the traffic condition of vehicles. The purpose of the chapter is to introduced the intelligent data aggregation & fusion technique during the image/video comparisons in vehicle monitoring, hence the duplicity can be remove and accurate information can be stored & fast processing can be done while the whole process of any vehicle surveillance for an specific road sections and, in the case of queues or traffic jams, a mechanism is activated to detect traffic.

3.1 Data Aggregation in Vehicular Sensor Network

1. Data generated by adjacent sensors is often redundant and highly correlated.

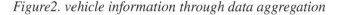

Figure2. vehicle information through data aggregation

2. The amount of data generated in large sensor networks is normally difficult for the base station to handle.

Data aggregation seeks to collect the most important data from sensors and to provide energy-efficient synchronization.

Data Aggregation Schemes can be classified into four categories:

1. The tree-based data aggregation schemes
2. The cluster-based data aggregation schemes
3. The chain-based data aggregation schemes
4. The sector-based data aggregation schemes

VANETs are one of the basic techniques for efficient, secure, informative and recreational transport systems. In current scenario and days, people spend a significant amount of their life's time in vehicles, to utilized time, more efficient, more enjoyable and make safer, greener and more economical. The intelligent vehicles based on Wireless VANETs have been developed for all these features and high security can be ensured by the reliable exchange of important events. The event can be exchange using the cloud computing for better communication, accessibility and with minimum transition error. Higher efficiency can be achieved by reducing congestion, environmental noise and pollution these are making driving times more predictable. In addition, VWSNs can be connected to the Internet to make traveling safer, enjoyable by offering downloadable and social networking files. VANETs use two types of messages:

i) Beacon messages and
ii) Security messages.

The vehicles periodically can be use transmissions through cloud based wireless sensor network using IoT and provide accurate their position and status information to their adjacent and nearby vehicles at every 100 ms intervals. The status information includes the speed of vehicle, location of the vehicle along with their pseudo ID. This type of information which are sending to neighboring vehicles known as Beacon Messages.

On the other side, safety notifications received by the vehicles pseudo ID which are help to the vehicles on the road by providing emergency information so that appropriate action can be taken to prevent accidents and protect people from deadly situations. When encountering incidents on the road, the vehicles send a WAV Short Message (WSM) to adjacent vehicles, nearby police station, nearby hospital even nearby vehicles service center, this technology also become popular as blue ray technology.

The message payload contains information about the status of the vehicle, the time of sending the message, the location of the vehicle and the events on the nearby road, etc. (X. Lin et al., 2007), and (H. Sarvada et al., 2013). Each vehicle collects information about neighboring vehicles within the communication range.

3.2 Cluster Based Data Aggregation Schemes

First most question is arise that why chosen the cluster based aggregation schemes for the Vehicle Monitoring and Surveillance through Vehicular Sensor Network, so the further is answer; The applications of the wireless sensor network and the challenges which are faced by the environment, while the nodes of the networks are deployed heterogeneously. The processing of the information has to undergo the specific mode of refraining in the network being the process, filter and data compression for the improvement of the signal ability through the sensor nodes which are variable. The information is collected together and merged into one content and communicated further. The working of the wireless sensor network is performed using the small devices named as nodes. The size and the work of the nodes vary according to the various fields. The main source of receiving the network sensor waves are microcontrollers playing a typical part in controlling waves and making the process of the network powerful. Many Studies suggest that the routing based on clustering is an effective way to decrease the utilization of energy and expand the lifespan of network within a single cluster also easily adapted and enhanced with artificial intelligent (ANN-Artificial Neural Network) techniques (Dreiseitl, S et al., 2002) and (Enami, N et al., 2010).

Thus, using KSOM (KohonenSelf Organizing Map) [Figure5] the sensor nodes clustering is evaluated for different nodes by acquiring varied sensor node parameters (W. Heinzelman et al., 2000). Also, it has been noted that the intelligent components neural networks reveals greater compatibility with wireless sensor networks features and can be used in varied schemes of energy conservation.

In clustering schemes, sensor nodes are partitioned into a number of small clusters. Each cluster contain a cluster head. Each cluster head gathers information from its group of sensor nodes, perform data aggregation and relay only relevant information to the sink. The sensed data is redundant if the node is within the range of sensing and transmitting with respect to other neighboring nodes and the parameter of interest is well within the gradient value of deviation. Therefore, clustering schemes are widely used in wireless sensor networks, not only due to their simple node coordination, but also because they use multi-hop routing between CHs to avoid long-range transmissions.

Here the cluster head will be playing a major role as the decision from the system will be made according to this network. Because of incorporation of KMOS and ANN networks the efficiency will be higher as well as for the performance which could be evaluated with the factors like Efficiency in power, PSNR.

4. INTELLIGENT WSN IN VEHICULAR SENSOR NETWORK

The technique of neural networks have are gaining popularity in the field of wireless sensor networks [figure 3], mainly because of the simple and parallel distributed computation and storage. Also, the data robustness, automatic sensor reading and the auto-classification of sensor nodes is considered as an added advantage of the neural network technique. The ability of this technique for the purpose of dimensionality reduction as well as prediction of sensor data which is easily obtained from the outputs of the neural-networks algorithms are considered as a potential prospect for the lower communication costs as well as the energy conservation. Thus, with these features of the neural network technique, it can be easily used with the wireless sensor networks which also known as Intelligent WSN.

Figure 3. Collaboration of WSN and ANN as an intelligent WSN

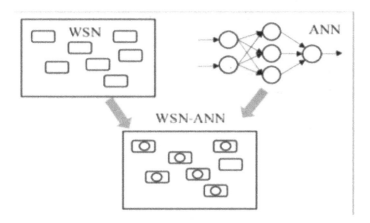

Neural networks employed and represented an important role for many applications such as image processing. Offered another significant contribution, he has offered a nerve-limit-based vehicle detection and classification approach. Knowledge of characteristics of traffic criteria, vehicle velocity, vehicle numbering, and vehicle category is extracting by merging the results of movement edge detection and background removal, this characteristic knowledge mining method is called seed-filling. Subsequently, the mining characteristic used as the recorded data of the neural network for an accurate vehicle recognition and hierarchical vehicle process.

Various types of neural networks are there and thus, selecting the most appropriate neural network still can be termed as a challenging task. This selection process is majorly depending upon the characteristics of the problem which is involved as well as on the properties of NN. The neural network which is selected must be trained for the purpose of decision making which may be done with different types of rules. These training rules for neural networks are essentially inspired from various systems occurring in the field of biological sciences (Dreiseitl, & Ohno-Machado, 2002). Also, learning from an example consists of the major ways of training a neural network. Thus an example which has a set of correct input-output data is usually fed to the network and by the usage and analysis of this illustrative data, the network should manipulate the values of the weights. So, the correct output is resulted when new data is given as an input and this process is known as learning.

Over and above the intelligence which is imparted to a neural network by training and learning, a major and important property of the NNs is its ability to differentiate between the data affected by noise or an intentional change in the data and also the capability to remove those changes after a successful process of learning.

There are many different types of Artificial Neural Network topologies having variety of capabilities which can be tapped according to the application [figure 4] in which they are needed. However, they all have nearly the same components, each unit performs a relatively simple job: receive input from neighbor's or external sources and use this to compute an output signal which units. This task is the adjustment of the weights is another vital part of processing. The system undetakes inherently parallel computations at the same time which is distinguished as follows:

1. Input Layer which gets the data in the neural network for processing
2. Output Layer which send data out of the neural network
3. Hidden Layer whose input and output signals remains within the neural network.

For the purpose of energy conservation in the wireless networks, there are numerous stages where the technique of neural networks can be applied for energy optimization (E.g. Energy efficient node clustering, data association, data fusion, data prediction, cluster head selection, etc.).

Figure 4. Apply ANN for WSNs Cluster Formation

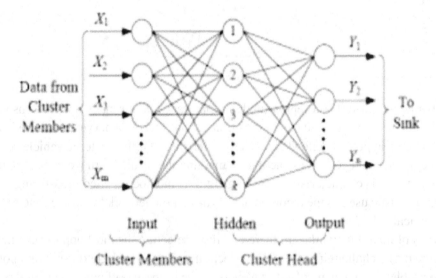

But there are various studies which show that when comparing various other neural topologies, the Self Organizing Map neural networks are considered highly applicable when the area of application is energy conservation methods.

On-road vehicle detection novel computational system uses K-SOM mapping for cluster formation and Feed Forward Back Propagation algorithm (FFBPA) system utilized from texture and geometric features of vehicles during the recognition process. FFBPA included on two parts of classifiers: the first one is a K-SOM mapping which informs about the vehicle texture features, and a Bayesian network that informs about volumes, position and confidence values of vehicle generated by Data Fusion.

4.1 Utilization of KSOM in Vehicular Sensor Network

The Self-Organizing Map (SOM) (Vesanto, J., 1999) is necessarily a neural network structure which is unsupervised and consists of neurons (sensor nodes in this case) arranged on a grid which is regularly low dimensional [Figure 5]. Each neuron is represented by a multi-dimensional weight vector according to the dimensions of input vectors. The Weight vectors (also known as synapses) are seen as a connecting link between the input layer and the output layer also known as map or the competitive layer. For the connection of these neurons, there is a specific neighborhood relationship which neither is nor dictated by the distance but many other parameters (Younis, M et al., 2008) thereby helping the optimum consumption of energy and increasing the life of the network. This study proposed the utilization of a self-organizing map for clustering of the sensor nodes because it has an enhanced capability to reduce the dimension of the input data from multiple dimensions to lower dimensional values, and it can also help in the visualization of the clusters in the form of a map.

Figure 5. Low Dimensional K-SOM Mapping

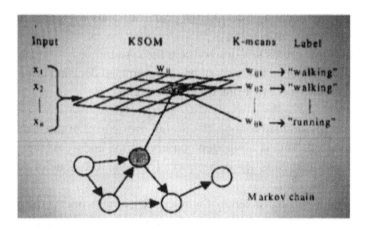

The Kohonen self-organizing map neural networks which is utilized for the purpose of clustering in this study as well as their examination for the purpose of learning the random behaviors of network applications and parameters. Thus, this is KSOM is required for the training of the neural network. The clustering of the sensor nodes which is done with the help of the Kohonen SOM is evaluated to get different number of nodes with the help of acquisition of varied parameters of sensor nodes. The set of data is first clustered using self-organizing map and then self-organizing map is clustered by K-means which reduces the multi dimensionality of the nodes to lower numbers as well as the map organization is much more lucid (Ultsch, A., 1993) and (Lee, S et al., 2004).

4.2 The technique of data fusion

In the field of wireless sensor networks, the technique of data fusion is posed by a challenge of intelligently fusing heterogeneous data which is collected from variety of sensors (Chen, Y et al., 2009). Thus, an intelligent system has to be designed for the purpose of efficient utilization and fusion after critical examination of heterogeneous information which has been acquired from a variety of sensory sources. This process must be carried out with high efficiency, accuracy and must be automatic without user intervention. The main advantage of data fusion (Chen, Y et al., 2009) is that it can considerably reduce the size of the heterogeneous data. Also, with the help of intelligent fusing, this technique can even classify noise and other influencing estimations from the data. Data fusion is the technique where the data which is locally sensed by the regular sensor nodes is collected, intelligently merged and finally transmitted to the base station. The cluster head sensor nodes are responsible to carry out the function of data fusion. This technique of data fusion is of prime importance here because it gathers all the data locally sensed and packs it in a single quantum (Liu Y et al., 2014 which is transferred to the base station thereby reducing the energy expenditure which could be incurred while sending the data individually. Thus size reduction and intelligent fusion helps conserve the energy win the process of data transmission which is generally the most energy expensive part in the system having heterogeneous wirelessly connected sensors.

Data Fusion technologies [figure 6] are intended to reduce and remove redundant information.

The node performing the function of data fusion primarily deals with three tasks:

1. Collection of data from various sensory nodes in the system.
2. Fusion of the collected data on the basis of pre-programmed decision criteria.
3. Transmission of the fused data to a sink or a base station.

By the performance of these three actions, the overall traffic load of the data transmission between nodes in a system is reduced. This is a big step conserving the energy of the sensory nodes thereby increasing the lifetime of the wireless sensor network. Thus, the technique of data fusion caters to the primary aim of the given study.

One of the essential data fusion problems of wireless sensor networks is the importance of utilizing an intelligent system which fuses heterogeneous information acquired from varied sources efficiently, automatically and accurately. Data fusion can reduce the data size. Even if the data had been influenced by intentional estimation or noise, the method of data fusion must be capable to identify and classify the data.

Thus, the system designed is an optimum trade-off between node-wise energy expense and computational performance. The technique of KSOM (Dehni, L et al., 2005) is applied for designing the learning algorithm which is of utmost importance in the training of the neural networks.

The system that is described above is implemented in using a step by step process which consists of three vital steps as follows:

1. Cluster setup phase (organization of cluster)
2. Cluster Head selection phase (subsequent step after the formation of cluster)
3. Transmission phase (data transmission from simple nodes to cluster heads which is further relayed to base station post aggregation)

Figure 6. Data Fusion Process flowchart

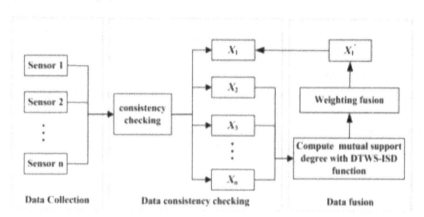

These steps are described in detail in the subsequent sections.

4.3 Cluster Setup Phase

Firstly, clustering is an important technique in the field of wireless sensor networks. Clustering fundamentally means forming clusters or group of sensor nodes wherein data from all nodes defined in one cluster is aggregated at a cluster head and further, this aggregated data is transmitted to the sink (or base station in this case). As data is sent to the base station after the process of aggregation, the energy efficiency of the system increases because of the reducing the communication overhead. Another key advantage by using this technique is that it can be scaled for large number of nodes with ease.

There are various algorithms which have been devised for the initial step of cluster formation or organization in order to extend the life of wireless sensor networks. The literature is evident to various protocols which present the clustering schemes mostly forming the clusters based the utilization of the topological neighborhood or adjacency as the prime parameter of importance. The protocol uses a 2 phase method of clustering Self Organizing Map followed by the algorithm of K-means which had been suggested with a precise assessment amid the direct clustering outcomes of clustering and prototype vectors data of self-organizing map.

The Self-Organizing Map (SOM) is necessarily a neural network structure (Enami N et al., 2010) and (Aslam M et al., 2013) which is unsupervised and consists of neurons (sensor nodes in this case) arranged on a grid which is regularly low dimensional. Each neuron is represented by a multi-dimensional weight vector according to the dimensions of input vectors. The Weight vectors (also known as synapses) are seen as a connecting link between the input layer and the output layer also known as map or the competitive layer. For the connection of these neurons, there is a specific neighborhood relationship which neither is nor dictated by the distance but many other parameters thereby helping the optimum consumption of energy and increasing the life of the network. This study proposed the utilization of a self-organizing map for clustering of the sensor nodes because it has an enhanced capability to reduce the dimension of the input data from multiple dimensions to lower dimensional values, and it can also help in the visualization of the clusters in the form of a map.

The self-organization map technique of cluster formation (Aslam M et al., 2012) is a function of multiple parameters and does not take just the proximate neighbor for the formation of the clusters.

Thus, the clusters formed using this technique is not necessarily adjacent neighboring sensor nodes. The dimension of input data associates to several parameters which the author requires to consider for clustering. The approach or algorithm helps in the formation of energy balanced clusters thereby resulting in equal distribution of energy for the consumption in various clusters. In the preliminary phase the reason for using self-organizing map is to make data pretreatment (which may consist of reduction of dimension, regrouping, map based visualization formation, etc.) use acquired by self-organizing map.

After the preliminary phase which is sorted by the SOM, the technique of Neural Networks is an apt tool which can be applied for getting effective results when considering various aspects of reduction in energy consumption like the duty cycling, the data driving and mobility based methods which are used in WSNs.

With the purpose of improvement of the SOM, the application of Kohenon algorithmis utlized in Kohonen self-organizing map neural networks used clustering and their examination to learn random behaviors of network applications and parameters. The sensor nodes' clustering using Kohonen SOM is evaluated for different number of nodes by acquiring varied parameters of sensor nodes (like, position, direction, energy levels, number of hops, latency, sensitivity among many others). KSOM is an excellent component for clustering of WSN because it is capable to lessen multi-dimensional input data dimensions and view clusters into a map. Therefore the set of data is first clustered usingself-organizing map and then self-organizing map (Thein M et al., 2010) is clustered by K-means.

The Kohenon technique for the application in context of SOM will be based on the study by (Aslam M et al., 2011) (Thein M et al., 2010) and (Aslam M et al., 2011). Here, the initial staged set of assumptions in regard to then WSNs are given in the subsequent list.

4.4 Cluster Head Selection Phase

The primary step involving the formation of clusters is explained in depth in the precceding section. After the formation of clusters, for each and ecery cluster, a cluster head is selected or elected. This cluster head is situated in the said cluster and is assigned with the responsibility of collection of data from various nodes in the cluster and relay the bundled data to the base station. A major challenenge is thus the apprpriate selection of cluster head so that minimum energy is spent in the relaying function.

The selection of a cluster head (Dehni L et al., 2005) is an important decision while considering any clustering algortihm because this step dictates the disspiation of the system energy in any given sensor deployed environment. Tehre a re various algorithms having a random method for the election of acluster head randomly based on probability. However, these algorithms cannot ensure with guarentee that the cluster head so elected are having a proper distribution and are covering the said area of sensor depoloyment in uniform fashion. This particular consideration is not particularly efficient which can be evidently seen from the example of the study by (Heinzelman W et al., 2000) which has proposed a system for the cluster heads selection with random way by using pre-defined Kopt number with an aim to randomize the distribution of energy consumption as well as the load among the sensors. Thus, the following is prposed for a more systematic way for the purpose of cluster head selection.

The selection of cluster head from the formed cluster [figure 7] is done keeping in mind various parameters. Above the many criterions defined for the selction of cluster head, three main paramters are regarded for the same:

1.   Geographically nearest located sensor to the base station.

Figure 7. Formation of Cluster Head

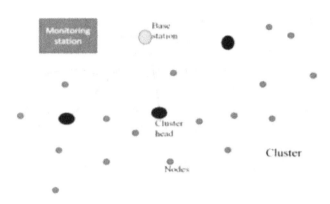

2. The sensor which has the highest energy level
3. The sensor which has highest adjacency to the center of gravity of the cluster.

There are various reasons which dictate the selection according to the above three rules. Considering the first criteria which dictates that the sensor be located nearest to the base station, it can be ensured that least amount of energy is utilized while relaying the messages to the base station. Considering the sensor which is the center of gravity of the cluster ensures that the intra cluster communication is most energy efficient, at the same time, the overhead reduction with respect to the cluster head neither is nor ensured in this case. Both these above stages ensure the stability of the cluster head during the transmission process or until the formation of new clusters by the effect of the re-clustering process. This re-clustering process usually lasts for many rounds which may result in the quick reduction of that cluster heads; however utilizing the above two methods ensures outcomes with longer life span.

Considereing various optimisation parameters for the puropse of energy ssaving, finally a cluster head is chosen which is the best trade-off between energy utlization and efficiency. Post the selecton of the cluster head, roles are assigned by the cluster head to all the cluster nodes through a propoer proposed protocol.

This study uses the second method which is selecting the nodes having highest energy level as the channel head, as the method for carrying out the election of cluster heads.The lack of concentration of algorithms dedicated to the clustering to nodes energy levels as the prime parameter in the development of clusters of networks could be termed as the primay motivation for the conception of this system is. This study utilizes the energy based clustering for the purpose of extension of the the network lifetime along with the faciluty of adequate coverage of network.

4.5 Transmission Phase

The transmission phase is the final step in the algortihm which is proposed in the said study. In this transmission phase, the pricipal objective is the passing or the relaying of data from the cluster heads to the base station. This step utilizes the data which is locally sesned by the regular nodes and sent to the cluster heads which after the application of data fusion technique is transmittedto the base station. The cluster heads perform the function of data fusion. This technique of data fusion is of prime importance here because it gathers all the data locally sensed and packs it in a single quantum which is transferred to the base station thereby reducing the energy expenditure which could be incurred while sending the data individually.

After the clusters formation and choosing their associated CH (cluster heads) now it is the time to pass the packets of data sensed at usual nodes to their associated cluster head and after using the functions of data fusion to acquired packets by cluster heads the messages are passedto the BS (base station). The utilization of energy of entire nodes is evaluated. One of the essential data fusion problems of wireless sensor networks is the importance of utilizing an intelligent system which fuses heterogeneous information acquired from varied sources efficiently, automatically and accurately. Data fusion can reduce the data size (Smith, D et al., 2006). Even if the data had been influenced by intentional estimation or noise, the method of data fusion must be capable to identify and classify the data. Sensor data fusion is a some need of tracking applications and target detection in wireless sensor networks. The consumed energy for data transmission over a distance is evaluated. After every phase of transmission the author counts a new round and they also has a rotation of clusters in using criterion of maximum energy. Since their aim is to create clusters with equal levels of energy the author must have threshold for the phase of re-clustering according to difference of nodes energy level. So the energy level of greater nodes of energy is verified regularly. These nodes arecluster head of the phase of last set up. The conditions are the predefined percent reduction of their energy level. When the re-clustering threshold is fulfilled the base station sends a message of re-clustering to the complete network.

After all the commands of the transmission are executed, the transmission stage is declared completed following which a new round begins with the adjustment of the cluster head by taking into consideration the previously proposed protocols. If it is observed during the adjustment process that the cluster head is not meeting the requirements laid down per the protocol, the system resorts to an a re-clustering phenomenon under which the new cluster head would be elected following the above described procedure. The entire process described above for all the three vital steps is then repeated step by step till required results are not obtained.

5. LIMITATION OF WSN IN TERM OF VEHICLES SURVEILLANCE

It is difficult to determine in wireless sensor networks for several reasons:

- Sensors with limited power, energy, storage and processing capacity
- Node asymmetry: Each node must manage different functions and hardware
- The network topology may change over time due to node mobility, deletion, or addition of nodes.
- Ambient conditions where sensor work is often unpredictable

All these conditions may cause the "delay" and / or "packet loss rate" to be too high to affect the prediction and reliability of the system requirements. It is therefore necessary to use the QoS management paradigm to ensure network flexibility, adaptability, and scalability.

Summary

This study was undertaken with the objectives of analysis of vehicle monitoring and surveillance through wireless Vehicular sensor network. Finally, the system is implemented based in an algorithm which is an intended integration of the KSOM and data fusion technique to vehicle monitoring and surveillance through vehicular sensor network.

The major aim of the chapter is designing an inventive method which is based on the approaches of the neural network being the self-organizing mapping and data fusion techniques for the optimization at nodes. The current research inculcates the back propagation algorithm method in which the artificial neural network is used for the purpose of training and optimization of network by reducing the function of loss. The main purpose of this technique is to acknowledge the best input corresponding to the outputs classifying the odes and the main profit of this method is upgrading the weights of the hidden layer weights of the network. The optimization of the consumption of energy and the performance of network involving the Data Fusion, Artificial Neural Network and the KSOM algorithms is the novel idea of this particular research. The creation of the energy efficient wireless network takes place where mapping of the nodes in the network is done by the KSOM technique and classification of the nodes is done by ANN. There are several rounds constituted and the formulation of cluster of nodes is done in each round which is further followed by data transmission phase.

Future Work

There are lots of challenges in term of future enhancement for the technology as per our current technological life style based on cloud and on IoT, there are some challenges will be not avoidable such as:

1) Latency: latency will be needed low level for the better run of real time applications with security enhancement and for safe messages.
2) Bandwidth: As smart vehicle having the navigation properties and it will be modified by 3D maps and visualizations in future to achieve that purpose the bandwidth should be very high.
3) Connectivity: Due to space concern and charging problems, in future there are must needed the seamless connectivity's between the vehicles for the fast communication between them.

Apart from these there are lots of application can be done in future to make vehicle sensor technology more attractive, easily meet the drivers requirements and will be more enhanced for daily life style to connected the Home IoT; infotainment (Wu He et al., 2014) and (Kim Younsun et al., 2017) are cloud based.

Some scenario can be defined as follows [figures 8,9,10 and 11]:

i) When any person leaving the home for office or any particular place there will be voice based personal assistant on their smart phone which are connected to the their car and will help about the minimize routing task with playing favorite entertainment's based on routing life style.
ii) When any person reached about the home, the smart voice based personal assistant ask for the home light on/off, parking place etc.

Figure 8. Infotainment: Cloud Based [Kim Younsun et al., 2017]

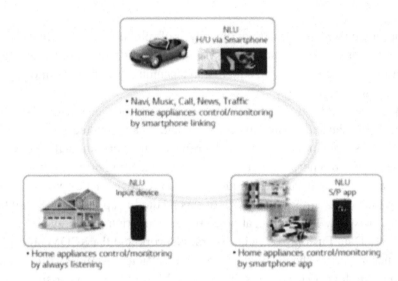

Figure 9. Cloud connectivity in vehicle using IoT[Kim Younsun et al., 2017]

Case Study: Intelligent Transport System

Here (figure: 12), try to explain how the intelligent sensor routing makes the intelligent transport system. In the following figure, there are denoting numbering which are further describe in deatils.

(1) The vehicle monitoring system identifies a potentially hazardous situation for occupants using vehicle and off-board sensors and portable sensors (accelerometer that measures the vehicle's horizontal position, LIDAR scale detection effects, and effects). The sensor measures the distance), Accident, however, is inevitable and the car gets stuck in a newly formed road cavity. The car will immediately initiate the security protocol provided to make an initial assessment of the situation.

(2) The vehicle's central system starts a broadcast alarm protocol to inform nearby drivers and pedestrians about the accident and to take additional safety precautions (eg low or alternative routes).

Figure 10. Applications of Infotainment system [Kim Younsun et al., 2017]

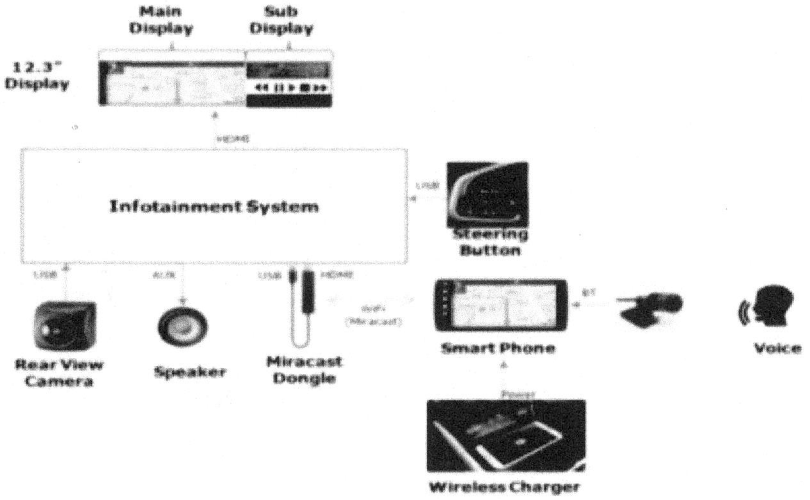

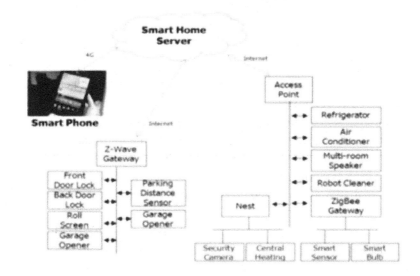

Figure 11. smart phone connectivity through cloud using IoT [Kim Younsun et al., 2017]

(2a) At the same time, the traffic infrastructure recognizes the situation by means of pattern recognition algorithms running in surveillance cameras and activates various security measures for this situation, e.g. For example, entering a road or locking an access road to do.

(3)   Portable sensors on the occupant receive central vehicle information and evaluate the health of the occupants.

(4)   After assessing the damage to the vehicle and the health of the occupants, the Central System shall inform the person concerned of: (i) the vehicle insurer where the location, insurance number and initial damage result from the information provided by different sensors. Information such as assessment is communicated; And (ii) rescue services that send accident information, including

Figure 12. Case Study [Juan Guerrero et al., 2018]

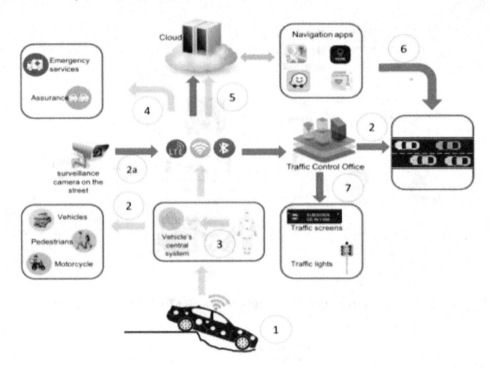

emergency services, but not only to passengers, the position of passengers in the vehicle and others, including major passenger signs.

(5)   All accident information generated by the vehicle's systems and protocols and road infrastructure will be sent in the cloud and stored and made available to the information system to provide other information and information to other drivers in real time.

(6)   Location services such as Google Maps, Apple Maps, Here We Go, and Waze may use information about new or alternative routes to avoid congestion or other accidents.

The central system sends a notification to the traffic infrastructure (traffic lights, warning screens, traffic signals) to send notifications and updates about the accident and to inform drivers and pedestrians about the situation.

REFERENCES

Abdelwahab, S., Hamdaoui, B., Guizani, M., & Znati, T. (2016). Replisom: disciplined tiny memory replication for massive IoT devices in LTE edge cloud. IEEE Internet of Things Journal, 3(3).

Alam, M., Fernandes, B., Almeida, J., Ferreira, J., & Fonseca, J. (2016). Integration of smart parking in distributed ITS architecture. *Proceedings of the 2016 International Conference on Open Source Systems & Technologies (ICOSST).* 10.1109/ICOSST.2016.7838582

Aslam, Rasheed, Shah, Rahim, Khan, Qasim, Qasim, Hassan, Khan, & Javaid. (2013). Energy optimization and Performance Analysis of Cluster Based Routing Protocols Extended from LEACH for WSNs. *International Journal of Modern Engineering Research, 3*(2).

Aslam, M., Shah, T., Javaid, N., Rahim, A., Rahman, Z., & Khan, Z. A. (2012). CEEC: Centralized energy efficient clustering a new routing protocol for WSNs. *Sensor, Mesh and Ad-Hoc Communications and Networks (SECON), 2012 9th Annual IEEE Communications Society Conference on IEEE.*

Aslam, N., Philips, W., Robertson, W., & Siva Kumar, S.H. (2011). A multi-criterion optimization technique for energy efficient cluster formation in Wireless Sensor networks. *Information Fusion, 12*(3).

Astarita, V., Vaiana, R., Iuele, T., Caruso, M. V., Vincenzo, P., & De Masi, F. (2014). 2014, "Automated Sensing System for Monitoring of Road Surface Quality by Mobile Devices. *Procedia: Social and Behavioral Sciences, 111*, 242–251. doi:10.1016/j.sbspro.2014.01.057

Atzori, Iera, & Morabito. (2010). The Internet of Things: A Survey. *Journal of Computer Networks, 54*(15).

Bandyopadhyay & Coyle. (2003). An Energy Efficient Hierarchical Clustering Algorithm for Wireless Sensor Networks. *IEEE INFOCOM.*

Bonomi, F., Milito, R., Natarajan, P., & Zhu, J. (2014). Fog Computing: A Platform for Internet of Things and Analytics. In Studies in Computational Intelligence, (vol. 546). Springer.

Bulumulle, G., & Bölöni, L. (2016). A study of the automobile blind-spots' spatial dimensions and angle of orientation on side-sweep accidents. *Proceedings of the 2016 Symposium on Theory of Modeling and Simulation (TMS-DEVS).*

Cai, H., & Lin, Y. (2011). Modelling of Operators' Emotion and Task Performance in a Virtual Driving Environment. *International Journal of Human-Computer Studies, 69*(9), 571–586. doi:10.1016/j.ijhcs.2011.05.003

Castanedo, F. (2013). A review of data fusion techniques. *Sci. World J.*

Chen, L., & Englund, C. (2016). A Survey. *IEEE Trans. Intell. Transport. Syst, 17*, 570–586.

Chen, L., Tseng, Y., & Syue, K. (2014). *Vehicular tracking and reporting by V2V communications. Surveillance on-the-road: Comput. Netw.*

Chen, Y., Shu, J., Zhang, S., Liu, L., & Sun, L. (2009). Data fusion in wireless sensor networks. *Electronic Commerce and Security, ISECS'09, 2.*

Dai, S., Jing, X., & Li, L. (2005). Research and Analysis on Routing Protocols for Wireless Sensor Networks. IEEE International Conference.

Dasarathy, B. V. (1997). *Sensor fusion potential exploitation-innovative architectures and illustrative applications. Proc. IEEE.*

Dehni, L., & Bennani, Y. (2005). LEA2C: low energy adaptive connectionist clustering for wireless sensor networks. In *International Workshop on Mobile Agents for Telecommunication Applications.* Springer.

Deng, Y., Hsu, D. F., Wu, Z., & Chu, C. H. (2012). Feature Selection and Combination for Stress Identification Using Correlation and Diversity. *Proceedings of the 12th International Symposium on Pervasive Systems, Algorithms and Networks*. 10.1109/I-SPAN.2012.12

Dolui, K., & Datta, S. K. (2017). Comparison of edge computing implementations: Fog computing, cloudlet and mobile edge computing. *Proceedings of the 2017 Global Internet of Things Summit, GIoTS 2017*, 1–6. 10.1109/GIOTS.2017.8016213

Dong, B., Wu, W., Yang, Z., & Li, J. (2016). Software Defined Networking Based On-Demand Routing Protocol in Vehicle Ad Hoc Networks. *Proceedings of the 12th International Conference on Mobile Ad-Hoc and Sensor Networks, MSN 2016*, 25. 10.1109/MSN.2016.041

Doolan, R., & Muntean, G.M. (2017). EcoTrec—A Novel VANET-Based Approach to Reducing Vehicle Emissions. *IEEE Trans. Intell. Transport. Syst.*

Dreiseitl, S., & Ohno-Machado, L. (2002). Logistic regression and artificial neural network classification models: a methodology review. *Journal of Biomedical Informatics*.

Durrant-Whyte, H. F. (1988). Sensor models and multisensor integration. *The International Journal of Robotics Research*, 7(6), 97–113. doi:10.1177/027836498800700608

Durrant-Whyte, H. F., & Stevens, M. (2001). Data fusion in decentralized sensing networks. *Proceedings of the 4th International Conference on Information Fusion*.

El Faouzi, N., & Klein, L.A. (2016). Data Fusion for ITS: Techniques and Research Needs. *Transport. Res. Procedia, 15*, 495–512.

Enami, Moghadam, & Dadashtabar. (2010). Neural Network Based Energy Efficiency In Wireless Sensor Networks: A Survey. *International Journal of Computer Science and Engineering Survey, 1*(1).

Enami, N., Moghadam, R. A., Dadashtabar, K., & Hoseini, M. (2010). Neural network based energy efficiency in wireless sensor networks. *International Journal of Computer Science and Engineering Survey, 1*(1), 39–53. doi:10.5121/ijcses.2010.1104

Farhady, Lee, & Nakao. (2015). Software-defined networking. *Computer Networks: The International Journal of Computer and Telecommunications Networking, 81*.

Fedele, R., Praticò, F. G., Carotenuto, R., & Giuseppe Della Corte, F. (2017). Instrumented infrastructures for damage detection and management. *Proceedings of the 2017 5th IEEE International Conference on Models and Technologies for Intelligent Transportation Systems (MT-ITS)*. 10.1109/MTITS.2017.8005729

Fong, A. C. M., Chan, C., Situ, L., & Fong, B. (2016). Wireless biosensing network for drivers' health monitoring. *Proceedings of the 2016 IEEE International Conference on Consumer Electronics (ICCE)*. 10.1109/ICCE.2016.7430600

Frenzel, L. (2018). *The Battle over V2V Wireless Technologies*. http://www.mwrf.com/systems/battle-over-v2v-wireless-technologies

Gojak, V., Janjatovic, J., Vukota, N., Milosevic, M., & Bjelica, M. Z. (2017). Informational bird's eye view system for parking assistance. *Proceedings of the 2017 IEEE 7th International Conference on Consumer Electronics-Berlin (ICCE-Berlin).* 10.1109/ICCE-Berlin.2017.8210604

Gond, S., & Gupta, N. (2012). Energy Efficient Deployment Techniques for Wireless Sensor Networks. *International Journal of Advanced Research in Computer Science and Software Engineering*, 2(7), 257–262.

Gruhn, H., Stöhr, D., Gövercin, M., & Glesner, S. (2013). Design and verification of a health-monitoring driver assistance system. *Proceedings of the 2013 7th International Conference on Pervasive Computing Technologies for Healthcare and Workshops.* 10.4108/icst.pervasivehealth.2013.252091

Hartenstein, H., & Laberteaux, K. P. (2010). *VANET: Vehicular Applications and Inter-Networking Technologies.* Wiley Online Library. doi:10.1002/9780470740637

He, Yan, & Xu. (2014). Developing Vehicular Data Cloud Services in the IoT Environment. *IEEE Transactions on Industrial Informatics.*

He, Z., Cao, J., & Liu, X. (2016). SDVN: Enabling rapid network innovation for heterogeneous vehicular communication. *IEEE Network*, 30(4). doi:10.1109/MNET.2016.7513858

Heinzelman, W., Chandrakasan, A., & Balakrishnan, H. (2000). Energy-efficient communication protocol for wireless microsensornetworks. In *System Sciences (HICSS '33) Proceedings of the 33rd Annual Hawaii International Conference on.* IEEE.

Heinzelman, W. R., Chandrakasan, A., & Balakrishnan, H. (2000). Energy-efficient communication protocol for wireless microsensor networks. In *System sciences, Proceedings of the 33rd annual Hawaii international conference on.* IEEE.

Hossain, E., Chow, G., & Leung, V. C. M. (2010). Vehicular telematics over heterogeneous wireless networks: A survey. *Computer Communications*, 33(7). doi:10.1016/j.comcom.2009.12.010

Hossan, A., Kashem, F. B., Hasan, M. M., Naher, S., & Rahman, M. I. (2016). A smart system for driver's fatigue detection, remote notification and semi-automatic parking of vehicles to prevent road accidents. *Proceedings of the 2016 International Conference on Medical Engineering, Health Informatics and Technology (MediTec).* 10.1109/MEDITEC.2016.7835371

Hu, Y. C., Patel, M., Sabella, D., Sprecher, N., & Young, V. (2015). *White paper: mobile edge computing a key technology towards 5G.* ETSI (European Telecommunications Standards Institute).

Huang, J., Zhang, T., & Metaxas, D. (2009). Learning with structured sparsity. *Proceedings of the International Conference on Machine Learning*, 417–424.

Intelligent Transport Systems (ITS). (2012). *Framework for public mobile networks in cooperative its (c-its)s.* Tech. Rep., European Telecommunications Standards Institute (ETSI), Palo Alto, CA.

James, L., & Nahl, D. (2000). Road Rage and Aggressive Driving: Steering Clear of Highway Warfare. Prometheus Books.

Jermsurawong, J., Ahsan, M. U., Haidar, A., Dong, H., & Mavridis, N. (2012). Car Parking Vacancy Detection and Its Application in 24-Hour Statistical Analysis. *Proceedings of the 2012 10th International Conference on Frontiers of Information Technology.* 10.1109/FIT.2012.24

Jiacheng, Haibo, Ning, Peng, Lin, & Xuemin. (2016). Software defined Internet of vehicles: architecture, challenges and solutions. *Journal of Communications and Information Networks, 1.*

Katsis, C. D., Katertsidis, N., Ganiatsas, G., & Fotiadis, D. E. (2008). *Toward Emotion Recognition in Car-Racing Drivers: A biosignal Processing Approach. IEEE Trans. Syst. Man Cybern. Part A Syst.*

Katzourakis, D. I., Lazic, N., Olsson, C., & Lidberg, M. R. (2015). *Driver Steering Override for Lane-Keeping Aid Using Computer-Aided Engineering. IEEE/ASME Trans. Mechatron.*

Kim, H., & Feamster, N. (2013). Improving network management with software defined networking. *IEEE Communications Magazine, 51*(2). doi:10.1109/MCOM.2013.6461195

Kim, S., Kim, J., Yi, K., & Jung, K. (2017). Detection and tracking of overtaking vehicle in Blind Spot area at night time. *IEEE International Conference on Consumer Electronics (ICCE)*, Las Vegas, NV.

Kim, Y., Oh, H., & Kang, S. (2017). Proof of Concept of Home IoT Connected Vehicles. *Sensors (Basel), 17*(6), 1289. doi:10.339017061289 PMID:28587246

Kyriakou, C., Christodoulou, S. E., & Dimitriou, L. (2016). Roadway pavement anomaly classification utilizing smartphones and artificial intelligence. *Proceedings of the 2016 18th Mediterranean Electrotechnical Conference (MELECON).* 10.1109/MELCON.2016.7495459

Lai, Y. K., Chou, Y. H., & Schumann, T. (2017). Vehicle detection for forward collision warning system based on a cascade classifier using adaboost algorithm. *Proceedings of the 2017 IEEE 7th International Conference on Consumer Electronics (ICCE).* 10.1109/ICCE-Berlin.2017.8210585

Lanatà, A., Valenza, G., Greco, A., Gentili, C., Bartolozzi, R., Bucchi, F., Frendo, F., & Scilingo, E. P. (2015). How the Autonomic Nervous System and Driving Style Change with Incremental Stressing Conditions During Simulated Driving. *IEEE Transactions on Intelligent Transportation Systems, 16*(3), 1505–1517. doi:10.1109/TITS.2014.2365681

Lecompte, D., & Gabin, F. (2012). Evolved multimedia broadcast/multicast service (eMBMS) in LTE-advanced: overview and Rel-11 enhancements. IEEE Communications, 50(11).

Lee, S., Yoo, J., & Chung, T. (2004). Distance-based energy efficient clustering for wireless sensor networks. *Local Computer Networks, 29th Annual IEEE International Conference.*

Li, H., Dong, M., & Ota, K. (2016). Control Plane Optimization in Software-Defined Vehicular Ad Hoc Networks. *IEEE Transactions on Vehicular Technology, 65*(10). doi:10.1109/TVT.2016.2563164

Lin, X., Sun, X., Ho, P.-H., & Shen, X. (2007). GSIS: A secure and privacy-preserving protocol for vehicular communications. *IEEE Transactions on Vehicular Technology, 56*(6).

Lin, Y., Nguyen, H. T., & Wang, C. (2017). Adaptive neuro-fuzzy predictive control for design of adaptive cruise control system. *Proceedings of the 2017 IEEE 14th International Conference on Networking, Sensing and Control (ICNSC).*

Liu, B., Jia, D., Wang, J., Lu, K., & Wu, L. (2015). Cloud-assisted safety message dissemination in VANET-cellular heterogeneous wireless network. IEEE Systems Journal.

Liu, K., Son, S. H., Lee, V. C. S., & Kapitanova, K. (2011). A token-based admission control and request scheduling in lane reservation systems. *Proceedings of the 14th International IEEE Conference on Intelligent Transportation Systems (ITSC)*. 10.1109/ITSC.2011.6082959

Liu, Y., Zeng, Q. A., & Wang, Y. H. (2014). *Data fusion in wireless sensor networks*. www.Journals.sagepub.com

Luan, T. H., Gao, L., Li, Z., Yang, W., Guiyi, S., & Sun, L. (2015). *Fog computing: focusing on mobile users at the edge, networking and internet architecture*. Networking and Internet Architecture.

Luo, F., Zhao, Y., & Yuan, Z. (2017). Fast and accurate vehicle detection by aspect ratio regression. *Proceedings of the 2017 Chinese Automation Congress (CAC)*. 10.1109/CAC.2017.8242943

Luo R.C., Yih C.-C., & Su K.L. (2002). Multisensor fusion and integration: Approaches, applications, and future research directions. *IEEE Sens. J.*

Manyika, J., & Durrant-Whyte, H. (1995). *Data Fusion and Sensor Management: A Decentralized Information-Theoretic Approach*. Prentice Hall.

McKeown, N., Anderson, T., & Balakrishnan, H. (2008). OpenFlow: Enabling innovation in campus networks. *Computer Communication Review*, *38*(2). doi:10.1145/1355734.1355746

Mehrabi, A., & Kim, K. (2015). Using a mobile vehicle for road condition surveillance by energy harvesting sensor nodes. *Proceedings of the 2015 IEEE 40th Conference on Local Computer Networks (LCN)*. 10.1109/LCN.2015.7366303

Meneguette, R. I., Bittencourt, L. F., & Madeira, E. R. M. (2013). A seamless flow mobility management architecture for vehicular communication networks. *Journal of Communications and Networks (Seoul)*, *15*(2). doi:10.1109/JCN.2013.000034

Mobile Edge Computing (MEC), ETSI, and Industry Specification Group (ISG). (2016). *White paper: mobile edge computing (MEC); framework and reference architecture*. ETSI (European Telecommunications Standards Institute).

Morgan, Y. L. (2010). Notes on DSRC & WAVE standards suite: Its architecture, design, and characteristics. *IEEE Communications Surveys and Tutorials*, *12*(4). doi:10.1109/SURV.2010.033010.00024

Niewolny, D. (2013). *How the Internet of Things is revolutionizing healthcare, Free scale Semiconductor*. http://www.freescale.com/healthcare

Oniga, S., & Suto, J. (2014). Human activity recognition using neural networks. *15th International Carpathian Control Conference - ICCC 2014*. 10.1109/CarpathianCC.2014.6843636

Padmavathi, G., Shanmugapriya, D., & Kalaivani, M. (2010). *A Study on Vehicle Detection and Tracking Using Wireless Sensor Networks*. WSN. https://m.scirp.org/papers/1385

Pu, L., Liu, Z., Meng, Z., Yang, X., Zhu, K., & Zhang, L. (2015). Implementing on-board diagnostic and GPS on VANET to safe the vehicle. *Proceedings of the 2015 International Conference on Connected Vehicles and Expo (ICCVE)*, 13–18. 10.1109/ICCVE.2015.64

Qi, G.-J., Tang, J., Zha, Z.-J., Chua, T.-S., & Zhang, H.-J. (2009). An efficient sparse metric learning in high-dimensional space via l1-penalized log determinant regularization. *Proceedings of the International Conference on Machine Learning.*

Qin, Y., Dong, M., Zhao, F., Langari, R., & Gu, L. (2015). Road profile classification for vehicle semi-active suspension system based on Adaptive Neuro-Fuzzy Inference System. *54th IEEE Conference on Decision and Control.* 10.1109/CDC.2015.7402428

Qu, L., Li, L., Zhang, Y., & Hu, J. (2009). PPCA-based missing data imputation for traffic flow volume: A systematical approach. *IEEE Trans. Intell. Transp. Syst.*

Rebolledo-Mendez, G., Reyes, A., Paszkowicz, S., Domingo, M. C., & Skrypchuk, L. (2014). *Developing a Body Sensor Network to Detect Emotions during Driving. IEEE Trans. Intell. Transport. Syst.*

Reyes, A., Barrado, C., & Guerrero, A. (2016). Communication technologies to design vehicle-to-vehicle and vehicle-to-infrastructures applications. *Latin American Applied Research*, *46*, 29–35.

Reyes-Muñoz, A., Domingo, M. C., López-Trinidad, M. A., & Delgado, J. L. (2016). Integration of Body Sensor Networks and Vehicular Ad-hoc Networks for Traffic Safety. *Sensors (Basel)*, *16*(1), 107. doi:10.339016010107 PMID:26784204

Rigas, G., Goletsis, Y., & Fotiadis, D.I. (2012). Real-time driver's stress event detection. *IEEE Trans. Intell. Transport. Syst.*

Safi, Q. K., Luo, S., Wei, C., Pan, L., & Chen, Q. (2017). Cloud-oriented secure and privacy-conscious parking information as a service using VANETs. *Computer Networks*, *124*, 33–45. doi:10.1016/j.comnet.2017.06.001

Salahuddin, M. A., Al-Fuqaha, A., & Guizani, M. (2015). Software-defined networking for rsu clouds in support of the internet of vehicles. IEEE Internet of Things Journal, 2(2). doi:10.1109/JIOT.2014.2368356

Sarvada, H., Nikhil, T. R., & Kulkarni, H. J. (2013). Identification of black spots and improvements to junctions in Bangalore city. *International Journal of Scientific Research (Ahmedabad, India)*, *2*(8).

Satyanarayanan, M., Bahl, P., Cáceres, R., & Davies, N. (2009). The case for VM-based cloudlets in mobile computing," pp. 14–23. *IEEE Pervasive Computing*, *8*(4), doi:10.1109/MPRV.2009.82

Satyanarayanan, M., Lewis, G., Morris, E., Simanta, S., Boleng, J., & Ha, K. (2013). The role of cloudlets in hostile environments. *IEEE Pervasive Computing*, *12*(4). doi:10.1109/MPRV.2013.77

Satyanarayanan, M., Schuster, R., & Ebling, M. (2015). "An open ecosystem for mobile-cloud convergence. *IEEE Communications Magazine*, *53*(3). doi:10.1109/MCOM.2015.7060484

Sengupta, S., Verma, S., Mull, S., & Paul, S. (2015). Comparative Study of Image Segmentation Using Variants of Self-Organizing Maps (SOM). *International Journal for Research in Emerging Science and Technology*, *2*(5).

Sharma, S., Sethi, D., & Bhattacharya, P. (2015). Artificial Neural Network based Cluster Head Selection in Wireless Sensor Network. *International Journal of Computers and Applications, 119*(4).

Shi, J., & Wu, J. (2017). Research on Adaptive Cruise Control based on curve radius prediction. *Proceedings of the 2017 2nd International Conference on Image, Vision and Computing (ICIVC).*

Simon, M., Schmidt, E. A., Kincses, W. E., Fritzsche, M., Bruns, A., Aufmuth, C., Bogdan, M., Rosenstiel, W., & Schrauf, M. (2011). EEG alpha spindle measures as indicators of driver fatigue under real traffic conditions. *Clinical Neurophysiology, 122*(6), 1168–1178. doi:10.1016/j.clinph.2010.10.044 PMID:21333592

Singh, R. K., Sarkar, A., & Anoop, C. S. (2016). A health monitoring system using multiple non-contact ECG sensors for automotive drivers. *Proceedings of the 2016 IEEE International Instrumentation and Measurement Technology Conference Proceedings.* 10.1109/I2MTC.2016.7520539

Smith, D., & Singh, S. (2016). Approaches to multisensor data fusion in target tracking: A survey. *IEEE Transactions on Knowledge and Data Engineering.*

Stallings. (2010). Software defined networks and openflow. *The Internet Protocol Journal, 16*(1).

Stallings, W. (2014). *Openflow switch specification.* Tech. Rep., Open Networking Foundation.

Tang, T., Lin, Z., & Zhang, Y. (2017). Rapid Forward Vehicle Detection Based on Deformable Part Model, *Proceedings of the 2017 2nd International Conference on Multimedia and Image Processing (ICMIP),* 27–31. 10.1109/ICMIP.2017.78

Thein, M. C. M., & Thein, T. (2010). An energy efficient cluster-head selection for wireless sensor networks. Intelligent systems, modelling and simulation (ISMS), 2010 international IEEE conference.

Truong, N. B., Lee, G. M., & Ghamri-Doudane, Y. (2015). Software defined networking-based vehicular Adhoc Network with Fog Computing. *Proceedings of the 14th IFIP/IEEE International Symposium on Integrated Network Management/International workshop on management of the future Internet.* 10.1109/INM.2015.7140467

Ultsch, A. (1993). Self-organizing neural networks for visualisation and classification. In Information and classification. Springer Berlin Heidelberg. doi:10.1007/978-3-642-50974-2_31

Vejlgaard, B., Lauridsen, M., Nguyen, H., Kovacs, I. Z., Mogensen, P., & Sorensen, M. (2017). Coverage and Capacity Analysis of Sigfox, LoRa, GPRS and NB-IoT. *Proceedings of the 2017 IEEE 85th Vehicular Technology Conference (VTC Spring).* 10.1109/VTCSpring.2017.8108666

Vermesan, O., Friess, P., & Furness, A. (2012). The Internet of Things 2012 New Horizons. Academic Press.

Vesanto, J. (1999). *SOM-based data visualization methods. Intelligent data analysis.* Volvo IntelliSafe System. https://www.volvocars.com/us/about/our-innovations/intellisafe

Wang, X., Wang, C., Zhang, J., Zhou, M., & Jiang, C. (2017). Improved rule installation for real-time query service in software-defined internet of vehicles. *IEEE Transactions on Intelligent Transportation Systems, 18*(2), 2017. doi:10.1109/TITS.2016.2543600

World Health Organization Report on Road Traffic Injury Prevention. (n.d.). https://apps.who.int/iris/bitstream/10665/42871/1/9241562609.pdf

Wu, X., & Zhu, X. (2008). Mining with noise knowledge: Error-aware data mining. *IEEE Trans. Syst. Man Cybern.*

Xu & Saadawi. (2001). Does the IEEE 802.11 MAC Protocol Work Well in Multihop Wireless Ad Hoc Networks. *IEEE Communications Magazine.*

Yang, J. Y., Chou, L. D., Li, Y. C., Lin, Y. H., Huang, S. M., Tseng, G., Wang, T. W., & Lu, S. P. (2010). Prediction of short-term average vehicular velocity considering weather factors in urban VANET environments. *Proceedings of the International Conference on Machine Learning and Cybernetics.* 10.1109/ICMLC.2010.5580743

Younis, M., & Akkaya, K. (2008). Strategies and techniques for node placement in wireless sensor networks: A survey. *Journal of Ad Hoc Networks, 6*(4).

Zhang, D., Yu, F. R., Wei, Z., & Boukerche, A. (2016). *Trust-based secure routing in software-defined vehicular ad hoc networks.* Networking and Internet Architecture.

Zhang, J., Wang, F., Wang, K., Lin, W., Xu, X., & Chen, C. (2011). Data-Driven Intelligent Transportation System: A survey. *IEEE Transactions on Intelligent Transportation Systems, 12*(4), 1624–1639. doi:10.1109/TITS.2011.2158001

Chapter 9
Routing in Vehicular Delay Tolerant Networks:
A Comparision

Anamika Chauhan
Delhi Technological University, India

Kapil Sharma
Delhi Technological University, India

Alka Aggarwal
Delhi Technological University, India

ABSTRACT

With the ever-escalating amount of vehicular traffic activity on the roads, the efficient management of traffic and safety of the drivers and passengers is of paramount gravity. Vehicular ad-hoc networks (VANETs) have emerged as the systems where vehicles would be perceptive of the locality and can supply the driver with required inputs to take necessary actions to alleviate the various issues. The system is designed to detect and identify essential traffic events and inform all concerned entities and take appropriate action. The characteristics of VANET are the topology is highly mobile, depends on city infrastructure, and the high speed of vehicles. These challenges result in frequent disruption of connections, long delays in delivering the messages. The challenges are overcome through the vehicular delay-tolerant network (VDTN) routing protocols are used that can facilitate communication under these network challenges. In this chapter, the authors evaluate the effect of the node density and message sizes on the performance of the various VDTN routing protocols.

DOI: 10.4018/978-1-7998-2764-1.ch009

INTRODUCTION

Now days the internet acts as the backbone network for most systems that require communication. The goal of a communication network is to deliver a message from the source to the destination successfully. The success of end to end delivery is dependent on finding the best possible path or route between the ends, and therefore a good routing strategy is the key to efficient communication. Routing in the internet uses a connected graph where there is always a path or route from a node to every other node. It can have single path or multiple paths to a destination. To communicate using the internet it is necessary and sufficient to have at least one device element of the network to have access to internet. If, at any point in time either the sender, receiver or the device connected to internet have no connection, then the message will get dropped. As an example, TCP (Fall, 2003) is a widely used connection oriented protocol, in this before starting the conversation, the sender and receiver must establish an end to end connection. TCP sends the data using IP addresses and port numbers of the sender and destination. To send the data TCP uses three way hand shake procedure. The network have continues connectivity, very low packet dropping rate, stable network topology and low packet delivery delay.

But as vehicles that are constantly in motion, they have no stable end to end path, but only have intermittent connectivity among nodes. Thus Vehicular networks have unstable topology and frequent disruption of the connections. Traditional internet works poorly in such a challenged environment. Vehicular Delay Tolerant Network(VDTN) which are adaptation of DTN can provide communication in this type of challenged network. Vehicular networks can have large and unpredictable delay in delivery of messages. VDTN have very low delivery probability and have limited resources. Communication range between the nodes is not long enough to connect all the nodes. Contacts between the nodes are for uncertain and varied durations. So VDTN uses the contact between nodes as the opportunity to deliver the messages. DTN network has many routing approaches. Most of them are replication based.

The network in challenging environment may or may not have continuous connections between the nodes of the network. But data is required to get transferred to the destination even when there is, not a single path leading to destination from source. In order to transfer the data, data needs to keep flowing until it reaches the destination. And to keep data flowing nodes need to interact with each other to transfer the data they have to each other (Keränen, 2009). VDTN can help in a great and efficient way to keep that data flowing in vehicular mobile challenged networks. DTN can provide an opportunistic network with mobile nodes such as a network built of moving sensors on pedestrians, animals and vehicles (Juang, 2002).

DTN overcomes all the problems like sporadic connectivity, prolonged and unpredictable delays, uneven data rates and high data rates by using Store-Carry-Forward Message Switching (Keränen, 2009). The whole packet (all complete blocks of application data) or the fragments of these messages are transferred or forwarded from a buffer storage of a node to the buffer storage of another node, on a path that will lastly reach to the destination. Due to frequent disruptions of the network, nodes need to communicate during the opportunistic contacts. Opportunistic contacts are the unscheduled contacts (Burleigh, 2007). DTN uses this property (mobility) of nodes as an opportunity for delivering messages between source end and the destination end by passing it on to any other nodes that comes within the range of communication of that node (Mealling, 2002). The mobile nodes then carry messages to help network to deliver them to destination. With growth in internet communication technology and advent of even 5G communication, vehicular networks will be able to use mobility to their advantage (Agrawal, 2016), (Agrawal, 2017), (Agrawal, 2018), (Agrawal, 2019).

VDTN OVERVIEW

DTN Architecture

The DTN architecture implements a new protocol that is bundle protocol (Burleigh, 2007). This protocol implements the store-carry-forward mechanism of message switching. As shown in figure 1, Bundle protocol is implemented above the lower layer protocols (Fall, 2003). It helps in tying the lower layer protocols together which in turn helps the application layer in communicating across lower layer protocols in a challenged environment.

This protocol stores and forwards the received or generated bundles among nodes. Throughout a DTN, only a single bundle protocol is used. That helps the lower layer protocols to work in each communication environment. The convergence layer protocol stack sits below the bundle protocol, this layer support exchange of the bundles (Mealling, 2002). The convergence layer interface is the boundary between the bundle protocol and the lower-layer protocols.

Figure 1. DTN protocol stack

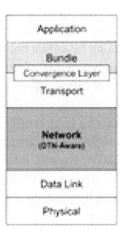

DTN Challenges

1. **Buffer size:** To overcome the issue of the sporadic connectivity, the nodes in the network have to save the messages or data in their buffer space until they find a node to transfer the message to or they find a better node to relay the message to. This delay that occur while nodes are waiting for their next candidate to transfer the messages to can be of few seconds, minutes, hours or days. It means that the nodes of the network need a large buffer capacity to be able to handle the messages waiting for getting relayed or delivered (Pan, 2013). It is too difficult to find the ideal buffer size so that no messages get dropped. Deciding the perfect buffer size also depends on the rate of messages generation. It is more difficult to find the buffer size that suits for all the applications. So, there are two options left, one is to either consider unlimited buffer space or the second option is to have an application specific buffer size.

2. **Contact capacity:** It specifies the data that can be forwarded or exchanged between the nodes during a contact before getting connection down (Sterbenz, 2002). In case of dynamic VDTN, usually the duration of contact at each encounter is short and limited. On this factor of the network, the performance of network depends largely as there can be scenarios in which the nodes have relatively small data to exchange than the capacity of the network to exchange data during the given or may be average contact phase of that network or nodes may have a large set of data to be exchanged than the capacity of network it can exchange data during the given or may be average contact phase of that network.

3. **Mobility:** The speed of the nodes with which they are moving may vary with different irregularities. The movement speed can be constant or variable (Juang, 2002). If the environment is highly dynamic then it may cause more frequent disruption of the connections and lower contact capacity than the less dynamic environments. The mobility of the nodes depends on the environment. Many routing protocols have been designed for different types of the mobility. The mobility can be classified into different types depending on how predictable it is. The predictable movement of the objects, helps in making the DTN routing algorithm perform efficiently by creating their schedules. Another instance of mobility is human or bus movements, their overall journey may be regular but their start and end time may vary depending on traffic or other obstructions (Chaintreau, 2007). The mobility schedule of these types of instances is not precise because of irregular traffic and other conditions. They show an implicit schedules of activities as there is no rigid time of the arrival of the bus or of a person reaching his office but their schedules are regular (Juang, 2002). That means the schedules are implicit but regular. So, to improve efficiency of the routing algorithms the mobility of the nodes and the pattern of the regularity of schedules can be observed to make decisions.

4. **Processing power and energy:** There is a large range of devices that can be used in DTN. They can be attached to people, animals or vehicles to transfer the data to their destination or to collect the data for study purpose (Juang, 2002). Usually these devices are small in size and they have limited power to process data and to gather it. Therefore, the DTN nodes cannot run a complex routing algorithm at each contact especially when the contact duration is short. As complex routing algorithm will consume more energy in processing.

ROUTING IN DTN

Routing is a challenging task due to lack of network topological information. Consequently, store-carry-forward mechanism is used in DTN to help routing amongst the mobile nodes. Routing algorithms helps the nodes of the network on making the best forwarding decision (Jones, 2007). There are some protocols that make simple decision to deliver the data to nodes which are reachable or in communication range for example epidemic, first contact (Vahdat, 2000). While other protocols make complex decisions by using the limited information they have it can be distance between nodes, mobility of nodes, energy remaining in the nodes, the buffer space available in the node or the number of copies to replicate. The routing decision depends on either some spatial or temporal condition (Small, 2005). It has been one of the main topics that has kept attracting research. Performance of a routing algorithm may vary largely by the some factors like the density of the network, mobility of nodes, distance between the source end and the destination end nodes and the amount and quality of information that nodes has. This is the reason that the forwarding strategy of the routing the protocols in DTN needs to be in accordance to the environment, they need to be adaptive to the requirement of network and should cover all the most possible scenarios that can happen in that environment. Till the date a number of routing protocols have been proposed by different researchers. According to the working of the routing protocols and the information they use foe making decision, they can be classified in two types. The first one is the flooding based routing protocols and the other one is estimation based routing protocols (Jones, 2007). The principal of flooding based routing protocols is replicating the messages and forwarding or relaying it to as many nodes or may be all nodes that has been in contact with the node that is carrying the message until the message reaches the destination. Flooding approach increases the chances of message delivery to destination. But it also uses a lot of network resource that causes the wastage of network resources. Estimation based routing protocols (Keränen, 2009)used kind of flooding approach but in limited way. These types of protocols try to reduce the flooding in the network by using the available local or global information to select the next best link to relay the message to. Below the detailed information of these types of routing approaches with some example has been given.

- **Direct Delivery Routing Protocol:** Direct Delivery routing protocol is one of the simplest routing protocols of DTN to send the data from source end to destination end. It is like a debased form of flooding in which the nodes tries to forward the message to minimum number of nodes (Keränen, 2009). This routing protocol will forward the message only if the source node and the destination node are in direct contact. Or we can say that the routing the message using Direct delivery routing protocol will be successful only if the source and the destination nodes are neighbours or are only just one-hop away from each other . Direct delivery routing protocol makes no relays because each message is delivered by the source node only. In the pros of this protocol is that it uses minimum amount of resources like buffer, energy and the bandwidth of the network (Juang, 2002). Because the intermediate nodes are not receiving message from other nodes to deliver them to some other node. So energy used in receiving and transmitting the message to other nodes is saved. And so is the buffer space and the bandwidth. But on other hand while counting for cons, this protocol limits the opportunities to deliver the message to the destination. Because this protocol is allowing only the original sender to deliver the message to destination. That causes a large delivery delay, data loss and delivery probability. Mostly Direct delivery protocol is used for comparing the lowest overhead ratio to other more practical routing protocols.

- **First Contact Routing Protocol:** First Contact routing Protocol is just as simple as the direct delivery routing protocol and in fact it uses the direct delivery strategy for delivering the message (Small, 2005). The sender node will create only one copy of the message and will relay it to the next node in which it comes in contact with. After that, no other node will replicate or relay the same message. And then this protocol follows the direct delivery strategy to deliver the message to the destination (Fall, 2003). So if the destination ever comes into the communication range of the relayed node or the sender node then the message will get successfully delivered. This protocol performed better than the direct delivery routing protocol in terms of the delivery probability as it is using more resources than the direct delivery routing protocol. Although this protocol makes a successful attempt in increasing the delivery probability while keeping the overhead and the use of resources to limited use, but it still shows a great scope of improvement.

- **Epidemic Routing protocol:** The Epidemic routing protocol is also a simplest but also a fastest routing protocol of DTN. The nodes that use this routing protocol replicate the messages and relay them to every node that comes in its path (Vahdat, 2000). Likewise, the node that receives that message will exhibit the same behavior. The nodes keep a summary vector, which helps in discarding the messages that are already stored in the nodes' buffer. This protocol follows the pure flooding approach as it is flooding the messages to all the nodes that are in communication range until it gets delivered to the destination. This protocol assumes that the messages are of small size and the network has unlimited resources like buffer capacity, energy and the network bandwidth. That's why the nodes keep sending their summary vector to other nodes on each contact. This protocol trades the high delivery probability at the cost of nodes and network resources. As this protocol is disseminating the messages to all possible paths, it decreases the delay of messages getting delivered to last destination. It also decreases the latency which is the time of a message from getting created at source node to getting delivered to destination node. Even though we say that the protocol keep flooding the message until it reaches the destination but the fact is that the destination node will not relay the message to any other node but the other nodes who still have this message and is not the destination node will keep relaying that message to other nodes until it get dropped from the buffer or get aborted because of some reasons. It provides the upper bound on delivery probability and delivery delay to compare the performance of other protocols.

- **ProPHET Routing Protocol**: ProPHET uses history of encounters (Lindgren, 2004) with other nodes to deliver messages to destination. It has statistical property that is used to find the next node to send messages. This protocol uses delivery predictability and transitivity. Each node maintains a delivery probability table that shows the probability of a message to get delivered to destination (Lindgren, 2004). Whenever nodes meet, they exchange their delivery predictability table and update their delivery probability table. Transitivity is, if a node X frequently encounters node Y and node Y frequently encounters node Z then node Z is a good relay to deliver message to node X. As each node calculates the delivery predictability for all known destination nodes where $P(x,y) \in [0,1]$. To calculate delivery predictability where a node encounter other node:

$$P(x,y) = P(x,y)_{old} + \left(1 - P(x,y)_{old}\right) \times P_{init} \tag{1}$$

Where P_{init} [2, 3] is initial Predictability and $P_{init}[0,1]$. So, whenever node x encounter node y, they exchange their delivery predictability tables to update their delivery predictabilities. The recommended value for P_{init} is 0.75.

If node x has not encountered node y for a long time then node x will update its delivery predictability by using following formula:

$$P(x,y) = P(x,y)_{old} \times \gamma^{k} \tag{2}$$

Where γ is aging constant and $\gamma \in [0,1]$ and k is aging factor that depict the time that has been elapsed since the last encounter.

Next equation shows the effect of transitivity on delivery predictability. Transitivity (Grasic, 2011) is, if any node x encounters another node y frequently and that node y encounters any other node z frequently, then node z is a good relay to deliver message to node x. Where $\beta \in [0,1]$, it is scaling constant that depicts the transitivity impact on delivery predictability.

$$P(x,y) = P(x,y)_{old} + \left(1 - P(x,y)_{old}\right) \times P(x,y) \times P(y,z) \times \beta \qquad (3)$$

This protocol assumes that the bandwidth is unlimited so time taken to deliver messages is ignored. The transitivity property decreases the message dropping rate and it also helps in decreasing the time a message waste in queue of a node. It lowers the load and the pressure of a node.

- **Spray and Wait routing protocol**: The spray and wait protocol (Spyropoulos, 2005)reduces the flooding while using the combination of epidemic and direct delivery routing protocol. This protocol replicates a fixed number L, of copies of messages. This protocol have two versions of it, vanilla and the binary, they both differ in the way they disperse the L number of copies of the messages in their spray phase. The vanilla version of this protocol disseminates the L copies of the message to first L different nodes that has been encountered while the binary version of this protocol disseminates the half of the L copies of messages to very first encountered node and other copies of the message to very second node that is encountered by the sending node. And then the receiving nodes repeat this process until the message reaches to the destination. This is the working of the protocol in its first phase that is spray phase. The second phase of the protocol is wait phase. The working of the both versions of the protocol is same in this phase of the protocol. In this phase, when the relaying and the source nodes of the network are left with only one copy of the message then they enter into the wait phase in which the message is transferred by the node by using the direct delivery strategy in which, the node carrying the message will deliver the message to destination by itself only. So the node will carry the message until either it reaches the destination or TTL expires. This routing protocol solves the problem of the epidemic routing protocol of unbounded replication of the messages. It also reduces the use of the network bandwidth by L. The disadvantage of this routing protocol is the long delivery delays and may be the node to which the message has been relayed may never be able to make it to the destination node.

SIMULATION AND RESULT

For the simulation of this work, ONE Simulator is used. The simulation time was set to 43200s which is 12 hrs. For simulation six node groups were defined. Each node group can have specific settings. For evaluating the performance based on message size, total nodes are 126. Group 1, 2 and 3 have 40 nodes and other three groups have 2 nodes each. But for evaluating the performance based on the node density, number of nodes in group 3, 4 and 6 will remain same for each scenario but the number of nodes in group 1, 2 and 3 are changing for each scenario but each group will have same number of nodes. The nodes in each group are increasing for every next scenario. The number of nodes for 1st, 2nd, 3rd, 4th and 5th scenario are 40, 60, 80, 100, 120 and 150 in each group from 1 to 3. The nodes in group 1 to 3 can go along all the paths of the map. Such nodes can be used to specify pedestrians. Group 1 consist of pedestrian nodes. Group 2 uses only route 1 which is roads. Group 2 is for vehicles that can travel only on roads. Group 3 is of pedestrians. Other groups are used for the trams. The mobility model used for the simulation is ShortestPathMapBasedMovement. In this simulation one new message is generated for every 25-35 seconds. Table 1. Shows the parameters used for the simulation of the protocols.

Table 1. Simulation parameters

Parameters	Values
Simulation area	4500*3400
Simulation time	43200
Mobility model	ShortestPathMapBasedMovement
TTL	300
Buffer size	5mb
Transmission range	10
No. Of nodes	126
Bundle creation rate	25 to 35 seconds
Bundle size	500kb - 1mb

Figure 2 shows the effect of node density on the delivery rate for each protocol. It can be seen that the delivery rate of first contact, spray and wait protocols are increasing on increasing the number of nodes while the delivery rate of other protocols is decreasing as on increasing the number of nodes the overhead in the network will also increase because of the flooding. So delivery probability is decreasing for other protocols.

Figure 2. Delivery Probability As Per Number Of Nodes

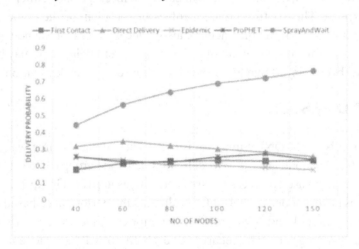

Figure 3 shows the effect of node density on overhead in the network. It is observed that the overhead is increasing for each protocol on increasing the node density. As on flooding each node will further replicate the messages which will increase the traffic on the network that will result, more overhead in the network.

Latency is the total time from message generation at the source to the finally receiving the message at destination node. It should be minimum to lower the delivery delay. As it can be observed from the figure 4 shown below that the latency is decreasing for routing protocols. But for first contact and spray & wait routing protocol, it is increasing.

Figure 3. Overhead Ratio As Per Node Density

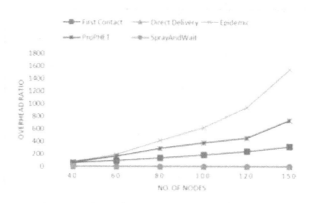

Figure 4. Latency Average As Per Node Density

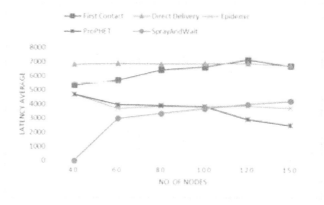

Figure 5 shows the effect of message size on the delivery rate of each protocol. As it can be seen that the delivery rate is decreasing for each routing protocol on increasing the message size.

Figure 5. Delivery Probability On Changing Message Size

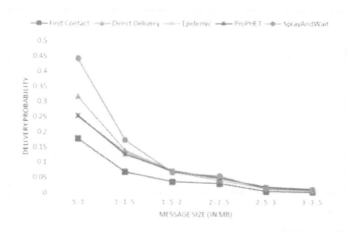

Figure 6 Shows the effect of message size on overhead in network for each protocol. Overhead is increasing for each protocol on increasing the message size.

Figure 6. Overhead Ratio As Per Message Size

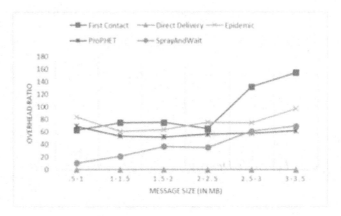

Figure 7 shows the effect of message size on latency of each protocol.

Figure 7. Latency Average As Per Message Size

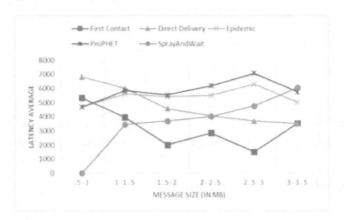

FUTURE RESEARCH DIRECTIONS

A lot can be done to further improve the algorithms. As observed, there is trade-off between the delivery probability and the resources. If the allocated resources are increased such as buffer space, TTL and energy then it will surely increase the delivery probability of the system. But there is a limit to these resources depending on the environment of the network and the application. For further improvement, delivery probability can be improved while keeping the use of resources to minimum. To improve the routing protocols researchers need to think about the strategy that will keep the use of resources to minimum while increasing the performance of the network and the retaining low overhead in the network.

CONCLUSION

In this work, authors have evaluated the performance of five routing protocols based on the effect of the message size and the node density. For the evaluation of the protocols, authors have considered the delivery probability, overhead ratio and the latency average as the parameter metrics. The performance showed:

- Effect of node density:
  1. Delivery probability decreases with the increase of number of nodes in the network for each protocol except for first contact and the spray and wait routing protocol.
  2. Overhead ratio increases for each protocol.
  3. Latency average is decreasing for each protocol except for first contact and spray and wait for which it is increasing.
- Effect of message size:
  1. Delivery probability is decreasing on increasing the message size for each protocol.
  2. Overhead is increasing on increasing the message size for each protocol.
  3. The behaviour of Latency average is different for each protocol on increasing the message size. For spray and wait, it is increasing while for direct delivery and epidemic, it is decreasing on increasing the message size.

ACKNOWLEDGMENT

Acknowledgment to Delhi Technological University and Dept of IT, DTU.

This research received no specific grant from any funding agency in the public, commercial, or not-for-profit sectors.

REFERENCES

Agrawal, S. K. (2016). 5G Millimeter Wave (mmWave) communication system with software defined radio (SDR). *Proceedings of the International Conference on Recent Trends in Engineering & Science (ICRTES-16)*.

Agrawal, S. K. (2016). 5G millimeter wave (mmWave) communications. In *3rd International Conference on Computing for Sustainable Global Development (INDIACom)* (pp. 3630-3634). IEEE.

Agrawal, S. K. (2017). Software Defined Millimeter Wave 5th Generation Communications System. *Application and Theory of Computer Technology, 2*(1), 46-56.

Agrawal, S. K. (2018). *Intelligent Software Defined Atmospheric Effect Processing for 5th Generation (5G) Millimeter Wave (MMWave)*. Communication System. doi:10.5815/ijwmt.2018.02.02

Agrawal, S. K. (2019). 5th generation millimeter wave wireless communication propagation losses dataset for indian metro cities based on corresponding weather conditions. Data in Brief, 23.

Burgess, J. G. (2006). *MaxProp: Routing for Vehicle-Based Disruption-Tolerant Networks* (Vol. 6). Infocom.

Burleigh, S. &. (2007). *Bundle protocol specification*. IETF Request for Comments RFC 5050.

Cao, Y. (2012). Routing in delay/disruption tolerant networks: A taxonomy, survey and challenges. *IEEE Communications Surveys & Tutorials, 15*(2), 654-677.

Chaintreau, A. H. (2007). Impact of human mobility on opportunistic forwarding algorithms. IEEE Transactions on Mobile Computing, 6, 606-620. doi:10.1109/TMC.2007.1060

Daly, E. M. (2007). Social network analysis for routing in disconnected delay-tolerant manets. In *Proceedings of the 8th ACM international symposium on Mobile ad hoc networking and computing* (pp. 32-40). ACM. 10.1145/1288107.1288113

Fall, K. (2003). A delay-tolerant network architecture for challenged internets. In *Proceedings of the 2003 conference on Applications, technologies, architectures, and protocols for computer communications* (pp. 27-34). ACM. 10.1145/863955.863960

Grasic, S. D. (2011). The evolution of a DTN routing protocol-PRoPHETv2. In *Proceedings of the 6th ACM workshop on Challenged networks* (pp. 27-30). ACM. 10.1145/2030652.2030661

Hui, P. C. (2010). Bubble rap: Social-based forwarding in delay-tolerant networks. *IEEE Transactions on Mobile Computing, 10*(11), 1576-1589.

Jones, E. P., Li, L., Schmidtke, J. K., & Ward, P. A. S. (2007). Practical routing in delay-tolerant networks. *IEEE Transactions on Mobile Computing, 6*(8), 943–959. doi:10.1109/TMC.2007.1016

Juang, P. O. (2002). Energy-efficient computing for wildlife tracking: Design tradeoffs and early experiences with ZebraNet. ACM SIGARCH Computer Architecture News, 30(5), 96-107. doi:10.1145/605397.605408

Keränen, A. J. (2009). The ONE simulator for DTN protocol evaluation. In *Proceedings of the 2nd international conference on simulation tools and techniques* (p. 55). ICST (Institute for Computer Sciences, Social-Informatics and Telecommunications Engineering). 10.4108/ICST.SIMUTOOLS2009.5674

LeBrun, J. C. (2005). Knowledge-based opportunistic forwarding in vehicular wireless ad hoc networks. In *2005 IEEE 61st Vehicular Technology Conference* (pp. 2289-2293). IEEE. 10.1109/VETECS.2005.1543743

Lindgren, A. A. (2004). Probabilistic routing in intermittently connected networks. In *International Workshop on Service Assurance with Partial and Intermittent Resources* (pp. 239-254). Springer. 10.1007/978-3-540-27767-5_24

Lu, R. L. (2010). Spring: A social-based privacy-preserving packet forwarding protocol for vehicular delay tolerant networks. In 2010 Proceedings IEEE INFOCOM (pp. 1-9). IEEE.

McMahon, A. &. (2009). Delay-and disruption-tolerant networking. *IEEE Internet Computing, 13*(6), 82-87.

Mealling, M. (2002). *Report from the Joint W3C/IETF URI Planning Interest Group: Uniform Resource Identifiers (URIs), URLs, and Uniform Resource Names (URNs): Clarifications and Recommendations*. RFC 3305.

Musolesi, M. (2008). Car: context-aware adaptive routing for delay-tolerant mobile networks. *IEEE Transactions on Mobile Computing, 8*(2), 246-260.

Pan, D. R., Ruan, Z., Zhou, N., Liu, X., & Song, Z. (2013). A comprehensive-integrated buffer management strategy for opportunistic networks. *EURASIP Journal on Wireless Communications and Networking, 2013*(1), 103. doi:10.1186/1687-1499-2013-103

Pentland, A. F. (2004). Daknet: Rethinking connectivity in developing nations. *Computer, 37*(1), 78-83.

Pereira, P. R.-P. (2011). From delay-tolerant networks to vehicular delay-tolerant networks. *IEEE Communications Surveys & Tutorials, 14*(4), 1166-1182.

Sharma, D. K. (2016). A machine learning-based protocol for efficient routing in opportunistic networks. *IEEE Systems Journal, 12*(3), 2207-2213.

Small, T. a. (2005). Resource and performance tradeoffs in delay-tolerant wireless networks. In *Proceedings of the 2005 ACM SIGCOMM workshop on Delay-tolerant networking. ACM.* 10.1145/1080139.1080144

Spyropoulos, T. P. (2005). Spray and wait: an efficient routing scheme for intermittently connected mobile networks. In *Proceedings of the 2005 ACM SIGCOMM workshop on Delay-tolerant networking* (pp. 252-259). ACM. 10.1145/1080139.1080143

Sterbenz, J. P. (2002). Survivable mobile wireless networks: issues, challenges, and research directions. In *Proceedings of the 1st ACM workshop on Wireless security* (pp. 31-40). ACM. 10.1145/570681.570685

Vahdat, A. a. (2000). *Epidemic routing for partially connected ad hoc networks.* Academic Press.

KEY TERMS AND DEFINITIONS

Bundle: A contiguous series of the data blocks is known as bundle where each bundle contains sufficient information to allow the application to make progress that individual data block may not contain.

Effectiveness and Efficiency: While retaining the limited resources (buffer space, energy and bandwidth), the effectiveness of any routing algorithm is to achieve maximum and sufficient delivery probability keeping delivery delay within range or minimum, and for efficiency keeping the network overhead to lowest.

QoS Awareness: For QoS based applications, the routing algorithms should prioritize the messages according to the application.

Scalability: For scalability, routing algorithm should work effectively in sparse and dense, both type of networks.

Chapter 10
Energy Harvesting for Wireless Sensor Nodes Using Rectenna

Sanjeev Kumar

Ambedkar Institute of Advanced Communication Technologies and Research, India

Jyotsna Sharma

Ambedkar Institute of Advanced Communication Technologies and Research, India

Arvind Kumar

Ambedkar Institute of Advanced Communication Technologies and Research, India

ABSTRACT

Wireless sensor nodes generally operate using energy from source line batteries, which need to be replaced or recharge from time to time. The connection of electromagnetic energy to DC energy, which is called radiofrequency (RF) energy harvesting, is one of the best techniques to act as an energy source for this equipment. An ambient amount of RF energy is present in our environment radiated from numerous sources so that it can act as a much predictable source of energy as compared to other techniques of energy harvesting. This system eliminates the periodic replacement of energy batteries for these sensor nodes. Despite the enormous RF energy present in the environment, the power per unit area is quite low. Hence, the major barrier is to increase the output of the rectifier circuit, even though the power density is low.

INTRODUCTION

Wireless sensor nodes generally operate using energy from source line batteries which needs to be replaced or recharge from time to time. Connection of electromagnetic energy to DC energy which is called Radio frequency (RF) energy harvesting is one of the best techniques to act as energy source to these equipments. Ambient amount of RF energy is present in our environment radiated from numerous sources so it can act as much predictable source of energy as compared to other techniques of energy harvesting. This system eliminates the periodic replacement of energy batteries for these sensor nodes.

DOI: 10.4018/978-1-7998-2764-1.ch010

Despite the enormous RF energy present in environment, the power per unit area is quite low. Hence, the major barrier is to increase the output of rectifier circuit even though the power density is low.

Different antenna designs are placed forward for higher efficiencies, line dipole, wide band and so on. Circular patch antenna provides higher gain for a given size of an antenna. Though wideband antennas provide higher efficiency by reception of larger amount of RF energy but impedance mismatching and lower output voltage may occur as compared to single band antenna. Diode in the rectifier circuit operates on the basis of frequency and input power levels, hence the rectifying effect of diode have impedance mismatch and lower output voltage in wide band antennas. Hence, to harvest more and more energy from environment, an array antenna is employed in this paper based on superposition of energy from each antenna in the form of exponentials.

The gain of antenna is ratio of intensity of given antenna in given direction to radiation intensity of isotropic antenna.

$$G = \frac{\grave{E}(\theta, \cancel{E})}{\omega_r / 4\pi} \quad \text{---} \tag{1}$$

Where ψ (θ, φ) is intensity of given antenna and ω_r is the power radiated by isotropic antenna.

1. Related work

"Wireless ambient radio power". TV, radio, cellular and Wi-Fi transmitters in our environment provides with huge energy. It is possible to harvest and store the energy signals to be used in various applications. It is four step procedure i.e. electromagnetic wave incident on antenna providing excitation current, rectification of resulting power, optimal voltage and current conversion with last stage of energy storage with use of capacitors for sensors (Sample, 2013).

For IoT thing environment, wireless sensor nodes are required to be constructed but we need to replace batteries which make its economic prospective weak. Power harvested from environment is very low to be used for exciting the sensor nodes. They provide power of range from 0- 80 nw which depends upon frequency of antenna in case of loop and spiral antennas. So the need of system is to increase the power output. This power can be increased by use of antenna array system. When antenna are arranged in array, mutual coupling exist between them. Mutual coupling effects the distribution of current on antennas. Impedance is governed by this current which eventually affects the power of system. The mutual coupling phenomena affects the power in two ways i.e. one positive and the other negative which depends on the nature of equivalent impedance of circuit when coupling is considered. Spacing of antenna with range equal to d/λ<1 increase the mutual coupling effect whereas the range of d/λ>1decreases the mutual coupling Mutual coupling provides an advantage of increasing the power of system when the equivalent impedance of system consist of capacitive reactance .Around 0.55λ spacing provides 1.5 times more power as compared to uncoupled power (Kim, 2016).

Due to long distance between the transmitter and the receiving antenna there are chances of power loss in harvesting system so the objective of this paper was to minimize the loss due to distance. Therefore, antenna array was employed to increase the power gain of the system. The bandwidth of the system increased up to 11% (Keyrouz, 2012).

In (Nayna, 2014) the chosen frequency was 10 GHz for the various applications. A rectangular patch antenna shows about 3dB higher return loss as compared to circular patch antenna. An improved VSWR is shown by rectangular patch antenna of value 1.18 as compared to circular patch antenna of value 1.27. However, the bandwidth offered by circular patch antenna is higher as compare to rectangular antenna with almost 8% higher value and nearly 2dB lower power level of side lobe. The circular and rectangular patch antennas are shown in fig1 and fig2.

Figure 1. Rectangular Patch Antenna

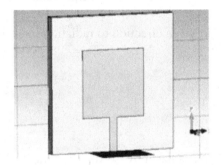

Figure 2. Circular Patch Antenna

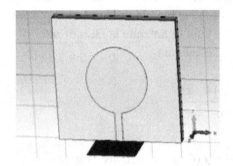

"Realization of efficient RF energy harvesting circuits employing different matching techniques" Matching networks can be designed in two ways i.e. with lumped elements and another is with distributed elements. Lumped consist of elements like resistor, inductor and capacitor whereas distributed has micro strip lines (Agarwal, 2014).

2. Methodology and Concepts

2.1 Radiation from the Hertzian Dipole

An infinitesimally small current element is called the hertz dipole. A hertzian dipole is 'an elementary source consisting of a time harmonic electric current element of a specified direction and infinitesimal length' (IEEE Trans. Antenna and Propagation 1983). A single current element cannot be supported by free space, but because the Maxwell's equations follow linearity, it can be represented by any arbitrary current distribution in terms of the current elements of the type a Hertzian dipole is made of. If the for a given current element the field is known, the field due to any current distribution can be computed using a superposition integral or summing the contributions due to all the current elements comprising the current distribution. Although an infinitesimally current element is not of much importance, it forms the basis of any complex radiating structures. After all radiating structure can be thought of as collection of small current elements. The Hertzian dipole is the basic antenna element and the starting point of antenna analysis. The analysis of a Hertz dipole, therefore, is an important subject in the antenna theory (Shevgaonkar).

$$E_0 = \frac{IdlSin\theta e^{j\omega t}e^{-j\beta r}}{4\pi\varepsilon} \frac{j\beta^2}{\omega r} \text{---} \tag{2}$$

$$H_\varphi = \frac{IdlSin\theta e^{j\omega t}e^{-j\beta r}}{4\pi r}\left(j\beta + 1/r\right)\text{---} \tag{3}$$

$$E_\theta = \frac{IdlSin\theta e^{j\omega t}e^{-j\beta r}}{4\pi\varepsilon}\frac{j\beta^2}{\omega r}\text{---} \tag{4}$$

If we look at the expressions of the electric field and magnetic fields, we note that the fields can be classified in three From above equation we see that the electric field E lies in (r, θ) plane whereas the magnetic field H lies in ø plane. That is to say that electric field and magnetic fields are perpendicular to each other at every point in space categories on the basis of their variation as a function of distance. The three fields have spatial variation as $1/r$ (radiation field), $1/r^2$ (induction field) and $1/r^3$ (electrostatic field). $^{\text{Noting that}}$ $\beta = \omega^2\sqrt{\mu\varepsilon}$ i. e. β is proportional to ω we, observe that the magnitude of the field which varies as $1/r^3$ is inversely proportional to the frequency. The field which varies as $1/r^2$ is independent of frequency, and the field which varies as $1/r$ is proportional to frequency. The $1/r^2$ and $1/r^3$ fields are dominant only for small values of r whereas $1/r$ fields are dominant for large values of r. it is interesting to note that at low frequencies, the fields are more localized around the source whereas, at high frequencies the field reach out at far away distances from the source. In other words, for same current I and same distance r, the $1/r$ field becomes stronger as the frequency increases.

Secondly we note that the near field is only the electric field. There is no magnetic field component which varies as $1/r^3$. The magnetic field is due to current and not due to accumulated charges and consequently it does not have a variation of $1/r^3$.

Thirdly, the power flow in the medium is solely due to the radiation field. This can be shown by computing the average Pointing vector at some point in space.

$$P = \frac{1}{2}\left(EXH\right)\text{ ---} \tag{5}$$

2.2 Total Power Radiated by the Hertz Dipole

The total power radiated by the antenna is obtained by integrating the Pointing vector over a spherical surface of say radius r. The elemental surface area is given as r²sinθdθdø and total power can be written as (Shevgaonkar).

$$W = 40\ \pi^2\ I0^2\ (dl/\lambda)^2\text{ ---} \tag{6}$$

The power radiated by the dipole is proportional to the square of the dipole length normalized with respect to the wavelength. An electrical component starts radiating more and more power as the frequency increases, and the power reaches out to farther distances.

2.3 Radiation Pattern of the Hertz Dipole

The radiation pattern is a plot of magnitude of the radiation electric field as a function of θ and ø. It essentially describes the way the power flow varies as a function of direction. Since the purpose of radiation pattern is to provide the directional dependence of the radiation field, the absolute field amplitudes are not of much concern. Consequently, the radiation field can be normalized with respect to its maximum value. The radiation pattern for the Hertz dipole therefore is

$$F(\theta, ø) = \sin \theta \quad --- \tag{7}$$

When plotted in the spherical coordinate system (ρ, θ, ø) with ρ=|*F(θ, ø)*| generates a radiation pattern. This shape of radiation pattern is similar to an apple though it is always correct to visualize the radiation pattern as a 3 dimensional figure, many times, just the two principal section of the figure are adequate to describe the gross radiation characteristics of an antenna.

2.4 Antenna Array

The radiation characteristics of monopole and dipole antennas have broad radiating beams and therefore lower directivity. The directivity of such antennas can be increased by enhancing their physical dimensions. However, an increase in the size of antenna not only increases the directivity but the radiation pattern also gets modified in an undesirable manner. Also, while controlling the radiation pattern, the terminal characteristics of antenna may get altered in an unpleasant manner. In fact, one does not know how precisely a radiation pattern is modified by shaping antenna of particular type. We can also find radiation pattern for a given antenna structure but finding the antenna shape to realize a given radiation pattern is rather an impossible to carry out. In practice, depending upon the application, the radiation pattern for an antenna is specified and the engineer has to design the radiating structure for the same.

Referring to the fundamental Fourier relationship between the current distribution on an antenna and the radiation pattern, we can say that, if we control the current distribution on an antenna surface, we will be able to get away with the desired radiation characteristics. Unfortunately, for those antennas discussed above, one does not have control over current distributions. Once the antenna is exited by voltage or current source at its feed point, the current distributions is automatically adjusted to satisfy the basic laws of electromagnetism. It is then clear that for better control of radiation pattern, one must find a mechanism of controlling spatial distribution of the current. Antenna array is mechanism which gives us the precise control of spatial current distribution. Using the spatial configuration of basic antenna elements one can realize arbitrarily complex radiation patterns with help of arrays. Also while manipulating the radiation pattern, the terminal characteristics of basic antenna elements alter only up to some margins. The input impedance of the antenna therefore gets decoupled from the radiation pattern.

If we consider the two element array of isotropic antennas, although isotropic antenna does not exist in practice, its use helps in understanding the principle of arrays.

The line joining the two elements as shown is called the axis of the array. All the angles φ is measured from the axis of the array. Note that the measurement of the angle φ from the axis of the array is random, and it has nothing to do with the standard spherical coordinate system (r, θ, φ)

2.5 Two isotropic sources (Shevgaonkar)

$$E_{Total} = E_0 + E_0 k e^{j\cdots} \quad \text{---} \qquad (8)$$

Ψ is the phase difference due to currents + phase difference due to path difference.

If the magnitude of two currents is same then k = 1 and the path difference is given by d $\cos\theta$ where θ is the angle which the radiation pattern makes with horizontal axis.

Phase difference $= \dfrac{2\pi d \cos\theta}{\lambda}$ where d is the distance between two antennas.

$\Psi = \alpha + \beta$ d $\cos\theta$ where $\beta = \dfrac{2\pi}{\lambda}$

So, Etotal = E0$[1 + e^{\psi}]$

$= E0[1 + \cos\ddot{}\ e^{\psi} + j\sin\ddot{}\ ]$

$|E(Total)| = 2E_0 \cos(\Psi/2)$

2.6 Impedance Matching

While discussing characteristics of a transmission line, we have seen that if a line is terminated in the characteristic impedance Z_0. Also, in this case there is no reflection on the line and the power is maximally transferred to the load. In practice, however, it is not always possible to design a circuit whose input or output impedance is matched to the adjacent circuits. For example, there may be a circuit which is to be connected to a signal generator of 50 Ω output impedance but the input impedance of the circuit is not 50 Ω. When this connection is made, not only the maximum power is not being transferred by the generator to the load, but the reflected wave might enter the generator and may alter its characteristics like frequency, etc. it is, therefore, essential to devise a technique which can avoid reflections from the circuits. Transmission lines can be used for matching two impedances. Due to low-loss the transmission line provides impedance matching with negligible loss of power.

2.7 Quarter-Wavelength Transformer

This technique is generally used for matching two resistive loads or for matching a resistive load to a transmission line or for matching two transmission lines with unequal characteristic impedances.

All the cases are identical in principle as all require matching between two purely resistive impedances. The principle here is very simple. We introduce a section of transmission line (transformer) between two resistances to be matched, such that the transformed impedances perfectly mater at either end of the transformer section. That is, in fig say, the impedance seen towards right at A appears to be Z_0, and impedance seen towards left of B appears to be R. So, when seen from transmission line side it appears to be terminated in Z_0, and when seen from load resistance side it appears to be connected to a conjugate matched load R.

Since, pure resistances are to be matched here; the impedance transformation in the transformer has to be from resistive impedance to resistive impedance. This is possible when only in the following two cases.

Figure 3. Different types of quarter wave transformer

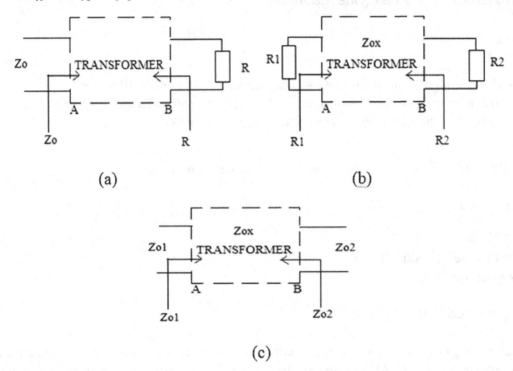

(a)

(b)

(c)

When length of the transforming line is λ/2.
When length of the transforming line is λ/4.

A λ/2 section of a transmission line transforms impedance into itself and hence does not serve any purpose for matching. So, the only possibility is that the transformer must be λ/4 long.

Let us assume that the characteristic impedance of the transformer section is Z_0X. For λ/4 length, the transformer inverts the normalized impedance. Therefore, the impedance seen at A towards right in fig would be

$$Z_A = \frac{1}{\left(\dfrac{R}{ZoX}\right)} Z_{0X} = Z_{0X^2} / R \text{ ---} \tag{9}$$

For matching at A, Z_A should be equal to Z_0 i.e.

$$Z_{0X} = \sqrt{RZ0} \text{ ---} \tag{10}$$

So, in general we can say that two resistive impedances can be matched by section of a transmission line which is quarter-wavelength long and has characteristic impedance equal to the geometric mean of the two resistances.

In the first look, it appears from the above discussion that a quarter wavelength transformer can be used to match only pure resistive impedances. However, if we see carefully, we find that it is not true. This is due to the fact that we can always transform a complex impedance into a purely a real one by adding an appropriate section of a transmission line. Let us consider matching of a complex impedance $R + jX$ to the characteristic impedance of a transmission line Z_0. To transform impedance $R + jX$ to some real value let an extra length 'L' of a transmission line be added between the quarter wavelength transformer and impedance as shown in fig

Figure 4. Quarter Wave Transformer

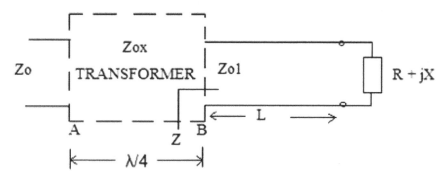

The characteristic impedance of the extra length of the line will be say $Z_0 1$ (one can use a line of characteristic impedance Z_0 as well). The length L should be chosen such that the transformed impedance Z' seen toward right at B is purely real. This can be done easily by using Smith Chart.

First the impedance $Z = R + jX$ is normalized with respect to $Z_0 1$ to give $\check{Z} = (R+jX)/Z_0 1 \equiv r+jx$. Let this point be denoted by P. Draw the constant VSWR circle through P. The circle will intersect the real axis at points S and T. These points represent location on the transmission line where the impedance is purely resistive. At point T the normalized impedance is rmax and at point S the normalized impedance is rmin.

If we take $L = Lmax$ then impedance $Z' = Z_0 1 rmax$ and then for matching we get

$$Z_{0X} = \sqrt{ZoZo1rmax}. \text{---} \tag{11}$$

Similarly, if we take $L = Lmin$ then $Z' = Z_0 1 rmin$ and we get

$$Z_{0X} = \sqrt{ZoZo1rmin} \text{---} \tag{12}$$

Theoretically, both solutions are equally acceptable and only their numerical values will decide which is practically more realizable.

The quarter-wavelength transformer although can match any impedance, has a very serious drawback. For every impedance to be matched, one needs a line with different $Z_0 X$ since the characteristic impedance of a line is decided by the physical structure of the line like conductor size, dielectric constant, separation between conductors etc. for every impedance $Z_0 X$, one need a special transmission line. Realizing a line with particular $Z_o X$ may not be always possible in practice. To overcome this drawback, the stub matching techniques have been proposed. These techniques make use of the standard transmission line section for matching arbitrary impedances. Smith chart is shown in Figure 5.

Figure 5. Stub matching using smith chart

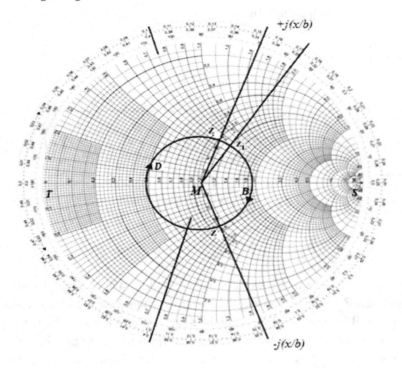

2.8 Terms and Definitions

(a) Isotropic antenna

It radiates in all direction uniformly i.e. omnidirectional in nature. Its electric field pattern is independent of θ and φ. Example: Broadcast towers.

(b) Radiation power density

It is the strength of the radiated power in any direction at any distance from antenna i.e. power/area.

$$P(r,,\varphi) = \frac{dWr}{ds} \text{ (Watts/m}^2) \text{ ---}$$

(13)

Also given by:

$$\frac{E^2\left(r,,,\cancel{E}\right)}{2\cdot}$$

Where η is wave impedance

(c) Radiation power intensity

It is the strength of radiated power in any direction from the antenna. It is power per unit solid angle (Watts / Steradians). It is given by

$$\psi\left(\theta,\varphi\right) = dWr / d\Omega \text{ ---}$$ (14)

Where $d\Omega = r^2\sin\theta\ d\theta\ d\ \varphi$

(d) Effective Length

If an antenna radiates W_r power over its physical length having non-uniform currents, then the length required to radiate same power assuming uniform currents define effective length.

(e) Radiation Parameters of an Antenna

The radiation pattern of antenna describes the directional dependence of the power radiated by the antenna. In general a radiation pattern has a direction of maximum radiation. Then, there are certain directions called nulls, along which no radiation goes, and there are directions in which the radiation is locally maximum. The local maxima in the radiation pattern are called the 'side lobes' of the radiation pattern. A typical radiation pattern in some plane, therefore, appears like that shown.

Figure 6. Radiation pattern as a (a) polar plot (b) Cartesian plot

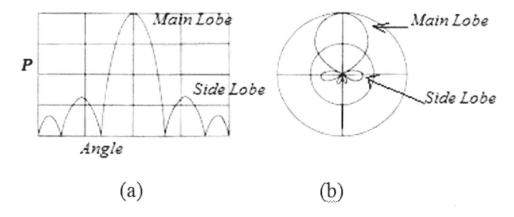

Fig6 (a) shows that radiation pattern as the polar plot and Fig10 (b) shows the radiation pattern as the Cartesian plot. It is rather a representation of the actual radiation pattern taking θ as an independent parameter and plotting |E| as a function of θ in regular plot. The radiation pattern indeed is periodic over 360° i.e. 2π radians.

Although the radiation pattern is a complete description of the directional properties of antenna radiation, its utility is rather restricted due to its too detailed nature. One would instead like to derive certain quantitative parameters from the radiation pattern which can be used for comparisons of different antennas. These parameters are as follows:

(f) Direction of the Main Beam

It is the direction in which the radiation field strength is maximum. Generally it is denoted by θ_{max}.

(g) Half-Power Beam Width (HPBW)

The main beam is the angular region where effective radiation from the antenna goes. The effective width of the main beam is the angular width of the pattern between the points on the radiation pattern where the field magnitude reduces to $E_{max}/\sqrt{2}$, where E_{max} is the maximum field. From fig, the HPBW = $(\theta_1 - \theta_2)$. Since, the field in direction θ_1 and θ_2 reduces to $\dfrac{1}{\sqrt[2]{2}}$ of its maximum value; the pointing vector in this direction reduces to one half or -3 dB compared to that in the direction of the maximum radiation. The half power beam width therefore is many times referred to as 3dB Beam width of the antenna. Generally, the half power beam widths are measured in the E and H planes of the radiation pattern.

Figure 7. Half-power beam width of a radiation pattern

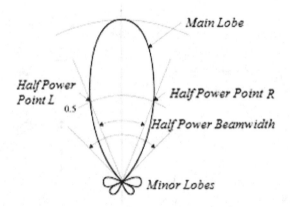

For the case of uniform linear array, as ϕ_{max} increases from 0 to π/2, the beam width ϕ_{HPBW} decreases monotonically. That is, when ϕ_{max} = 0, (end fire array) the HPBW is maximum and when ϕ_{max} = π/2 (broad side array) the HPBW is minimum. For a broad side array (ϕm_{ax} = π/2), the HPBW is

$$\varnothing_{HPBW} = \frac{\gg}{dN} = \frac{\gg}{\text{Length of the Array}} \text{ ---} \tag{15}$$

For the end fire array ($\varnothing_{max} = 0$), the HPBW is

$$\varnothing_{HPBW} = \sqrt{2\lambda / dN} = \sqrt{\frac{2\gg}{\text{Length of the Array}}} \text{ ---} \tag{16}$$

The length of the array is (N-1)d. However, for N>>1 the length of the array is approximated to dN. It is important to note that, for a broadside array, the HPBW is inversely proportional to the length of the array, whereas, it is inversely proportional to the square root of the length of the array for an end fire array. We, therefore, find that for a given array length, the broad side array has much smaller HPBW compared to that for the end fire array.

(h) Beam Width First Nulls

Occasionally, the width of the main beam (also called main lobe) is measured by angular separation between the first nulls on either side of the direction of maximum radiation. From fig, BWFN = θn2-θn1. It should be mentioned here that the HPBW is better measure of the effective width of the main beam compared to the BWFN as there are cases where the HPBW changes but the BWFN remains fixed.

The presence of side lobes essentially indicates the leakage of power in the undesired directions. An antenna system is primarily designed to transmit radiation in the direction along the main beam. However, since in any practical antenna system we have side lobes, the total radiated power is not focused into the main beam but a part of it leaks in the directions of the side lobes. Obviously, one would like to keep this leakage minimal. In other words, the side lobe amplitude should be as small as possible compared to the amplitude of the main beam. The amplitude of the highest side lobe compared to that of the main beam is called the side lobe level (SLL). For good satellite communication antennas The SLL is -30dB to -40dB. Generally the amplitude of the side lobes reduces as we go away from the main beam and hence the first side lobe on either side of the main beam defines the SLL.

(i) Directivity

The directivity is the parameter which quantifies the radiation focusing capability of an antenna. The HPBW in some sense has similar information but it does not quantify how much of the total radiated power has been confined into the main beam. A part of radiated power leaks through the side lobes and the remaining power is spread over the HPBW. Since, here we are investigating the angular distribution of the radiated power, it is appropriate to define a quantity called the Radiation Intensity as the power per unit solid angle. The radiation intensity in general is a function of θ and ø and is given by (Lin, 2018)

$$U(\theta,\varnothing) = \frac{Power \ along \ direction(\theta,\varnothing) \ in \ solif \ angle \ d\copyright}{Solid \ angle(d\copyright)} \text{ ---} \tag{17}$$

Now the solid angle on the surface of a sphere is defined as

$$d© = \frac{dA}{r^2} ---$$ (18)

Where dA is the area on the surface of the sphere and r is the radius of the sphere. dΩ=sinθ dθ dø.

$$U(\theta,\varnothing) = \frac{Power\,along\,(\theta,\varnothing)}{dA} r^2 ---$$ (19)

= (Power density) r²

If W watts of power is uniformly radiated in all directions, i.e. over 4π solid angle, we get the average radiation intensity as

$$U(\theta,\varnothing) = \frac{W}{4\pi} = \frac{1}{4\pi}\iint U(\theta,\varnothing)d\Omega ---$$ (20)

The directive gain of the antenna is defined as

$$G(\theta,\varnothing) = \frac{U(\theta,\varnothing)}{U_{av}} = \frac{4\pi U(\theta,\varnothing)}{\iint U(\theta,\varnothing)} ---$$ (21)

It is obvious that G(θ,ø) can be less than or greater than unity with no bounds on either side. That is, theoretically G(θ,ø) can vary from 0 to infinity. In the direction of the nulls E(θ,ø) and consequently U(θ,ø) and G(θ,ø) are zero, whereas, in the direction of the main beam G(θ,ø) is maximum.

The maximum directive gain is called the 'Directivity' of the antenna and is denoted by D.

D=Max(G(θ, ø))

The directivity D lies between 1 and infinity. For D=1, Umax= Uav and the antenna does not exhibit any directional characteristics. The antenna is called the 'isotropic antenna'. It may be noted that isotropic antenna is only hypothetical and in practice one cannot realize an isotropic antenna. Hence, for practical antenna D is always greater than 1. As the directivity D increases, the radiation gets more and more focused is the direction of the main beam. Directivity can also be defined by

$$D = \frac{4\pi}{\varnothing_{HP}\theta_{HP}} ---$$ (22)

Where, θ_{HP} and $\varnothing_{HP}$ are the half power beam width in radians in the θ and ø planes respectively. This can be seen from fig we can note that the volume under the actual main beam is approximately equal to the volume of the box with height unity and lengths and widths respectively θ_{HP} and $\varnothing_{HP}$.

For an N- element uniform array the directivity is given by

$$D = \frac{4\pi}{\iint |AF|^2 \, d\Omega} \text{---} \tag{23}$$

Where, AF is the normalized radiation pattern of the array. Fig shows main beam of the array in the three dimensional space. It is apparent that although the planar radiation patterns looks similar for the broad side and end fire arrays, in three dimensions they have totally different appearances. The three dimensional for the broad side array looks almost like a disk, whereas, for the end fire array, it appears like an elongated balloon. For any arbitrary direction of maximum radiation, the main beam looks like hollow cone as shown.

Figure 8. View of the radiation patterns of the broad side and end fire

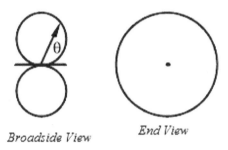

Broadside View   *End View*

If we denote the directivity of the broad side and the end fire array respectively by DBS and DEF, then from above equation we get

$$D_{BS} = \frac{2dN}{\lambda} \text{---} \tag{24}$$

$$D_{EF} = \frac{8dN}{\lambda} \text{---} \tag{25}$$

The result is quite interesting. The directivity of the end fire array is about 4 times higher than that of the broad side array of the same length.

(j) Antenna Gain

As seen above, the directivity is parameter which totally depends upon the radiation pattern. Indirectly it assumes that the total power radiated, W, is same as that supplied to the antenna input. In practice however, the antennas are not, made of ideal conductor and consequently when the current flows along the antenna surface, there is an ohmic loss. A part of the power supplied to the antenna input is therefore lost in heating the antenna due to the ohmic loss. If we assume that the power actually radiated by the antenna is W, the power supplied to the input of the antenna will be

$$P_i = W + P_l \text{ ---} \tag{26}$$

Where, P_l is the ohmic loss due to finite conductivity of the antenna. Let us define power efficiency of an antenna as

$$\eta_r = \frac{W}{P_i} = \frac{W}{W + P_l} \text{ ---} \tag{27}$$

The antenna power gain is defined as $GP = D\eta_r$. We have, Power gain = Directivity *Efficiency.

3. Simulation in HFSS

3.1 Antenna design

The antenna is designed using HFSS (High Frequency Simulation Software) 2011. Circular patch antenna is employed in the circuit due to high gain for a given size of antenna. Designing involve numerous steps which are as follows:

Open HFSS window and click on project icon where a user can insert the new HFSS design as shown.

Figure 9. HFSS project window

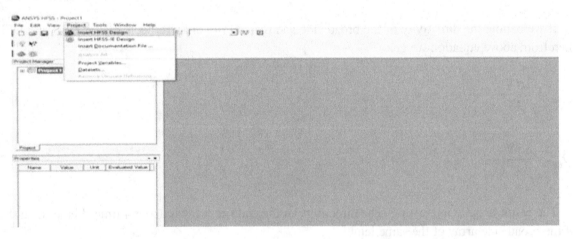

After inserting the design, a project window opens up with three axis to start the design of the desired antenna system as shown.

First of all a circle is formed to give rise to circular patch antenna with radius of 17 mm and the radius of patch is calculated using formula given below (Agarwal, 2014).

$$A = \cfrac{F}{\left\{1 + \cfrac{2h}{\prod \varepsilon F}\left(ln\left(\cfrac{\prod F}{2h}\right) + 1.7726\right)\right\}} \quad --- \tag{28}$$

Where, $F = \dfrac{8.791 * 10^{\wedge}9}{fr^2 \sqrt[2]{\varepsilon}}$ and ε is the relative permittivity of the antenna.

Another circle with same radius is formed at a distance of 62.5mm because the inter atomic spacing should be between λ/2 to λ and λ=c/f where f is the resonant frequency for which the antenna is designed.

Width of feed lines are calculated using formula (Agarwal, 2014)

Figure 10. Design inserted window

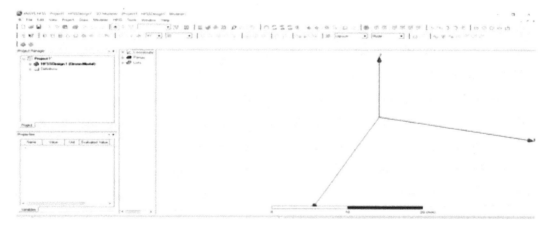

Figure 11. Circular Patch

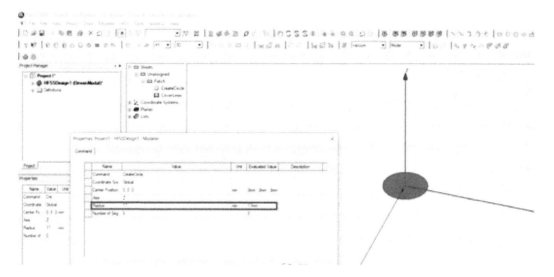

$$Z = \frac{60}{\sqrt[2]{\varepsilon reff}} ln\left(\frac{8h}{w} + \frac{w}{4h}\right) ---$$ (29)

The widths of 100 Ω and 50 Ω feed lines are calculated to be 0.7 mm for Z = 100 Ω and 3 mm for Z = 50 Ω.

1. Each of the patch is connected to 100 Ω feed line by drawing a rectangle at position (0,.35, 0)
   Axis Z
   X size -20 mm
   Y size -0.7 mm

Figure 12. Circular patch 2 * 1 array

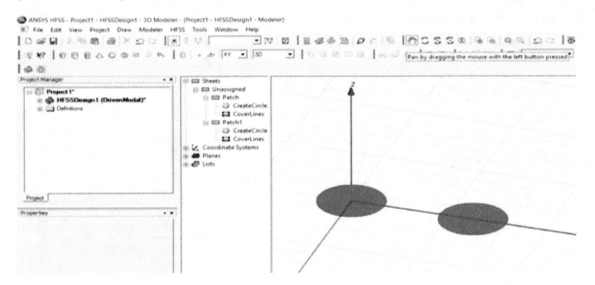

2. The rectangle is copied to form another rectangle to 2nd patch at a distance of 62.5 mm
3. Another rectangle connecting these two rectangles positioned at (-20, -.35, 0)
   Axis Z
   X size -0.7 mm
   Y size 63.2 mm
4. The equivalent at the junction of two 100 Ω lines is 50 Ω feed line connected to edge feed. Length of these 100 Ω and 50 Ω lines does not depend on impedance. Only width is dependent on impedance as discussed earlier. A rectangle is drawn with position (-20.7, 30.1, 0)
   Axis Z
   X axis -3 mm
   Y axis 3 mm

Figure 13. Feedline 1

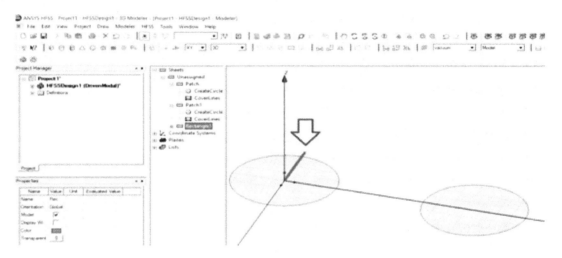

5.   Now another rectangle is drawn covering all the elements drawn till now. Patch is selected with all rectangles and are united and a ground plane is formed with position (26.6, 89.1, -1.6) i.e. (17+9.6, 62.5+17+9.6, -1.6) mm.

6.   Length and width of ground plane is greater than patch by 6h, where h is height of substrate i.e. 6*1.6= 9.6 mm.

Axis Z

X size -50.3

Y size -115.7

50.3 mm= (23.7+26.6) mm

Figure 14. Feedline 2

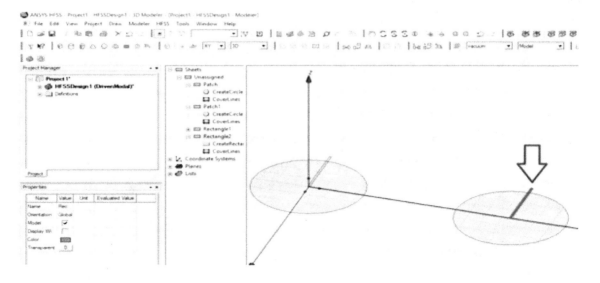

7. Now, a cuboidal structure is selected to form substrate of material FR4_epoxy with relative permittivity ξr =4.4 with dimensions same as that of ground plane along with height/thickness.

Figure 15. 50 Ω feedline equivalent

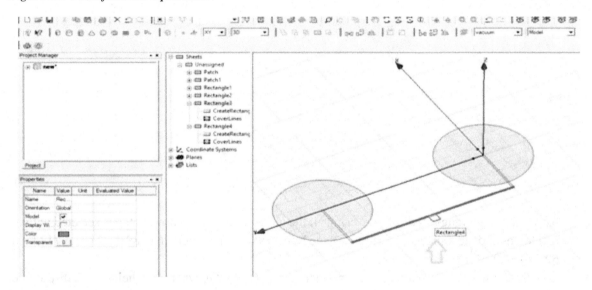

8. YZ plane is selected to form source with positions (-23.7, 32.75, 0)
    Axis X
    Y size -3.75 mm
    Z size -1.6mm

Figure 16. Patch as a single unit

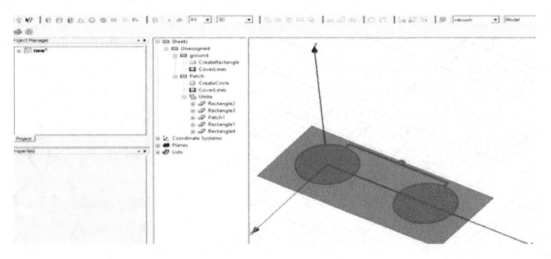

Figure 17. Substrate and Ground plane

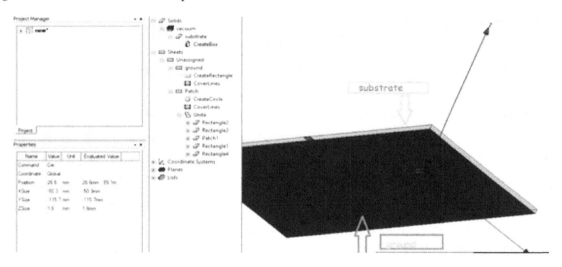

9. Return to XY plane. All faces of radiation box are quarter wavelength away from radiating pattern. To form radiating box copy substrate and paste to rename to rad box of material as vacuum and positions (57.85, 120.35, 32.85)
    X size -112.8 mm
    Y Size -178.2 mm
    Z size -64.1 mm

Figure 18. Source to patch antenna

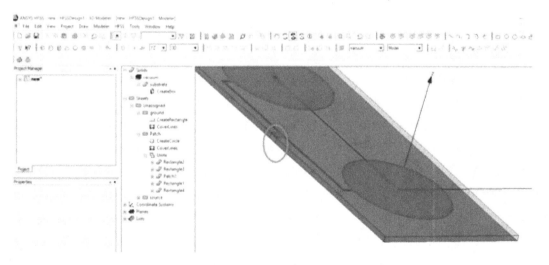

Here an addition of λ/4 is done to each position of substrate.

Figure 19. (a)Radiation box (b) Electric field pattern

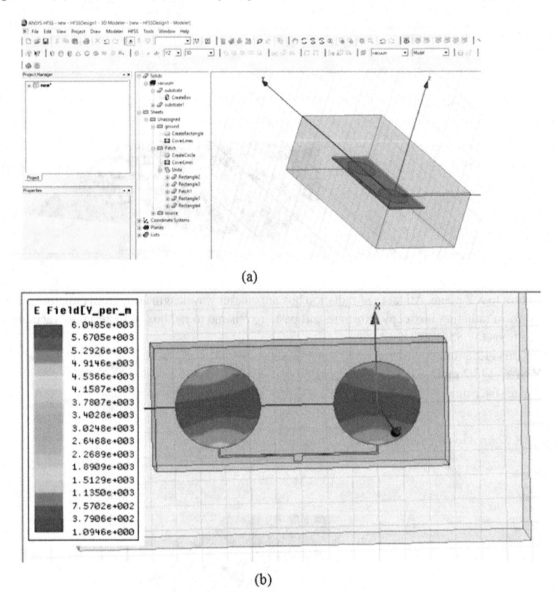

(a)

(b)

4. Simulation in ADS

4.1 Rectifier Circuits

One important application of diode is in the design of rectifier circuit. A rectifier circuit forms the first stage of a power supply circuit. It is rectifying of an AC (alternating voltage) into one of the polarity either positive or negative. The diode is useful for this feature because of its non linear characteristics, that is, current exist for one voltage polarity, but value of voltage for the other polarity is zero. Rectification is classified as half-wave rectifier or full-wave with half-wave with simpler structure and full-wave with more efficiency.

Half wave rectifier and its transfer characteristics with Vγ the cut in voltage of diode below which it is non conducting. When the supply voltage is greater than the Vγ of the diode, the diode becomes forward biased and a current diode is induced in the circuit. In this case, we can write (Matsunaga, 2013)

$$i_D = \frac{Vs - V\gamma}{R} \text{ ---} \tag{30}$$

We see that input signal has alternate polarity and has time averaged value equal to zero, the output voltage is unidirectional and has an average value that is not zero. The input voltage is hence rectified.

Figure 20. Half wave rectifier

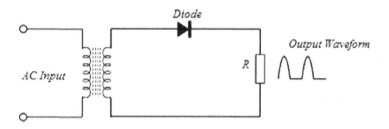

Figure 21. Output waveform from HW rectifier

Full-wave rectifier

During the positive half cycle of the input voltage diode D1 and D2 are forward biased and D3 and D4 are reverse biased and reverse happens for negative half cycle.

Figure 22. Full wave bridge rectifier

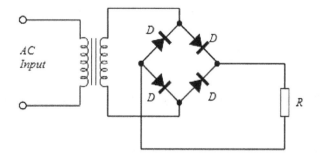

The rectifier circuit employed is basically a voltage quadrupler circuit which consists of two diodes and two capacitors (Matsunaga, 2013). The working of the circuit and a voltage quadrupler circuit are shown in the fig24.

1. In the negative half cycle, the diode D1 conducts and diode D2 is non-conducting, capacitor C1 is charged to maximum value of voltage being applied.
2. In the positive half cycle, the diode D2 conducts and D1 forms open circuit with capacitor C1, diode D2 and capacitor C2 all in series.
3. The circuit output voltage is calculated using KVL with capacitor C1 having charged up to maximum applied voltage in the previous cycle. So it is the form:

-Vm -Vm + Vo = 0

Where Vm is the maximum voltage applied to the circuit with capacitor being charged to this value.

Figure 23. Waveform for FW rectifier

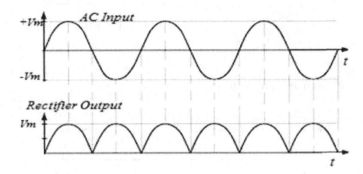

Figure 24. Voltage Quadrupler Circuit

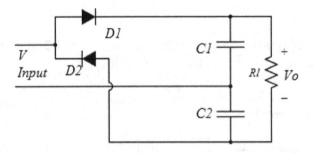

4.2 Simulation in ADS

The Software used for the simulation of circuit is The Advanced Design System (ADS).
Getting started with ADS needs one to follow following steps:

1. ADS window starts with displaying a new work space option along with other acquiring knowledge options and one need to select the New work space option to start a project.
2. The user need to add workspace name and add libraries in the next step which contain analog, digital and user defined libraries
3. A window opens up, we need to select the schematic icon which further ask for the cell name and design templates which are optional to select.
4. The workspace with window with tutorials, knowledge centre is shown below.

Figure 25. ADS work space

5. When new workspace is formed an option appears to select templates where if choose simulation template then following circuit appears.

Figure 26. Simulation template schematic

6. Then the system designed is the voltage quadrupler schematic by placing capacitor C1 and C2 at desired locations and Diodes D1 and D2. Diodes need to be defined by their model which has same name as the diode selected for the circuit as shown in fig..

Figure 27. Voltage Quadrupler Circuit

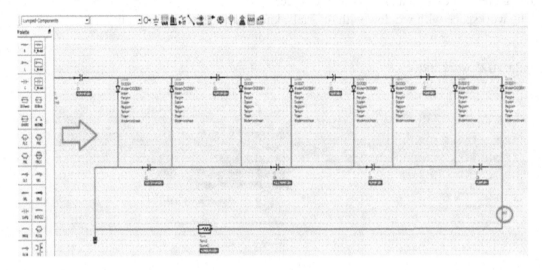

7. The antenna system is represented by receiving equivalent in ADS by a power source with value calculated from the output of HFSS design.
8. In HFSS, the 3D plot is described in earlier sections which displays the gain as 4.287 dB which when converted to Watt is 2.6834 w as shown in fig..
9. The output impedance of the antenna system can be seen in solution data which shows the output impedance of the network and that value is used in receiving antenna circuit of ADS.
10. Both the networks need to be joined by a matching network in order to avoid mismatch. The impedance matching network matches the input impedance of rectifier circuit and the antenna output impedance.
11. The input impedance of rectifier is calculated using frequency 5.5 GHz for calculating reactance of the capacitor as $1/j\omega$ and the dynamic resistance of the diode is 25 Ω and after drawing the equivalent circuit as shown fig.
12. Single stub matching is used to match the network by placing it between the two and then placing the source impedance and load impedance in the matching window. The W and L values are synthesized according to value of frequency and the network
13. The smith chart matching builds the values for inductor and capacitor to match the two parts. After giving input to source and load impedance of the circuit the ADS design is build.
14. This design is build between the two separate networks of receiving antenna and rectifier circuit as mentioned above. The build matching network is shown in figure.

Figure 28. Source frequency port

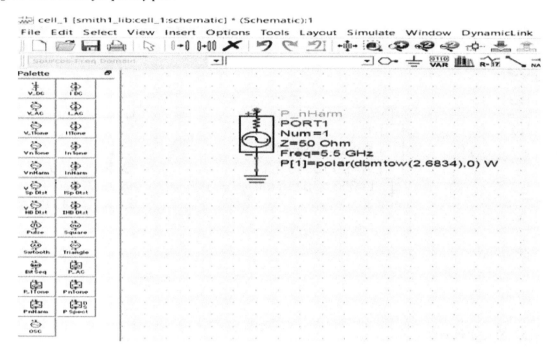

Figure 29. Equivalent impedance circuit for input impedance

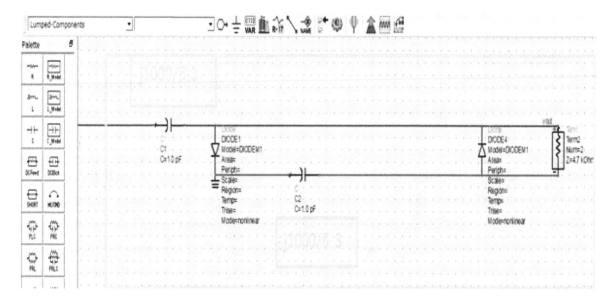

Figure 30. Stub matching

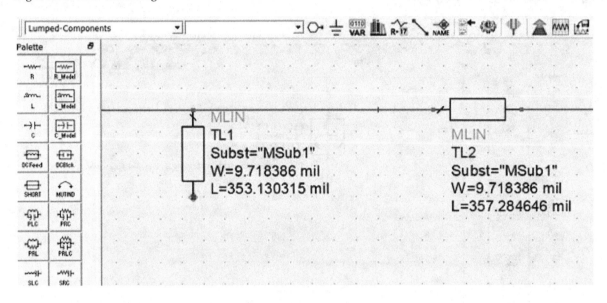

Figure 31. System circuit

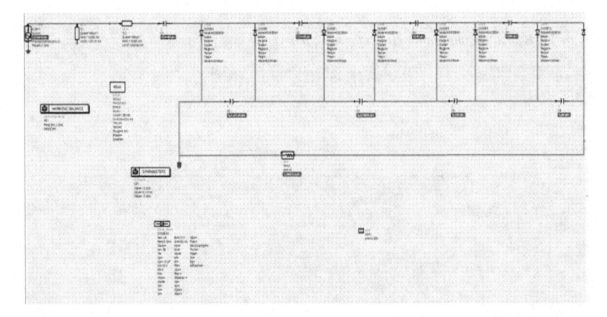

5. CONCLUSION

A 2*1 circular patch array antenna is used in this chapter which provides higher gain. The fundamental concept of radiation from antenna is explained using building blocks of an antenna i.e. hertzian dipole with its electric field equations and magnetic field too. Radiation pattern of antenna system provides with the power gain of the system because it signifies the directivity of antenna which is given by the maximum power gain in particular direction. The HFSS (High Frequency Simulation Software) working methods starting with simple circle to a complete 2 * 1 circular patch array antenna is formed. In ADS the three basic sub systems are designed starting with how to create a new workspace in ADS.

REFERENCES

Agarwal, S., Pandey, S. K., & Singh, J. (2014). Realization of efficient RF energy harvesting circuits employing different matching techniques. *Int. Symp on Quality Electronic Design (ISDEQ)*, 754-761.

Keyrouz, S., Perotto, G., & Visser, H. J. (2012). Novel broadband Yagi-Uda antenna for ambient energy harvesting. *IEEE European Microwave Conf.*, 518-521.

Khang, S.-T., Lee, D.-J., Hwang, I.-J., Yeo, T.-D., & Yu, J.-W. (2017). Microwave Power Transfer with Optimal Number of Rectenna Arrays for Mid-Range Applications. *IEEE Antennas and Wireless Propagation Letters*, 1–1. doi:10.1109/LAWP.2017.2778507

Kim, J. H., Cho, S. I., & Kim, H. J. (2016). Exploiting the mutual coupling effect on dipole antennas for RF energy harvesting. *IEEE Antennas and Wireless Propagation Letters*, 1301–1304.

Li, X., Yang, L., & Huang, L. (2019). Novel Design of 2.45-GHz Rectenna Element and Array for Wireless Power Transmission. *IEEE Access: Practical Innovations, Open Solutions*, 1–1. doi:10.1109/ACCESS.2019.2900329

Lin, Chiu, & Gong. (2018). *A Wearable Rectenna to Harvest Low-Power RF Energy for Wireless Healthcare Applications*. doi:10.1109/CISP-BMEI.2018.8633222

Matsunaga, T., Nishiyama, E., & Toyoda, I. (2013). 5.8-GHz Stacked Differential Rectenna Suitable for Large-Scale Rectenna Arrays With DC Connection. *IEEE Transactions on Antennas and Propagation*, *63*, 1200–1202. doi:10.1109/APMC.2013.6695070

Nayna, T. F., Baki, A. K., & Ahmed, F. (2014). *Comparative study of Rectangular and Circular micro strip patch antenna*. ICEEICT.

Neaman. (n.d.). *Electronic Circuits* (3rd ed.). MGH.

Niotaki, K., Kim, S., Giuppi, F., Collado, A., Georgiadis, A., & Tentzeris, M. (2014). Optimized design of multiband and solar rectennas. *WiSNet 2014 - Proceedings: 2014 IEEE Topical Conference on Wireless Sensors and Sensor Networks*, 31-33. 10.1109/WiSNet.2014.6825507

Olgun, U., Chen, C.-C., & Volakis, J. (2011). Investigation of Rectenna Array Configurations for Enhanced RF Power Harvesting. *Antennas and Wireless Propagation Letters. IEEE.*, *10*, 262–265. doi:10.1109/LAWP.2011.2136371

Sample, A. P., Parks, A. N., & Southwood, S. (2013). *Wireless ambient radio power in smith J.P. In Wirelessly powered sensor networks and computational RFID*. Springer.

Shevgaonkar, R. K. (n.d.). *Electromagnetic waves* (12th ed.). MGH.

Singh, M., Agarwal, S., & Parikar, M. S. (2017). Design of rectenna system for GSM-900 band using novel broadside 2*1 array antenna. *Journal of Engineering (Stevenage, England)*.

Takacs, A., Okba, A. & Aubert, H. (2018). *Compact Planar Integrated Rectenna for Batteryless IoT Applications*. doi:10.23919/EuMC.2018.8541764

Takhedmit, H., Cirio, L., Costa, F., & Picon, O. (2014). Transparent rectenna and rectenna array for RF energy harvesting at 2.45 GHz. *8th European Conference on Antennas and Propagation (EuCAP)*, 2970-2972. 10.1109/EuCAP.2014.6902451

Chapter 11
Cloud Computing Technologies

Shweta Kaushik
JIIT Sector 128, Noida, India

Charu Gandhi
JIIT Sector 128, Noida, India

ABSTRACT

In today's world, cloud computing and e-commerce are complementary to each other in terms of their vast effectiveness. E-commerce allows the business to move and grow on the internet without having or buying any physical space. Cloud computing helps e-commerce by securing the investment of IT infrastructure. That is the only reason why most of the organizations are moving their business towards cloud computing. Many organizations are getting much more benefit from the usage of cloud computing. But before adopting this, they must understand its trade-off also. In this chapter, the authors present the requirements of e-commerce organizations for adoption of cloud computing, benefit after the adoption of cloud computing in the e-commerce business, and what difficulties e-commerce organizations feel after the usage of this technology.

Cloud Computing

In last few years cloud computing become a most promising area in the field of IT and shift from a theoretical knowledge to real life applications. Nowadays, almost in every industrial area it is used at large scale such as healthcare, academics and telecommunication.

Cloud computing is a type of technology that allows to easily access and use the required services and information stored at some other remote location, which can be accessed via internet. It is a pool of resources shared among multiple users such as storage, network infrastructure, application and services over distributed environment. It is also beneficial for organizations or individual to access the data and services on the pay-per-use basis i.e, user needs to pay only for the amount of data or services which is utilized by an organization or individual and not for entire data, resource and services. One of the attractive features of cloud computing is that the user's data is stored at some other remote location, i.e.

DOI: 10.4018/978-1-7998-2764-1.ch011

cloud and the cloud service provider is responsible for the data maintenance and security as the cloud is owned by the cloud service provider whereas the data operation are controlled by the data owner. Today many organizations based on education, healthcare and banking domain are moving towards cloud to provide various services to their clients on the pay-per -use basis. Some major cloud service providers are Google, Amazon, Salesforce, Microsoft etc. Cloud users don't claim the physical framework rather they rent the usage from a third-party provider.

In today's world cloud computing and e-commerce are complementary each other in terms of their vast effectiveness. E-commerce allows the business to move and grow on internet without having or buying any physical space and cloud computing helps the e-commerce by securing the investment of IT infrastructure. That is the only reason why most of the organizations are moving their business towards cloud computing. Many organizations are getting much more benefit from the usage of cloud computing. But before adopting this, they must understand its tradeoff also. In this chapter the primary focus is to present that what are the requirement of e-commerce organization for adoption of cloud computing, benefit after adoption of cloud environment in e-commerce organization and what difficulties e-commerce organizations feels after the usage of this technology.

Cloud Entities

In general, basically three entities are involved under the concept of cloud computing environment as shown in figure 1-

- **Owner:** Owner is the entity who has some data or services which is required by the user. Owner will store all the data and services on the cloud from where any user can access them. Owner also decides the access criteria and type of access such as: read, write or update to the user on data, resources or services. After deciding the access, the access criteria owner is free from any data handling tasks such as- its storage, maintenance, transformation etc. As all these tasks are further handles by the CSP. Owner make itself free and contact with service provider only when either new update / addition required to the previously stored data or any modification in user access criteria.
- **Cloud Service Provider (CSP):** Cloud service provider act as an intermediate layer between the owner and the user. Cloud service provider is that entity who maintains the data and services and setup the security protocols. Cloud service provider allows the authorized user to access their required data and services according to access criteria that is based on the role, capability, access control or authorization, etc. as decided by the owner. This entity plays an important role in entire cloud environment. Both the owner and user can contact this entity regarding their services.
- **User:** It is the entity who actually required the data and services and acquired it from the cloud service provider according to their requirement and pay only for the amount of data or resource they used. Users do not have any direct contact with owner, only with CSP after cross verification of access criteria. Only after that users will be able to use its required data or service and pay for only that much data utilized by them.

Figure 1. Entities in Cloud Computing Environment

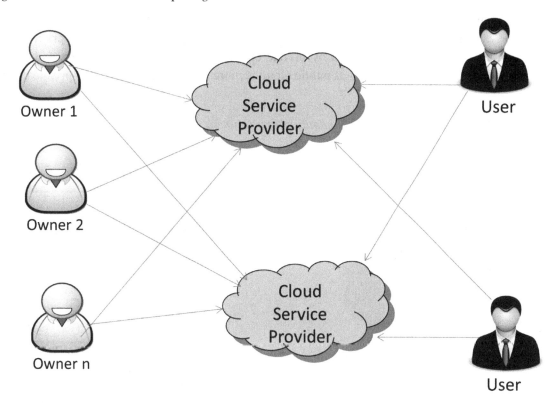

Cloud Deployment Models

According to the development of cloud in various organizations and for social usage, it can be classified as shown in figure 2-

- **Public Cloud:** It is an infrastructure provided to the user or many organizations in order to utilize the various available resources without any firewall implementation to deliver the cloud data. This type of model is managed and provided by the third party who is responsible for handling all the request and issues. There is no access restriction, authorization and authentication mechanism.
- **Private Cloud:** It is an infrastructure which is provided within an organization to utilize its resources under the firewall implementation. This type of model is either owned or leased from a third party and managed by the organization to deliver the resources to the user according to some security criteria such as access control, authentication etc. The resources used by the user in private cloud are not much cost effective in comparison to public cloud and also it provides more productivity in terms of data, resources rather than public cloud.
- **Community Cloud:** Many organizations are working together on the same service and also follows the same policies, values and requirements. This cloud model is either owned by an external third party or any organization involved in the community. It is much secure than public cloud and also help the different organizations to come together in the community.

- **Hybrid Cloud:** This type of infrastructure is a combination of two or more deployment models, in such a manner that the data transfer between them does not affect each other i.e. formed with the both private and public. The sensitive data under hybrid cloud generally handled by private cloud while non- sensitive data is handled by private cloud. This combination of public and private cloud will also help in cost saving as public cloud is more costly in comparison to private cloud.

Figure 2. Deployment Models in Cloud Computing Environment

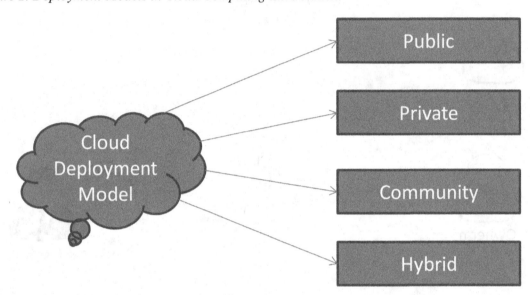

CLOUD DELIVERY MODELS

According to which type of service, out of many available services provided by cloud environment, it can be classified as shown in figure 3-

- **Software as a Service (SaaS):** It can be described as delivery of any application or software service to the intended user as per their requirement over the cloud environment and allows to use, maintain and operating them at the cloud server end virtually. This delivery model does not require any installation at the user machine, as all the application or services are handled at the service provider end. Example-
- **Platform as a Service (PaaS):** It can be described as delivery of the various computing services to the user for the purpose of their application or program implementation and execution. The various services come under this delivery model are as: database for data storage and operating system to provide the execution environment. All these tasks are handled on the internet/ service provider end without any installation at user machine. This will also reduce the task related to software maintenance and its support. In general, it provides the user with Application Programming Interface (API) which help in developing a customized application. The primary element in PaaS is point- and-snap which encourages the user to make new web applications easily and effectively within time and cost constraints. Example- Force.com, Microsoft Azure.

- **Infrastructure as a Service (IaaS):** It can be described as delivery of resources related to hardware to the user as per to the requirement of user using virtualization to execute their application. It enables the user to find out its required infrastructure over the internet in a practical way. Example- Amazon EC2, GoGrid.

Figure 3. Service Delivery Models in Cloud Computing Environment

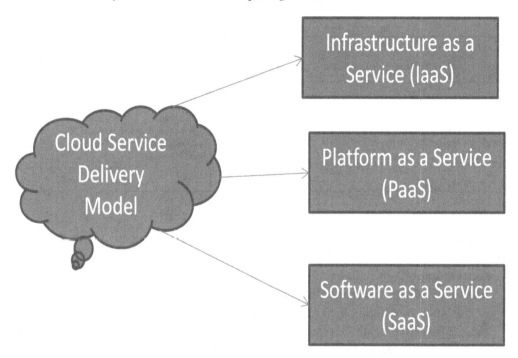

The comparative analysis of all these three-cloud delivery model based on its various kay characteristics can be summarized as shown in table 1.

Cloud Computing BENEFIT FOR ENTITIES

All the entities involved in cloud computing are gaining much benefit from cloud computing as shown in figure 4.

- **Benefit for Owner:** Owners are the organizations who are moving towards the acceptance of cloud computing applications and after its utilization getting the benefit as-
    a. **Payment as need**: For the small organization it is not feasible to invest a large amount in IT infrastructure. For this reason, adoption of cloud is beneficial for them. They need to pay only for that service or resource which is utilized by them not else.
    b. **Reduction in operation cost**: for the startup company it is beneficiary to use cloud computing as they can skip the hardware/ software purchasing and installation cost and use them with the help of cloud computing.

Table 1. Comparative Analysis of cloud delivery model

Delivery model	Paradigm	Key Characteristics	Key Terms	Pros	Cons	When not to use
Software as a Service (SaaS)	Software as strength	Communication by API, Service Level Agreement (SLA)	Client- server application	Avoid investment on software and development resources, reduced risk, iterative updates	Centralization of data requires new/ different security measures	Can be utilized in almost each and every application
Platform as a Service (PaaS)	License obtaining	Consumes cloud infrastructure	Solution stack	Rationalized version distribution	Centralization requires security measures	N / A
Infrastructure as a Service (IaaS)	Infrastructure as strength	Usually platform independent, infrastructure costs are shared, pay by usage;	Grid computing, utility computing, hypervisor, multi-tenant computing,	Avoid capital expenditure on hardware and human resources	Business efficiency and productivity largely depends on the vendor's capabilities; potentially greater long-term cost	When capital budget is greater than operating budget

- **Benefit for Service Provider**: Cloud service provider gets lot of incentive after providing service to the user as-
  a. **Getting incentive**: Getting profit is always the prime requirement for any organization.
  b. **Authority of large customer**: Organizations are getting a healthy relationship with number of customers by offering their resources as service.
  c. **Franchise distribution**: Service provider also motivate different vendors to provide a cloud option to their users by distributing their franchise.
  d. **Getting benefit from existing investment**: Many service providers creates an infrastructure once and then utilize it by servicing many requests. For example- Google established once and serve many users at the same time and also moving from private to public cloud for getting more attention and publicity.
- **Benefit for Users**: These entities are the actual beneficiary of cloud computing as it reduces the cost, data availability 24*7, easily access by just connecting with internet and service elasticity.

CLOUD COMPUTING CHARACTERISTICS

Based on the relation of cloud computing with other traditional technology the characteristics of cloud can be classified under two categories as:

- **Essential Characteristics**
  a) **On-request self-administration:** Customers have some arrangement in registering capacities, for example, server time and system stockpiling.

Figure 4. Benefits of Cloud Computing Environment

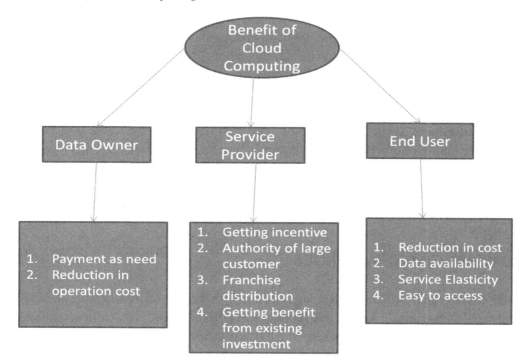

b) **Broad network access:** As the abilities are accessible over the system and got to through standard instruments, it implies that entrance to client is accessible through the web from a wide scope of gadgets, for example, PCs, workstations, and cell phones.

c) **Resource pooling or shared Infrastructure:** The mechanical assets of cloud specialist cooperatives are pooled to serve various customers utilizing a multi-inhabitant model, with various physical and virtual assets powerfully appointed and reassigned by buyer request. The client has no control or information about the precise area of the gave assets yet might have the option to indicate area at a more elevated level of deliberation. Instances of assets incorporate stockpiling, handling, memory, arrange transmission capacity, and virtual machines.

d) **Rapid Elasticity:** Abilities can be quickly and flexibly provisioned, cloud gives boundless provisioning of capacities to client whenever.

e) **Measured Service:** Cloud frameworks naturally controls and improves asset utilized by utilizing an estimating/metering ability suitable to the kind of administration. Asset utilization can be checked, controlled, and revealed giving straightforwardness to both the supplier and buyer of the used assistance.

- **Key Characteristics**
  a) **Agility:** Mechanical foundation assets could be re-provisioned effectively and reasonably by the client.
  b) **Cost:** Cost can be significantly limited and costs acquired in capital are changed over to operational costs. Rather than buy the assets, clients can utilize assets given by an outsider and pay according to use.

c) **Gadget and area freedom:** capable clients to get to frameworks utilizing an internet browser paying little respect to their area or what gadget they are utilizing (e.g., PC, mobile).

d) **Dependability:** information can be put away in various servers, which makes cloud appropriate for business coherence and fiasco recuperation.

e) **Maintainability:** comes to fruition through improved asset use, increasingly effective frameworks, and carbon lack of bias. Regardless, PCs and related framework are significant buyers of energy.

f) **Maintenance:** Application upkeep of cloud isn't so troublesome; cloud doesn't require any application to be introduced in the customer machine. In the event that any progressions happened, it would arrive at the client immediately.

g) **Metering:** Use of cloud assets must be estimated and metered per customer, in view of an application on an every day, week after week, month to month, and yearly premise.

CLOUD COMPUTING CHALLENGES

The present selection of distributed computing is related with various difficulties since clients are as yet distrustful about its realness. In light of an overview led by IDC in 2008, the significant difficulties that forestall Cloud Computing from being received are perceived by associations are as per the following:

- **Security:** It is evident that the security issue has assumed the most significant job in thwarting Cloud registering acknowledgment. Without uncertainty, putting your information, running your product on another person's hard circle utilizing another person's CPU seems overwhelming to many. Understood security issues, for example, information misfortune, phishing, botnet (running remotely on a gathering of machines) pose genuine dangers to association's information and programming. Also, the multi-tenure model and the pooled processing assets in distributed computing has presented new security challenges that require novel methods to handle with. For instance, programmers can utilize Cloud to compose botnet as Cloud frequently gives progressively dependable foundation administrations at a moderately less expensive cost for them to start an attack (Ramgovind, 2010).

- **Costing Model**: Cloud shoppers must consider the exchange offs amongst computation, communication, and combination. While moving to the Cloud can altogether diminish the framework cost, it raises the expense of information correspondence, for example the expense of moving an association's information to and from general society and network Cloud and the expense per unit of registering asset utilized is probably going to be higher. This issue is especially unmistakable if the buyer utilizes the cross-breed cloud arrangement model where the association's information is circulated among various open/private (in-house IT framework)/network mists. Instinctively, on interest figuring bodes well just for CPU serious jobs (Ramgovind, 2010).

- **Charging Model**: The flexible asset pool has made the cost investigation much more confused than normal server farms, which regularly ascertains their cost dependent on utilizations of static processing. In addition, a launched virtual machine has turned into the unit of cost investigation instead of the fundamental physical server. For SaaS cloud suppliers, the expense of creating multi occupancy inside their offering can be exceptionally significant. These include: re-plan and redevelopment of the product that was initially utilized for single-occupancy, cost of giving new highlights that permit to concentrated customization, execution and security upgrade for simultaneous client access, and managing complexities prompted by the above changes. Consequently, SaaS suppliers need to weigh up the exchange off between the arrangement of multi tenure and the cost-reserve funds yielded by multi-tenure, for example, decreased overhead through amortization, diminished number of on location programming licenses, and so forth. Accordingly, a vital and feasible charging model for SaaS supplier is critical for the gainfulness and maintainability of SaaS cloud providers (Ramgovind, 2010).

- **System Level Agreement (SLA):** Although cloud purchasers don't have authority over the fundamental registering assets, they do need to guarantee the quality, accessibility, dependability, and execution of these assets when customers have moved their centre business capacities onto their endowed cloud. As it were, it is imperative for purchasers to acquire ensures from suppliers on administration conveyance. Commonly, these are given through Service Level Agreements (SLAs) consulted between the suppliers and purchasers. The absolute first issue is the meaning of SLA details so that has a suitable degree of granularity, specifically the tradeoffs among expressiveness and complicatedness, with the goal that they can cover the greater part of the purchaser desires and is moderately easy to be weighted, checked, assessed, and authorized by the asset assignment system on the cloud. Likewise, unique cloud contributions (IaaS, PaaS and SaaS) should characterize various SLA meta determinations. This additionally raises various execution issues for the cloud suppliers. Moreover, propelled SLA instruments need to always consolidate client criticism and customization highlights into the SLA evaluation framework (Weinhardt, 2009).

- **What to move**: Based on an overview (Sample size = 244) led by IDC in 2008, the seven IT frameworks/applications being moved to the cloud are: IT Management Applications(26.2%),Collaborative Applications (25.4%), Personal Applications (25%), Business Applications (23.4%), Applications Development and Deployment (16.8%), Server Capacity (15.6%), and Storage Capacity (15.5%). This outcome uncovers that associations still have security/protection worries in moving their information on to the Cloud. As of now, fringe capacities, for example, IT the board and individual applications are the most effortless IT frameworks to move. Associations are moderate in utilizing IaaS contrasted with SaaS. This is somewhat on the grounds that negligible capacities are regularly re-appropriated to the Cloud, and center exercises are kept in-house. The review likewise demonstrates that in three years time, 31.5% of the association will move their Storage Capacity to the cloud. However this number is still moderately low contrasted with Collaborative Applications (46.3%) at that time (Gens, 2009).

- **Cloud Interoperability Issue**: Currently, each cloud offering has its own specific manner on how cloud customers/applications/clients connect with the cloud, prompting the "Dim Cloud" marvel. This seriously frustrates the improvement of cloud environments by driving seller locking, which restricts the capacity of clients to look over elective merchants/offering all the while so as to enhance assets at various levels inside an association. All the more significantly, exclusive cloud API smakes it exceptionally hard to coordinate cloud administrations with an association's very own current heritage frameworks (for example an on-premise server farm for exceptionally intelligent displaying applications in apharmaceutical company). The essential objective of interoperability is to understand the consistent liquid information crosswise over mists and among cloud and nearby applications. There are various levels that interoperability is fundamental for distributed computing. To start with, to enhance the IT resource and processing assets, an association regularly needs to keep in-house IT resources and abilities related with their center skills while re-appropriating peripheral capacities and exercises (for example the human asset framework) on to the cloud. Second, as a general rule, with the end goal of optimization,an association may need to redistribute various negligible capacities to cloud administrations offered by various merchants. Institutionalization seems, by all accounts, to be a decent answer for location the interoperability issue. Be that as it may, as distributed computing just begins to remove, the interoperability issue has notappeared on the squeezing motivation of significant industry cloud merchants (Ramgovind, 2010).

CLOUD COMPUTI NG ATTRIBUTES

For the adoption of cloud computing environment by any organization there are mainly few requirements needs to be followed properly. These basic requirements are also termed as attributes or drivers for the successful execution and usage of cloud computing. These all attributes are described as: data availability, elasticity, collaboration, mobility, lower cost, scalability, risk reduction and virtualization as shown in figure 5. Table 2 describe all these attributes along with the description of how they are related to the organization and used by them for solving their various issues.

Table 2. Cloud Computing Attributes

Attribute	Description
Data Availability	Usage of cloud computing allows the user to access their required data at anytime and any where by just connecting with the internet, data is available all the time.
Elasticity	User can add or remove the resources at anytime as the requirement arise. Thus, it can be easy to use the resources dynamically rather than statically. Allows the user not to specify the complete requirement at initial stage only.
Collaboration	Cloud computing bring multiple organizations at the same place if they all accessing simultaneously over the same data or information. This feature will also help in maintaining the data consistency also.
Mobility	User will be able to access the data anywhere, no need to fix at a particular location only. Data will be available across the world.
Lower Cost	The pay-per-use feature of cloud computing allows the user to invest only for those resources or data which is utilized by them not for anything else. Also, the user need not to pay any amount for the infrastructure cost and physical resource settlement.
Scalability	User can access the resource as per the demand that are accessible in large amount also by increasing their scalability.
Risk Reduction	User can test their idea on cloud infrastructure without investing any cost in actual setup environment. This will reduce the risk occurrence as user have complete idea about all the possibility of any risk appearance.
Virtualization	Each user in cloud environment has an impression that the available resources are utilized by itself without knowing that how they are arranged physically. But in actual, same resources are utilized by multiple users at the same time. Therefore, it is highly required that service provider will support multiple users at the same time with less resources available with it.

Figure 5. Drivers for Cloud Computing

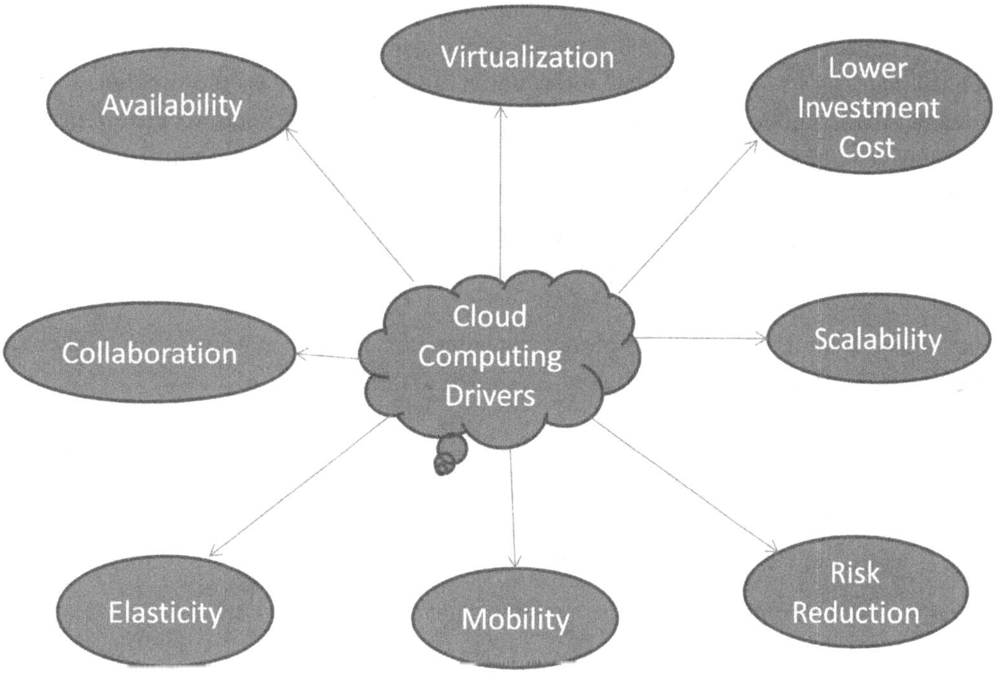

CLOUD SECURITY

The cloud is a place to keep the client's data at remote location; normally the clients are exceptionally delicate to store their private information in cloud. It is also possible that the business rationale and different business-related exchanges are to be put away in the spot of cloud, so the cloud clients need high security to keep their own private information in the cloud. The distributed computing should set out the IT security game plans that the client requires. The encryption of information preceding transmission between the client's premises and the specialist organization's premises is especially significant, for instance, where the web is utilized for transmission. Customers may likewise necessitate that their applications are facilitated on equipment that is explicit to them, instead of on shared equipment. There ought to be an entrance benefits between cloud suppliers and cloud customers. This will secure the unapproved get to, validation strategy are pursued for enabling client to get to their information in cloud.

Brodkin (2008) specify various security issues that can be raised by the customer while selecting any service provider for a particular service. These can be summarized as:

- **Privileged user access:** Data transmitted from the customer through the Internet represents a specific level of hazard, due to issues of information ownership; enterprises should invest in energy for becoming more acquainted with their suppliers and their guidelines however much as could be expected before allocating some trifling applications first to try things out.
- **Regulatory compliance:** Customers are responsible for the security of their answer, as they can pick between suppliers that permit to be evaluated by outsider associations that check levels of security and suppliers that don't.

- **Data location:** Information area relying upon agreements, a few customers may never comprehend what nation or what locale their information is found.
- **Data Segregation:** Encrypted data from different organizations might be put away on the equivalent hard plate, so a system to isolate information ought to be sent by the supplier.
- **Recovery:** Each supplier ought to have a disaster recovery convention to secure client information.
- **Investigative support:** If a customer speculates flawed action from the supplier, it might not have numerous lawful ways seek after an examination.
- **Long-term viability:** It alludes to the capacity to withdraw an agreement and all information if the present supplier is purchased out by another firm.

A comparative analysis of different solution techniques, used for securing the Cloud environment under different parameters is explained below, as shown in table 3.

Table 3. Comparison table of security techniques in cloud environment

Security Parameters/ Model	Architecture	Security Techniques	Security achieved as	Type	Pros	Cons	Similar Application
Intrusion Detection system (IDS)	Integrated, Layered	Honey pot & signature generation	Log management, Cyber-attack, /distributed denial of service attack	Network, Host	Compatible, efficient and scalable	Time consuming, higher resource utilization	Oracle SOA suit, IBM open cloud architecture
Hadoop Distributed File System (HDFS)	Master-Slave	Pattern matching algorithm	Occasional failure from loss of data	MapReduce & HDFS	High availability & reliability of cluster node and fault tolerance	Reduced performance	Yahoo, Facebook
Virtual Private Network (VPN)	Hub and spoke model	Border Gateway Protocol (BGP) & Autonomous System Numbers (ASN)	Traffic inspection after data decryption	multiple service host-server, to single-service host-server	One to one connectivity & perfect forward secrecy	User credential stick	NCP, Amazon
Secure Socket Layer (SSL)	Cloud server behaves like proxy server	Public key cryptography & Handshake message	Tampering & Monitoring	OpenSSL & Apache	Google will increase the site rank that have high SSL rating	PODDLE bite attack	Windows, Azure
Multi tenancy-based access control	Identity based and role-based access control	Segmentation of each tenant securely	Identity crises among different tenant	MAC, DAC, RBAC	Assigning the role and restrict the number of user and transaction per role	Side channel attack	NASA, XACML's library

ATTACKS IN CLOUD

- **Denial of Service (DoS) attack**: In DoS attack, an invader over-burdens the objective cloud framework with administration demands so it quit reacting to any new solicitations and thus made assets inaccessible to its clients. Some Cloud Security Alliance has distinguished that the cloud is progressively helpless against DoS assaults, since it is utilized by such many clients which makes it considerably more harming. DOS attacks are of numerous types, 1) An invader can over-burden the objective with enormous measure of garbage information that devour the system data transfer capacity and assets, for instance UDP floods, ICMP floods and so forth. 2) An invader can utilize clear space that related with different systems administration convention to over-burden target asset, for instance SYN floods, section parcel assault, ping of death and so forth. 3) An invader can make HTTP demand in enormous sum with the goal that it cannot be handle by the server for instance HTTP DDOS assault, XML DDOS assault and so on.

Solution: For confining DoS assault we can order traffic based on approval, so we can square traffic that are recognize as unapproved and permit traffic that are distinguish as approved. For this firewall can be utilized to permit or deny traffic on the premise of access conventions, ports or IP addresses.

- **Cloud malware Injection attack**: In Cloud Malware Injection Attack an invader attempts to infuse vindictive assistance or virtual machine into the cloud. In this kind of assault assailant makes its own pernicious assistance execution module (SaaS or PaaS) or virtual machine occurrence (IaaS) and attempt to add it to the Cloud framework. At that point, the invader needs to carry on in order to make it a legitimate assistance to the Cloud framework that it is some new help usage occurrence among the substantial cases. If the invader succeeds in this, the Cloud consequently diverts the solicitations of legitimate client to the malignant assistance execution, and the aggressor code begins to execute. The primary situation behind the Cloud Malware Injection assault is that an invader moves a malevolent help example into cloud with the goal that it can accomplish access to the administration solicitations of the unfortunate casualty's administration. To accomplish this, the attacker needs to infer authority over the unfortunate casualty's information in the cloud. As per order, this assault is the significant agent of misusing the support of cloud assault surface.

Solution: In order to keep cloud from malware infusion assault we can join the uprightness with equipment or can utilize equipment for trustworthiness reason because for an assailant it is hard to meddle in the IaaS level. For this we can use a record designation table (FAT) framework, by utilizing it we can decide the legitimacy and trustworthiness of new example by contrasting the current and past case.

- **Side channel attack**: An invader endeavors to bargain the cloud framework by setting a noxious virtual machine in nearness to a target cloud server framework and afterward propelling a side channel assault. Side-channel assaults have developed as a sort of viable security risk focusing on framework usage of cryptographic calculations. Assessing cryptographic frameworks flexibility to side-channel assaults is consequently significant for secure framework structure. Side channel assaults use two stages to assault VM CO-Residence and Placement for example an aggressor can regularly put their example on the equivalent physical machine as an objective example and VM Extraction i.e., the capacity of a malignant occasion to use side channels to learn data about co-occupant occasions. It tends to be anything but difficult to increase mystery data from a gadget so protection from side divert assault in distributed computing ought to be given.

Solution: To keep cloud from side channel assault we can utilize blend of virtual firewall apparatus. Another methodology is to utilize arbitrarily encryption unscrambling (utilizing idea of perplexity dispersion) since it anticipates second step extraction of side channel assault.

- **Man in Middle attack:** A man in the middle attack is one in which the aggressor captures messages in an open key trade and afterward retransmits them, substituting his own open key for the mentioned one, with the goal that the two unique gatherings still seem, by all accounts, to be speaking with one another. All the while, the two unique gatherings seem to convey typically. The message sender doesn't perceive that the beneficiary is an obscure assailant attempting to get to or change the message previously retransmitting to the collector. Subsequently, the assailant controls the whole correspondence. Some sort of MIM assaults are:
  - **Address Resolution Protocol Communication (ARP):** In the ordinary ARP correspondence, the host PC will send a parcel which has the source and goal IP address inside the bundle and will communicate it to every one of the gadgets associated with the system. The gadget which has the objective IP address will just send the ARP answer with its Macintosh address in it and afterward correspondence happens. The ARP convention isn't a verified convention and the ARP store doesn't have a secure system which results in a major issue.
  - **ARP Cache Poisoning:** In ARP store harming, the assailant would sniff onto the system by controlling the system change to screen the system traffic and farce the ARP parcels between the host and the goal PC and play out the MIM assault.
  - **DNS Spoofing:** The objective, for this situation, will be furnished with counterfeit data which would prompt loss of qualifications. As clarified before this is a sort of online MIM assault where the aggressor has made a phony site of your bank, so when you visit your bank site you will be diverted to the site made by the assailant and afterward the aggressor will increase every one of your qualifications.
  - **Session Hijacking:** In this once the session is set up between the host PC and the web server the assailant can acquire certain pieces of the session foundation which is finished by catching the treats that were utilized for the session foundation.
- **Authentication attack:** Confirmation is a frail point in distributed computing administrations which is often focused by an assailant. Today the vast majority of the administrations still utilize basic username and secret phrase kind of learning based confirmation, yet some special case are budgetary foundations which are utilizing different types of auxiliary validation, (for example, shared mystery questions, site keys, virtual consoles, and so forth.) that make it progressively hard for mainstream phishing assaults. Some validation assaults are:
  - **Brute Force Attacks**: In this kind of assault, every single imaginable blend of secret key applies to break the secret key. The animal power assault is commonly applied to split the encoded passwords where the passwords are spared in the type of scrambled content.
  - **Dictionary Attack**: This kind of Attack is generally quicker than beast power assault. Not at all like checking all conceivable outcomes utilizing savage power assault, the lexicon assault attempts to coordinate the secret phrase with generally happening words or expressions of everyday life use.

- ○ **Shoulder Surfing**: Shoulder Surfing is an elective name of "spying" in which the aggressor sees the client's developments to get his/her secret phrase. In this kind of assault, the assailant watches the client; how he enters the secret phrase for example what keys of console the client has squeezed.
- ○ **Replay Attacks**: The replay assaults are otherwise called the reflection assaults. It is an approach to assault challenge reaction client confirmation system.
- ○ **Phishing Attacks**: It is an electronic assault where the assailant diverts the client to the phony site to get passwords/Pin Codes of the client.
- ○ **Key Loggers**: The key lumberjacks are the product programs which screens the client exercises by recording each furthermore, every key squeezed by the client.

Solution: 1) Deferred reaction: Given a login-name/secret word pair the server gives a marginally postponed yes/no answer (say not quicker than one answer for every second). This ought to keep an aggressor from checking adequately numerous passwords in a sensible time. **2) Record locking:** Accounts are bolted after a couple of fruitless login endeavors (for instance, a record is bolted for an hour after five fruitless endeavors). Like the past measure, this measure is intended to keep assailants from checking adequately numerous passwords in a sensible time. **3) Biometrics:** Biometric is a picture-based verification framework in which fingerprints, face, iris, retinal, discourse, signature check are utilized to confirm against the first example. The picture is preprocessed first and afterward the order of pictures is finished.

What is E- Commerce?

E-commerce is also known as electronic commerce. It is a type of an organization which deals with selling or buying its product through the online environment. This may include either any computer network or internet. For example, Microsoft Outlook, which allows the end users to send and receive faxes using email accounts. Nowadays, it is widely accepted in almost all the area such as- online payment transactions, supply chain management, automated information collection system, mobile commerce, electronic data interchange etc. in order to facilitate any business smooth processing it allows to exchange the data to resolve the financial and payment issue. It seems as one of the effective and efficient way for calculating any business. Many researchers share their own view regarding the e-commerce and how it can be utilized by small organizations to establish their business.

According to Raymond (2001), describe e-commerce as- "The function of information are exchange and commercial transaction support that operate on telecommunication, networks linking business customers and suppliers". On the other hand, Turbon et al. (2002), describes e-commerce as: "An emerging concept that describes the process of buying, selling or exchanging service and information via computer also".

Inclusion of e-commerce in business also bring many advantages to any organization such as-

1. It helps organization to have a profit by decreasing the cost and incrementing the sale of their product.
2. With the help of e-commerce any business organization can work 24*7 without any stoppage.
3. Use of e-commerce makes it feasible and easy to shop for customer by just sitting at one place only.
4. It helps the organization to have their customer from all over the world not to a particular region based on the internet.

E-commerce is used by almost all the organization from small, medium scale to large scale organization. Table 4 describe the various categories for e-commerce-based applications ranging from medium to small level organizations-

Table 4. E-commerce Applications

E-commerce Application	Description
Electronic Marketing	• Allow the customer to contact with sales officer. • Use internet to find out the customer requirements. • Use internet for satisfying the customer needs. • Satisfy the customer through the use of electronic channel. • Show the required information with intended customer or supplier.
Electronic order and delivery of product	• Customer can order the required data or service online. • Customer can track the outgoing and incoming of their data delivery. • The business transaction cost is also minimized.
Electronic Advertising	• Only those products are displayed to the customers which are accordance to their requirements. • The broacher or guide of the entire product is available online. • All the product information is also maintained online. • Corresponding company name of product is also accessible.
Electronic Payment System	• Facilitate Electronic Fund Transfer (EFT) • Provide the facilities for electronic card, online credit card processing and prepaid card processing.
Customer Support Service Centre	• Availability of Frequently Asked Questions (FAQ) • Handling the customer queries online, new customer registration, feedback evaluation online.

Difficulties Faced by E-Commerce

Nowadays, each and every organization tries to using e-commerce for their product selling and gaining higher profit from the customers. But still they are facing many problems as shown in figure 6 and to resolve this all e-commerce organization are adopting the cloud computing. These difficulties can be summarized as-

- **Low Capital:** In order to smooth functioning of any e-commerce-based organization, a great investment is a primary requirement for purchasing and maintaining the hardware. And when the organization grows due to large data flow a greater number of end user's interaction, there is also a need arise to update the various hardware as well as software characteristics requirements for maintaining the same infrastructure. It is not easy for much e-commerce organization to scale their hardware/ software after a limit. In this case, a, low capital will be generated for organization as most of the meeting part is spend in maintenance.
- **Security & Privacy of data:** Due to the large number of cases of fraud, data leakage, hacking details and software security holes many organizations are hesitating for the movement to cloud.
- **Lack of Technical People:** E-commerce business organization is totally depending upon the usage of web technology. For any e-business there is need of skill people in this area. They all responsible for the management and conservation. Because of increasing demand of e-business

there are various technical issue already resolved at such as data integration, data mining, data store, information security and so on. But many issues are still hindered and become a challenging task for medium to small scale organization due to lack of technical & technology support.

- **Mobile Terminal:** With the incoming of 3G era, mobile communication is become a necessity in our life. The mobile terminal will also become a prime source of e-commerce in future also. Therefore, a switching requirement to the mobile terminal is also a big challenge in front of e-commerce application with lot of challenges such as information security and processing.

Figure 6. Cloud Computing with E-commerce

Difficulties faced by E-commerce	Cloud Computing benefit for E commerce	Difficulties faced by E-commerce after using Cloud Computing
1. Low Capital 2. Security & Privacy of data 3. Lack of technical people 4. Mobile Terminal	1. Security & Trust 2. Construction & operation cost 3. Mobility 4. Decision making model 5. Quality 6. Tailored in investment 7. Global Expansion 8. Scalability of Cloud Computing	1. Lack of rules & Regulations 2. Cloud Computing Security Issues 3. Regulatory of Service Provider

Cloud Computing for E-Commerce

E-commerce come into the limelight since 1970s. the primary focus of e-commerce is to allow the various organization to do their all business-related task such as transactions, data handling etc. are managed electronically. It allows the organizations to sell and buy their product online without any physical setup of business space. Cloud computing helps the e-commerce business application by lowering their infrastructure cost and increase the deployment speed. The usage of cloud computing in e-commerce business application reduce the cost for hardware and software installations as well as it allows the business to dynamically add or remove their required resources as the business grows with the passage of time.

Cloud Computing Benefit for E-commerce

The usage of cloud computing with e-commerce bring many benefits for e-commerce organization as shown in figure 6-

- **Security & Trust:** Any owner who store its data over cloud environment, the first concern is its data security Babar (2011). Apart from privacy the other issue is to maintain the trust among different entities to encourage a number of users towards the usage of cloud computing. Any organization which adopting the cloud computing service always ensures that service provider will strictly follow all the security policies and standards. Any e-commerce application uses the best choice regarding the security standard while storing the data in cloud.

- **Construction & Operation Cost:** As any organization grows, simultaneously there is an increment in its data. It will raise the requirement of new hardware and software to maintain their data. After using the cloud computing all these issues related to data storage, operation and maintenance are resolved by service provider without any involvement of organization.

- **Mobility:** Usage of cloud computing helps the e-commerce applications in accessing their data or service at anytime and anywhere with the usage of mobile devices by just connecting with the internet.

- **Decision Making Model:** Nowadays many business organizations which are using e-commerce facing a number of problems as- a) with the large number of users, data volume becoming large and large. Therefore, for storage, management and data mining large capabilities is required. b) Secondly, the user's requirements are changing rapidly which require business intelligence real time property. The usage of Business Intelligence (BI) will help in taking the decision regarding the business.

- **Quality:** The quality of any service is depending upon its reliability, flexibility and accessibility of it's to the users from anywhere and anytime. Many of the CSP such as Google, IBM, Amazon data centres are scattered all over the world to provide the reliability of their data and maintain its quality in case of any failure also Buyya (2008).

- **Tailored in Investment:** The usage of cloud computing saves the total investment cost of any e-commerce organization by up to 70- 80%. This will help the e-commerce to improve their infrastructure and future development. Out of many features two most important are data flexibility and scalability of cloud computing which encourage the various e-commerce organization to move towards its adaption.

- **Global Expansion:** It require that e-commerce data is available and accessible to the whole world through the usage of cloud technology. Use of cloud technique helps in handling many e-commerce applications to be available to the customers at anytime and anywhere.

- **Resource scalability in Cloud Computing:** Out of many advantages the popular advantage after adapting the cloud computing is to scale the resources or upgrade the resources as need arise and after using dispose them if they no needed for longer time. This will help the e-commerce organization not to worry about required resources at initial stage only.

Difficulties Faced by E-commerce after using Cloud Computing

Usage of cloud computing in e-commerce not only brings advantages only but still come with many difficulties also as shown in figure 6, which need to be solved.

- **Lack of rules & Regulation:** There are no specific guidelines regarding any rules or regulation for the usage of cloud computing in e-commerce. Because of this limitation of law and regulation sometime many problems will not be able to solve in specific time period.
- **Cloud Computing security issue:** Under the cloud environment it is easier to solve many security issues such as end user authenticity, data integrity, repudiation etc. but still many security issues are still unsolved as- network security, trust maintenance among different parties, data confidentiality etc.
- **Regulation of Service Provider:** In cloud environment all the tasks related to data storage, data processing, maintenance is handled by the service provider only. But there is no way to monitor the service provider, control them and regulate their services.

RELATED WORK

Darwazeh et. Al (2015) proposed a productive distributed cloud storage model that gives classification and honesty through information arrangement and limits the multifaceted nature and handling time expected to scramble the information by applying TLS, AES and SHA security instrument dependent on the sort of arranged information. They tried the proposed model with arranged encryption calculations, and their recreation results indicated the effectiveness and unwavering quality. This paper is built up on the possibility of manual order of information and not the programmed order and other encryption calculations, for example, RSA, Elliptic Curve cryptography, and uneven open key can be utilized to give the higher level of security and secrecy.

Sengupta et al. (2015), planned an encryption calculation Hybrid DESCAST to give the security to the huge measure of information sent through the web. Through proposed calculation, they handled the constraints of the two DES and CAST Block Cipher Algorithm and broke down that the calculation time and multifaceted nature for encryption and unscrambling is higher than the separate DES and CAST calculation. What's more, they reasoned that consolidating 128-piece key and 64-piece key figure calculations, the savage power assault and assaults through birthday issues were turned away and the calculation is progressively strong.

Ko et al. (2013), proposed a security model that keeps the most secret and basic information on the private cloud also, lay of it on the general population cloud and for checking the honesty of the information at general society cloud this model uses the hash codes. The author proposed cloud security model that partners a job to every client and stores the job of the client in the database for client approval process and activities can be performed by the client as for their jobs. Additionally, for security reason, this model uses double check conspire for key confirmation on one layer what's more, client validation by utilizing username and secret key on another layer. A cryptographic procedure is proposed for keeping information secure on the cloud. Author also dissected the model against different sorts of assaults. This model is thought about with different existing cloud security structures and the recreation results demonstrated that this procedure is a lot increasingly hearty, effective and quicker than other existing models. Besides, this model is effective regarding cost since it stores exceptionally touchy information on the private cloud and less basic information on people in general cloud, where capacity cost of information is moderately very less.

Hwang et al. (2011), has proposed an information security model utilizing encryption what's more, unscrambling calculations. The model utilized such a instrument that the cloud specialist organization can perform capacity and encryption/unscrambling errands. The downside of this strategy is that the client or information proprietor has no control of information.

Prakash et al. (2014), proposed a proficient information encryption and decoding utilizing 256 piece symmetric key with revolution for verifying the exceptionally basic remote information in cloud worldview. They directed an examination on the variable size content documents store and it indicated that the proposed technique is better than existing techniques. Additionally, they presented the system for verifying the cloud server from unapproved clients. Likewise, they have too exhibited the presentation investigation of encryption and decoding calculations.

Lai et al. (2013), proposed an Attribute-Based Encryption (ABE) and unscrambling strategy in the cloud-based framework to give information security. They have been planned such a decoding calculation which depends on the client mentioned properties of the redistributed encoded information. The constraint of this strategy is that it accentuation increasingly computational and capacity overhead on cloud specialist organization for checking the client qualities with the re-appropriated encoded information. Despite the fact that these overheads of the cloud server can be limited by presenting outsider examiner.

Liu et al. (2012), talked about the security issues in distributed computing, methodologies to battle security issues what's more, exhibited different cloud borders. He broke down that the administration accessibility and information protection in the cloudbased frameworks are of the base worry in security and through relative investigation he made a decision about that security issue can't be handled through single security technique furthermore, numerous customary and late innovations and methodologies must be required for ensuring the cloud-based frameworks.

Moghaddam et al. (2013), evaluated the near investigation of six extraordinary symmetric key cryptographic calculations in a cloud-based condition. They proposed two sorts of cloud servers; that is cloud and information servers. The confinement of this technique is that it makes stockpiling and calculation overheads of keeping up two separate servers.

REFERENCES

Babar, M. A., & Chauhan, M. A. (2011, May). A tale of migration to cloud computing for sharing experiences and observations. In *Proceedings of the 2nd international workshop on software engineering for cloud computing* (pp. 50-56). ACM. 10.1145/1985500.1985509

Brodkin, J. (2008). Gartner: Seven cloud-computing security risks. *InfoWorld, 2008*, 1–3.

Buyya, R., Yeo, C. S., & Venugopal, S. (2008, September). Market-oriented cloud computing: Vision, hype, and reality for delivering it services as computing utilities. In *2008 10th IEEE international conference on high performance computing and communications* (pp. 5-13). IEEE.

Darwazeh, N. S., Al-Qassas, R. S., & AlDosari, F. (2015). A secure cloud computing model based on data classification. *Procedia Computer Science, 52*, 1153–1158. doi:10.1016/j.procs.2015.05.150

Gens, F. (2009). New IDC IT cloud services survey: Top benefits and challenges. *IDC exchan.*

Hwang, J. J., Chuang, H. K., Hsu, Y. C., & Wu, C. H. (2011, April). A business model for cloud computing based on a separate encryption and decryption service. In *2011 International Conference on Information Science and Applications* (pp. 1-7). IEEE.

Ko, R. K., Jagadpramana, P., Mowbray, M., Pearson, S., Kirchberg, M., Liang, Q., & Lee, B. S. (2011, July). TrustCloud: A framework for accountability and trust in cloud computing. In *2011 IEEE World Congress on Services* (pp. 584-588). IEEE. 10.1109/SERVICES.2011.91

Lai, J., Deng, R. H., Guan, C., & Weng, J. (2013). Attribute-based encryption with verifiable outsourced decryption. *IEEE Transactions on Information Forensics and Security*, 8(8), 1343–1354. doi:10.1109/TIFS.2013.2271848

Liu, W. (2012, April). Research on cloud computing security problem and strategy. In *2012 2nd International Conference on Consumer Electronics, Communications and Networks (CECNet)* (pp. 1216-1219). IEEE. 10.1109/CECNet.2012.6202020

Malik, M. I., & Wani, S. H. (2018). Cloud Computing Technologies. *International Journal of Advanced Research in Computer Science*, 9(2), 379–384. doi:10.26483/ijarcs.v9i2.5760

Moghaddam, F. F., Karimi, O., & Alrashdan, M. T. (2013, November) A comparative study of applying real-time encryption in cloud computing environments. In *2013 IEEE 2nd International Conference on Cloud Networking (CloudNet)* (pp. 185-189). IEEE. 10.1109/CloudNet.2013.6710575

Prakash, G. L., Prateek, M., & Singh, I. (2014, July). Data encryption and decryption algorithms using key rotations for data security in cloud system. In *2014 International Conference on Signal Propagation and Computer Technology (ICSPCT 2014)* (pp. 624-629). IEEE. 10.1109/ICSPCT.2014.6884895

Ramgovind, S., Eloff, M. M., & Smith, E. (2010, August). *The management of security in cloud computing. In 2010 Information Security for South Africa.* IEEE.

Raymond, L. (2001). Determinants of Web site implementation in small business. *Internet Research: Electronic Network Applications and Policy*, 411.

Sengupta, N., & Chinnasamy, R. (2015). Contriving hybrid DESCAST algorithm for cloud security. *Procedia Computer Science*, 54, 47–56. doi:10.1016/j.procs.2015.06.006

Turban, E., King, D., Lee, J., & Viehland, D. (2002). *Electronic commerce: A managerial perspective 2002.* Prentice Hall.

Weinhardt, C., Anandasivam, A., Blau, B., & Stößer, J. (2009). Business models in the service world. *IT Professional*, 11(2), 28–33. doi:10.1109/MITP.2009.21

Compilation of References

Abdelwahab, S., Hamdaoui, B., Guizani, M., & Znati, T. (2016). Replisom: disciplined tiny memory replication for massive IoT devices in LTE edge cloud. IEEE Internet of Things Journal, 3(3).

Abdoos, M., Mozayani, N., & Bazzan, A. L. (2011, October). Traffic light control in non-stationary environments based on multi agent Q-learning. In *2011 14th International IEEE conference on intelligent transportation systems (ITSC)* (pp. 1580-1585). IEEE.

Abomhara, M., & Køien, G. M. (2015). Cyber Security and the Internet ofThings: Vulnerabilities, Threats, Intruders and Attacks. *Journal of Cyber Security*, *4*, 65–88. doi:10.13052/jcsm2245-1439.414

Adu-Gyamfi, Y. O., Asare, S. K., Sharma, A., & Titus, T. (2017). Automated vehicle recognition with deep convolutional neural networks. *Transportation Research Record: Journal of the Transportation Research Board*, *2645*(1), 113–122. doi:10.3141/2645-13

Agarwal, S., Pandey, S. K., & Singh, J. (2014). Realization of efficient RF energy harvesting circuits employing different matching techniques. *Int. Symp on Quality Electronic Design (ISDEQ)*, 754-761.

Agrafiotis, I., Nurse, J. R. C., Goldsmith, M., Creese, S., & Upton, D. (2018). A taxonomy of cyber-harms: Defining the impacts of cyber-attacks and understanding how they propagate. *Journal of Cybersecurity*, *4*(1), 1–15. doi:10.1093/cybsec/tyy006

Agrawal, S. K. (2017). Software Defined Millimeter Wave 5th Generation Communications System. *Application and Theory of Computer Technology, 2*(1), 46-56.

Agrawal, S. K. (2019). 5th generation millimeter wave wireless communication propagation losses dataset for indian metro cities based on corresponding weather conditions. Data in Brief, 23.

Agrawal, A., Alenezi, M., Pandey, D., Kumar, R., & Khan, R. A. (2019). Usable-Security Assessment through a Decision Making Procedure. *ICIC Express Letters*, *10*(8), 665–672.

Agrawal, A., Zarour, M., Alenezi, M., Kumar, R., & Khan, R. A. (2019). Security durability assessment through fuzzy analytic hierarchy process. *Peer J. Computer Science*, *5*, 1–44. doi:10.7717/peerj-cs.215

Agrawal, S. K. (2016). 5G Millimeter Wave (mmWave) communication system with software defined radio (SDR). *Proceedings of the International Conference on Recent Trends in Engineering & Science (ICRTES-16)*.

Agrawal, S. K. (2016). 5G millimeter wave (mmWave) communications. In *3rd International Conference on Computing for Sustainable Global Development (INDIACom)* (pp. 3630-3634). IEEE.

Agrawal, S. K. (2018). *Intelligent Software Defined Atmospheric Effect Processing for 5th Generation (5G) Millimeter Wave (MMWave)*. Communication System. doi:10.5815/ijwmt.2018.02.02

Ahmad, N., & Habib, K. (2010). *Analysis of Network Security Threats and Vulnerabilities by Development & Implementation of a Security Network Monitoring Solution.* Blekinge Institute of Technology.

Akyildiz, I. F., Lee, W. Y., & Chowdhury, K. R. (2009). CRAHNs: Cognitive radio ad hoc networks. *Ad Hoc Networks*, *7*(5), 810–836. doi:10.1016/j.adhoc.2009.01.001

Alam, M., Fernandes, B., Almeida, J., Ferreira, J., & Fonseca, J. (2016). Integration of smart parking in distributed ITS architecture. *Proceedings of the 2016 International Conference on Open Source Systems & Technologies (ICOSST).* 10.1109/ICOSST.2016.7838582

Aldosari, W., & Taeib, T. E. (2015). Secure Key Establishment for Device-To-Device Communications among Mobile Devices. *International Journal of Engineering Research and Reviews*, *3*(2), 43–47.

Alenezi, M., Kumar, R., Agrawal, A., & Khan, R. A. (2019). Usable-security attribute evaluation using fuzzy analytic hierarchy process. *ICIC Express Letter-An International Journal of Research and Survey.*, *13*(6), 1–17.

Allal & Boudjit. (2013, February). Geocast Routing Protocols for VANETs: Survey and Geometry-Driven Scheme Proposal. *Journal of Internet Services and Information Security, 3*(1-2), 20-36.

Allal, S., & Boudjit, S. (2012). Geocast Routing Protocols for VANETs: Survey and Guidelines. *2012 Sixth International Conference on Innovative Mobile and Internet Services in Ubiquitous Computing*, 323–328. 10.1109/IMIS.2012.133

Altayeb & Mahgoub. (2013, July). A Survey of Vehicular Ad hoc Networks Routing Protocols. *International Journal of Innovation and Applied Studies, 3*(3), 829-846.

Amaral, P., Dinis, J., Pinto, P., Bernardo, L., Tavares, J., & Mamede, H. S. (2016). Machine learning in software defined networks: Data collection and traffic classification. *Proceedings - International Conference on Network Protocols, ICNP.* 10.1109/ICNP.2016.7785327

Analoui, M., Mirzaei, A., & Kabiri, P. (2005). Intrusion detection using multivariate analysis of variance algorithm. *Third International Conference on Systems, Signals & Devices SSD*, 3.

Answer & Guy. (2014). A Survey of VANET Technologies. *Journal of Emerging Trends in Computing and Information Sciences.*

Antoniou, J., & Pitsillides, A. (2007). *4G converged environment: Modeling network selection as a game. In 16th IST Mobile and Wireless Communications Summit.* IEEE. doi:10.1109/ISTMWC.2007.4299242

Anwer, S., & Guy, C. (2014). A Survey of Vehicular technologies. *Journal of Emerging Trends in Computing and Information Science, 5*(9).

Araghi, S., Khosravi, A., & Creighton, D. (2014, July). Optimal design of traffic signal controller using neural networks and fuzzy logic systems. In *2014 International Joint Conference on Neural Networks (IJCNN)* (pp. 42-47). IEEE. 10.1109/IJCNN.2014.6889477

Araghi, S., Khosravi, A., Johnstone, M., & Creighton, D. (2013, October). Intelligent traffic light control of isolated intersections using machine learning methods. In *2013 IEEE International Conference on Systems, Man, and Cybernetics* (pp. 3621-3626). IEEE. 10.1109/SMC.2013.617

Arzil, S., Hosseinpour, M., & Jabraeil Jamali, M. (2010). *Adaptive routing protocol for VANETs in city environments using real-time traffic information.* Academic Press.

Aslam, M., Shah, T., Javaid, N., Rahim, A., Rahman, Z., & Khan, Z. A. (2012). CEEC: Centralized energy efficient clustering a new routing protocol for WSNs. *Sensor, Mesh and Ad-Hoc Communications and Networks (SECON), 2012 9th Annual IEEE Communications Society Conference on IEEE.*

Aslam, N., Philips, W., Robertson, W., & Siva Kumar, S.H. (2011). A multi-criterion optimization technique for energy efficient cluster formation in Wireless Sensor networks. *Information Fusion, 12*(3).

Aslam, Rasheed, Shah, Rahim, Khan, Qasim, Qasim, Hassan, Khan, & Javaid. (2013). Energy optimization and Performance Analysis of Cluster Based Routing Protocols Extended from LEACH for WSNs. *International Journal of Modern Engineering Research, 3*(2).

Astarita, V., Vaiana, R., Iuele, T., Caruso, M. V., Vincenzo, P., & De Masi, F. (2014). 2014, "Automated Sensing System for Monitoring of Road Surface Quality by Mobile Devices. *Procedia: Social and Behavioral Sciences, 111*, 242–251. doi:10.1016/j.sbspro.2014.01.057

Atéchian, T., & Brunie, L. (2008). *DG-Castor: Direction-Based Geocast Routing Protocol for Query Dissemination in Vanet. IADIS International Telecommunications. Networks and Systems.*

Ateniese, G. (2007). Proble Data Posseon.atUntrued and Store. *Proc. 14th ACM Conf. Computer and Comm. Security (CCS '07)*, 598-609.

Atzori, Iera, & Morabito. (2010). The Internet of Things: A Survey. *Journal of Computer Networks, 54*(15).

Awodele, O., Onuiri, E. E., & Okolie, S. (2012). Vulnerabilities in Network Infrastructures and Prevention/Containment Measures. Informing Science & IT Education Conference (InSITE), 53-67.

Azzouni, A., & Pujolle, G. (2018). NeuTM: A neural network-based framework for traffic matrix prediction in SDN. In *IEEE/IFIP Network Operations and Management Symposium: Cognitive Management in a Cyber World, NOMS 2018* (pp. 1–5). Institute of Electrical and Electronics Engineers Inc. 10.1109/NOMS.2018.8406199

Babar, M. A., & Chauhan, M. A. (2011, May). A tale of migration to cloud computing for sharing experiences and observations. In *Proceedings of the 2nd international workshop on software engineering for cloud computing* (pp. 50-56). ACM. 10.1145/1985500.1985509

Bai, Y., Mai, Y., & Wang, N. (2017). Performance comparison and evaluation of the proactive and reactive routing protocols for MANETs. *IEEE Wireless Telecommunications Symposium (WTS).* 10.1109/WTS.2017.7943538

Bandyopadhyay & Coyle. (2003). An Energy Efficient Hierarchical Clustering Algorithm for Wireless Sensor Networks. *IEEE INFOCOM.*

Bays, L. R., Oliveira, R. R., Barcellos, M. P., Gaspary, L. P., & Madeira, E. R. M. (2015). Virtual network security: Threats, countermeasures, and challenges. *Journal of Internet Services and Applications, 6*(1), 1–19. doi:10.118613174-014-0015-z

Behal, S., & Kumar, K. (2016). Trends in Validation of DDoS Research. *Procedia Computer Science, 85*, 7–15. doi:10.1016/j.procs.2016.05.170

Ben Jaballah, W., Conti, M., & Lal, C. (2019). *A Survey on Software-Defined VANETs: Benefits, Challenges, and Future Directions.* Retrieved from https://arxiv.org/abs/1904.04577

Bendaoud, F., Abdennebi, M., & Didi, F. (2015). Network selection using game theory. In *3rd International Conference on Control, Engineering & Information Technology (CEIT)* (pp. 1–6). IEEE. 10.1109/CEIT.2015.7233014

Bennett, K., Rigby, M., & Budgen, D. (2006). Role Based Access Control – a Solution with Its Own Challenges. *IEEE Proceedings - Software, 153*(1), 1-3.

Berner, B. (2011). Seven unforgivable errors in network security. *Binesh Magazine*, 53-55.

Bhadoria & Jaiswal. (2016). Performance Analysis of Traffic Type and Routing Protocols in VANET for City Scenario. *International Journal of Urban Design for Ubiquitous Computing, 4*(1).

Bhoi, S. K., & Khilar, P. M. (2014). Vehicular communication: A survey. *IET Network, 3*(3), 204–217. doi:10.1049/iet-net.2013.0065

Birge, J. R., Khabazian, A., & Peng, J. (2018). Optimization Modeling and Techniques for Systemic Risk Assessment and Control in Financial Networks. *Tutorials in Operations Research (INFORMS)*, 64-84.

Biswas, S., Tatchikou, R., & Dion, F. (2006). Vehicle-to-vehicle wireless communication protocols for enhancing highway traffic safety. *IEEE Communications Magazine, 44*(1), 74–82. doi:10.1109/MCOM.2006.1580935

Blum, J., Eskandarian, A., & Hoffman, L. (2003, June). Mobility management in IVC networks. *Proceedings of IEEE Intelligent Vehicles Symposium*. 10.1109/IVS.2003.1212900

Bonomi, F., Milito, R., Natarajan, P., & Zhu, J. (2014). Fog Computing: A Platform for Internet of Things and Analytics. In Studies in Computational Intelligence, (vol. 546). Springer.

Bowers, K. D. (2009). A High Availabe& Integrity based Layers for Cloud Storage. *Proc. ACM Conf. Comput& Comm. Security (CCS '09)*, 187-198.

Brenton, C., & Hunt, C. (n.d.). *Mastering Network Security* (2nd ed.). Wiley.

Brodkin, J. (2008). Gartner: Seven cloud-computing security risks. *InfoWorld, 2008*, 1–3.

Buckley, J. J. (1985). Fuzzy hierarchical analysis. *Fuzzy Sets and Systems, 17*(3), 233–247. doi:10.1016/0165-0114(85)90090-9

Budhraja, K. K., Malvankar, A., Bahrami, M., Kundu, C., Kundu, A., & Singhal, M. (2017). Risk-Based Packet Routing for Privacy and Compliance-Preserving SDN. In *IEEE International Conference on Cloud Computing, CLOUD* (pp. 761–765). 10.1109/CLOUD.2017.109

Bui, K. H. N., Lee, O. J., Jung, J. J., & Camacho, D. (2016, June). Dynamic Traffic Light Control System Based on Process Synchronization Among Connected Vehicles. In *International Symposium on Ambient Intelligence* (pp. 77-85). Springer. 10.1007/978-3-319-40114-0_9

Bulumulle, G., & Bölöni, L. (2016). A study of the automobile blind-spots' spatial dimensions and angle of orientation on side-sweep accidents. *Proceedings of the 2016 Symposium on Theory of Modeling and Simulation (TMS-DEVS)*.

Burgess, J. G. (2006). *MaxProp: Routing for Vehicle-Based Disruption-Tolerant Networks* (Vol. 6). Infocom.

Burleigh, S. &. (2007). *Bundle protocol specification*. IETF Request for Comments RFC 5050.

Buttler, J., & Akchurina, N. (2013). Nash Equilibria in Normal Games via Optimization Methods. *2013 European Control Conference (ECC)*. 10.23919/ECC.2013.6669658

Buyya, R., Yeo, C. S., & Venugopal, S. (2008, September). Market-oriented cloud computing: Vision, hype, and reality for delivering it services as computing utilities. In *2008 10th IEEE international conference on high performance computing and communications* (pp. 5-13). IEEE.

Cai, F., Gao, Y., Cheng, L., Sang, L., & Yang, D. (2016). Spectrum sharing for LTE and WiFi coexistence using decision tree and game theory. *IEEE Wireless Communications and Networking Conference, WCNC*. 10.1109/WCNC.2016.7565015

Cai, H., & Lin, Y. (2011). Modelling of Operators' Emotion and Task Performance in a Virtual Driving Environment. *International Journal of Human-Computer Studies, 69*(9), 571–586. doi:10.1016/j.ijhcs.2011.05.003

Camp, T., & Liu, Y. (2003). An Adaptive Mesh-based Protocol for Geocast Routing. *Journal of Parallel and Distributed Computing: Special Issue on Mobile Ad-Hoc Networking and Computing, 63*(2), 196–213. doi:10.1016/S0743-7315(02)00064-3

Canavan, J. E. (2000). *Fundamentals of Network Security.* Artech House Telecommunications Library.

Cao, Y. (2012). Routing in delay/disruption tolerant networks: A taxonomy, survey and challenges. *IEEE Communications Surveys & Tutorials, 15*(2), 654-677.

Casado, M., Foster, V. N., & Guha, A. (2014). Abstractions for Software-Defined Networks. *Communications of the ACM, 57*(10), 86–95. doi:10.1145/2661061.2661063

Castanedo, F. (2013). A review of data fusion techniques. *Sci. World J.*

Cesana, M., Malanchini, I., & Capone, A. (2008). Modelling network selection and resource allocation in wireless access networks with non-cooperative games. In *5th IEEE International Conference on Mobile Ad Hoc and Sensor Systems* (pp. 404–409). IEEE. 10.1109/MAHSS.2008.4660055

Chaintreau, A. H. (2007). Impact of human mobility on opportunistic forwarding algorithms. IEEE Transactions on Mobile Computing, 6, 606-620. doi:10.1109/TMC.2007.1060

Chandramouli, R. (2001). A framework for multiple authorization types in a healthcare application system. *17th Annual Computer Security Applications Conference.* 10.1109/ACSAC.2001.991530

Chang, C.-J., Tsai, T.-L., & Chen, Y.-H. (2009). *Utility and Game-Theory Based Network Selection Scheme in Heterogeneous Wireless Networks. In 2009 IEEE Wireless Communications and Networking Conference.* IEEE. doi:10.1109/WCNC.2009.4918016

Chang, C., Wu, C., & Lin, H. (2008). Integrating fuzzy theory and hierarchy concepts to evaluate software quality. *Springer Software Qual. J., 16*(2), 263–276. doi:10.100711219-007-9035-2

Chang, S. H. (2012). *Fuzzy Multi-Criteria Evaluation and Statistics.* Wunan Books.

Chao, K. H., Lee, R. H., & Wang, M. H. (2008, September). An intelligent traffic light control based on extension neural network. In *International Conference on Knowledge-Based and Intelligent Information and Engineering Systems* (pp. 17-24). Springer. 10.1007/978-3-540-85563-7_8

Charilas, D. E., & Panagopoulos, A. D. (2010). A survey on game theory applications in wireless networks. *Computer Networks, 54*(18), 3421–3430. doi:10.1016/j.comnet.2010.06.020

Charles, P., & Pñeeger, S. L. (2012). *Analyzing Computer Security: A Threat / Vulnerability / Countermeasure Approach.* Prentice Hall.

Chen, H. L., Tseng, C. C., & Hu, S. H. (2006). An adaptive handshaking-based geocasting protocol in MANETs. *IWCMC 2006 - Proceedings of the 2006 International Wireless Communications and Mobile Computing Conference, 2006,* 413–418. 10.1145/1143549.1143632

Chen, L., & Englund, C. (2016). A Survey. *IEEE Trans. Intell. Transport. Syst, 17,* 570–586.

Chen, Lin, & Ling. (2009). A Mobicast Routing Protocol in Vehicular Ad-Hoc Networks. *GLOBECOM, IEEE Global Telecommunications Conference.*

Chen, Y. R., Chen, K. P., & Hsiungy, P. A. (2016, November). Dynamic traffic light optimization and Control System using model-predictive control method. In *2016 IEEE 19th International Conference on Intelligent Transportation Systems (ITSC)* (pp. 2366-2371). IEEE 10.1109/ITSC.2016.7795937

Chen, Y., Shu, J., Zhang, S., Liu, L., & Sun, L. (2009). Data fusion in wireless sensor networks. *Electronic Commerce and Security, ISECS'09, 2*.

Chen, L., Tseng, Y., & Syue, K. (2014). *Vehicular tracking and reporting by V2V communications. Surveillance on-the-road: Comput. Netw.*

Chen, M., Li, F., & Wang, J. (2011). A game theoretical approach of network selection algorithm in heterogeneous wireless networks. In *IET International Communication Conference on Wireless Mobile and Computing (CCWMC 2011)* (pp. 148–153). IET. 10.1049/cp.2011.0865

Chen, Q.-B., Zhou, W.-G., Chai, R., & Tang, L. (2011). Game-theoretic approach for pricing strategy and network selection in heterogeneous wireless networks. *IET Communications, 5*(5), 676–682. doi:10.1049/iet-com.2010.0249

Chen, X., Zhao, P., Peng, Y., Liu, B., Li, W., Xie, Y., Chen, X., & Yuan, M. (2018). Risk analysis and optimization for communication transmission link interruption in Smart Grid cyberphysical system. *International Journal of Distributed Sensor Networks, 14*(2), 1–12. doi:10.1177/1550147718756035

Cherdantseva, Y., Burnap, P., Blyth, A., Eden, P., Jones, K., Soulsby, H., & Stoddart, K. (2016). A review of cyber security risk assessment methods for SCADA systems. *Computers & Security, 56*, 1–27. doi:10.1016/j.cose.2015.09.009

Chiang, C. C., Wu, H. K., & Liu, W. (1997). Routing in Clustered MultiHop Mobile Wireless Networks with Fading Channel. *Proceedings of IEEE SICON*, 197–211.

Chopra, A. (2016). Security Issues of Firewall. *International Journal of P2P Network Trends and Technology, 6*(1).

Chung, B. D., & Seo, K. K. (2015). A Cloud Service Selection Model Based On Analytic Network Process. *Indian Journal of Science and Technology, 8*(18), 1-5.

CISCO Systems. (2001). *A beginner's guide to network security.* http://www.cisco.com/ warp/public/cc/so/neso/sqso/beggu_pl.pdf

Clancy, T. C., Kiyavash, N., & Lin, D. J. (2003). Secure smartcard-based fingerprint authentication. *Proceedings of the ACM SIGMM 2003 Multimedia, Biometrics Methods and Workshop*, 45–52.

Clausen, T., & Jacquet, P. (2003). *RFC 3626 - Optimized Link State Routing Protocol.* OLSR.

Correia, S., Boukerche, A., & Meneguette, R. I. (2017). An architecture for hierarchical software-defined vehicular networks. *IEEE Communications Magazine, 55*(7), 80–86. doi:10.1109/MCOM.2017.1601105

Corson & Macker. (1999, January). *Mobile Ad hoc Networking (MANET): Routing Protocol Performance Issues and Evaluation Considerations.* RFC 2501.

Curtmolaand. (2008). MR-PDP: MultileReplicationProvale Data Posssion. *Proc. IEEE Int. Conf. Distrtd Computing Systs (ICDCS '08)*, 411-420.

Curtmola, R., Khan, O., & Burns, R. (2008). Robust Remote Data Checking. *Proc. Fourth ACM Int. Worksp Storage Security systems & Survivability*, 63-68.

Dai, S., Jing, X., & Li, L. (2005). Research and Analysis on Routing Protocols for Wireless Sensor Networks. IEEE International Conference.

Daly, E. M. (2007). Social network analysis for routing in disconnected delay-tolerant manets. In *Proceedings of the 8th ACM international symposium on Mobile ad hoc networking and computing* (pp. 32-40). ACM. 10.1145/1288107.1288113

Dark Reading. (2011). *Sony data breach cleanup to cost $171 million*. http://www.darkreading.com/attacks-and-breaches/sony-data-breach-cleanupto-cost-\$171-million/d/d-id/1097898

Darwazeh, N. S., Al-Qassas, R. S., & AlDosari, F. (2015). A secure cloud computing model based on data classification. *Procedia Computer Science, 52*, 1153–1158. doi:10.1016/j.procs.2015.05.150

Dasarathy, B. V. (1997). *Sensor fusion potential exploitation-innovative architectures and illustrative applications. Proc. IEEE.*

Das, S. (2012). Analysis of neighbour and isolated node of intersection area based geocasting protocol (IBGP) in VANET. *International Journal of Wireless & Mobile Networks, 1*(1), 7–15. doi:10.5121/ijwmn.2012.4120

Das, S., & Lobiyal, D. K. (2012). *Intersection area based geocasting protocol (IBGP) for Vehicular Ad hoc networks. Lecture Notes of the Institute for Computer Sciences, Social-Informatics and Telecommunications Engineering.* doi:10.1007/978-3-642-27317-9_40

Daya, B. (2010). *Network Security: History, Importance, and Future.* University of Florida Department of Electrical and Computer Engineering.

Daya, B. (2013). *Network Security: History, Importance, and Future.* University of Florida Department of Electrical and Computer Engineering. http://web.mit.edu/~bdaya/www/Network%20Security.pdf

Dehni, L., & Bennani, Y. (2005). LEA2C: low energy adaptive connectionist clustering for wireless sensor networks. In *International Workshop on Mobile Agents for Telecommunication Applications.* Springer.

Deng, H. (1999). Multi criteria analysis with fuzzy pair wise comparisons. *International Journal of Approximate Reasoning, 21*(3), 215–231. doi:10.1016/S0888-613X(99)00025-0

Deng, Y., Hsu, D. F., Wu, Z., & Chu, C. H. (2012). Feature Selection and Combination for Stress Identification Using Correlation and Diversity. *Proceedings of the 12th International Symposium on Pervasive Systems, Algorithms and Networks.* 10.1109/I-SPAN.2012.12

Dhaka, Poonia, & Raja. (2014, April). The realistic mobility evaluation of vehicular ad-hoc network for indian automotive networks. *International Journal of Ad hoc, Sensor & Ubiquitous Computing, 5*(2).

Dhankhar & Agrawal. (2014, June). VANETs: A Survey on Routing Protocols and Issues. *International Journal of Innovative Research in Science, Engineering and Technology, 3*(6).

Dinesha, H. A., & Agrawal, V. K. (2012a). Formal Modeling for Multi-Level Authentication in Sensor-Cloud Integration System. *International Journal of Applied Information Systems, 2*(1), 16–21.

Dinesha, H. A., & Agrawal, V. K. (2012b). Multi-dimensional Password Generation Technique for accessing cloud services. Special Issue on: Cloud Computing and Web Services. *International Journal on Cloud Computing: Services and Architecture, 2*(3), 31–39.

Dolui, K., & Datta, S. K. (2017). Comparison of edge computing implementations: Fog computing, cloudlet and mobile edge computing. *Proceedings of the 2017 Global Internet of Things Summit, GIoTS 2017*, 1–6. 10.1109/GIOTS.2017.8016213

Domingos da Cunha, F., Villas, L., Boukerche, A., Maia, G., Viana, A. C., & …. (2016). Data Communication in VANETs: Survey, Applications and Challenges. *Ad Hoc Networks, Elsevier, 44*(C), 90–103. doi:10.1016/j.adhoc.2016.02.017

Dong, B., Wu, W., Yang, Z., & Li, J. (2016). Software Defined Networking Based On-Demand Routing Protocol in Vehicle Ad Hoc Networks. *Proceedings of the 12th International Conference on Mobile Ad-Hoc and Sensor Networks, MSN 2016*, 25. 10.1109/MSN.2016.041

Dong, L., & Peng, Y. (2012). Network Security and Firewall Technology. *Proceedings of 2010 3rd International Conference on Computer and Electrical Engineering (ICCEE2010no.2)*.

Doolan, R., & Muntean, G.M. (2017). EcoTrec—A Novel VANET-Based Approach to Reducing Vehicle Emissions. *IEEE Trans. Intell. Transport. Syst.*

Dreiseitl, S., & Ohno-Machado, L. (2002). Logistic regression and artificial neural network classification models: a methodology review. *Journal of Biomedical Informatics.*

Driving Tests. (2019, July). *How do traffic jams form.* Retrieved from: https://www.drivingtests.co.nz/resources/how-do-traffic-jams-form/

Dua, A., Kumar, N., & Bawa, S. (2014). A systematic review on routing protocols for Vehicular Ad Hoc Networks. *Vehicular Communications, 1*(1), 33–52. doi:10.1016/j.vehcom.2014.01.001

Dube, R., Rais, C. D., Wang, K.-Y., & Tripathi, S. K. (1996). *Signal Stability based Adaptive Routing (SSA) for Ad-Hoc Mobile Networks.* Academic Press.

Durrant-Whyte, H. F. (1988). Sensor models and multisensor integration. *The International Journal of Robotics Research, 7*(6), 97–113. doi:10.1177/027836498800700608

Durrant-Whyte, H. F., & Stevens, M. (2001). Data fusion in decentralized sensing networks. *Proceedings of the 4th International Conference on Information Fusion.*

Durresi, M., & Durresi, A. (2005). Emergency Broadcast Protocol for Inter-Vehicle Communications. *IEEE International Conference on Parallel and Distributed Systems (ICPADS'05).* 10.1109/ICPADS.2005.147

El Faouzi, N., & Klein, L.A. (2016). Data Fusion for ITS: Techniques and Research Needs. *Transport. Res. Procedia, 15*, 495–512.

Elleithy, K. M., Blagovic, D., Cheng, W., & Sideleau, P. (2006). Denial of Service Attack Techniques: Analysis, Implementation and Comparison. *Systemics, Cybernetics and Informatics, 3*(1), 66–71.

Enami, Moghadam, & Dadashtabar. (2010). Neural Network Based Energy Efficiency In Wireless Sensor Networks: A Survey. *International Journal of Computer Science and Engineering Survey, 1*(1).

Enami, N., Moghadam, R. A., Dadashtabar, K., & Hoseini, M. (2010). Neural network based energy efficiency in wireless sensor networks. *International Journal of Computer Science and Engineering Survey, 1*(1), 39–53. doi:10.5121/ijcses.2010.1104

Erway, C. (2009). Dynic Proable Data Possson. *Proc. ACM Conf. Computer and Comm. Security (CCS '09)*, 213-222.

Face Detection Using OpenCV With Haar Cascade Classifiers. (2019, August). Retrieved from https://becominghuman.ai/face-detection-using-opencv-with-haar-cascade-classifiers-941dbb25177

Fall, K. (2003). A delay-tolerant network architecture for challenged internets. In *Proceedings of the 2003 conference on Applications, technologies, architectures, and protocols for computer communications* (pp. 27-34). ACM. 10.1145/863955.863960

Farhady, Lee, & Nakao. (2015). Software-defined networking. *Computer Networks: The International Journal of Computer and Telecommunications Networking, 81.*

Farrow, R. (n.d.). *Network Security Tools.* http://sageweb.sage.org/pubs/whitepapers/ farrow.pdf

Features of Smart Cities. (2019, July). Retrieved from: https://www.bestcurrentaffairs.com/features-of-smart-cities/

Fedele, R., Praticò, F. G., Carotenuto, R., & Giuseppe Della Corte, F. (2017). Instrumented infrastructures for damage detection and management. *Proceedings of the 2017 5th IEEE International Conference on Models and Technologies for Intelligent Transportation Systems (MT-ITS).* 10.1109/MTITS.2017.8005729

Ferraiolo, D. F., Cugini, J. A., & Kuhn, D. R. (1999). *Role-Based Access Control (RBAC): Features and Motivations.* National Institute of Standards and Technology.

Ferraiolo, D. F., Kuhn, D. R., & Chandramouli, R. (2003). *Role-Based Access Control.* Artech House.

Festag, A. (2008). NoW - Network on wheels: Project objectives, technology and achievements. *5th International Workshop on Intelligent Transportation (WIT)*, 211-216.

Flauzac, O., Nolot, F., Rabat, C., & Steffenel, L. A. (2009). Grid of Security: A New Approach of the Network Security. *Proc. of Int. Conf. on Network and System Security, NSS '09*, 67-72. 10.1109/NSS.2009.53

Fong, A. C. M., Chan, C., Situ, L., & Fong, B. (2016). Wireless biosensing network for drivers' health monitoring. *Proceedings of the 2016 IEEE International Conference on Consumer Electronics (ICCE).* 10.1109/ICCE.2016.7430600

Forderer, D. (2005, May). *Street-Topology Based Routing* (Master's thesis). University of Mannheim.

Franco, L., Sahama, T., & Croll, P. (2008). Security Enhanced Linux to Enforce Mandatory Access Control in Health Information Systems. *Australasian Workshop on Health Data and Knowledge Management, the Australian Computer Science Week, Conference in Research and Practice in Information Technology Series, 327*, 27-33.

Franz, W., Hartenstein, H., & Mauve, M. (Eds.). (2005, November). *Inter-Vehicle-Communications Based on Ad Hoc Networking Principles-The Fleet Net Project.* Universitatverlag Karlsuhe.

Frenzel, L. (2018). *The Battle over V2V Wireless Technologies.* http://www.mwrf.com/systems/battle-over-v2v-wireless-technologies

Fubler, H., Hartenstein, H., Mauve, M., Effelsberg, W., & Widmer, J. (2004). Contention-based forwarding for street scenarios. In *1st International workshop in intelligent transportation (WIT 2004)* (No. LCA-CONF-2004-005). Academic Press.

Fu, S., Li, J., Li, R., & Ji, Y. (2014). A Game Theory Based Vertical Handoff Scheme for Wireless Heterogeneous Networks. In *10th International Conference on Mobile Ad-hoc and Sensor Networks* (pp. 220–227). 10.1109/MSN.2014.37

Garcia-Luna-Aceves, J. J., & Spohn, M. (n.d.). *Source-Tree Routing in Wireless Networks £.* Academic Press.

Gens, F. (2009). New IDC IT cloud services survey: Top benefits and challenges. *IDC exchan.*

Ghafoor, H., & Koo, I. (2018). CR-SDVN: A Cognitive Routing Protocol for Software-Defined Vehicular Networks. *IEEE Sensors Journal, 18*(4), 1761–1772. doi:10.1109/JSEN.2017.2788014

Gojak, V., Janjatovic, J., Vukota, N., Milosevic, M., & Bjelica, M. Z. (2017). Informational bird's eye view system for parking assistance. *Proceedings of the 2017 IEEE 7th International Conference on Consumer Electronics-Berlin (ICCE-Berlin).* 10.1109/ICCE-Berlin.2017.8210604

Goli, D. (2013). Group fuzzy TOPSIS methodology in computer security software selection. *International Journal of Fuzzy Logic Systems, 3*(2), 29–48. doi:10.5121/ijfls.2013.3203

Gond, S., & Gupta, N. (2012). Energy Efficient Deployment Techniques for Wireless Sensor Networks. *International Journal of Advanced Research in Computer Science and Software Engineering, 2*(7), 257–262.

Goyal, P., & Saxena, S. (2008). A dynamic decision model for vertical handoffs across heterogeneous wireless networks. In *World academy of science, engineering and Technology* (Vol. 31, pp. 677–682). Retrieved from http://citeseerx.ist. psu.edu/viewdoc/download?doi=10.1.1.306.7734&rep=rep1&type=pdf

Goyal, P., Lobiyal, D. K., & Katti, C. P. (2017). Vertical handoff in heterogeneous wireless networks: A tutorial. In *2017 International Conference on Computing, Communication and Automation (ICCCA)* (pp. 551–566). IEEE. 10.1109/ CCAA.2017.8229862

Goyal, P., Lobiyal, D. K., & Katti, C. P. (2018c). Game Theory for Vertical Handoff Decisions in Heterogeneous Wireless Networks: A Tutorial. In S. Bhattacharyya, T. Gandhi, K. Sharma, & P. Dutta (Eds.), Advanced Computational and Communication Paradigms (1st ed., Vol. 475). Singapore: Springer Singapore. doi:10.1007/978-981-10-8240-5

Goyal, P., Lobiyal, D. K., & Katti, C. P. (2018a). Dynamic user preference based group vertical handoffs in heterogeneous wireless networks: A non-cooperative game approach. *Wireless Networks*. Advance online publication. doi:10.100711276-018-1826-9

Goyal, P., Lobiyal, D. K., & Katti, C. P. (2018b). Dynamic User Preference Based Network Selection for Vertical Handoff in Heterogeneous Wireless Networks. *Wireless Personal Communications, 98*(1), 725–742. doi:10.100711277-017-4892-x

Granelli, F., Boato, G., & Kliazovich, D. (2006). MORA: A movement-based routing algorithm for vehicle ad hoc networks. *Proceeding in 1st IEEE Workshop AutoNet*.

Grasic, S. D. (2011). The evolution of a DTN routing protocol-PRoPHETv2. In *Proceedings of the 6th ACM workshop on Challenged networks* (pp. 27-30). ACM. 10.1145/2030652.2030661

Gray, D., Allen, J., Cois, C., Connell, A., Ebel, E., Gulley, W., & Wisniewski, B. D. (2015). *Improving federal cyber security governance through data driven decision making and execution.* Technical report–CMU/SEI-2015-TR-011, Software Engineering Institute, Carnegie Mellon University United States.

Grimaldo, J., & Mart, R. (2018). Performance comparison of routing protocols in VANETs under black hole attack in Panama City. *IEEE International Conference on Electronics, Communications and Computers (CONIELECOMP)*. 10.1109/CONIELECOMP.2018.8327187

Grover, J., Prajapati, N. K., Laxmi, V., & Gaur, M. S. (2011). Machine learning approach for multiple misbehavior detection in VANET. In *Communications in Computer and Information Science* (Vol. 192, pp. 644–653). CCIS. doi:10.1007/978-3-642-22720-2_68

Gruhn, H., Stöhr, D., Gövercin, M., & Glesner, S. (2013). Design and verification of a health-monitoring driver assistance system. *Proceedings of the 2013 7th International Conference on Pervasive Computing Technologies for Healthcare and Workshops*. 10.4108/icst.pervasivehealth.2013.252091

Haas, Pearlman, & Samar. (2002, July). *The Zone Routing Protocol (ZRP) for Ad Hoc Networks*. Internet Draft.

Haas, Z. J. (n.d.). *A new routing protocol for the reconfigurable wireless networks*. Retrieved from http://www.ee.cornell. edu/~haas/wnl.html

Hahn, W. J., Seaman, S. L., & Bikel, R. (2012). Making decisions with multiple attributes: A case in sustainability planning. *Graziadio Business Review, 15*(2), 365–381.

Hamedani, A. R. F. (2010). *Network Security Issues, Tools for Testing*. School of Information Science, Halmstad University.

Hamoud, O. N., Kenaza, T., & Challal, Y. (2017). Security in Device-to-Device communications (D2D): A survey. IET Networks, 1-10.

Hartenstein, H., & Laberteaux, K. P. (2010). *VANET: Vehicular Applications and Inter-Networking Technologies*. Wiley Online Library. doi:10.1002/9780470740637

Haw, R., Alam, M. G. R., & Hong, C. S. (2014). A context-aware content delivery framework for QoS in mobile cloud. In *APNOMS 2014 - 16th Asia-Pacific Network Operations and Management Symposium* (pp. 1–6). 10.1109/APNOMS.2014.6996607

Hawi, R., Okeyo, G., & Kimwele, M. (2017, July). Smart traffic light control using fuzzy logic and wireless sensor network. In *2017 Computing Conference* (pp. 450-460). IEEE. 10.1109/SAI.2017.8252137

He, M., Kalmbach, P., Blenk, A., Kellerer, W., & Schmid, S. (2017). Algorithm-data driven optimization of adaptive communication networks. In *Proceedings - International Conference on Network Protocols, ICNP* (pp. 1–6). 10.1109/ICNP.2017.8117592

He, Y., Yu, F. R., Zhao, N., Yin, H., & Boukerche, A. (2017). Deep reinforcement learning (DRL)-based resource management in software-defined and virtualized vehicular ad hoc networks. In *DIVANet 2017 - Proceedings of the 6th ACM Symposium on Development and Analysis of Intelligent Vehicular Networks and Applications, Co-located with MSWiM 2017* (Vol. 17, pp. 47–54). 10.1145/3132340.3132355

He, Yan, & Xu. (2014). Developing Vehicular Data Cloud Services in the IoT Environment. *IEEE Transactions on Industrial Informatics*.

Heinzelman, W. R., Chandrakasan, A., & Balakrishnan, H. (2000). Energy-efficient communication protocol for wireless microsensor networks. In *System sciences, Proceedings of the 33rd annual Hawaii international conference on*. IEEE.

Heinzelman, W., Chandrakasan, A., & Balakrishnan, H. (2000). Energy-efficient communication protocol for wireless microsensornetworks. In *System Sciences (HICSS '33) Proceedings of the 33rd Annual Hawaii International Conference on*. IEEE.

Henricksen, H., Caelli, W., & Croll, P. R. (2007). Securing Grid Data Using Mandatory Access Controls. *Proceedings of the fifth Australasian symposium on ACSW, ACM Intnl. Conf., 68*, 25-32.

He, Z., Cao, J., & Liu, X. (2016). SDVN: Enabling rapid network innovation for heterogeneous vehicular communication. *IEEE Network, 30*(4), 10–15. doi:10.1109/MNET.2016.7513858

Hilbrich, R. (n.d.). *Eclipse SUMO–Simulation of Urban Mobility*. Retrieved August 3, 2019 from https://www.dlr.de/ts/en/desktopdefault.aspx/tabid-9883/16931_read-41000

Hindustan Times. (2019, July). Retrieved from: https://www.hindustantimes.com/india-news/20-smart-cities-may-be-ready-only-by-2021/story-g3WNnnHEj8VSDROkTKYWjJ.html

Hossain, E., Chow, G., & Leung, V. C. M. (2010). Vehicular telematics over heterogeneous wireless networks: A survey. *Computer Communications, 33*(7). doi:10.1016/j.comcom.2009.12.010

Hossan, A., Kashem, F. B., Hasan, M. M., Naher, S., & Rahman, M. I. (2016). A smart system for driver's fatigue detection, remote notification and semi-automatic parking of vehicles to prevent road accidents. *Proceedings of the 2016 International Conference on Medical Engineering, Health Informatics and Technology (MediTec)*. 10.1109/MEDITEC.2016.7835371

Hu, V. C., Kahn, D. R., & Ferraiolo, D. (2014). *Guide to Attribute Based Access Control (ABAC) Definition and Considerations*. NIST Special Publication 800-162, Nat'l Institute of Standards and Technology.

Hu, Y. C., Patel, M., Sabella, D., Sprecher, N., & Young, V. (2015). *White paper: mobile edge computing a key technology towards 5G*. ETSI (European Telecommunications Standards Institute).

Hua, J. (2009). The Application of Artificial Neural Networks in Risk Assessment on High-tech Project Investment. *International Conference on Business Intelligence and Financial Engineering*, 17-20.

Huang, J., Zhang, T., & Metaxas, D. (2009). Learning with structured sparsity. *Proceedings of the International Conference on Machine Learning*, 417–424.

Hu, C., Hong, Y., & Hou, J. (2003). On mitigating the broadcast storm problem with directional antennas. *IEEE International Conference on Communications, 1*, 104–110. 10.1109/icc.2003.1204151

Hui, P. C. (2010). Bubble rap: Social-based forwarding in delay-tolerant networks. *IEEE Transactions on Mobile Computing, 10*(11), 1576-1589.

Hwang, J. J., Chuang, H. K., Hsu, Y. C., & Wu, C. H. (2011, April). A business model for cloud computing based on a separate encryption and decryption service. In *2011 International Conference on Information Science and Applications* (pp. 1-7). IEEE.

Ibrahim, K., Weigle, M. C., & Abuelela, M. (2009). P-IVG: Probabilistic inter-vehicle geocast for dense vehicular networks. *IEEE Vehicular Technology Conference*. 10.1109/VETECS.2009.5073804

IEEE 1609 - Family of Standards for Wireless Access in Vehicular Environments (WAVE). (n.d.). Retrieved July 25, 2019 from https://www.standards.its.dot.gov/factsheets/factsheet/80

Intelligent Transport Systems (ITS). (2012). *Framework for public mobile networks in cooperative its (c-its)s*. Tech. Rep., European Telecommunications Standards Institute (ETSI), Palo Alto, CA.

ITS Research Fact Sheets - Benefits of Intelligent Transportation Systems. (2019, July). Retrieved from: https://www.its.dot.gov/factsheets/benefits_factsheet.htm

Iwata, Chiang, Pei, Gerla, & Chen. (1999, August). Scalable Routing Strategies for Ad Hoc Wireless Networks. *IEEE Journal on Selected Areas in Communications*, 1369-79.

Izaddoost, A., Othman, M., & Rasid, M. F. A. (2007). Accurate ICMP traceback model under DoS/DDoS attack. *Proceedings of the international conference on advanced computing and communications, (ADCOM 2007)*, 441–446.

James, L., & Nahl, D. (2000). Road Rage and Aggressive Driving: Steering Clear of Highway Warfare. Prometheus Books.

Jermsurawong, J., Ahsan, M. U., Haidar, A., Dong, H., & Mavridis, N. (2012). Car Parking Vacancy Detection and Its Application in 24-Hour Statistical Analysis. *Proceedings of the 2012 10th International Conference on Frontiers of Information Technology*. 10.1109/FIT.2012.24

Jiacheng, Haibo, Ning, Peng, Lin, & Xuemin. (2016). Software defined Internet of vehicles: architecture, challenges and solutions. *Journal of Communications and Information Networks, 1*.

Jiang, X., & Camp, T. (2002). A Review of Geocasting Protocols for a Mobile Ad Hoc Network. *Proceedings of the Grace Hopper Celebration (GHC)*.

Jindal & Bedi. (2016, March). Vehicular Ad-Hoc Networks: Introduction, Standards, Routing Protocols and Challenges. *IJCSI International Journal of Computer Science Issues, 13*(2).

Joa-Ng, M., Member, S., Lu, I.-T., & Member, S. (1999). A Peer-to-Peer Zone-Based Two-Level Link State Routing for Mobile Ad Hoc Networks. *IEEE Journal on Selected Areas in Communications, 17*(8), 1415–1425. doi:10.1109/49.779923

Johnson, Maltz, & Hu. (2004, July). *The Dynamic Source Routing Protocol for Mobile Ad Hoc Networks (DSR)*. draft-ietf-manetdsr-10.txt.

Johnson, D. B., & Maltz, D. A. (n.d.). Dynamic Source Routing in Ad Hoc Wireless Networks. In *Mobile Computing* (pp. 153–181). Springer US. doi:10.1007/978-0-585-29603-6_5

Jones, E. P., Li, L., Schmidtke, J. K., & Ward, P. A. S. (2007). Practical routing in delay-tolerant networks. *IEEE Transactions on Mobile Computing*, *6*(8), 943–959. doi:10.1109/TMC.2007.1016

Joshi, H. P. (2007). *Distributed Robust Geocast: A Multicast Protocol for Inter-vehicle Communication*. Dept. of Computer Networking and Electrical Engineering, Master's T.

Joshi, H., Sichitiu, M., & Kihl, M. (2007). Distributed Robust Geocast Multicast Routing for Inter-Vehicle Communication. *Proceedings of WEIRD Workshop on WiMax, Wireless and Mobility*.

Juang, P. O. (2002). Energy-efficient computing for wildlife tracking: Design tradeoffs and early experiences with ZebraNet. ACM SIGARCH Computer Architecture News, 30(5), 96-107. doi:10.1145/605397.605408

Juels. (2007). Pors: Proofs of Retrievability for Large Files. *Proc. 14th ACM Conf. Comptr & Comm. Security*, 584-597.

Juels. (2017). PORs: Proof of Retrievability of Large File. *Proc. ACM Conf. Computer and Comm. Security (CCS '07)*, 584-597.

Karabey, B., & Baykal, N. (2013). Attack Tree Based Information Security Risk Assessment Method Integrating Enterprise Objectives with Vulnerabilities. *The International Arab Journal of Information Technology*, *10*(3), 297–304.

Karimi, Ithnin, Razak, & Najafzadeh (2011b, September). Non DTN Geographic Routing Protocols for Vehicular Ad Hoc Networks. *International Journal of Computer Science Issues, 8*(5), 86-91.

Karimi, Ithnin, Razak, & Najafzadeh. (2011a, November). DTN Routing Protocols for VANETs: Issues and Approaches. *International Journal of Computer Science Issues, 8*(6), 89-93.

Karp, B., & Kung, H. T. (2000, August). GPSR: Greedy perimeter stateless routing for wireless networks, In *Proceedings of the 6th annual international conference on mobile computing and networking* (pp. 243–254). ACM. 10.1145/345910.345953

Katsis, C. D., Katertsidis, N., Ganiatsas, G., & Fotiadis, D. E. (2008). *Toward Emotion Recognition in Car-Racing Drivers: A biosignal Processing Approach. IEEE Trans. Syst. Man Cybern. Part A Syst.*

Katzourakis, D. I., Lazic, N., Olsson, C., & Lidberg, M. R. (2015). *Driver Steering Override for Lane-Keeping Aid Using Computer-Aided Engineering. IEEE/ASME Trans. Mechatron.*

Kelly, D., & Smith, C. (2011). *Bayesian Inference for Probabilistic Risk Assessment: A Practitioner's Guidebook*. Springer. doi:10.1007/978-1-84996-187-5

Kenney, J. B. (2011, July). Dedicated short-range communications (DSRC) standards in the United States. *Proceedings of the IEEE*, *99*(7), 1162–1182. doi:10.1109/JPROC.2011.2132790

Keränen, A. J. (2009). The ONE simulator for DTN protocol evaluation. In *Proceedings of the 2nd international conference on simulation tools and techniques* (p. 55). ICST (Institute for Computer Sciences, Social-Informatics and Telecommunications Engineering). 10.4108/ICST.SIMUTOOLS2009.5674

Keyrouz, S., Perotto, G., & Visser, H. J. (2012). Novel broadband Yagi-Uda antenna for ambient energy harvesting. *IEEE European Microwave Conf.*, 518-521.

Khan, A. A. (n.d.). *Cognitive-radio-based internet of things: Applications, architectures, spectrum related functionalities, and future research directions.* Retrieved from https://ieeexplore.ieee.org/abstract/document/7955907/

Khan, A. A., Stojmenovic, I., & Zaguia, N. (2008). Parameterless broadcasting in static to highly mobile wireless ad hoc, sensor and actuator networks. *Proceeding of 22nd International Conference on Advanced Information Networking and Applications(AINA -2008).*

Khan, A., Khan, A. A., Abolhasan, M., & Ni, W. (2018). *5G Next generation VANETs using SDN and Fog Computing Framework.* Retrieved from https://www.researchgate.net/publication/323570830

Khang, S.-T., Lee, D.-J., Hwang, I.-J., Yeo, T.-D., & Yu, J.-W. (2017). Microwave Power Transfer with Optimal Number of Rectenna Arrays for Mid-Range Applications. *IEEE Antennas and Wireless Propagation Letters,* 1–1. doi:10.1109/LAWP.2017.2778507

Khan, M. W., Pandey, D., & Khan, S. A. (2018a). Measuring the Security Testing Attributes through Fuzzy Analytic Network Process: A Design Perspective. *Journal of Advance Research in Dynamical & Control Systems, 10*(12), 1514–1523.

Khan, M. W., Pandey, D., & Khan, S. A. (2018b). Test Plan Specification using Security Attributes: A Design Perspective. *ICIC Express Letters, 12*(10), 1061–1069.

Kihl, M., Sichitiu, M., Ekeroth, T., & Rozenberg, M. (2007). Reliable Geographical Multicast Routing in Vehicular Ad-hoc Networks. *Proceeding in WWIC '07 Proceedings of the 5th international conference on Wired/Wireless Internet Communications,* 315 – 325. 10.1007/978-3-540-72697-5_27

Kim, H., & Feamster, N. (2013). Improving network management with software defined networking. *IEEE Communications Magazine, 51*(2). doi:10.1109/MCOM.2013.6461195

Kim, J. H., Cho, S. I., & Kim, H. J. (2016). Exploiting the mutual coupling effect on dipole antennas for RF energy harvesting. *IEEE Antennas and Wireless Propagation Letters,* 1301–1304.

Kim, M., Jang, I., Choo, S., Koo, J., & Pack, S. (2017). Collaborative security attack detection in software-defined vehicular networks. In *19th Asia-Pacific Network Operations and Management Symposium: Managing a World of Things, APNOMS 2017* (pp. 19–24). 10.1109/APNOMS.2017.8094172

Kim, S., Kim, J., Yi, K., & Jung, K. (2017). Detection and tracking of overtaking vehicle in Blind Spot area at night time. *IEEE International Conference on Consumer Electronics (ICCE),* Las Vegas, NV.

Kim, Y., Oh, H., & Kang, S. (2017). Proof of Concept of Home IoT Connected Vehicles. *Sensors (Basel), 17*(6), 1289. doi:10.339017061289 PMID:28587246

Kizza, J. M. (2005). Computer Network Security. New York: Springer Science+Business Media, Inc.

Kizza, J. M. (2013). Guide to Computer Network Security. Springer.

Koçak, S. A., Alptekin, G. I., & Bener, A. B. (2014). Evaluation of Software Product Quality Attributes and Environmental Attributes using ANP Decision Framework. *3rd International Workshop on Requirements Engineering for Sustainable Systems.* 1-8.

Ko, R. K., Jagadpramana, P., Mowbray, M., Pearson, S., Kirchberg, M., Liang, Q., & Lee, B. S. (2011, July). TrustCloud: A framework for accountability and trust in cloud computing. In *2011 IEEE World Congress on Services* (pp. 584-588). IEEE. 10.1109/SERVICES.2011.91

Ko, Y. B., & Vaidya, N. H. (2000). GeoTORA: a protocol for geocasting in mobile ad hoc networks. *International Conference on Network Protocols,* 240–250. 10.1109/icnp.2000.896308

Ko, Y. B., & Vaidya, N. H. (2000). Location-aided routing (LAR) in mobile ad hoc networks. *Wireless Networks*, 6(4), 307–321. doi:10.1023/A:1019106118419

Ko, Y. B., & Vaidya, N. H. (2002). Flooding-Based Geocasting Protocols for Mobile Ad Hoc Networks. *Mobile Networks and Applications*, 7(6), 471–480. doi:10.1023/A:1020712802004

Ko, Y., & Vaidya, N. H. (1998). Location-aided routing (LAR) in mobile ad hoc networks. *Proceedings of the ACM/IEEE International Conference on Mobile Computing and Networking (MOBICOM'98)*, 3112, 1–16. 10.1145/288235.288252

Kreutz, D., Ramos, F. M. V., Verissimo, P. E., Rothenberg, C. E., Azodolmolky, S., & Uhlig, S. (2015). Software-defined networking: A comprehensive survey. *Proceedings of the IEEE*, 103(1), 14–76. doi:10.1109/JPROC.2014.2371999

Krishnan, K. (2004). *Computer Networks and Computer Security*. North Carolina State University.

Kumar, R., & Dave, M. (2012). A Review of Various VANET Data Dissemination Protocols. International Journal of u- and e- Service, Science and Technology, 5(3).

Kumar, R., Khan, S. A., & Khan, R. A. (2016). Analytical Network Process for Software Security: A Design Perspective. CSI Transactions on ICT1-4.

Kumar, R., Khan, S. A., & Khan, R. A. (2017). Fuzzy Analytic Hierarchy Process for Software Durability: Security Risks Perspective. Advances in Intelligent Systems and Computing (Originally Published with the Title: Advances in Intelligent and Soft Computing), 469-478.

Kumar, A. (2012). *Enhanced Routing in Delay Tolerant Enabled Vehicular Ad Hoc Networks. International Journal of Scientific and Research Publications* , 2.

Kumar, R., Zarour, M., Alenezi, M., Agrawal, A., & Khan, R. A. (2019). Measuring Security Durability of Software through Fuzzy-Based Decision-Making Process. *International Journal of Computational Intelligence Systems*, 12(2), 627–642. doi:10.2991/ijcis.d.190513.001

Kyriakou, C., Christodoulou, S. E., & Dimitriou, L. (2016). Roadway pavement anomaly classification utilizing smartphones and artificial intelligence. *Proceedings of the 2016 18th Mediterranean Electrotechnical Conference (MELECON)*. 10.1109/MELCON.2016.7495459

Lai, J., Deng, R. H., Guan, C., & Weng, J. (2013). Attribute-based encryption with verifiable outsourced decryption. *IEEE Transactions on Information Forensics and Security*, 8(8), 1343–1354. doi:10.1109/TIFS.2013.2271848

Lai, Y. K., Chou, Y. H., & Schumann, T. (2017). Vehicle detection for forward collision warning system based on a cascade classifier using adaboost algorithm. *Proceedings of the 2017 IEEE 7th International Conference on Consumer Electronics (ICCE)*. 10.1109/ICCE-Berlin.2017.8210585

Lanatà, A., Valenza, G., Greco, A., Gentili, C., Bartolozzi, R., Bucchi, F., Frendo, F., & Scilingo, E. P. (2015). How the Autonomic Nervous System and Driving Style Change with Incremental Stressing Conditions During Simulated Driving. *IEEE Transactions on Intelligent Transportation Systems*, 16(3), 1505–1517. doi:10.1109/TITS.2014.2365681

LeBrun, J. C. (2005). Knowledge-based opportunistic forwarding in vehicular wireless ad hoc networks. In *2005 IEEE 61st Vehicular Technology Conference* (pp. 2289-2293). IEEE. 10.1109/VETECS.2005.1543743

Lecompte, D., & Gabin, F. (2012). Evolved multimedia broadcast/multicast service (eMBMS) in LTE-advanced: overview and Rel-11 enhancements. IEEE Communications, 50(11).

Lee, S., Yoo, J., & Chung, T. (2004). Distance-based energy efficient clustering for wireless sensor networks. *Local Computer Networks, 29th Annual IEEE International Conference.*

Lee, S.-H., & Ko, Y.-B. (2006). Geometry driven Scheme for Geocast Routing in Mobile Ad hoc Networks. *IEEE 63rd Vehicular Technology Conference*, 638–642. 10.1109/VETECS.2006.1682902

Lee, J. H., Hancock, M. G., & Hu, M. C. (2014). Towards an effective framework for building smart cities: Lessons from Seoul and San Francisco. *Technological Forecasting and Social Change, 89*, 80–99. doi:10.1016/j.techfore.2013.08.033

Lee, U., & Gerla, M. (2010). A survey of urban vehicular sensing platforms. *Computer Networks, 54*(4), 527–544. doi:10.1016/j.comnet.2009.07.011

Lemke, C. E., & Howson, J. T. Jr. (1964). Equilibrium Points of Bimatrix Games. *Journal of the Society for Industrial and Applied Mathematics, 12*(2), 413–423. doi:10.1137/0112033

Li, Y., & Li, J. (2015). MultiClassifier: A combination of DPI and ML for application-layer classification in SDN. In *2014 2nd International Conference on Systems and Informatics, ICSAI 2014* (pp. 682–686). doi:10.1109/ICSAI.2014.7009372

Li, Y., Li, X., & Yoshie, O. (2014). Traffic engineering framework with machine learning based meta-layer in software-defined networks. In *Proceedings of 2014 4th IEEE International Conference on Network Infrastructure and Digital Content, IEEE IC-NIDC 2014* (pp. 121–125). 10.1109/ICNIDC.2014.7000278

Liang, X., Du, X., Wang, G., & Han, Z. (2019). A Deep Reinforcement Learning Network for Traffic Light Cycle Control. *IEEE Transactions on Vehicular Technology, 68*(2), 1243–1253. doi:10.1109/TVT.2018.2890726

Liao, W. H., Sheu, J. P., & Tseng, Y. C. (2001). GRID: A fully location-aware routing protocol for mobile ad hoc networks. *Telecommunication Systems, 18*(1–3), 37–60. doi:10.1023/A:1016735301732

Liao, W., Tseng, Y., Lo, K., & Sheu, J. (2000). GeoGRID: A Geocasting Protocol for Mobile Ad Hoc Networks Based on GRID. *Journal of Internet Technology, 1*(2), 23–32. http://www.citeulike.org/user/s-fujii/article/2246138

Li, F., & Wang, Y. (2007, June). Routing in Vehicular Ad Hoc Networks: A Survey. *IEEE Vehicular Technology Magazine, 2*(2), 12–22. doi:10.1109/MVT.2007.912927

Li, H., Dong, M., & Ota, K. (2016). Control Plane Optimization in Software-Defined Vehicular Ad Hoc Networks. *IEEE Transactions on Vehicular Technology, 65*(10). doi:10.1109/TVT.2016.2563164

Lin, Chiu, & Gong. (2018). *A Wearable Rectenna to Harvest Low-Power RF Energy for Wireless Healthcare Applications*. doi:10.1109/CISP-BMEI.2018.8633222

Lin, S. C., Akyildiz, I. F., Wang, P., & Luo, M. (2016). QoS-aware adaptive routing in multi-layer hierarchical software defined networks: A reinforcement learning approach. In *Proceedings - 2016 IEEE International Conference on Services Computing, SCC 2016* (pp. 25–33). 10.1109/SCC.2016.12

Lin, Y., Nguyen, H. T., & Wang, C. (2017). Adaptive neuro-fuzzy predictive control for design of adaptive cruise control system. *Proceedings of the 2017 IEEE 14th International Conference on Networking, Sensing and Control (ICNSC)*.

Lin, C., & Gerla, M. (1997). Adaptive clustering for mobile wireless networks. *IEEE Journal on Selected Areas in Communications, 15*(7), 1265–1275. doi:10.1109/49.622910

Lindgren, A. A. (2004). Probabilistic routing in intermittently connected networks. In *International Workshop on Service Assurance with Partial and Intermittent Resources* (pp. 239-254). Springer. 10.1007/978-3-540-27767-5_24

Lin, X., Sun, X., Ho, P.-H., & Shen, X. (2007). GSIS: A secure and privacy-preserving protocol for vehicular communications. *IEEE Transactions on Vehicular Technology, 56*(6).

Lious, T. S., & Wang, M. J. J. (1992). Ranking fuzzy numbers with integral value. *Fuzzy Sets and Systems, 50*(3), 247–255. doi:10.1016/0165-0114(92)90223-Q

Liu, B., Jia, D., Wang, J., Lu, K., & Wu, L. (2015). Cloud-assisted safety message dissemination in VANET-cellular heterogeneous wireless network. IEEE Systems Journal.

Liu, S., & Liu, Y. (2016). Network security risk assessment method based on HMM and attack graph model. *17th IEEE/ACIS, International Conference on Software Engineering, Artificial Intelligence, Networking and Parallel/Distributed Computing (SNPD)*, 1-6.

Liu, W. (2012, April). Research on cloud computing security problem and strategy. In *2012 2nd International Conference on Consumer Electronics, Communications and Networks (CECNet)* (pp. 1216-1219). IEEE. 10.1109/CECNet.2012.6202020

Liu, Y., Zeng, Q. A., & Wang, Y. H. (2014). *Data fusion in wireless sensor networks.* www.Journals.sagepub.com

Liu, B., Tian, H., Wang, B., & Fan, B. (2014). AHP and Game Theory based Approach for Network Selection in Heterogeneous Wireless Networks. *Consumer Communications and Networking Conf. (CCNC)*, 973–978. 10.1109/CCNC.2014.6866617

Liu, J., Wan, J., Zeng, B., Wang, Q., Song, H., & Qiu, M. (2017). A scalable and quick-response software defined vehicular network assisted by mobile edge computing. *IEEE Communications Magazine*, *55*(7), 94–100. doi:10.1109/MCOM.2017.1601150

Liu, K., Son, S. H., Lee, V. C. S., & Kapitanova, K. (2011). A token-based admission control and request scheduling in lane reservation systems. *Proceedings of the 14th International IEEE Conference on Intelligent Transportation Systems (ITSC)*. 10.1109/ITSC.2011.6082959

Liu, Y. C., Chen, C., & Chakraborty, S. (2015). A Software Defined Network architecture for GeoBroadcast in VANETs. *IEEE International Conference on Communications*, 6559–6564. 10.1109/ICC.2015.7249370

Li, X., Yang, L., & Huang, L. (2019). Novel Design of 2.45-GHz Rectenna Element and Array for Wireless Power Transmission. *IEEE Access: Practical Innovations, Open Solutions*, 1–1. doi:10.1109/ACCESS.2019.2900329

Lochert, C., Hartenstein, H., Tian, J., Fussler, H., Hermann, D., & Mauve, M. (2003, June). A routing strategy for vehicular ad hoc networks in city environments. In *Intelligent vehicles symposium, 2003, proceedings IEEE* (pp. 156–161). IEEE. doi:10.1109/IVS.2003.1212901

Lu, R. L. (2010). Spring: A social-based privacy-preserving packet forwarding protocol for vehicular delay tolerant networks. In 2010 Proceedings IEEE INFOCOM (pp. 1-9). IEEE.

Luan, T. H., Gao, L., Li, Z., Yang, W., Guiyi, S., & Sun, L. (2015). *Fog computing: focusing on mobile users at the edge, networking and internet architecture.* Networking and Internet Architecture.

Luo R.C., Yih C.-C., & Su K.L. (2002). Multisensor fusion and integration: Approaches, applications, and future research directions. *IEEE Sens. J.*

Luo, Y., Zhang, W., & Hu, Y. (2010). A new cluster based routing protocol for vanet. *IEEE Second International Conference on Networks Security Wireless Communications and Trusted Computing (NSWCTC)*. 10.1109/NSWCTC.2010.48

Luo, F., Zhao, Y., & Yuan, Z. (2017). Fast and accurate vehicle detection by aspect ratio regression. *Proceedings of the 2017 Chinese Automation Congress (CAC)*. 10.1109/CAC.2017.8242943

Maheshwari, P., Suneja, D., Singh, P., & Mutneja, Y. (2015, October). Smart traffic optimization using image processing. In *2015 IEEE 3rd International Conference on MOOCs, Innovation and Technology in Education (MITE)* (pp. 1-4). IEEE. 10.1109/MITE.2015.7375276

Mahjabin, T., Xiao, Y., Sun, G., & Jiang, W. (2017). A survey of distributed denial-of-service attack, prevention, and mitigation techniques. *International Journal of Distributed Sensor Networks, 13*(12), 1–33. doi:10.1177/1550147717741463

Maihoefer, C., & Leinmueller, T. (2005). *Abiding Geocast : Time – stable Geocast for Ad Hoc Networks*. Academic Press.

Maihöfer, C., Eberhardt, R., & Schoch, E. (2004). *CGGC: cached greedy geocast.* . doi:0.1007/978-3-540-24643-5_2

Maihöfer, C., Eberhardt, R., & Schoch, E. (2004). CGGC: Cached greedy geocast. Lecture Notes in Computer Science (Including Subseries Lecture Notes in Artificial Intelligence and Lecture Notes in Bioinformatics), 2957, 13–25. doi:10.1007/978-3-540-24643-5_2

Maihöfer, C., Franz, W., & Eberhardt, R. (2003). Stored Geocast. *Proceedings of Kommunikation in Verteilten Systemen (KiVS)*, 257–268. doi:10.1007/978-3-642-55569-5_21

Maihöfer, C. (2004). A survey of geocast routing protocols. *IEEE COMMUNICATIONS SURVEYS, 6*(2), 32–42. doi:10.1109/COMST.2004.5342238

Maihöfer, C., Cseh, C., Franz, W., & Eberhardt, R. (2003). Performance evaluation of stored geocast. *IEEE Vehicular Technology Conference, 58*(5), 2901–2905. 10.1109/vetecf.2003.1286151

Maihöfer, C., & Eberhardt, R. (2004). Geocast in vehicular environments: Caching and transmission range control for improved efficiency. *IEEE Intelligent Vehicles Symposium, Proceedings*, 951–956. 10.1109/IVS.2004.1336514

Malik, M. I., & Wani, S. H. (2018). Cloud Computing Technologies. *International Journal of Advanced Research in Computer Science, 9*(2), 379–384. doi:10.26483/ijarcs.v9i2.5760

Malik, M., & Singh, Y. (2015). A Review: DoS and DDoS Attacks. *International Journal of Computer Science and Mobile Computing, 4*(6), 260–265.

Manyika, J., & Durrant-Whyte, H. (1995). *Data Fusion and Sensor Management: A Decentralized Information-Theoretic Approach*. Prentice Hall.

Marin, G. A. (2005). Network security basics. *In Security & Privacy, IEEE, 3*(6), 68-72.

Marina, M. K., & Das, S. R. (2006). Ad hoc on-demand multipath distance vector routing. *Wireless Communications and Mobile Computing, 6*(7), 969–988. doi:10.1002/wcm.432

Matsunaga, T., Nishiyama, E., & Toyoda, I. (2013). 5.8-GHz Stacked Differential Rectenna Suitable for Large-Scale Rectenna Arrays With DC Connection. *IEEE Transactions on Antennas and Propagation, 63*, 1200–1202. doi:10.1109/APMC.2013.6695070

McClure, S., Scambray, J., & Kurtz, G. (2009). *Hacking Exposed: Network Security Secrets & Solutions* (6th ed.). TMH.

McKeown, N., Anderson, T., & Balakrishnan, H. (2008). OpenFlow: Enabling innovation in campus networks. *Computer Communication Review, 38*(2). doi:10.1145/1355734.1355746

McMahon, A. &. (2009). Delay-and disruption-tolerant networking. *IEEE Internet Computing, 13*(6), 82-87.

Mealling, M. (2002). *Report from the Joint W3C/IETF URI Planning Interest Group: Uniform Resource Identifiers (URIs), URLs, and Uniform Resource Names (URNs): Clarifications and Recommendations*. RFC 3305.

Mehrabi, A., & Kim, K. (2015). Using a mobile vehicle for road condition surveillance by energy harvesting sensor nodes. *Proceedings of the 2015 IEEE 40th Conference on Local Computer Networks (LCN)*. 10.1109/LCN.2015.7366303

Mehta, S., & Kumar, A. (2019). *Towards Inclusive and Sustainable Smart Cities: The Case of Ranchi*. ORF Special Report No. 81. Observer Research Foundation.

Mell, P., & Grance, T. (2009). *Above clouds: A review of cloud comptg.* Univ. of California, Berkeley, Technology. Rep. UCBEECS-2009-28.

Meneguette, R. I., Bittencourt, L. F., & Madeira, E. R. M. (2013). A seamless flow mobility management architecture for vehicular communication networks. *Journal of Communications and Networks (Seoul)*, *15*(2). doi:10.1109/JCN.2013.000034

Meng, S., Wang, P., & Wang, J. (2011). Application of Fuzzy Logic in the Network Security Risk Evaluation. *Advanced Materials Research*, *282*(283), 359–362. doi:10.4028/www.scientific.net/AMR.282-283.359

Mikhailov, L. (2003). Deriving priorities from fuzzy pairwise comparison judgments. *Fuzzy Sets and Systems*, *134*(3), 365–385. doi:10.1016/S0165-0114(02)00383-4

Ministry of Road Transport and Highways. (2018, October 1). *Road accidents in India – 2017*. Retrieved July 10,2019 from http://www.indiaenvironmentportal.org.in/content/459084/road-accidents-in-india-2017

Mir & Ravindran. (2017). Role of IoT in Smart City Applipn: A Review. *Int. Jornl of Advd Research in Comptr Engg. & Tech*, *6*(7), 1099–1104.

Mobile Edge Computing (MEC), ETSI, and Industry Specification Group (ISG). (2016). *White paper: mobile edge computing (MEC); framework and reference architecture.* ETSI (European Telecommunications Standards Institute).

Moghaddam, F. F., Karimi, O., & Alrashdan, M. T. (2013, November). A comparative study of applying real-time encryption in cloud computing environments. In *2013 IEEE 2nd International Conference on Cloud Networking (CloudNet)* (pp. 185-189). IEEE. 10.1109/CloudNet.2013.6710575

Moghaddam, M. J., Hosseini, M., & Safabakhsh, R. (2015, March). Traffic light control based on fuzzy Q-leaming. In *2015 The International Symposium on Artificial Intelligence and Signal Processing (AISP)* (pp. 124-128). IEEE. 10.1109/AISP.2015.7123500

Mohammed, O. S., & Taha, D. B. (2016). Conducting multi-class security metrics from enterprise architect class diagram. *International Journal of Computer Science and Information Security*, *14*(4), 56–61.

Morgan, Y. L. (2010). Notes on DSRC & WAVE standards suite: Its architecture, design, and characteristics. *IEEE Communications Surveys and Tutorials*, *12*(4). doi:10.1109/SURV.2010.033010.00024

Morris, R., Jannotti, J., Kaashoek, F., Li, J., & Decouto, D. (2000, September). CarNet: A scalable ad hoc wireless network system. *9th ACM SIGOPS European Workshop*, Kolding, Denmark. 10.1145/566726.566741

Mougouei, D. (2017). PAPS: A scalable framework for prioritization and partial selection of security requirements. *ArXiv*, 1–12.

Moustafa, H., & Yan, Z. (2009). *Vehicular networks: Techniques, Standards, and Applications.* CRC Press. doi:10.1201/9781420085723

Mu~noz-Gonz'alez, L., & Lupu, E. C. (2017). Bayesian Attack Graphs for Security Risk Assessment. *IST-153 Workshop on Cyber Resilience*, 1-5.

Murray, P. (2004). *Network Security.* http://www.pandc.org/peter/presentations/ohio-tech-2004/Ohio-tech-security-handout.pdf

Murthy, S., & Garcia-Luna-Aceves, J. J. (1996). An efficient routing protocol for wireless networks. *Mobile Networks and Applications*, *1*(2), 183–197. doi:10.1007/BF01193336

Musolesi, M. (2008). Car: context-aware adaptive routing for delay-tolerant mobile networks. *IEEE Transactions on Mobile Computing*, *8*(2), 246-260.

Nakao, A., & Du, P. (2018). Toward in-network deep machine learning for identifying mobile applications and enabling application specific network slicing. *IEICE Transactions on Communications, E101B*(7), 1536–1543. doi:10.1587/transcom.2017CQI0002

Nakorn & Rojviboonchai. (2010). *DECA: Density-Aware Reliable Broadcasting in Vehicular Ad Hoc Networks.* In International Conference on Electrical Engineering/Electronics, Computer, Telecommunications and Information Technology (ECTI-CON2010), Chiang Mai, Thailand.

Nash, J. (1951). Non-Cooperative Games. *Annals of Mathematics, 54*(2), 286. Advance online publication. doi:10.2307/1969529

Nayna, T. F., Baki, A. K., & Ahmed, F. (2014). *Comparative study of Rectangular and Circular micro strip patch antenna.* ICEEICT.

Neaman. (n.d.). *Electronic Circuits* (3rd ed.). MGH.

Neural Network Tutorial. (2019, August). Retrieved from https://www.simplilearn.com/neural-networks-tutorial-article

News. (2019, February). Retrieved from: https://www.news18.com/news/india/the-single-statistic-that-shows-why-indian-roads-are-getting-more-congested-each-passing-month-2031835.html

Niewolny, D. (2013). *How the Internet of Things is revolutionizing healthcare, Free scale Semiconductor.* http://www.freescale.com/healthcare

Niotaki, K., Kim, S., Giuppi, F., Collado, A., Georgladis, A., & Tentzeris, M. (2014). Optimized design of multiband and solar rectennas. *WiSNet 2014 - Proceedings: 2014 IEEE Topical Conference on Wireless Sensors and Sensor Networks*, 31-33. 10.1109/WiSNet.2014.6825507

Nitti, M., Stelea, G. A., Popescu, V., & Fadda, M. (2015). When Social Networks Meet D2D Communications: A Survey. *International Journal of Advanced Networking and Applications, 7*(1), 2576–2581.

Niyato, D., & Hossain, E. (2008). A Noncooperative Game-Theoretic Framework for Radio Resource Management in 4G Heterogeneous Wireless Access Networks. *IEEE Transactions on Mobile Computing, 7*(3), 332–345. doi:10.1109/TMC.2007.70727

Niyato, D., & Hossain, E. (2009). Dynamics of Network Selection in Heterogeneous Wireless Networks: An Evolutionary Game Approach. *IEEE Transactions on Vehicular Technology, 58*(4), 2008–2017. doi:10.1109/TVT.2008.2004588

Obayiuwana, E., & Falowo, O. E. (2016). Network selection in heterogeneous wireless networks using multi-criteria decision-making algorithms: A review. *Wireless Networks*, 1–33. doi:10.100711276-016-1301-4

Olgun, U., Chen, C.-C., & Volakis, J. (2011). Investigation of Rectenna Array Configurations for Enhanced RF Power Harvesting. *Antennas and Wireless Propagation Letters. IEEE., 10*, 262–265. doi:10.1109/LAWP.2011.2136371

Onifade, F. W., Ojo, K., & Akande, O. (2008). Angular Displacement Scheme (ADS): Providing Reliable Geocast Transmission for Mobile Ad-Hoc Networks (MANETs). *IJCSNS International Journal of Computer Science and Network Security, 8*(8), 334–339.

Oniga, S., & Suto, J. (2014). Human activity recognition using neural networks. *15th International Carpathian Control Conference - ICCC 2014.* 10.1109/CarpathianCC.2014.6843636

Open Networking Foundation. (2012). Software-Defined Networking : The New Norm for Networks. *ONF White Paper, 2*, 2–6. Retrieved from https://www.opennetworking.org/images/stories/downloads/sdn-resources/white-papers/wp-sdn-newnorm.pdf

Open Networking Foundation. (2013). OpenFlow 1.4 Specifications. *Onf, 0,* 1–36. doi:10.1002/2014GB005021

OpenStreetMap. (n.d.). Retrieved August 5, 2019 from https://en.wikipedia.org/wiki/OpenStreetMap

OWASP. (2017). *OWASP Top 10. The Ten Most Critical Web Application Security Risks.* https://www.owasp.org/images/7/72/OWASP Top 102017%28en%29.pdf.pdf

Padmavathi, G., Shanmugapriya, D., & Kalaivani, M. (2010). *A Study on Vehicle Detection and Tracking Using Wireless Sensor Networks.* WSN. https://m.scirp.org/papers/1385

Pan, D. R., Ruan, Z., Zhou, N., Liu, X., & Song, Z. (2013). A comprehensive-integrated buffer management strategy for opportunistic networks. *EURASIP Journal on Wireless Communications and Networking, 2013*(1), 103. doi:10.1186/1687-1499-2013-103

Park, V., & Corson, S. (2001). Temporally-ordered routing algorithm (TORA). In Internet Draft: draft-ietf-manet-tora-spec-04.txt.

Park, V. D., & Corson, M. S. (1997). A highly adaptive distributed routing algorithm for mobile wireless networks. *Proceedings of the INFOCOM '97.* 10.1109/INFCOM.1997.631180

Paul & Islam. (2012). Survey over VANET Routing Protocols for Vehicle to Vehicle Communication. *IOSR Journal of Computer Engineering, 7*(5), 1-9.

Paul, Paul, & Bikas. (2011, April). VANET Routing Protocols: Pros and Cons. *International Journal of Computer Applications, 20*(3).

Pei, G., Gerla, M., & Chen, T.-W. (2000). Fisheye state routing: a routing scheme for ad hoc wireless networks. *IEEE International Conference on Communications.*

Pentland, A. F. (2004). Daknet: Rethinking connectivity in developing nations. *Computer, 37*(1), 78-83.

Pereira, P. R.-P. (2011). From delay-tolerant networks to vehicular delay-tolerant networks. *IEEE Communications Surveys & Tutorials, 14*(4), 1166-1182.

Perkins & Bhagwat. (1994). Highly Dynamic Destination Sequenced Distance-Vector Routing (DSDV) for Mobile Computers. *ACM Conference on SIGCOMM.*

Perkins, C. E. (n.d.). *Highly Dynamic Destination-Sequenced Distance-Vector Routing (DSDV) for Mobile Computers.* Academic Press.

Perkins, C. E., & Royer, E. M. (1999). Ad-hoc On-Demand Distance Vector Routing. In *Proceedings of WMCSA '99. Second IEEE Workshop on Mobile Computer Systems and Applications.* Washington, DC: IEEE Computer Society.

Piamrat, K., Ksentini, A., Bonnin, J.-M., & Viho, C. (2011). Radio resource management in emerging heterogeneous wireless networks. *Computer Communications, 34*(9), 1066–1076. doi:10.1016/j.comcom.2010.02.015

Podio, L., & Jeffrey, S. D. (2002). *Biometric Authentication Technology: From the Movies to Your Desktop. National Institute of Standards and Technology (NIST).* Information Technology Laboratory.

Prabhakar, S. (2017). Network Security In Digitalization: Attacks And Defence. *International Journal of Research in Computer Applications and Robotics, 5*(5), 46–52.

Prakash, G. L., Prateek, M., & Singh, I. (2014, July). Data encryption and decryption algorithms using key rotations for data security in cloud system. In *2014 International Conference on Signal Propagation and Computer Technology (ICSPCT 2014)* (pp. 624-629). IEEE. 10.1109/ICSPCT.2014.6884895

Pu, L., Liu, Z., Meng, Z., Yang, X., Zhu, K., & Zhang, L. (2015). Implementing on-board diagnostic and GPS on VANET to safe the vehicle. *Proceedings of the 2015 International Conference on Connected Vehicles and Expo (ICCVE)*, 13–18. 10.1109/ICCVE.2015.64

Punter, A., Coburn, A., & Ralph, D. (2016). *Evolving risk frameworks: modelling resilient business systems as interconnected networks.* Centre for Risk Studies, University of Cambridge. http://cambridgeriskframework.com/ page/17

Qazi, Z. A., Lee, J., Jin, T., Bellala, G., Arndt, M., & Noubir, G. (2013). Application-awareness in SDN. Computer Communication Review, 43, 487–488. doi:10.1145/2486001.2491700

Qi, G.-J., Tang, J., Zha, Z.-J., Chua, T.-S., & Zhang, H.-J. (2009). An efficient sparse metric learning in high-dimensional space via l1-penalized log determinant regularization. *Proceedings of the International Conference on Machine Learning.*

Qin, Y., Dong, M., Zhao, F., Langari, R., & Gu, L. (2015). Road profile classification for vehicle semi-active suspension system based on Adaptive Neuro-Fuzzy Inference System. *54th IEEE Conference on Decision and Control.* 10.1109/CDC.2015.7402428

Qu, L., Li, L., Zhang, Y., & Hu, J. (2009). PPCA-based missing data imputation for traffic flow volume: A systematical approach. *IEEE Trans. Intell. Transp. Syst.*

Radhika, K. (2011). Vertical Handoff Decision using Game Theory Approach for Multi-mode Mobile Terminals in Next Generation Wireless Networks. *International Journal of Computers and Applications, 36*(11), 31–37. doi:10.5120/4535-6451

Rahbar, H., & Naik, K. (2010). *DTSG: Dynamic time-stable geocast routing in vehicular ad hoc networks.* doi:10.1109/MEDHOCNET.2010.5546872

Rajput, S. K., & Patil, M. (2018). Waste Mangnt in IoT- Facilitated Smart Cities- A Suvery. *Internl Journal of Computer Apps, 182*(24), 21–26.

Ramgovind, S., Eloff, M. M., & Smith, E. (2010, August). *The management of security in cloud computing. In 2010 Information Security for South Africa.* IEEE.

Rana, Rana, & Purohit. (2014, June). A Review of Various Routing Protocols in VANET. *International Journal of Computer Applications, 96*(18).

Rana, N. P., Luthra, S., Mangla, S. K., Islam, R., Roderick, S., & Dwivedi, Y. K. (2018). Barriers to the development of smart cities in Indian context. *Information Systems Frontiers*, 1–23.

Rani, P., Sharma, N., & Singh, P. K. (2011). Performance Comparison of VANET Routing Protocols. *7th International Conference on Wireless Communications, Networking and Mobile Computing*, Wuhan, China.

Rani, P., Sharma, N., & Singh, P. K. (2011). *Performance Comparison of VANET Routing Protocols.* IEEE. doi:10.1109/wicom.2011.6040428

Rawashdeh & Mahmud. (2012). A novel algorithm to form stable clusters in vehicular ad hoc networks on highways. *EURASIP Journal on Wireless Communications and Networking,* (1), 1–13.

Raw, R. S., Kumar, M., & Singh, N. (2013). Security challenges, issues and their solutions for VANET. *International Journal of Network Security & Its Applications, 5*(5). Advance online publication. doi:10.5121/ijnsa.2013.5508

Raya, M., & Hubaux, J.-P. (2007). Securing vehicular ad hoc networks. *Journal of Computer Security, 15*(1), 39–68. doi:10.3233/JCS-2007-15103

Raymond, L. (2001). Determinants of Web site implementation in small business. *Internet Research: Electronic Network Applications and Policy*, 411.

Rebolledo-Mendez, G., Reyes, A., Paszkowicz, S., Domingo, M. C., & Skrypchuk, L. (2014). *Developing a Body Sensor Network to Detect Emotions during Driving. IEEE Trans. Intell. Transport. Syst.*

Reichardt, D., Miglietta, M., Moretti, L., Morsink, P., & Schulz, W. (2002). CarTALK 2000 – safe and comfortable driving based upon inter-vehicle-communication. In *Intelligent Vehicle Symposium*. IEEE.

Reid, P. (2003). *Biometrics for Network Security*. Prentice Hall PTR.

Reid, J., Cheong, I., Henricksen, M., & Smith, J. (2003). A novel use of RBAC to protect privacy in distributed health care information systems. *8th Australasian Conference on Information Security and Privacy*, 403-415. 10.1007/3-540-45067-X_35

Reyes. (2014). Vehicle density in VANET application. *Journal of Ambient Intelligence and Smart Environments, 6*, 469-481.

Reyes, A., Barrado, C., & Guerrero, A. (2016). Communication technologies to design vehicle-to-vehicle and vehicle-to-infrastructures applications. *Latin American Applied Research, 46*, 29–35.

Reyes-Muñoz, A., Domingo, M. C., López-Trinidad, M. A., & Delgado, J. L. (2016). Integration of Body Sensor Networks and Vehicular Ad-hoc Networks for Traffic Safety. *Sensors (Basel), 16*(1), 107. doi:10.339016010107 PMID:26784204

Rigas, G., Goletsis, Y., & Fotiadis, D.I. (2012). Real-time driver's stress event detection. *IEEE Trans. Intell. Transport. Syst.*

Rodrigo, A., & Edirisinghe, L. (2015, May). A Study on electronic toll collection systems in expressways in Sri Lanka. In *Proceedings of 8th International Research Conference*. KDU.

Roozbahani, F. S., & Azad, R. (2015). Security Solutions against Computer Networks Threats. *International Journal of Advanced Networking and Applications, 7*(1), 2576–2581.

Royani, T., Haddadnia, J., & Alipoor, M. (2013). Control of traffic light in isolated intersections using fuzzy neural network and genetic algorithm. *International Journal of Computer and Electrical Engineering, 5*(1), 142–146. doi:10.7763/IJCEE.2013.V5.682

Ruhil, A. P., Lobiyal, D. K., & Stojmenovic, I. (2005). Performance Evaluation of Geocasting Protocols in Mobile Ad Hoc Networks. *11th National Conference on Communication (NCC-2005)*, 46–50. Retrieved from http://www.tjprc.org/view-archives.php

Saaty, T. L. (1996). *Decision Making with Dependence and Feedback the Analytic Network Process*. RWS Publications.

Saaty, T. L. (1980). *The Analytic Hierarchy Process*. McGraw Hill.

Safi, Q. K., Luo, S., Wei, C., Pan, L., & Chen, Q. (2017). Cloud-oriented secure and privacy-conscious parking information as a service using VANETs. *Computer Networks, 124*, 33–45. doi:10.1016/j.comnet.2017.06.001

Sailer, R., Jaeger, T., Valdez, E., C'aceres, R., Perez, R., Berger, S., Grifõn, J., & van Doorn, L. (2005). Building a MAC based security architecture for the Xen opensource hypervisor. *Proceedings of the Annual Computer Security Applications Conference*, 1-10.

Salahuddin, M. A., Al-Fuqaha, A., & Guizani, M. (2015). Software-Defined Networking for RSU Clouds in Support of the Internet of Vehicles. *IEEE Internet of Things Journal, 2*(2), 133–144. doi:10.1109/JIOT.2014.2368356

Salih, Y. K., See, O. H., Ibrahim, R. W., Yussof, S., & Iqbal, A. (2015). A user-centric game selection model based on user preferences for the selection of the best heterogeneous wireless network. *Annales des Télécommunications, 70*(5-6), 239–248. doi:10.100712243-014-0443-6

Sample, A. P., Parks, A. N., & Southwood, S. (2013). *Wireless ambient radio power in smith J.P. In Wirelessly powered sensor networks and computational RFID.* Springer.

Santhi, S. (2019). *SoS Emergency Ad-Hoc Wireless Network, Computational Intelligence and Sustainable Systems (CISS).* EAI/Springer Innovations in Comm and Computing.

Santns, R. A., Edwards, R. M., Edwards, A., & Belis, D. (2004). A novel cluster-based location routing algorithm for inter-vehicular communication. *IEEE 15th International Symposium on Personal, Indoor and Mobile Radio Communications.*

Santos, P. M. (2018). Porto Living Lab: An IoT-Based Sensing Platform for Smart Cities. IEEE Internet of Things Journal, 5(2), 523-532.

Sarvada, H., Nikhil, T. R., & Kulkarni, H. J. (2013). Identification of black spots and improvements to junctions in Bangalore city. *International Journal of Scientific Research (Ahmedabad, India), 2*(8).

Satyanarayanan, M., Bahl, P., Cáceres, R., & Davies, N. (2009). The case for VM-based cloudlets in mobile computing," pp. 14–23. *IEEE Pervasive Computing, 8*(4), doi:10.1109/MPRV.2009.82

Satyanarayanan, M., Lewis, G., Morris, E., Simanta, S., Boleng, J., & Ha, K. (2013). The role of cloudlets in hostile environments. *IEEE Pervasive Computing, 12*(4). doi:10.1109/MPRV.2013.77

Satyanarayanan, M., Schuster, R., & Ebling, M. (2015). "An open ecosystem for mobile-cloud convergence. *IEEE Communications Magazine, 53*(3). doi:10.1109/MCOM.2015.7060484

Schwarz, T., & Miller, E. L. (2006). Store, Forget & Check: using Algbric Signtres to Chck Remtel Admnied Storge. *Proc. IEEE Int Conf. Distribtd Comptng Sytms*, 1-6.

Schwingenschlogl, C., & Kosch, T. (2002). Geocast enhancements of AODV for vehicular networks. *Mobile Computing and Communications Review, 6*(3), 96–97. doi:10.1145/581291.581307

Sebe, F. (2008). Efficnt Remote Data Possen Checkg in Critical Inf. Infrastes. *Trans. Knowledge and Data Eng, 20*(8), 1034–1038. doi:10.1109/TKDE.2007.190647

Seet, B. C., Liu, G., Lee, B. S., Foh, C. H., Wong, K. J., & Lee, K. K. (2004). A-STAR: A mobile ad hoc routing strategy for metropolis vehicular communications. In *NETWORKING 2004, networking technologies, services, and protocols; performance of computer and communication networks; mobile and wireless communications* (pp. 989–999). Springer. doi:10.1007/978-3-540-24693-0_81

Sekar, R., Gupta, A., Frullo, J., Shanbhag, T., Tiwari, A., Yang, H., & Zhou, S. (2002). Specification-based anomaly detection: a new approach for detecting network intrusions. *Proceedings of the 9th ACM conference on Computer and communication security*, 265– 274.

Sendra, S., Rego, A., Lloret, J., Jimenez, J. M., & Romero, O. (2017). Including artificial intelligence in a routing protocol using Software Defined Networks. In *2017 IEEE International Conference on Communications Workshops, ICC Workshops 2017* (pp. 670–674). 10.1109/ICCW.2017.7962735

Sengupta, S., Verma, S., Mull, S., & Paul, S. (2015). Comparative Study of Image Segmentation Using Variants of Self-Organizing Maps (SOM). *International Journal for Research in Emerging Science and Technology, 2*(5).

Sengupta, N., & Chinnasamy, R. (2015). Contriving hybrid DESCAST algorithm for cloud security. *Procedia Computer Science, 54*, 47–56. doi:10.1016/j.procs.2015.06.006

Shah, M. A. (2008). Privacy-Preserving Audit & Extracting of Digital Content. Cryptology based Print of the Report.

Shamsher, R., & Abdullah, M. N. (2015). Traffic congestion in Bangladesh-causes and solutions: A study of Chittagong metropolitan city. *Asian Business Review, 2*(1), 13–18. doi:10.18034/abr.v2i1.309

Sharma & Gupta. (2012, October). Comparison based Performance Analysis of UDP/CBR and TCP/FTP Traffic under AODV Routing Protocol in MANET. *International Journal of Computer Applications, 56*(15).

Sharma, D. K. (2016). A machine learning-based protocol for efficient routing in opportunistic networks. *IEEE Systems Journal, 12*(3), 2207-2213.

Sharma. (2019). A survey: issues and challenges of vehicular ad hoc networks (VANETs). *International conf on sustainable computing in science, technology and management (SUSCOM-2019)*, 2491-2503.

Sharma, S., Sethi, D., & Bhattacharya, P. (2015). Artificial Neural Network based Cluster Head Selection in Wireless Sensor Network. *International Journal of Computers and Applications, 119*(4).

Sharma, T., & Yadav, R. (2015). Security in Virtual private network. *International Journal of Innovations & Advancement in Computer Science, 4*, 669–675.

Shevgaonkar, R. K. (n.d.). *Electromagnetic waves* (12th ed.). MGH.

Shi, J., & Wu, J. (2017). Research on Adaptive Cruise Control based on curve radius prediction. *Proceedings of the 2017 2nd International Conference on Image, Vision and Computing (ICIVC)*.

Shrinivas. (2011). Privacy-Preserving Public Auditing in Cloud Storage security. *Intl Jornl of Computer Science and Information Technology, 2*(6), 2691-2693.

Simon, M., Schmidt, E. A., Kincses, W. E., Fritzsche, M., Bruns, A., Aufmuth, C., Bogdan, M., Rosenstiel, W., & Schrauf, M. (2011). EEG alpha spindle measures as indicators of driver fatigue under real traffic conditions. *Clinical Neurophysiology, 122*(6), 1168–1178. doi:10.1016/j.clinph.2010.10.044 PMID:21333592

Singh & Verma. (2013, September). Simulation and analysis of AODV, DSDV, ZRP in VANET. *International Journal in Foundations of Computer Science & Technology, 3*(5).

Singh, M., Agarwal, S., & Parikar, M. S. (2017). Design of rectenna system for GSM-900 band using novel broadside 2*1 array antenna. *Journal of Engineering (Stevenage, England)*.

Singh, R. K., Sarkar, A., & Anoop, C. S. (2016). A health monitoring system using multiple non-contact ECG sensors for automotive drivers. *Proceedings of the 2016 IEEE International Instrumentation and Measurement Technology Conference Proceedings*. 10.1109/I2MTC.2016.7520539

Singh, S., & Silakari, S. (2009). A Survey of Cyber Attack Detection Systems. *International Journal of Computer Science and Network Security, 9*(5), 1–10.

Sitting & fuming: traffic congestion statistics. (2019, July). https://static.nationwide.com/static/road-congestion-infographic.pdf?r=52

Siva Ram Murthy, C., & Manoj, B. S. (n.d.). *Ad Hoc Wireless Networks Architectures and Protocols C*. Siva Ram Murthy B. S. Manoj.

Sivaganesan, S. (2020). An Event based Neural Network Architecture with Content Addressable Memory. *International Journal of Embedded and Real-Time Communication Systems, IGI Global, 11*(1), 23–40. doi:10.4018/IJERTCS.2020010102

Sivakumar, R., Sinha, P., & Bharghavan, V. (1999). CEDAR: A Core-Extraction Distributed Ad Hoc Routing Algorithm. *IEEE Journal on Selected Areas in Communications, 17*(8), 1454–1465. doi:10.1109/49.779926

Small, T. a. (2005). Resource and performance tradeoffs in delay-tolerant wireless networks. In *Proceedings of the 2005 ACM SIGCOMM workshop on Delay-tolerant networking. ACM.* 10.1145/1080139.1080144

Smart Cities Definition. (2019, August). Retrieved from https://www.techopedia.com/definition/31494/smart-city

Smart Cities Mission. (2016, August). *Ministry of Urban Development, Government of India.* Retrieved from http://smartcities.gov.in/

Smart City Mission. (2019, July), Retrieved from https://en.wikipedia.org/wiki/Smart_Cities_Mission

Smart City. (2019, August). Retrieved from https://en.wikipedia.org/wiki/Smart_city

Smith, D., & Singh, S. (2016). Approaches to multisensor data fusion in target tracking: A survey. *IEEE Transactions on Knowledge and Data Engineering.*

Sodiya, A. S., & Onashoga, A. S. (2009). Components-Based Access Control Architecture. *Issues in Informing Science and Information Technology, 6,* 699–706. doi:10.28945/1090

Soh, A. C., Rahman, R. Z. A., Rhung, L. G., & Sarkan, H. M. (2011, September). Traffic signal control based on adaptive neural-fuzzy inference system applied to intersection. In *2011 IEEE Conference on Open Systems* (pp. 231-236). IEEE. 10.1109/ICOS.2011.6079251

Song, T., Xia, W., Song, T., & Shen, L. (2010). *A Cluster-Based Directional Routing Protocol in VANET.* IEEE 12th International Conference on Communication Technology, Nanjing, China.

Soutar, C., Roberge, D., Stojanov, S. A., Gilroy, R., & Kumar, B. V. (1998). Biometric encryption using image processing. *Proceedings of the SPIE - Optical Security and Counterfeit Deterrence Techniques II, 3314,* 178–188.

Spyropoulos, T. P. (2005). Spray and wait: an efficient routing scheme for intermittently connected mobile networks. In *Proceedings of the 2005 ACM SIGCOMM workshop on Delay-tolerant networking* (pp. 252-259). ACM. 10.1145/1080139.1080143

Srihari. (2015). Automatic Battery Replacement of Robot. *Advances in Natural and Applied Sciences, 9*(7), 33-38.

Stallings. (2010). Software defined networks and openflow. *The Internet Protocol Journal, 16*(1).

Stallings, W. (2006). *Cryptography and Network Security* (4th ed.). Prentice Hall.

Stallings, W. (2007). *Network security essentials: applications and standards* (3rd ed.). Prentice Hall.

Stallings, W. (2011). *Network Security Essentials: Applications And Standards.* Pearson Education *Inc.*

Stallings, W. (2014). *Openflow switch specification.* Tech. Rep., Open Networking Foundation.

Sterbenz, J. P. (2002). Survivable mobile wireless networks: issues, challenges, and research directions. In *Proceedings of the 1st ACM workshop on Wireless security* (pp. 31-40). ACM. 10.1145/570681.570685

Stojmenovic, I., Ruhil, A. P., & Lobiyal, D. K. (2003). Voronoi diagram and convex hull based geocasting and routing in wireless networks. *Proceedings - IEEE Symposium on Computers and Communications,* 51–56. 10.1109/ISCC.2003.1214100

Su, W., & Gerla, M. (n.d.). IPv6 Flow Handoff In Ad Hoc Wireless Networks Using Mobility Prediction. In *Seamless Interconnection for Universal Services. Global Telecommunications Conference. GLOBECOM'99. (Cat. No. 99CH37042)* (pp. 271–275). Academic Press.

Sudheera, K. L. K., Ma, M., & Chong, P. H. J. (2019). Link Stability Based Optimized Routing Framework for Software Defined Vehicular Networks. *IEEE Transactions on Vehicular Technology, 68*(3), 2934–2945. doi:10.1109/TVT.2019.2895274

Sumathi, M., Sharvani, G. S., & Dinesha, H. A. (2013). Implementation of Multifactor Authentication System for Accessing Cloud Service. *International Journal of Scientific and Research Publications, 3*(6), 1–8.

SUMO Traffic Simulator. (2019, August). Retrieved from http://sumo.sourceforge.net/

Sun, M.-T., & Feng, W.-C. (2000). GPS-based message broadcast for adaptive inter-vehicle communications. *52nd Vehicular Technology Conference Fall (IEEE VTS Fall VTC).*

Syal & Kaur. (2014). A Study of Routing Protocols for Vehicular Ad-Hoc Networks. *International Journal of Engineering Trends and Technology, 15*(1).

Takacs, A., Okba, A. & Aubert, H. (2018). *Compact Planar Integrated Rectenna for Batteryless IoT Applications.* doi:10.23919/EuMC.2018.8541764

Takhedmit, H., Cirio, L., Costa, F., & Picon, O. (2014). Transparent rectenna and rectenna array for RF energy harvesting at 2.45 GHz. *8th European Conference on Antennas and Propagation (EuCAP),* 2970-2972. 10.1109/EuCAP.2014.6902451

Tang, T., Lin, Z., & Zhang, Y. (2017). Rapid Forward Vehicle Detection Based on Deformable Part Model, *Proceedings of the 2017 2nd International Conference on Multimedia and Image Processing (ICMIP),* 27–31. 10.1109/ICMIP.2017.78

Tang, Y., Cheng, N., Wu, W., Wang, M., Dai, Y., & Shen, X. (2019). Delay-Minimization Routing for Heterogeneous VANETs with Machine Learning Based Mobility Prediction. *IEEE Transactions on Vehicular Technology, 68*(4), 3967–3979. doi:10.1109/TVT.2019.2899627

Tan, W., Yang, M., Feng, Y., & Wei, R. (2009). A security framework for wireless network based on public key infrastructure. *Proc. of Computing, Communication, Control, and Management. CCCM, 9*(2), 567–570.

The Network Simulator – ns-2. (n.d.). Retrieved July 30, 2019 from https://www.isi.edu/nsnam/ns/

Thein, M. C. M., & Thein, T. (2010). An energy efficient cluster-head selection for wireless sensor networks. Intelligent systems, modelling and simulation (ISMS), 2010 international IEEE conference.

Toh, C. K. (1997). Associativity-Based Routing for Ad-Hoc Mobile Networks. *Wireless Personal Communications, 4*(2), 103–139. doi:10.1023/A:1008812928561

Tonguz, O., Wisitpongphan, N., Bai, F., Mudalige, P., & Sadekar, V. (2007). Broadcasting in VANET. *2007 Mobile Networking for Vehicular Environments, MOVE,* 7–12. doi:10.1109/MOVE.2007.4300825

Tonguz, O. K., Wisitpongphan, N., Bai, F., Mudalige, P., & Sadekar, V. (2007,May). Broadcasting in VANET. *Proc. IEEE INFOCOM MOVE Workshop 2007.*

Traffic Congestion Costs. (2018, April). Retrieved from: https://timesofindia.indiatimes.com/india/traffic-congestion-costs-four-major-indian-cities-rs-1-5-lakh-crore-a-year/articleshow/63918040.cms

Traffic Congestion. (2015, Sept.). Retrieved from: https://www.mapsofindia.com/my-india/society/traffic-congestion-in-delhi-causes-outcomes-and-solutions

Trestian, R., Ormond, O., & Muntean, G. M. (2012). Game theory-based network selection: Solutions and challenges. *IEEE Communications Surveys and Tutorials, 14*(4), 1212–1231. doi:10.1109/SURV.2012.010912.00081

Truong, N. B., Lee, G. M., & Ghamri-Doudane, Y. (2015a). Software defined networking-based vehicular Adhoc Network with Fog Computing. *Proceedings of the 2015 IFIP/IEEE International Symposium on Integrated Network Management, IM 2015,* 1202–1207. 10.1109/INM.2015.7140467

Tseng, Y. C., Ni, S. Y., Chen, Y. S., & Sheu, J. P. (2002). The broadcast storm problem in a mobile ad hoc network. *Wireless Networks, 8*(2–3), 153–167. doi:10.1023/A:1013763825347

Tseng, Y. C., Ni, S. Y., & Shih, E. Y. (2003). Adaptive approaches to relieving broadcast storms in a wireless multihop mobile ad hoc network. *IEEE Transactions on Computers, 52*(5), 545–557. doi:10.1109/TC.2003.1197122

Turban, E., King, D., Lee, J., & Viehland, D. (2002). *Electronic commerce: A managerial perspective 2002.* Prentice Hall.

Udayakumar, E., & Krishnaveni, V. (2019). A Review on Interference management in Millimeter-Wave MIMO Systems for future 5G Networks. *Proceedings of International Conference on Innovations in Electrical and Electronics Engineering (ICIEEE 2019),* 1-6.

Udayakumar, E., & Krishnaveni, V. (2019). Analysis of various Interference in Millimeter- Wave Communication Systems: A Survey. *Proceedings of IEEE International Conference on Computing, Communication and Networking Technologies (ICCCNT 2019),* 1-6. 10.1109/ICCCNT45670.2019.8944417

Uddin, M., & Nadeem, T. (2017). Traffic Vision: A Case for Pushing Software Defined Networks to Wireless Edges. In *Proceedings - 2016 IEEE 13th International Conference on Mobile Ad Hoc and Sensor Systems, MASS 2016* (pp. 37–46). 10.1109/MASS.2016.016

Ultsch, A. (1993). Self-organizing neural networks for visualisation and classification. In Information and classification. Springer Berlin Heidelberg. doi:10.1007/978-3-642-50974-2_31

UN Report. (2019, July). Retrieved from https://www.un.org/development/desa/en/news/population/2018-world-urbanization-prospects.html

Vahdat, A. a. (2000). *Epidemic routing for partially connected ad hoc networks.* Academic Press.

Vats. (2017). Vanet. A future technology. *International Journal of Science and Research Publications, 7*(2), 378-389.

VDOT. (2019, July). Retrieved from http://www.virginiadot.org/infoservice/smart-default.asp

Vejlgaard, B., Lauridsen, M., Nguyen, H., Kovacs, I. Z., Mogensen, P., & Sorensen, M. (2017). Coverage and Capacity Analysis of Sigfox, LoRa, GPRS and NB-IoT. *Proceedings of the 2017 IEEE 85th Vehicular Technology Conference (VTC Spring).* 10.1109/VTCSpring.2017.8108666

Venkatesh, A., & Indra, M. (2014, January). Routing Protocols for Vehicular Adhoc Networks (VANETs): A Review. *Journal of Emerging Trends in Computing and Information Sciences, 5*(1).

Vermesan, O., Friess, P., & Furness, A. (2012). The Internet of Things 2012 New Horizons. Academic Press.

Vesanto, J. (1999). *SOM-based data visualization methods. Intelligent data analysis.* Volvo IntelliSafe System. https://www.volvocars.com/us/about/our-innovations/intellisafe

Vetrivelan, P (2019). *A Neural Network based Automatic Crop Monitoring Robot for Agriculture. In The IoT and the Next Revolutions Automating the World.* IGI Global.

Vetrivelan, P. (2015). PAPR Reduction for OQAM/OFDM Signals by using Neural Networks. *International Journal of Applied Engineering Research, 10*(41), 30292–30297.

Vetrivelan, P. (2015). PAPR Reduction for OQAM/OFDM Signals using Optimized Iterative Clipping and Filtering Technique. *Proceedings of IEEE International Conference on Soft-Computing and Network Security (ICSNS'15)*, 72.

Viduto, V., Maple, C., Huang, W., & López-Peréz, D. (2012). A novel risk assessment and optimisation model for a multi-objective network security countermeasure selection problem. *Decision Support Systems, 53*(3), 599–610. doi:10.1016/j.dss.2012.04.001

Viola, P., & Jones, M. (2001). Rapid object detection using a boosted cascade of simple features. *CVPR, 1*(511-518), 3.

Wang, C. (2012). Towards the Secure& Dependable Storage Service in the Cloud Comptng. *IEEE Trans. Service Computing, 5*(2), 220-232.

Wang, C., Ma, X., Jiang, W., Zhao, L., Lin, N., & Shi, J. (2019). IMCR: Influence maximisation-based cluster routing algorithm for SDVN. In *Proceedings - 21st IEEE International Conference on High Performance Computing and Communications, 17th IEEE International Conference on Smart City and 5th IEEE International Conference on Data Science and Systems, HPCC/SmartCity/DSS 2019* (pp. 2580–2586). 10.1109/HPCC/SmartCity/DSS.2019.00361

Wang, P., Lin, S. C., & Luo, M. (2016). A framework for QoS-aware traffic classification using semi-supervised machine learning in SDNs. In *Proceedings - 2016 IEEE International Conference on Services Computing, SCC 2016* (pp. 760–765). 10.1109/SCC.2016.133

Wang, T., & Wang, G. (2010). *TIBCRPH: Traffic Infrastructure Based Cluster Routing Protocol with Handoff in VANET.* IEEE The 19th Annual Wireless and Optical Communications Conference (WOCC 2010), Shanghai, China.

Wang, Y., Tian, L., & Chen, Z. (2019). Game Analysis of Access Control Based on User Behavior Trust. *Information'19, 10*(132), 1-13.

Wang, C., Chow, S. S. M., Wang, Q., Ren, K., & Lou, W. (2013). Privacy_preserving Public Auditing for Secure Cloud Storage. *IEEE Transactions on Computers, 62*(2), 362–375. doi:10.1109/TC.2011.245

Wang, L., & Kuo, G.-S. G. S. (2013). Mathematical Modeling for Network Selection in Heterogeneous Wireless Networks—A Tutorial. *IEEE Communications Surveys and Tutorials, 15*(1), 271–292. doi:10.1109/SURV.2012.010912.00044

Wang, Q., & Wang, C. (2011). Enabling Public Audita & Data Dynamic for Storage in the Cloud Comptg. *IEEE Transactions on Parallel and Distributed Systems, 22*, 847–859. doi:10.1109/TPDS.2010.183

Wang, X., Wang, C., Zhang, J., Zhou, M., & Jiang, C. (2017). Improved rule installation for real-time query service in software-defined internet of vehicles. *IEEE Transactions on Intelligent Transportation Systems, 18*(2), 2017. doi:10.1109/TITS.2016.2543600

Watersand, B. (2008). Compact the Proofs of the Retrievability. *Proc. Int. Conf. Theory &Applicn of Cryptology &Infn Security: Advan of Cryptology, 5350*, 90-107.

Weinhardt, C., Anandasivam, A., Blau, B., & Stößer, J. (2009). Business models in the service world. *IT Professional, 11*(2), 28–33. doi:10.1109/MITP.2009.21

Weisstein, E. W. (2019). *Fermat Points.* Retrieved December 12, 2019, from https://mathworld.wolfram.com/FermatPoints.html

Wilton, C. (2017). Sony, Cyber Security, and Free Speech. *Preserving the First Amendment in the Modern World., 7*(1), 1–43.

WiMAX - 802.16 - Worldwide Interoperability for Microwave Access. (n.d.). Retrieved July 28, 2019 from https://ccm. net/contents/808-wimax-802-16-worldwide-interoperability-for-microwave-access

Wisitpongphan, N., Tonguz, O. K., Parikh, J. S., Mudalige, P., Bai, F., & Sadekar, V. (2007). Broadcast storm mitigation techniques in vehicular ad hoc networks. *IEEE Wireless Communications, 14*(6), 84–94. doi:10.1109/MWC.2007.4407231

World Health Organization Report on Road Traffic Injury Prevention. (n.d.). https://apps.who.int/iris/bit-stream/10665/42871/1/9241562609.pdf

Wu, X., & Zhu, X. (2008). Mining with noise knowledge: Error-aware data mining. *IEEE Trans. Syst. Man Cybern.*

Wu, K., Tong, Z., Li, W., & Ma, G. (2009). Security Model Based on Network Business Security. *Proc. of Int. Conf. on Computer Technology and Development, ICCTD '09, 1,* 577-580.

Xiao, P., Qu, W., Qi, H., Xu, Y., & Li, Z. (2015). An efficient elephant flow detection with cost-sensitive in SDN. In *Proceedings of the 2015 1st International Conference on Industrial Networks and Intelligent Systems, INISCom 2015* (pp. 24–28). 10.4108/icst.iniscom.2015.258274

Xia, Y., Yeo, C. K., & Lee, B. S. (2009). *Hierarchical Cluster Based Routing for Highly Mobile Heterogeneous MANET. IEEE International Conference on Network and Service Security*, Paris, France.

Xu & Saadawi. (2001). Does the IEEE 802.11 MAC Protocol Work Well in Multihop Wireless Ad Hoc Networks. *IEEE Communications Magazine.*

Xu, P., Fang, X., & Liu, X. (2010). A Non-cooperative Pairwise Matrices Game Model for Heterogeneous Network Selection. In *International Conference on Communications and Mobile Computing* (Vol. 3, pp. 387–391). IEEE. 10.1109/CMC.2010.29

Yan, F., & Yang, J. YLin, C. (2015). Computer Network Security and Technology Research. *Seventh International Conference on Measuring Technology and Mechatronics Automation*, 293-296. 10.1109/ICMTMA.2015.77

Yang, C., Xu, Y., Xu, R., & Sha, X. (2011). A heterogeneous wireless network selection algorithm based on non-cooperative game theory. In *6th International ICST Conference on Communications and Networking in China (CHINACOM)* (pp. 720–724). IEEE. 10.1109/ChinaCom.2011.6158248

Yang, J. Y., Chou, L. D., Li, Y. C., Lin, Y. H., Huang, S. M., Tseng, G., Wang, T. W., & Lu, S. P. (2010). Prediction of short-term average vehicular velocity considering weather factors in urban VANET environments. *Proceedings of the International Conference on Machine Learning and Cybernetics.* 10.1109/ICMLC.2010.5580743

Yao, P. (2004). Evaluation of Three Geocasting Protocols for a MANET. *Grace Hopper Celebration of Women in Computing*, 1–6.

Yao, P., Krohne, E., & Camp, T. (2004). Performance comparison of geocast routing protocols for a MANET. *Proceedings - International Conference on Computer Communications and Networks, ICCCN*, 213–220. 10.1109/icccn.2004.1401631

Yin, C., Xiong, Z., Chen, H., Wang, J., Cooper, D., & David, B. (2015). A literature survey on smart cities. *Science China. Information Sciences, 58*(10), 1–18. doi:10.100711432-015-5397-4

Younis, M., & Akkaya, K. (2008). Strategies and techniques for node placement in wireless sensor networks: A survey. *Journal of Ad Hoc Networks, 6*(4).

You, Z., Cheng, G., Wang, Y., Chen, P., & Chen, S. (2019). Cross-layer and SDN Based routing scheme for P2P communication in vehicular Ad-hoc networks. *Applied Sciences (Switzerland), 9*(22), 4734. doi:10.3390/app9224734

Yu, Q., & Heijenk, G. (2008). Abiding geocast for warning message dissemination in vehicular ad hoc networks. *IEEE International Conference on Communications*, 400–404. 10.1109/ICCW.2008.81

Zaimi, Houssaini, Boushaba, Oumsis, & Aboutajdine. (2017, August). *An Evaluation of Routing Protocols for Vehicular Ad-Hoc Network Considering the Video Stream*. Springer.

Zanakis, S. H., Solomon, A., Wishart, N., & Dublish, S. (1998). Multi-attribute decision making: A simulation comparison of select methods. *European Journal of Operational Research*, *107*(3), 507–529. doi:10.1016/S0377-2217(97)00147-1

Zang, L., Jia, L., & Luo, Y. (2006, June). An intelligent control method for urban traffic signal based on fuzzy neural network. In *2006 6th World Congress on Intelligent Control and Automation* (Vol. 1, pp. 3430-3434). IEEE.

Zhang, D., Yu, F. R., Wei, Z., & Boukerche, A. (2016). *Trust-based secure routing in software-defined vehicular ad hoc networks*. Networking and Internet Architecture.

Zhang, D., Yu, F. R., & Yang, R. (2018). A Machine Learning Approach for Software-Defined Vehicular Ad Hoc Networks with Trust Management. *2018 IEEE Global Communications Conference, GLOBECOM 2018 - Proceedings*. 10.1109/GLOCOM.2018.8647426

Zhang, G., Chen, W., Xu, Z., Liang, H., Mu, D., & Gao, L. (2009). Geocast routing in urban vehicular ad hoc networks. *Studies in Computational Intelligence*, *208*, 23–31. doi:10.1007/978-3-642-01209-9_3

Zhang, J., Wang, F., Wang, K., Lin, W., Xu, X., & Chen, C. (2011). Data-Driven Intelligent Transportation System: A survey. *IEEE Transactions on Intelligent Transportation Systems*, *12*(4), 1624–1639. doi:10.1109/TITS.2011.2158001

Zhiyong, L., Zhihua, D., & Peili, Q. (2011). Formal Description of IPSec Security Policy in VPN Networks. *Journal of Hua Zhong University of Science and Technology*, 14-16.

Zhu, M., Cai, Z., Cao, J., & Xu, M. (2015). Efficient multiple-copy routing in software. *Proc. Int. Conf. Inf. Commun. Technol.*, 1–6.

Zhu, M., Cao, J., Pang, D., & He, Z. (2015). SDN-Based Routing for Efficient Message Propagation in VANET Min. *Proc. 10th Int. Conf. Wireless Algorithms, Syst. Appl.*, 788–797. doi:10.1007/978-3-319-21837-3

Related References

To continue our tradition of advancing academic research, we have compiled a list of recommended IGI Global readings. These references will provide additional information and guidance to further enrich your knowledge and assist you with your own research and future publications.

Abed, S., Khir, T., & Ben Brahim, A. (2016). Thermodynamic and Energy Study of a Regenerator in Gas Turbine Cycle and Optimization of Performances. *International Journal of Energy Optimization and Engineering*, 5(2), 25–44. doi:10.4018/IJEOE.2016040102

Abu Bakar, W. A., Abdullah, W. N., Ali, R., & Mokhtar, W. N. (2016). Polymolybdate Supported Nano Catalyst for Desulfurization of Diesel. In T. Saleh (Ed.), *Applying Nanotechnology to the Desulfurization Process in Petroleum Engineering* (pp. 263–280). Hershey, PA: IGI Global. doi:10.4018/978-1-4666-9545-0.ch009

Addo-Tenkorang, R., Helo, P., & Kantola, J. (2016). Engineer-To-Order Product Development: A Communication Network Analysis for Supply-Chain's Sustainable Competitive Advantage. In R. Addo-Tenkorang, J. Kantola, P. Helo, & A. Shamsuzzoha (Eds.), *Supply Chain Strategies and the Engineer-to-Order Approach* (pp. 43–59). Hershey, PA: IGI Global. doi:10.4018/978-1-5225-0021-6.ch003

Adebiyi, I. D., Popoola, P. A., & Pityana, S. (2016). Mitigation of Wear Damage by Laser Surface Alloying Technique. In E. Akinlabi, R. Mahamood, & S. Akinlabi (Eds.), *Advanced Manufacturing Techniques Using Laser Material Processing* (pp. 172–196). Hershey, PA: IGI Global. doi:10.4018/978-1-5225-0329-3.ch007

Ahmad, W. (2016). Sulfur in Petroleum: Petroleum Desulfurization Techniques. In T. Saleh (Ed.), *Applying Nanotechnology to the Desulfurization Process in Petroleum Engineering* (pp. 1–52). Hershey, PA: IGI Global. doi:10.4018/978-1-4666-9545-0.ch001

Ahmed, I., Ahmad, N., Mehmood, I., Haq, I. U., Hassan, M., & Khan, M. U. (2016). Applications of Nanotechnology in Transportation Engineering. In A. Khitab & W. Anwar (Eds.), *Advanced Research on Nanotechnology for Civil Engineering Applications* (pp. 180–207). Hershey, PA: IGI Global. doi:10.4018/978-1-5225-0344-6.ch006

Aikhuele, D. (2018). A Study of Product Development Engineering and Design Reliability Concerns. *International Journal of Applied Industrial Engineering, 5*(1), 79–89. doi:10.4018/IJAIE.2018010105

Al-Najar, B. T., & Bououdina, M. (2016). Bioinspired Nanoparticles for Efficient Drug Delivery System. In M. Bououdina (Ed.), *Emerging Research on Bioinspired Materials Engineering* (pp. 69–103). Hershey, PA: IGI Global. doi:10.4018/978-1-4666-9811-6.ch003

Al-Shebeeb, O. A., Rangaswamy, S., Gopalakrishan, B., & Devaru, D. G. (2017). Evaluation and Indexing of Process Plans Based on Electrical Demand and Energy Consumption. *International Journal of Manufacturing, Materials, and Mechanical Engineering, 7*(3), 1–19. doi:10.4018/IJMMME.2017070101

Alexakis, H., & Makris, N. (2016). Validation of the Discrete Element Method for the Limit Stability Analysis of Masonry Arches. In V. Sarhosis, K. Bagi, J. Lemos, & G. Milani (Eds.), *Computational Modeling of Masonry Structures Using the Discrete Element Method* (pp. 292–325). Hershey, PA: IGI Global. doi:10.4018/978-1-5225-0231-9.ch012

AlMegren, H. A., Gonzalez-Cortes, S., Huang, Y., Chen, H., Qian, Y., Alkinany, M., ... Xiao, T. (2016). Preparation of Deep Hydrodesulfurzation Catalysts for Diesel Fuel using Organic Matrix Decomposition Method. In H. Al-Megren & T. Xiao (Eds.), *Petrochemical Catalyst Materials, Processes, and Emerging Technologies* (pp. 216–253). Hershey, PA: IGI Global. doi:10.4018/978-1-4666-9975-5.ch009

Alshammari, A., Kalevaru, V. N., Bagabas, A., & Martin, A. (2016). Production of Ethylene and its Commercial Importance in the Global Market. In H. Al-Megren & T. Xiao (Eds.), *Petrochemical Catalyst Materials, Processes, and Emerging Technologies* (pp. 82–115). Hershey, PA: IGI Global. doi:10.4018/978-1-4666-9975-5.ch004

Amel, M. (2016). Synthesis, Characterizations, and Biological Effects Study of Some Quinoline Family. In M. Bououdina (Ed.), *Emerging Research on Bioinspired Materials Engineering* (pp. 160–196). Hershey, PA: IGI Global. doi:10.4018/978-1-4666-9811-6.ch006

Amna, T., Haasan, M. S., Khil, M., & Hwang, I. (2016). Impact of Electrospun Biomimetic Extracellular Environment on Proliferation and Intercellular Communication of Muscle Precursor Cells: An Overview – Intercellular Communication of Muscle Precursor Cells with Extracellular Environment. In M. Bououdina (Ed.), *Emerging Research on Bioinspired Materials Engineering* (pp. 247–265). Hershey, PA: IGI Global. doi:10.4018/978-1-4666-9811-6.ch009

Amuda, M. O., Lawal, T. F., & Akinlabi, E. T. (2017). Research Progress on Rheological Behavior of AA7075 Aluminum Alloy During Hot Deformation. *International Journal of Materials Forming and Machining Processes, 4*(1), 53–96. doi:10.4018/IJMFMP.2017010104

An, M., & Qin, Y. (2016). Challenges of Railway Safety Risk Assessment and Maintenance Decision Making. In B. Rai (Ed.), *Handbook of Research on Emerging Innovations in Rail Transportation Engineering* (pp. 173–211). Hershey, PA: IGI Global. doi:10.4018/978-1-5225-0084-1.ch009

Anil, M., Ayyildiz-Tamis, D., Tasdemir, S., Sendemir-Urkmez, A., & Gulce-Iz, S. (2016). Bioinspired Materials and Biocompatibility. In M. Bououdina (Ed.), *Emerging Research on Bioinspired Materials Engineering* (pp. 294–322). Hershey, PA: IGI Global. doi:10.4018/978-1-4666-9811-6.ch011

Related References

Armutlu, H. (2018). Intelligent Biomedical Engineering Operations by Cloud Computing Technologies. In U. Kose, G. Guraksin, & O. Deperlioglu (Eds.), *Nature-Inspired Intelligent Techniques for Solving Biomedical Engineering Problems* (pp. 297–317). Hershey, PA: IGI Global. doi:10.4018/978-1-5225-4769-3.ch015

Arokiyaraj, S., Saravanan, M., Bharanidharan, R., Islam, V. I., Bououdina, M., & Vincent, S. (2016). Green Synthesis of Metallic Nanoparticles Using Plant Compounds and Their Applications: Metallic Nanoparticles Synthesis Using Plants. In M. Bououdina (Ed.), *Emerging Research on Bioinspired Materials Engineering* (pp. 1–34). Hershey, PA: IGI Global. doi:10.4018/978-1-4666-9811-6.ch001

Atik, M., Sadek, M., & Shahrour, I. (2017). Single-Run Adaptive Pushover Procedure for Shear Wall Structures. In V. Plevris, G. Kremmyda, & Y. Fahjan (Eds.), *Performance-Based Seismic Design of Concrete Structures and Infrastructures* (pp. 59–83). Hershey, PA: IGI Global. doi:10.4018/978-1-5225-2089-4.ch003

Aydin, A., Akyol, E., Gungor, M., Kaya, A., & Tasdelen, S. (2018). Geophysical Surveys in Engineering Geology Investigations With Field Examples. In N. Ceryan (Ed.), *Handbook of Research on Trends and Digital Advances in Engineering Geology* (pp. 257–280). Hershey, PA: IGI Global. doi:10.4018/978-1-5225-2709-1.ch007

Azevedo, N. M., Lemos, J. V., & Rocha de Almeida, J. (2016). Discrete Element Particle Modelling of Stone Masonry. In V. Sarhosis, K. Bagi, J. Lemos, & G. Milani (Eds.), *Computational Modeling of Masonry Structures Using the Discrete Element Method* (pp. 146–170). Hershey, PA: IGI Global. doi:10.4018/978-1-5225-0231-9.ch007

Bamufleh, H. S., Noureldin, M. M., & El-Halwagi, M. M. (2016). Sustainable Process Integration in the Petrochemical Industries. In H. Al-Megren & T. Xiao (Eds.), *Petrochemical Catalyst Materials, Processes, and Emerging Technologies* (pp. 150–163). Hershey, PA: IGI Global. doi:10.4018/978-1-4666-9975-5.ch006

Banerjee, S., Gautam, R. K., Gautam, P. K., Jaiswal, A., & Chattopadhyaya, M. C. (2016). Recent Trends and Advancement in Nanotechnology for Water and Wastewater Treatment: Nanotechnological Approach for Water Purification. In A. Khitab & W. Anwar (Eds.), *Advanced Research on Nanotechnology for Civil Engineering Applications* (pp. 208–252). Hershey, PA: IGI Global. doi:10.4018/978-1-5225-0344-6.ch007

Bas, T. G. (2017). Nutraceutical Industry with the Collaboration of Biotechnology and Nutrigenomics Engineering: The Significance of Intellectual Property in the Entrepreneurship and Scientific Research Ecosystems. In T. Bas & J. Zhao (Eds.), *Comparative Approaches to Biotechnology Development and Use in Developed and Emerging Nations* (pp. 1–17). Hershey, PA: IGI Global. doi:10.4018/978-1-5225-1040-6.ch001

Beale, R., & André, J. (2017). *Design Solutions and Innovations in Temporary Structures*. Hershey, PA: IGI Global. doi:10.4018/978-1-5225-2199-0

Behnam, B. (2017). Simulating Post-Earthquake Fire Loading in Conventional RC Structures. In P. Samui, S. Chakraborty, & D. Kim (Eds.), *Modeling and Simulation Techniques in Structural Engineering* (pp. 425–444). Hershey, PA: IGI Global. doi:10.4018/978-1-5225-0588-4.ch015

Ben Hamida, I., Salah, S. B., Msahli, F., & Mimouni, M. F. (2018). Distribution Network Reconfiguration Using SPEA2 for Power Loss Minimization and Reliability Improvement. *International Journal of Energy Optimization and Engineering*, 7(1), 50–65. doi:10.4018/IJEOE.2018010103

Benjamin, S. R., de Lima, F., & Rathoure, A. K. (2016). Genetically Engineered Microorganisms for Bioremediation Processes: GEMs for Bioremediaton. In A. Rathoure & V. Dhatwalia (Eds.), *Toxicity and Waste Management Using Bioremediation* (pp. 113–140). Hershey, PA: IGI Global. doi:10.4018/978-1-4666-9734-8.ch006

Bhaskar, S. V., & Kudal, H. N. (2017). Effect of TiCN and AlCrN Coating on Tribological Behaviour of Plasma-nitrided AISI 4140 Steel. *International Journal of Surface Engineering and Interdisciplinary Materials Science*, 5(2), 1–17. doi:10.4018/IJSEIMS.2017070101

Bhowmik, S., Sahoo, P., Acharyya, S. K., Dhar, S., & Chattopadhyay, J. (2016). Effect of Microstructure Degradation on Fracture Toughness of 20MnMoNi55 Steel in DBT Region. *International Journal of Manufacturing, Materials, and Mechanical Engineering*, 6(3), 11–27. doi:10.4018/IJMMME.2016070102

Bhutto, A. W., Abro, R., Abbas, T., Yu, G., & Chen, X. (2016). Desulphurization of Fuel Oils Using Ionic Liquids. In H. Al-Megren & T. Xiao (Eds.), *Petrochemical Catalyst Materials, Processes, and Emerging Technologies* (pp. 254–284). Hershey, PA: IGI Global. doi:10.4018/978-1-4666-9975-5.ch010

Bhuyan, D. (2018). Designing of a Twin Tube Shock Absorber: A Study in Reverse Engineering. In K. Kumar & J. Davim (Eds.), *Design and Optimization of Mechanical Engineering Products* (pp. 83–104). Hershey, PA: IGI Global. doi:10.4018/978-1-5225-3401-3.ch005

Bouloudenine, M., & Bououdina, M. (2016). Toxic Effects of Engineered Nanoparticles on Living Cells. In M. Bououdina (Ed.), *Emerging Research on Bioinspired Materials Engineering* (pp. 35–68). Hershey, PA: IGI Global. doi:10.4018/978-1-4666-9811-6.ch002

Brunetti, A., Sellaro, M., Drioli, E., & Barbieri, G. (2016). Membrane Engineering and its Role in Oil Refining and Petrochemical Industry. In H. Al-Megren & T. Xiao (Eds.), *Petrochemical Catalyst Materials, Processes, and Emerging Technologies* (pp. 116–149). Hershey, PA: IGI Global. doi:10.4018/978-1-4666-9975-5.ch005

Bügler, M., & Borrmann, A. (2016). Simulation Based Construction Project Schedule Optimization: An Overview on the State-of-the-Art. In F. Miranda & C. Abreu (Eds.), *Handbook of Research on Computational Simulation and Modeling in Engineering* (pp. 482–507). Hershey, PA: IGI Global. doi:10.4018/978-1-4666-8823-0.ch016

Calderon, F. A., Giolo, E. G., Frau, C. D., Rengel, M. G., Rodriguez, H., Tornello, M., ... Gallucci, R. (2018). Seismic Microzonation and Site Effects Detection Through Microtremors Measures: A Review. In N. Ceryan (Ed.), *Handbook of Research on Trends and Digital Advances in Engineering Geology* (pp. 326–349). Hershey, PA: IGI Global. doi:10.4018/978-1-5225-2709-1.ch009

Carmona-Murillo, J., & Valenzuela-Valdés, J. F. (2016). Motivation on Problem Based Learning. In D. Fonseca & E. Redondo (Eds.), *Handbook of Research on Applied E-Learning in Engineering and Architecture Education* (pp. 179–203). Hershey, PA: IGI Global. doi:10.4018/978-1-4666-8803-2.ch009

Ceryan, N. (2016). A Review of Soft Computing Methods Application in Rock Mechanic Engineering. In P. Samui (Ed.), *Handbook of Research on Advanced Computational Techniques for Simulation-Based Engineering* (pp. 1–70). Hershey, PA: IGI Global. doi:10.4018/978-1-4666-9479-8.ch001

Ceryan, N., & Can, N. K. (2018). Prediction of The Uniaxial Compressive Strength of Rocks Materials. In N. Ceryan (Ed.), *Handbook of Research on Trends and Digital Advances in Engineering Geology* (pp. 31–96). Hershey, PA: IGI Global. doi:10.4018/978-1-5225-2709-1.ch002

Ceryan, S. (2018). Weathering Indices Used in Evaluation of the Weathering State of Rock Material. In N. Ceryan (Ed.), *Handbook of Research on Trends and Digital Advances in Engineering Geology* (pp. 132–186). Hershey, PA: IGI Global. doi:10.4018/978-1-5225-2709-1.ch004

Chandrasekaran, S., Silva, B., Patil, A., Oo, A. M., & Campbell, M. (2016). Evaluating Engineering Students' Perceptions: The Impact of Team-Based Learning Practices in Engineering Education. *International Journal of Quality Assurance in Engineering and Technology Education*, 5(4), 42–59. doi:10.4018/IJQAETE.2016100103

Chen, H., Padilla, R. V., & Besarati, S. (2017). Supercritical Fluids and Their Applications in Power Generation. In L. Chen & Y. Iwamoto (Eds.), *Advanced Applications of Supercritical Fluids in Energy Systems* (pp. 369–402). Hershey, PA: IGI Global. doi:10.4018/978-1-5225-2047-4.ch012

Chen, L. (2017). Principles, Experiments, and Numerical Studies of Supercritical Fluid Natural Circulation System. In L. Chen & Y. Iwamoto (Eds.), *Advanced Applications of Supercritical Fluids in Energy Systems* (pp. 136–187). Hershey, PA: IGI Global. doi:10.4018/978-1-5225-2047-4.ch005

Clementi, F., Di Sciascio, G., Di Sciascio, S., & Lenci, S. (2017). Influence of the Shear-Bending Interaction on the Global Capacity of Reinforced Concrete Frames: A Brief Overview of the New Perspectives. In V. Plevris, G. Kremmyda, & Y. Fahjan (Eds.), *Performance-Based Seismic Design of Concrete Structures and Infrastructures* (pp. 84–111). Hershey, PA: IGI Global. doi:10.4018/978-1-5225-2089-4.ch004

Cortés-Polo, D., Calle-Cancho, J., Carmona-Murillo, J., & González-Sánchez, J. (2017). Future Trends in Mobile-Fixed Integration for Next Generation Networks: Classification and Analysis. *International Journal of Vehicular Telematics and Infotainment Systems*, 1(1), 33–53. doi:10.4018/IJVTIS.2017010103

Cui, X., Zeng, S., Li, Z., Zheng, Q., Yu, X., & Han, B. (2018). Advanced Composites for Civil Engineering Infrastructures. In K. Kumar & J. Davim (Eds.), *Composites and Advanced Materials for Industrial Applications* (pp. 212–248). Hershey, PA: IGI Global. doi:10.4018/978-1-5225-5216-1.ch010

Dalgıç, S., & Kuşku, İ. (2018). Geological and Geotechnical Investigations in Tunneling. In N. Ceryan (Ed.), *Handbook of Research on Trends and Digital Advances in Engineering Geology* (pp. 482–529). Hershey, PA: IGI Global. doi:10.4018/978-1-5225-2709-1.ch014

de la Varga, D., Soto, M., Arias, C. A., van Oirschot, D., Kilian, R., Pascual, A., & Álvarez, J. A. (2017). Constructed Wetlands for Industrial Wastewater Treatment and Removal of Nutrients. In Á. Val del Río, J. Campos Gómez, & A. Mosquera Corral (Eds.), *Technologies for the Treatment and Recovery of Nutrients from Industrial Wastewater* (pp. 202–230). Hershey, PA: IGI Global. doi:10.4018/978-1-5225-1037-6.ch008 del Valle-Zermeño, R., Chimenos, J. M., & Formosa, J. (2016). Flue Gas Desulfurization: Processes and Technologies. In T. Saleh (Ed.), *Applying Nanotechnology to the Desulfurization Process in Petroleum Engineering* (pp. 337–377). Hershey, PA: IGI Global. doi:10.4018/978-1-4666-9545-0.ch011

Delgado, J. M., Henriques, A. A., & Delgado, R. M. (2016). Structural Non-Linear Models and Simulation Techniques: An Efficient Combination for Safety Evaluation of RC Structures. In F. Miranda & C. Abreu (Eds.), *Handbook of Research on Computational Simulation and Modeling in Engineering* (pp. 540–584). Hershey, PA: IGI Global. doi:10.4018/978-1-4666-8823-0.ch018

Delgado, P. S., Arêde, A., Pouca, N. V., & Costa, A. (2016). Numerical Modeling of RC Bridges for Seismic Risk Analysis. In F. Miranda & C. Abreu (Eds.), *Handbook of Research on Computational Simulation and Modeling in Engineering* (pp. 457–481). Hershey, PA: IGI Global. doi:10.4018/978-1-4666-8823-0.ch015

Deng, Y., & Liu, S. (2016). Catalysis with Room Temperature Ionic Liquids Mediated Metal Nanoparticles. In H. Al-Megren & T. Xiao (Eds.), *Petrochemical Catalyst Materials, Processes, and Emerging Technologies* (pp. 285–329). Hershey, PA: IGI Global. doi:10.4018/978-1-4666-9975-5.ch011

Deperlioglu, O. (2018). Intelligent Techniques Inspired by Nature and Used in Biomedical Engineering. In U. Kose, G. Guraksin, & O. Deperlioglu (Eds.), *Nature-Inspired Intelligent Techniques for Solving Biomedical Engineering Problems* (pp. 51–77). Hershey, PA: IGI Global. doi:10.4018/978-1-5225-4769-3.ch003

Dias, G. L., Magalhães, R. R., Ferreira, D. D., & Vitoriano, F. A. (2016). The Use of a Robotic Arm for Displacement Measurements in a Cantilever beam. *International Journal of Manufacturing, Materials, and Mechanical Engineering*, 6(3), 45–57. doi:10.4018/IJMMME.2016070104

Dimitratos, N., Villa, A., Chan-Thaw, C. E., Hammond, C., & Prati, L. (2016). Valorisation of Glycerol to Fine Chemicals and Fuels. In H. Al-Megren & T. Xiao (Eds.), *Petrochemical Catalyst Materials, Processes, and Emerging Technologies* (pp. 352–384). Hershey, PA: IGI Global. doi:10.4018/978-1-4666-9975-5.ch013

Dixit, A. (2018). Application of Silica-Gel-Reinforced Aluminium Composite on the Piston of Internal Combustion Engine: Comparative Study of Silica-Gel-Reinforced Aluminium Composite Piston With Aluminium Alloy Piston. In K. Kumar & J. Davim (Eds.), *Composites and Advanced Materials for Industrial Applications* (pp. 63–98). Hershey, PA: IGI Global. doi:10.4018/978-1-5225-5216-1.ch004

Drei, A., Milani, G., & Sincraian, G. (2016). Application of DEM to Historic Masonries, Two Case-Studies in Portugal and Italy: Aguas Livres Aqueduct and Arch-Tympana of a Church. In V. Sarhosis, K. Bagi, J. Lemos, & G. Milani (Eds.), *Computational Modeling of Masonry Structures Using the Discrete Element Method* (pp. 326–366). Hershey, PA: IGI Global. doi:10.4018/978-1-5225-0231-9.ch013

Dutta, S., Roy, P. K., & Nandi, D. (2016). Optimal Allocation of Static Synchronous Series Compensator Controllers using Chemical Reaction Optimization for Reactive Power Dispatch. *International Journal of Energy Optimization and Engineering*, 5(3), 43–62. doi:10.4018/IJEOE.2016070103

Dutta, S., Roy, P. K., & Nandi, D. (2016). Quasi Oppositional Teaching-Learning based Optimization for Optimal Power Flow Incorporating FACTS. *International Journal of Energy Optimization and Engineering*, *5*(2), 64–84. doi:10.4018/IJEOE.2016040104

Eloy, S., Dias, M. S., Lopes, P. F., & Vilar, E. (2016). Digital Technologies in Architecture and Engineering: Exploring an Engaged Interaction within Curricula. In D. Fonseca & E. Redondo (Eds.), *Handbook of Research on Applied E-Learning in Engineering and Architecture Education* (pp. 368–402). Hershey, PA: IGI Global. doi:10.4018/978-1-4666-8803-2.ch017

Elsayed, A. M., Dakkama, H. J., Mahmoud, S., Al-Dadah, R., & Kaialy, W. (2017). Sustainable Cooling Research Using Activated Carbon Adsorbents and Their Environmental Impact. In T. Kobayashi (Ed.), *Applied Environmental Materials Science for Sustainability* (pp. 186–221). Hershey, PA: IGI Global. doi:10.4018/978-1-5225-1971-3.ch009

Ercanoglu, M., & Sonmez, H. (2018). General Trends and New Perspectives on Landslide Mapping and Assessment Methods. In N. Ceryan (Ed.), *Handbook of Research on Trends and Digital Advances in Engineering Geology* (pp. 350–379). Hershey, PA: IGI Global. doi:10.4018/978-1-5225-2709-1.ch010

Erinosho, M. F., Akinlabi, E. T., & Pityana, S. (2016). Enhancement of Surface Integrity of Titanium Alloy with Copper by Means of Laser Metal Deposition Process. In E. Akinlabi, R. Mahamood, & S. Akinlabi (Eds.), *Advanced Manufacturing Techniques Using Laser Material Processing* (pp. 60–91). Hershey, PA: IGI Global. doi:10.4018/978-1-5225-0329-3.ch004

Farag, H., & Kishida, M. (2016). Kinetic Models for Complex Parallel–Consecutive Reactions Assessment of Reaction Network and Product Selectivity. In H. Al-Megren & T. Xiao (Eds.), *Petrochemical Catalyst Materials, Processes, and Emerging Technologies* (pp. 330–351). Hershey, PA: IGI Global. doi:10.4018/978-1-4666-9975-5.ch012

Faroz, S. A., Pujari, N. N., Rastogi, R., & Ghosh, S. (2017). Risk Analysis of Structural Engineering Systems Using Bayesian Inference. In P. Samui, S. Chakraborty, & D. Kim (Eds.), *Modeling and Simulation Techniques in Structural Engineering* (pp. 390–424). Hershey, PA: IGI Global. doi:10.4018/978-1-5225-0588-4.ch014

Fernando, P. R., Hamigah, T., Disne, S., Wickramasingha, G. G., & Sutharshan, A. (2018). The Evaluation of Engineering Properties of Low Cost Concrete Blocks by Partial Doping of Sand with Sawdust: Low Cost Sawdust Concrete Block. *International Journal of Strategic Engineering*, *1*(2), 26–42. doi:10.4018/IJoSE.2018070103

Fragiadakis, M., Stefanou, I., & Psycharis, I. N. (2016). Vulnerability Assessment of Damaged Classical Multidrum Columns. In V. Sarhosis, K. Bagi, J. Lemos, & G. Milani (Eds.), *Computational Modeling of Masonry Structures Using the Discrete Element Method* (pp. 235–253). Hershey, PA: IGI Global. doi:10.4018/978-1-5225-0231-9.ch010

Gaines, T. W., Williams, K. R., & Wagener, K. B. (2016). ADMET: Functionalized Polyolefins. In H. Al-Megren & T. Xiao (Eds.), *Petrochemical Catalyst Materials, Processes, and Emerging Technologies* (pp. 1–21). Hershey, PA: IGI Global. doi:10.4018/978-1-4666-9975-5.ch001

Garg, H. (2016). Bi-Criteria Optimization for Finding the Optimal Replacement Interval for Maintaining the Performance of the Process Industries. In P. Vasant, G. Weber, & V. Dieu (Eds.), *Handbook of Research on Modern Optimization Algorithms and Applications in Engineering and Economics* (pp. 643–675). Hershey, PA: IGI Global. doi:10.4018/978-1-4666-9644-0.ch025

Gaspar, P. D., Dinho da Silva, P., Gonçalves, J. P., & Carneiro, R. (2016). Computational Modelling and Simulation to Assist the Improvement of Thermal Performance and Energy Efficiency in Industrial Engineering Systems: Application to Cold Stores. In F. Miranda & C. Abreu (Eds.), *Handbook of Research on Computational Simulation and Modeling in Engineering* (pp. 1–68). Hershey, PA: IGI Global. doi:10.4018/978-1-4666-8823-0.ch001

Ge, H., Tang, M., & Wen, X. (2016). Ni/ZnO Nano Sorbent for Reactive Adsorption Desulfurization of Refinery Oil Streams. In T. Saleh (Ed.), *Applying Nanotechnology to the Desulfurization Process in Petroleum Engineering* (pp. 216–239). Hershey, PA: IGI Global. doi:10.4018/978-1-4666-9545-0.ch007

Ghosh, S., Mitra, S., Ghosh, S., & Chakraborty, S. (2017). Seismic Reliability Analysis in the Framework of Metamodelling Based Monte Carlo Simulation. In P. Samui, S. Chakraborty, & D. Kim (Eds.), *Modeling and Simulation Techniques in Structural Engineering* (pp. 192–208). Hershey, PA: IGI Global. doi:10.4018/978-1-5225-0588-4.ch006

Gil, M., & Otero, B. (2017). Learning Engineering Skills through Creativity and Collaboration: A Game-Based Proposal. In R. Alexandre Peixoto de Queirós & M. Pinto (Eds.), *Gamification-Based E-Learning Strategies for Computer Programming Education* (pp. 14–29). Hershey, PA: IGI Global. doi:10.4018/978-1-5225-1034-5.ch002

Gill, J., Ayre, M., & Mills, J. (2017). Revisioning the Engineering Profession: How to Make It Happen! In M. Gray & K. Thomas (Eds.), *Strategies for Increasing Diversity in Engineering Majors and Careers* (pp. 156–175). Hershey, PA: IGI Global. doi:10.4018/978-1-5225-2212-6.ch008

Gopal, S., & Al-Hazmi, M. H. (2016). Advances in Catalytic Technologies for Selective Oxidation of Lower Alkanes. In H. Al-Megren & T. Xiao (Eds.), *Petrochemical Catalyst Materials, Processes, and Emerging Technologies* (pp. 22–52). Hershey, PA: IGI Global. doi:10.4018/978-1-4666-9975-5.ch002

Goyal, N., Ram, M., Bhardwaj, A., & Kumar, A. (2016). Thermal Power Plant Modelling with Fault Coverage Stochastically. *International Journal of Manufacturing, Materials, and Mechanical Engineering*, 6(3), 28–44. doi:10.4018/IJMMME.2016070103

Goyal, N., Ram, M., & Kumar, P. (2017). Welding Process under Fault Coverage Approach for Reliability and MTTF. In M. Ram & J. Davim (Eds.), *Mathematical Concepts and Applications in Mechanical Engineering and Mechatronics* (pp. 222–245). Hershey, PA: IGI Global. doi:10.4018/978-1-5225-1639-2.ch011

Gray, M., & Lundy, C. (2017). Engineering Study Abroad: High Impact Strategy for Increasing Access. In M. Gray & K. Thomas (Eds.), *Strategies for Increasing Diversity in Engineering Majors and Careers* (pp. 42–59). Hershey, PA: IGI Global. doi:10.4018/978-1-5225-2212-6.ch003

Guha, D., Roy, P. K., & Banerjee, S. (2016). Application of Modified Biogeography Based Optimization in AGC of an Interconnected Multi-Unit Multi-Source AC-DC Linked Power System. *International Journal of Energy Optimization and Engineering*, 5(3), 1–18. doi:10.4018/IJEOE.2016070101

Guha, D., Roy, P. K., & Banerjee, S. (2016). Grey Wolf Optimization to Solve Load Frequency Control of an Interconnected Power System: GWO Used to Solve LFC Problem. *International Journal of Energy Optimization and Engineering*, 5(4), 62–83. doi:10.4018/IJEOE.2016100104

Gupta, A. K., Dey, A., & Mukhopadhyay, A. K. (2016). Micromechanical and Finite Element Modeling for Composites. In S. Datta & J. Davim (Eds.), *Computational Approaches to Materials Design: Theoretical and Practical Aspects* (pp. 101–162). Hershey, PA: IGI Global. doi:10.4018/978-1-5225-0290-6.ch005

Guraksin, G. E. (2018). Internet of Things and Nature-Inspired Intelligent Techniques for the Future of Biomedical Engineering. In U. Kose, G. Guraksin, & O. Deperlioglu (Eds.), *Nature-Inspired Intelligent Techniques for Solving Biomedical Engineering Problems* (pp. 263–282). Hershey, PA: IGI Global. doi:10.4018/978-1-5225-4769-3.ch013

Hansman, C. A. (2016). Developing Mentoring Programs in Engineering and Technology Education. *International Journal of Quality Assurance in Engineering and Technology Education*, 5(2), 1–15. doi:10.4018/IJQAETE.2016040101

Hasan, U., Chegenizadeh, A., & Nikraz, H. (2016). Nanotechnology Future and Present in Construction Industry: Applications in Geotechnical Engineering. In A. Khitab & W. Anwar (Eds.), *Advanced Research on Nanotechnology for Civil Engineering Applications* (pp. 141–179). Hershey, PA: IGI Global. doi:10.4018/978-1-5225-0344-6.ch005

Hejazi, T., & Akbari, L. (2017). A Multiresponse Optimization Model for Statistical Design of Processes with Discrete Variables. In M. Ram & J. Davim (Eds.), *Mathematical Concepts and Applications in Mechanical Engineering and Mechatronics* (pp. 17–37). Hershey, PA: IGI Global. doi:10.4018/978-1-5225-1639-2.ch002

Hejazi, T., & Hejazi, A. (2017). Monte Carlo Simulation for Reliability-Based Design of Automotive Complex Subsystems. In M. Ram & J. Davim (Eds.), *Mathematical Concepts and Applications in Mechanical Engineering and Mechatronics* (pp. 177–200). Hershey, PA: IGI Global. doi:10.4018/978-1-5225-1639-2.ch009

Hejazi, T., & Poursabbagh, H. (2017). Reliability Analysis of Engineering Systems: An Accelerated Life Testing for Boiler Tubes. In M. Ram & J. Davim (Eds.), *Mathematical Concepts and Applications in Mechanical Engineering and Mechatronics* (pp. 154–176). Hershey, PA: IGI Global. doi:10.4018/978-1-5225-1639-2.ch008

Henao, J., & Sotelo, O. (2018). Surface Engineering at High Temperature: Thermal Cycling and Corrosion Resistance. In A. Pakseresht (Ed.), *Production, Properties, and Applications of High Temperature Coatings* (pp. 131–159). Hershey, PA: IGI Global. doi:10.4018/978-1-5225-4194-3.ch006

Huirache-Acuña, R., Alonso-Nuñez, G., Rivera-Muñoz, E. M., Gutierrez, O., & Pawelec, B. (2016). Trimetallic Sulfide Catalysts for Hydrodesulfurization. In T. Saleh (Ed.), *Applying Nanotechnology to the Desulfurization Process in Petroleum Engineering* (pp. 240–262). Hershey, PA: IGI Global. doi:10.4018/978-1-4666-9545-0.ch008

Ilori, O. O., Adetan, D. A., & Umoru, L. E. (2017). Effect of Cutting Parameters on the Surface Residual Stress of Face-Milled Pearlitic Ductile Iron. *International Journal of Materials Forming and Machining Processes*, 4(1), 38–52. doi:10.4018/IJMFMP.2017010103

Imam, M. H., Tasadduq, I. A., Ahmad, A., Aldosari, F., & Khan, H. (2017). Automated Generation of Course Improvement Plans Using Expert System. *International Journal of Quality Assurance in Engineering and Technology Education*, 6(1), 1–12. doi:10.4018/IJQAETE.2017010101

Injeti, S. K., & Kumar, T. V. (2018). A WDO Framework for Optimal Deployment of DGs and DSCs in a Radial Distribution System Under Daily Load Pattern to Improve Techno-Economic Benefits. *International Journal of Energy Optimization and Engineering*, 7(2), 1–38. doi:10.4018/IJEOE.2018040101

Ishii, N., Anami, K., & Knisely, C. W. (2018). *Dynamic Stability of Hydraulic Gates and Engineering for Flood Prevention*. Hershey, PA: IGI Global. doi:10.4018/978-1-5225-3079-4

J., J., Chowdhury, S., Goyal, P., Samui, P., & Dalkiliç, Y. (2016). Determination of Bearing Capacity of Shallow Foundation Using Soft Computing. In P. Saxena, D. Singh, & M. Pant (Eds.), *Problem Solving and Uncertainty Modeling through Optimization and Soft Computing Applications* (pp. 292-328). Hershey, PA: IGI Global. doi:10.4018/978-1-4666-9885-7.ch014

Jagan, J., Gundlapalli, P., & Samui, P. (2016). Utilization of Classification Techniques for the Determination of Liquefaction Susceptibility of Soils. In S. Bhattacharyya, P. Banerjee, D. Majumdar, & P. Dutta (Eds.), *Handbook of Research on Advanced Hybrid Intelligent Techniques and Applications* (pp. 124–160). Hershey, PA: IGI Global. doi:10.4018/978-1-4666-9474-3.ch005

Jayapalan, S. (2018). A Review of Chemical Treatments on Natural Fibers-Based Hybrid Composites for Engineering Applications. In K. Kumar & J. Davim (Eds.), *Composites and Advanced Materials for Industrial Applications* (pp. 16–37). Hershey, PA: IGI Global. doi:10.4018/978-1-5225-5216-1.ch002

Jeet, K., & Dhir, R. (2016). Software Module Clustering Using Bio-Inspired Algorithms. In P. Vasant, G. Weber, & V. Dieu (Eds.), *Handbook of Research on Modern Optimization Algorithms and Applications in Engineering and Economics* (pp. 445–470). Hershey, PA: IGI Global. doi:10.4018/978-1-4666-9644-0.ch017

Joshi, S. D., & Talange, D. B. (2016). Fault Tolerant Control for a Fractional Order AUV System. *International Journal of Energy Optimization and Engineering*, 5(2), 1–24. doi:10.4018/IJEOE.2016040101

Julião, D., Ribeiro, S., de Castro, B., Cunha-Silva, L., & Balula, S. S. (2016). Polyoxometalates-Based Nanocatalysts for Production of Sulfur-Free Diesel. In T. Saleh (Ed.), *Applying Nanotechnology to the Desulfurization Process in Petroleum Engineering* (pp. 426–458). Hershey, PA: IGI Global. doi:10.4018/978-1-4666-9545-0.ch014

Kamthan, P. (2016). On the Nature of Collaborations in Agile Software Engineering Course Projects. *International Journal of Quality Assurance in Engineering and Technology Education*, 5(2), 42–59. doi:10.4018/IJQAETE.2016040104

Karaman, O., Celik, C., & Urkmez, A. S. (2016). Self-Assembled Biomimetic Scaffolds for Bone Tissue Engineering. In M. Bououdina (Ed.), *Emerging Research on Bioinspired Materials Engineering* (pp. 104–132). Hershey, PA: IGI Global. doi:10.4018/978-1-4666-9811-6.ch004

Karkalos, N. E., Markopoulos, A. P., & Dossis, M. F. (2017). Optimal Model Parameters of Inverse Kinematics Solution of a 3R Robotic Manipulator Using ANN Models. *International Journal of Manufacturing, Materials, and Mechanical Engineering, 7*(3), 20–40. doi:10.4018/IJMMME.2017070102

Kesimal, A., Karaman, K., Cihangir, F., & Ercikdi, B. (2018). Excavatability Assessment of Rock Masses for Geotechnical Studies. In N. Ceryan (Ed.), *Handbook of Research on Trends and Digital Advances in Engineering Geology* (pp. 231–256). Hershey, PA: IGI Global. doi:10.4018/978-1-5225-2709-1.ch006

Khanh, D. V., Vasant, P. M., Elamvazuthi, I., & Dieu, V. N. (2016). Multi-Objective Optimization of Two-Stage Thermo-Electric Cooler Using Differential Evolution: MO Optimization of TEC Using DE. In F. Miranda & C. Abreu (Eds.), *Handbook of Research on Computational Simulation and Modeling in Engineering* (pp. 139–170). Hershey, PA: IGI Global. doi:10.4018/978-1-4666-8823-0.ch004

Kim, D., Hassan, M. K., Chang, S., & Bigdeli, Y. (2016). Nonlinear Vibration Control of 3D Irregular Structures Subjected to Seismic Loads. In P. Samui (Ed.), *Handbook of Research on Advanced Computational Techniques for Simulation-Based Engineering* (pp. 103–119). Hershey, PA: IGI Global. doi:10.4018/978-1-4666-9479-8.ch003

Knoflacher, H. (2017). The Role of Engineers and Their Tools in the Transport Sector after Paradigm Change: From Assumptions and Extrapolations to Science. In H. Knoflacher & E. Ocalir-Akunal (Eds.), *Engineering Tools and Solutions for Sustainable Transportation Planning* (pp. 1–29). Hershey, PA: IGI Global. doi:10.4018/978-1-5225-2116-7.ch001

Kose, U. (2018). Towards an Intelligent Biomedical Engineering With Nature-Inspired Artificial Intelligence Techniques. In U. Kose, G. Guraksin, & O. Deperlioglu (Eds.), *Nature-Inspired Intelligent Techniques for Solving Biomedical Engineering Problems* (pp. 1–26). Hershey, PA: IGI Global. doi:10.4018/978-1-5225-4769-3.ch001

Kostić, S. (2018). A Review on Enhanced Stability Analyses of Soil Slopes Using Statistical Design. In N. Ceryan (Ed.), *Handbook of Research on Trends and Digital Advances in Engineering Geology* (pp. 446–481). Hershey, PA: IGI Global. doi:10.4018/978-1-5225-2709-1.ch013

Kumar, A., Patil, P. P., & Prajapati, Y. K. (2018). *Advanced Numerical Simulations in Mechanical Engineering*. Hershey, PA: IGI Global. doi:10.4018/978-1-5225-3722-9

Kumar, G. R., Rajyalakshmi, G., & Manupati, V. K. (2017). Surface Micro Patterning of Aluminium Reinforced Composite through Laser Peening. *International Journal of Manufacturing, Materials, and Mechanical Engineering, 7*(4), 15–27. doi:10.4018/IJMMME.2017100102

Kumari, N., & Kumar, K. (2018). Fabrication of Orthotic Calipers With Epoxy-Based Green Composite. In K. Kumar & J. Davim (Eds.), *Composites and Advanced Materials for Industrial Applications* (pp. 157–176). Hershey, PA: IGI Global. doi:10.4018/978-1-5225-5216-1.ch008

Kuppusamy, R. R. (2018). Development of Aerospace Composite Structures Through Vacuum-Enhanced Resin Transfer Moulding Technology (VERTMTy): Vacuum-Enhanced Resin Transfer Moulding. In K. Kumar & J. Davim (Eds.), *Composites and Advanced Materials for Industrial Applications* (pp. 99–111). Hershey, PA: IGI Global. doi:10.4018/978-1-5225-5216-1.ch005

Lemos, J. V. (2016). The Basis for Masonry Analysis with UDEC and 3DEC. In V. Sarhosis, K. Bagi, J. Lemos, & G. Milani (Eds.), *Computational Modeling of Masonry Structures Using the Discrete Element Method* (pp. 61–89). Hershey, PA: IGI Global. doi:10.4018/978-1-5225-0231-9.ch003

Loy, J., Howell, S., & Cooper, R. (2017). Engineering Teams: Supporting Diversity in Engineering Education. In M. Gray & K. Thomas (Eds.), *Strategies for Increasing Diversity in Engineering Majors and Careers* (pp. 106–129). Hershey, PA: IGI Global. doi:10.4018/978-1-5225-2212-6.ch006

Macher, G., Armengaud, E., Kreiner, C., Brenner, E., Schmittner, C., Ma, Z., ... Krammer, M. (2018). Integration of Security in the Development Lifecycle of Dependable Automotive CPS. In N. Druml, A. Genser, A. Krieg, M. Menghin, & A. Hoeller (Eds.), *Solutions for Cyber-Physical Systems Ubiquity* (pp. 383–423). Hershey, PA: IGI Global. doi:10.4018/978-1-5225-2845-6.ch015

Maghsoodlou, S., & Poreskandar, S. (2016). Controlling Electrospinning Jet Using Microscopic Model for Ideal Tissue Engineering Scaffolds. *International Journal of Chemoinformatics and Chemical Engineering*, 5(2), 1–16. doi:10.4018/IJCCE.2016070101

Mahendramani, G., & Lakshmana Swamy, N. (2018). Effect of Weld Groove Area on Distortion of Butt Welded Joints in Submerged Arc Welding. *International Journal of Manufacturing, Materials, and Mechanical Engineering*, 8(2), 33–44. doi:10.4018/IJMMME.2018040103

Maiti, S. (2016). Engineered Gellan Polysaccharides in the Design of Controlled Drug Delivery Systems. In M. Bououdina (Ed.), *Emerging Research on Bioinspired Materials Engineering* (pp. 266–293). Hershey, PA: IGI Global. doi:10.4018/978-1-4666-9811-6.ch010

Majumdar, J. D., Weisheit, A., & Manna, I. (2016). Laser Surface Processing for Tailoring of Properties by Optimization of Microstructure. In E. Akinlabi, R. Mahamood, & S. Akinlabi (Eds.), *Advanced Manufacturing Techniques Using Laser Material Processing* (pp. 121–171). Hershey, PA: IGI Global. doi:10.4018/978-1-5225-0329-3.ch006

Maldonado-Macías, A. A., García-Alcaraz, J. L., Hernández-Arellano, J. L., & Cortes-Robles, G. (2016). An Ergonomic Compatibility Perspective on the Selection of Advanced Manufacturing Technology: A Case Study for CNC Vertical Machining Centers. In G. Alor-Hernández, C. Sánchez-Ramírez, & J. García-Alcaraz (Eds.), *Handbook of Research on Managerial Strategies for Achieving Optimal Performance in Industrial Processes* (pp. 137–165). Hershey, PA: IGI Global. doi:10.4018/978-1-5225-0130-5.ch008

Mamaghani, I. H. (2016). Application of Discrete Finite Element Method for Analysis of Unreinforced Masonry Structures. In V. Sarhosis, K. Bagi, J. Lemos, & G. Milani (Eds.), *Computational Modeling of Masonry Structures Using the Discrete Element Method* (pp. 440–458). Hershey, PA: IGI Global. doi:10.4018/978-1-5225-0231-9.ch017

Mansor, M. R., Sapuan, S. M., Salim, M. A., Akop, M. Z., Musthafah, M. T., & Shaharuzaman, M. A. (2016). Concurrent Design of Green Composites. In D. Verma, S. Jain, X. Zhang, & P. Gope (Eds.), *Green Approaches to Biocomposite Materials Science and Engineering* (pp. 48–75). Hershey, PA: IGI Global. doi:10.4018/978-1-5225-0424-5.ch003

Mansouri, I., & Esmaeili, E. (2016). Nanotechnology Applications in the Construction Industry. In A. Khitab & W. Anwar (Eds.), *Advanced Research on Nanotechnology for Civil Engineering Applications* (pp. 111–140). Hershey, PA: IGI Global. doi:10.4018/978-1-5225-0344-6.ch004

Manzoor, A. (2016). MOOCs for Enhancing Engineering Education. In D. Fonseca & E. Redondo (Eds.), *Handbook of Research on Applied E-Learning in Engineering and Architecture Education* (pp. 204–223). Hershey, PA: IGI Global. doi:10.4018/978-1-4666-8803-2.ch010

Martin, A., Kalevaru, V. N., & Radnik, J. (2016). Palladium in Heterogeneous Oxidation Catalysis. In H. Al-Megren & T. Xiao (Eds.), *Petrochemical Catalyst Materials, Processes, and Emerging Technologies* (pp. 53–81). Hershey, PA: IGI Global. doi:10.4018/978-1-4666-9975-5.ch003

Melnyczuk, J. M., & Palchoudhury, S. (2016). Introduction to Bio-Inspired Hydrogel and Their Application: Hydrogels. In M. Bououdina (Ed.), *Emerging Research on Bioinspired Materials Engineering* (pp. 133–159). Hershey, PA: IGI Global. doi:10.4018/978-1-4666-9811-6.ch005

Mitra-Kirtley, S., Mullins, O. C., & Pomerantz, A. E. (2016). Sulfur and Nitrogen Chemical Speciation in Crude Oils and Related Carbonaceous Materials. In T. Saleh (Ed.), *Applying Nanotechnology to the Desulfurization Process in Petroleum Engineering* (pp. 53–83). Hershey, PA: IGI Global. doi:10.4018/978-1-4666-9545-0.ch002

Moalosi, R., Uziak, J., & Oladiran, M. T. (2016). Using Blended Learning Approach to Deliver Courses in An Engineering Programme. *International Journal of Quality Assurance in Engineering and Technology Education*, 5(1), 23–39. doi:10.4018/IJQAETE.2016010103

Mohammadzadeh, S., & Kim, Y. (2017). Nonlinear System Identification of Smart Buildings. In P. Samui, S. Chakraborty, & D. Kim (Eds.), *Modeling and Simulation Techniques in Structural Engineering* (pp. 328–347). Hershey, PA: IGI Global. doi:10.4018/978-1-5225-0588-4.ch011

Mohanty, I., & Bhattacherjee, D. (2016). Artificial Neural Network and Its Application in Steel Industry. In S. Datta & J. Davim (Eds.), *Computational Approaches to Materials Design: Theoretical and Practical Aspects* (pp. 267–300). Hershey, PA: IGI Global. doi:10.4018/978-1-5225-0290-6.ch010

Mohebkhah, A., & Sarhosis, V. (2016). Discrete Element Modeling of Masonry-Infilled Frames. In V. Sarhosis, K. Bagi, J. Lemos, & G. Milani (Eds.), *Computational Modeling of Masonry Structures Using the Discrete Element Method* (pp. 200–234). Hershey, PA: IGI Global. doi:10.4018/978-1-5225-0231-9.ch009

Molina, G. J., Aktaruzzaman, F., Soloiu, V., & Rahman, M. (2017). Design and Testing of a Jet-Impingement Instrument to Study Surface-Modification Effects by Nanofluids. *International Journal of Surface Engineering and Interdisciplinary Materials Science*, 5(2), 43–61. doi:10.4018/IJSEIMS.2017070104

Montalvan-Sorrosa, D., de los Cobos-Vasconcelos, D., & Gonzalez-Sanchez, A. (2016). Nanotechnology Applied to the Biodesulfurization of Fossil Fuels and Spent Caustic Streams. In T. Saleh (Ed.), *Applying Nanotechnology to the Desulfurization Process in Petroleum Engineering* (pp. 378–389). Hershey, PA: IGI Global. doi:10.4018/978-1-4666-9545-0.ch012

Montillet, J., Yu, K., Bonenberg, L. K., & Roberts, G. W. (2016). Optimization Algorithms in Local and Global Positioning. In P. Vasant, G. Weber, & V. Dieu (Eds.), *Handbook of Research on Modern Optimization Algorithms and Applications in Engineering and Economics* (pp. 1–53). Hershey, PA: IGI Global. doi:10.4018/978-1-4666-9644-0.ch001

Moreira, F., & Ferreira, M. J. (2016). Teaching and Learning Requirements Engineering Based on Mobile Devices and Cloud: A Case Study. In D. Fonseca & E. Redondo (Eds.), *Handbook of Research on Applied E-Learning in Engineering and Architecture Education* (pp. 237–262). Hershey, PA: IGI Global. doi:10.4018/978-1-4666-8803-2.ch012

Mukherjee, A., Saeed, R. A., Dutta, S., & Naskar, M. K. (2017). Fault Tracking Framework for Software-Defined Networking (SDN). In C. Singhal & S. De (Eds.), *Resource Allocation in Next-Generation Broadband Wireless Access Networks* (pp. 247–272). Hershey, PA: IGI Global. doi:10.4018/978-1-5225-2023-8.ch011

Mukhopadhyay, A., Barman, T. K., & Sahoo, P. (2018). Electroless Nickel Coatings for High Temperature Applications. In K. Kumar & J. Davim (Eds.), *Composites and Advanced Materials for Industrial Applications* (pp. 297–331). Hershey, PA: IGI Global. doi:10.4018/978-1-5225-5216-1.ch013

Náprstek, J., & Fischer, C. (2017). Dynamic Stability and Post-Critical Processes of Slender Auto-Parametric Systems. In V. Plevris, G. Kremmyda, & Y. Fahjan (Eds.), *Performance-Based Seismic Design of Concrete Structures and Infrastructures* (pp. 128–171). Hershey, PA: IGI Global. doi:10.4018/978-1-5225-2089-4.ch006

Nautiyal, L., Shivach, P., & Ram, M. (2018). Optimal Designs by Means of Genetic Algorithms. In M. Ram & J. Davim (Eds.), *Soft Computing Techniques and Applications in Mechanical Engineering* (pp. 151–161). Hershey, PA: IGI Global. doi:10.4018/978-1-5225-3035-0.ch007

Nazir, R. (2017). Advanced Nanomaterials for Water Engineering and Treatment: Nano-Metal Oxides and Their Nanocomposites. In T. Saleh (Ed.), *Advanced Nanomaterials for Water Engineering, Treatment, and Hydraulics* (pp. 84–126). Hershey, PA: IGI Global. doi:10.4018/978-1-5225-2136-5.ch005

Nogueira, A. F., Ribeiro, J. C., Fernández de Vega, F., & Zenha-Rela, M. A. (2018). Evolutionary Approaches to Test Data Generation for Object-Oriented Software: Overview of Techniques and Tools. In M. Khosrow-Pour, D.B.A. (Ed.), Incorporating Nature-Inspired Paradigms in Computational Applications (pp. 162-194). Hershey, PA: IGI Global. doi:10.4018/978-1-5225-5020-4.ch006

Nunes, J. F., Moreira, P. M., & Tavares, J. M. (2016). Human Motion Analysis and Simulation Tools: A Survey. In F. Miranda & C. Abreu (Eds.), *Handbook of Research on Computational Simulation and Modeling in Engineering* (pp. 359–388). Hershey, PA: IGI Global. doi:10.4018/978-1-4666-8823-0.ch012

Ogunlaja, A. S., & Tshentu, Z. R. (2016). Molecularly Imprinted Polymer Nanofibers for Adsorptive Desulfurization. In T. Saleh (Ed.), *Applying Nanotechnology to the Desulfurization Process in Petroleum Engineering* (pp. 281–336). Hershey, PA: IGI Global. doi:10.4018/978-1-4666-9545-0.ch010

Ong, P., & Kohshelan, S. (2016). Performances of Adaptive Cuckoo Search Algorithm in Engineering Optimization. In P. Vasant, G. Weber, & V. Dieu (Eds.), *Handbook of Research on Modern Optimization Algorithms and Applications in Engineering and Economics* (pp. 676–699). Hershey, PA: IGI Global. doi:10.4018/978-1-4666-9644-0.ch026

Osho, M. B. (2018). Industrial Enzyme Technology: Potential Applications. In S. Bharati & P. Chaurasia (Eds.), *Research Advancements in Pharmaceutical, Nutritional, and Industrial Enzymology* (pp. 375–394). Hershey, PA: IGI Global. doi:10.4018/978-1-5225-5237-6.ch017

Padmaja, P., & Marutheswar, G. (2017). Certain Investigation on Secured Data Transmission in Wireless Sensor Networks. *International Journal of Mobile Computing and Multimedia Communications*, 8(1), 48–61. doi:10.4018/IJMCMC.2017010104

Paixão, S. M., Silva, T. P., Arez, B. F., & Alves, L. (2016). Advances in the Reduction of the Costs Inherent to Fossil Fuels' Biodesulfurization towards Its Potential Industrial Application. In T. Saleh (Ed.), *Applying Nanotechnology to the Desulfurization Process in Petroleum Engineering* (pp. 390–425). Hershey, PA: IGI Global. doi:10.4018/978-1-4666-9545-0.ch013

Palmer, S., & Hall, W. (2017). An Evaluation of Group Work in First-Year Engineering Design Education. In R. Tucker (Ed.), *Collaboration and Student Engagement in Design Education* (pp. 145–168). Hershey, PA: IGI Global. doi:10.4018/978-1-5225-0726-0.ch007

Panneer, R. (2017). Effect of Composition of Fibers on Properties of Hybrid Composites. *International Journal of Manufacturing, Materials, and Mechanical Engineering*, 7(4), 28–43. doi:10.4018/IJMMME.2017100103

Parker, J. (2016). Hubble's Expanding Universe: A Model for Quality in Technology Infused engineering and Technology Education. *International Journal of Quality Assurance in Engineering and Technology Education*, 5(2), 16–29. doi:10.4018/IJQAETE.2016040102

Paul, S., & Roy, P. (2018). Optimal Design of Power System Stabilizer Using a Novel Evolutionary Algorithm. *International Journal of Energy Optimization and Engineering*, 7(3), 24–46. doi:10.4018/IJEOE.2018070102

Pavaloiu, A. (2018). Artificial Intelligence Ethics in Biomedical-Engineering-Oriented Problems. In U. Kose, G. Guraksin, & O. Deperlioglu (Eds.), *Nature-Inspired Intelligent Techniques for Solving Biomedical Engineering Problems* (pp. 219–231). Hershey, PA: IGI Global. doi:10.4018/978-1-5225-4769-3.ch010

Peña, F. (2016). A Semi-Discrete Approach for the Numerical Simulation of Freestanding Blocks. In V. Sarhosis, K. Bagi, J. Lemos, & G. Milani (Eds.), *Computational Modeling of Masonry Structures Using the Discrete Element Method* (pp. 416–439). Hershey, PA: IGI Global. doi:10.4018/978-1-5225-0231-9.ch016

Penchovsky, R., & Traykovska, M. (2016). Synthetic Approaches to Biology: Engineering Gene Control Circuits, Synthesizing, and Editing Genomes. In M. Bououdina (Ed.), *Emerging Research on Bioinspired Materials Engineering* (pp. 323–351). Hershey, PA: IGI Global. doi:10.4018/978-1-4666-9811-6.ch012

Pieroni, A., & Iazeolla, G. (2016). Engineering QoS and Energy Saving in the Delivery of ICT Services. In P. Vasant & N. Voropai (Eds.), *Sustaining Power Resources through Energy Optimization and Engineering* (pp. 208–226). Hershey, PA: IGI Global. doi:10.4018/978-1-4666-9755-3.ch009

Pioro, I., Mahdi, M., & Popov, R. (2017). Application of Supercritical Pressures in Power Engineering. In L. Chen & Y. Iwamoto (Eds.), *Advanced Applications of Supercritical Fluids in Energy Systems* (pp. 404–457). Hershey, PA: IGI Global. doi:10.4018/978-1-5225-2047-4.ch013

Plaksina, T., & Gildin, E. (2017). Rigorous Integrated Evolutionary Workflow for Optimal Exploitation of Unconventional Gas Assets. *International Journal of Energy Optimization and Engineering*, 6(1), 101–122. doi:10.4018/IJEOE.2017010106

Puppala, A. J., Bheemasetti, T. V., Zou, H., Yu, X., Pedarla, A., & Cai, G. (2016). Spatial Variability Analysis of Soil Properties using Geostatistics. In P. Samui (Ed.), *Handbook of Research on Advanced Computational Techniques for Simulation-Based Engineering* (pp. 195–226). Hershey, PA: IGI Global. doi:10.4018/978-1-4666-9479-8.ch008

Ramdani, N., & Azibi, M. (2018). Polymer Composite Materials for Microelectronics Packaging Applications: Composites for Microelectronics Packaging. In K. Kumar & J. Davim (Eds.), *Composites and Advanced Materials for Industrial Applications* (pp. 177–211). Hershey, PA: IGI Global. doi:10.4018/978-1-5225-5216-1.ch009

Ramesh, M., Garg, R., & Subrahmanyam, G. V. (2017). Investigation of Influence of Quenching and Annealing on the Plane Fracture Toughness and Brittle to Ductile Transition Temperature of the Zinc Coated Structural Steel Materials. *International Journal of Surface Engineering and Interdisciplinary Materials Science*, 5(2), 33–42. doi:10.4018/IJSEIMS.2017070103

Razavi, A. M., & Ahmad, R. (2016). Agile Software Development Challenges in Implementation and Adoption: Focusing on Large and Distributed Settings – Past Experiences, Emergent Topics. In I. Ghani, D. Jawawi, S. Dorairaj, & A. Sidky (Eds.), *Emerging Innovations in Agile Software Development* (pp. 175–207). Hershey, PA: IGI Global. doi:10.4018/978-1-4666-9858-1.ch010

Reccia, E., Cecchi, A., & Milani, G. (2016). FEM/DEM Approach for the Analysis of Masonry Arch Bridges. In V. Sarhosis, K. Bagi, J. Lemos, & G. Milani (Eds.), *Computational Modeling of Masonry Structures Using the Discrete Element Method* (pp. 367–392). Hershey, PA: IGI Global. doi:10.4018/978-1-5225-0231-9.ch014

Ro, H. K., & McIntosh, K. (2016). Constructing Conducive Environment for Women of Color in Engineering Undergraduate Education. In U. Thomas & J. Drake (Eds.), *Critical Research on Sexism and Racism in STEM Fields* (pp. 23–48). Hershey, PA: IGI Global. doi:10.4018/978-1-5225-0174-9.ch002

Rodulfo-Baechler, S. M. (2016). Dual Role of Perovskite Hollow Fiber Membrane in the Methane Oxidation Reactions. In H. Al-Megren & T. Xiao (Eds.), *Petrochemical Catalyst Materials, Processes, and Emerging Technologies* (pp. 385–430). Hershey, PA: IGI Global. doi:10.4018/978-1-4666-9975-5.ch014

Rudolf, S., Biryuk, V. V., & Volov, V. (2018). Vortex Effect, Vortex Power: Technology of Vortex Power Engineering. In V. Kharchenko & P. Vasant (Eds.), *Handbook of Research on Renewable Energy and Electric Resources for Sustainable Rural Development* (pp. 500–533). Hershey, PA: IGI Global. doi:10.4018/978-1-5225-3867-7.ch021

Sah, A., Bhadula, S. J., Dumka, A., & Rawat, S. (2018). A Software Engineering Perspective for Development of Enterprise Applications. In A. Elçi (Ed.), *Handbook of Research on Contemporary Perspectives on Web-Based Systems* (pp. 1–23). Hershey, PA: IGI Global. doi:10.4018/978-1-5225-5384-7.ch001

Sahoo, P., & Roy, S. (2017). Tribological Behavior of Electroless Ni-P, Ni-P-W and Ni-P-Cu Coatings: A Comparison. *International Journal of Surface Engineering and Interdisciplinary Materials Science*, 5(1), 1–15. doi:10.4018/IJSEIMS.2017010101

Sahoo, S. (2018). Laminated Composite Hypar Shells as Roofing Units: Static and Dynamic Behavior. In K. Kumar & J. Davim (Eds.), *Composites and Advanced Materials for Industrial Applications* (pp. 249–269). Hershey, PA: IGI Global. doi:10.4018/978-1-5225-5216-1.ch011

Sahu, H., & Hungyo, M. (2018). Introduction to SDN and NFV. In A. Dumka (Ed.), *Innovations in Software-Defined Networking and Network Functions Virtualization* (pp. 1–25). Hershey, PA: IGI Global. doi:10.4018/978-1-5225-3640-6.ch001

Saikia, P., Bharadwaj, S. K., & Miah, A. T. (2016). Peroxovanadates and Its Bio-Mimicking Relation with Vanadium Haloperoxidases. In M. Bououdina (Ed.), *Emerging Research on Bioinspired Materials Engineering* (pp. 197–219). Hershey, PA: IGI Global. doi:10.4018/978-1-4666-9811-6.ch007

Saladino, R., Botta, G., & Crucianelli, M. (2016). Advances in Nanotechnology Transition Metal Catalysts in Oxidative Desulfurization (ODS) Processes: Nanotechnology Applied to ODS Processing. In T. Saleh (Ed.), *Applying Nanotechnology to the Desulfurization Process in Petroleum Engineering* (pp. 180–215). Hershey, PA: IGI Global. doi:10.4018/978-1-4666-9545-0.ch006

Saleh, T. A., Danmaliki, G. I., & Shuaib, T. D. (2016). Nanocomposites and Hybrid Materials for Adsorptive Desulfurization. In T. Saleh (Ed.), *Applying Nanotechnology to the Desulfurization Process in Petroleum Engineering* (pp. 129–153). Hershey, PA: IGI Global. doi:10.4018/978-1-4666-9545-0.ch004

Saleh, T. A., Shuaib, T. D., Danmaliki, G. I., & Al-Daous, M. A. (2016). Carbon-Based Nanomaterials for Desulfurization: Classification, Preparation, and Evaluation. In T. Saleh (Ed.), *Applying Nanotechnology to the Desulfurization Process in Petroleum Engineering* (pp. 154–179). Hershey, PA: IGI Global. doi:10.4018/978-1-4666-9545-0.ch005

Salem, A. M., & Shmelova, T. (2018). Intelligent Expert Decision Support Systems: Methodologies, Applications, and Challenges. In T. Shmelova, Y. Sikirda, N. Rizun, A. Salem, & Y. Kovalyov (Eds.), *Socio-Technical Decision Support in Air Navigation Systems: Emerging Research and Opportunities* (pp. 215–242). Hershey, PA: IGI Global. doi:10.4018/978-1-5225-3108-1.ch007

Samal, M. (2017). FE Analysis and Experimental Investigation of Cracked and Un-Cracked Thin-Walled Tubular Components to Evaluate Mechanical and Fracture Properties. In P. Samui, S. Chakraborty, & D. Kim (Eds.), *Modeling and Simulation Techniques in Structural Engineering* (pp. 266–293). Hershey, PA: IGI Global. doi:10.4018/978-1-5225-0588-4.ch009

Samal, M., & Balakrishnan, K. (2017). Experiments on a Ring Tension Setup and FE Analysis to Evaluate Transverse Mechanical Properties of Tubular Components. In P. Samui, S. Chakraborty, & D. Kim (Eds.), *Modeling and Simulation Techniques in Structural Engineering* (pp. 91–115). Hershey, PA: IGI Global. doi:10.4018/978-1-5225-0588-4.ch004

Santhanakumar, M., Adalarasan, R., & Rajmohan, M. (2016). An Investigation in Abrasive Waterjet Cutting of Al6061/SiC/Al2O3 Composite Using Principal Component Based Response Surface Methodology. *International Journal of Manufacturing, Materials, and Mechanical Engineering*, 6(4), 30–47. doi:10.4018/IJMMME.2016100103

Sareen, N., & Bhattacharya, S. (2016). Cleaner Energy Fuels: Hydrodesulfurization and Beyond. In T. Saleh (Ed.), *Applying Nanotechnology to the Desulfurization Process in Petroleum Engineering* (pp. 84–128). Hershey, PA: IGI Global. doi:10.4018/978-1-4666-9545-0.ch003

Sarhosis, V. (2016). Micro-Modeling Options for Masonry. In V. Sarhosis, K. Bagi, J. Lemos, & G. Milani (Eds.), *Computational Modeling of Masonry Structures Using the Discrete Element Method* (pp. 28–60). Hershey, PA: IGI Global. doi:10.4018/978-1-5225-0231-9.ch002

Sarhosis, V., Oliveira, D. V., & Lourenco, P. B. (2016). On the Mechanical Behavior of Masonry. In V. Sarhosis, K. Bagi, J. Lemos, & G. Milani (Eds.), *Computational Modeling of Masonry Structures Using the Discrete Element Method* (pp. 1–27). Hershey, PA: IGI Global. doi:10.4018/978-1-5225-0231-9.ch001

Satyam, N. (2016). Liquefaction Modelling of Granular Soils using Discrete Element Method. In P. Samui (Ed.), *Handbook of Research on Advanced Computational Techniques for Simulation-Based Engineering* (pp. 381–441). Hershey, PA: IGI Global. doi:10.4018/978-1-4666-9479-8.ch015

Sawant, S. (2018). Deep Learning and Biomedical Engineering. In U. Kose, G. Guraksin, & O. Deperlioglu (Eds.), *Nature-Inspired Intelligent Techniques for Solving Biomedical Engineering Problems* (pp. 283–296). Hershey, PA: IGI Global. doi:10.4018/978-1-5225-4769-3.ch014

Sezgin, H., & Berkalp, O. B. (2018). Textile-Reinforced Composites for the Automotive Industry. In K. Kumar & J. Davim (Eds.), *Composites and Advanced Materials for Industrial Applications* (pp. 129–156). Hershey, PA: IGI Global. doi:10.4018/978-1-5225-5216-1.ch007

Shah, M. Z., Gazder, U., Bhatti, M. S., & Hussain, M. (2018). Comparative Performance Evaluation of Effects of Modifier in Asphaltic Concrete Mix. *International Journal of Strategic Engineering*, 1(2), 13–25. doi:10.4018/IJoSE.2018070102

Shah, V. S., Shah, H. R., & Samui, P. (2016). Application of Meta-Models (MPMR and ELM) for Determining OMC, MDD and Soaked CBR Value of Soil. In S. Bhattacharyya, P. Banerjee, D. Majumdar, & P. Dutta (Eds.), *Handbook of Research on Advanced Hybrid Intelligent Techniques and Applications* (pp. 454–482). Hershey, PA: IGI Global. doi:10.4018/978-1-4666-9474-3.ch015

Sharma, N., & Kumar, K. (2018). Fabrication of Porous NiTi Alloy Using Organic Binders. In K. Kumar & J. Davim (Eds.), *Composites and Advanced Materials for Industrial Applications* (pp. 38–62). Hershey, PA: IGI Global. doi:10.4018/978-1-5225-5216-1.ch003

Sharma, T. K. (2016). Application of Shuffled Frog Leaping Algorithm in Software Project Scheduling. In P. Saxena, D. Singh, & M. Pant (Eds.), *Problem Solving and Uncertainty Modeling through Optimization and Soft Computing Applications* (pp. 225–238). Hershey, PA: IGI Global. doi:10.4018/978-1-4666-9885-7.ch011

Shivach, P., Nautiyal, L., & Ram, M. (2018). Applying Multi-Objective Optimization Algorithms to Mechanical Engineering. In M. Ram & J. Davim (Eds.), *Soft Computing Techniques and Applications in Mechanical Engineering* (pp. 287–301). Hershey, PA: IGI Global. doi:10.4018/978-1-5225-3035-0.ch014

Shmelova, T. (2018). Stochastic Methods for Estimation and Problem Solving in Engineering: Stochastic Methods of Decision Making in Aviation. In S. Kadry (Ed.), *Stochastic Methods for Estimation and Problem Solving in Engineering* (pp. 139–160). Hershey, PA: IGI Global. doi:10.4018/978-1-5225-5045-7.ch006

Shukla, R., Anapagaddi, R., Singh, A. K., Allen, J. K., Panchal, J. H., & Mistree, F. (2016). Integrated Computational Materials Engineering for Determining the Set Points of Unit Operations for Production of a Steel Product Mix. In S. Datta & J. Davim (Eds.), *Computational Approaches to Materials Design: Theoretical and Practical Aspects* (pp. 163–191). Hershey, PA: IGI Global. doi:10.4018/978-1-5225-0290-6.ch006

Siero González, L. R., & Romo Vázquez, A. (2017). Didactic Sequences Teaching Mathematics for Engineers With Focus on Differential Equations. In M. Ramírez-Montoya (Ed.), *Handbook of Research on Driving STEM Learning With Educational Technologies* (pp. 129–151). Hershey, PA: IGI Global. doi:10.4018/978-1-5225-2026-9.ch007

Singh, R., & Dutta, S. (2018). Visible Light Active Nanocomposites for Photocatalytic Applications. In K. Kumar & J. Davim (Eds.), *Composites and Advanced Materials for Industrial Applications* (pp. 270–296). Hershey, PA: IGI Global. doi:10.4018/978-1-5225-5216-1.ch012

Singh, R., & Lou, H. H. (2016). Safety and Efficiency Enhancement in LNG Terminals. In H. Al-Megren & T. Xiao (Eds.), *Petrochemical Catalyst Materials, Processes, and Emerging Technologies* (pp. 164–176). Hershey, PA: IGI Global. doi:10.4018/978-1-4666-9975-5.ch007

Sözbilir, H., Özkaymak, Ç., Uzel, B., & Sümer, Ö. (2018). Criteria for Surface Rupture Microzonation of Active Faults for Earthquake Hazards in Urban Areas. In N. Ceryan (Ed.), *Handbook of Research on Trends and Digital Advances in Engineering Geology* (pp. 187–230). Hershey, PA: IGI Global. doi:10.4018/978-1-5225-2709-1.ch005

Stanciu, I. (2018). Stochastic Methods in Microsystems Engineering. In S. Kadry (Ed.), *Stochastic Methods for Estimation and Problem Solving in Engineering* (pp. 161–176). Hershey, PA: IGI Global. doi:10.4018/978-1-5225-5045-7.ch007

Strebkov, D., Nekrasov, A., Trubnikov, V., & Nekrasov, A. (2018). Single-Wire Resonant Electric Power Systems for Renewable-Based Electric Grid. In V. Kharchenko & P. Vasant (Eds.), *Handbook of Research on Renewable Energy and Electric Resources for Sustainable Rural Development* (pp. 449–474). Hershey, PA: IGI Global. doi:10.4018/978-1-5225-3867-7.ch019

Subburaman, D., Jagan, J., Dalkiliç, Y., & Samui, P. (2016). Reliability Analysis of Slope Using MPMR, GRNN and GPR. In F. Miranda & C. Abreu (Eds.), *Handbook of Research on Computational Simulation and Modeling in Engineering* (pp. 208–224). Hershey, PA: IGI Global. doi:10.4018/978-1-4666-8823-0.ch007

Sun, J., Wan, S., Lin, J., & Wang, Y. (2016). Advances in Catalytic Conversion of Syngas to Ethanol and Higher Alcohols. In H. Al-Megren & T. Xiao (Eds.), *Petrochemical Catalyst Materials, Processes, and Emerging Technologies* (pp. 177–215). Hershey, PA: IGI Global. doi:10.4018/978-1-4666-9975-5.ch008

Tüdeş, Ş., Kumlu, K. B., & Ceryan, S. (2018). Integration Between Urban Planning and Natural Hazards For Resilient City. In N. Ceryan (Ed.), *Handbook of Research on Trends and Digital Advances in Engineering Geology* (pp. 591–630). Hershey, PA: IGI Global. doi:10.4018/978-1-5225-2709-1.ch017

Tyukhov, I., Rezk, H., & Vasant, P. (2016). Modern Optimization Algorithms and Applications in Solar Photovoltaic Engineering. In P. Vasant & N. Voropai (Eds.), *Sustaining Power Resources through Energy Optimization and Engineering* (pp. 390–445). Hershey, PA: IGI Global. doi:10.4018/978-1-4666-9755-3.ch016

Ulamis, K. (2018). Soil Liquefaction Assessment by Anisotropic Cyclic Triaxial Test. In N. Ceryan (Ed.), *Handbook of Research on Trends and Digital Advances in Engineering Geology* (pp. 631–664). Hershey, PA: IGI Global. doi:10.4018/978-1-5225-2709-1.ch018

Umar, M. A., Tenuche, S. S., Yusuf, S. A., Abdulsalami, A. O., & Kufena, A. M. (2016). Usability Engineering in Agile Software Development Processes. In I. Ghani, D. Jawawi, S. Dorairaj, & A. Sidky (Eds.), *Emerging Innovations in Agile Software Development* (pp. 208–221). Hershey, PA: IGI Global. doi:10.4018/978-1-4666-9858-1.ch011

Üzüm, O., & Çakır, Ö. A. (2016). A Bio-Inspired Phenomena in Cementitious Materials: Self-Healing. In M. Bououdina (Ed.), *Emerging Research on Bioinspired Materials Engineering* (pp. 220–246). Hershey, PA: IGI Global. doi:10.4018/978-1-4666-9811-6.ch008

Valente, M., & Milani, G. (2017). Seismic Assessment and Retrofitting of an Under-Designed RC Frame Through a Displacement-Based Approach. In V. Plevris, G. Kremmyda, & Y. Fahjan (Eds.), *Performance-Based Seismic Design of Concrete Structures and Infrastructures* (pp. 36–58). Hershey, PA: IGI Global. doi:10.4018/978-1-5225-2089-4.ch002

Vasant, P. (2018). A General Medical Diagnosis System Formed by Artificial Neural Networks and Swarm Intelligence Techniques. In U. Kose, G. Guraksin, & O. Deperlioglu (Eds.), *Nature-Inspired Intelligent Techniques for Solving Biomedical Engineering Problems* (pp. 130–145). Hershey, PA: IGI Global. doi:10.4018/978-1-5225-4769-3.ch006

Vergara, D., Lorenzo, M., & Rubio, M. (2016). On the Use of Virtual Environments in Engineering Education. *International Journal of Quality Assurance in Engineering and Technology Education*, 5(2), 30–41. doi:10.4018/IJQAETE.2016040103

Verrollot, J., Tolonen, A., Harkonen, J., & Haapasalo, H. J. (2018). Challenges and Enablers for Rapid Product Development. *International Journal of Applied Industrial Engineering*, 5(1), 25–49. doi:10.4018/IJAIE.2018010102

Wagner, C., & Ryan, C. (2016). Physical and Digital Integration Strategies of Electronic Device Supply Chains and Their Applicability to ETO Supply Chains. In R. Addo-Tenkorang, J. Kantola, P. Helo, & A. Shamsuzzoha (Eds.), *Supply Chain Strategies and the Engineer-to-Order Approach* (pp. 224–245). Hershey, PA: IGI Global. doi:10.4018/978-1-5225-0021-6.ch011

Wang, Z., Wu, P., Lan, L., & Ji, S. (2016). Preparation, Characterization and Desulfurization of the Supported Nickel Phosphide Catalysts. In H. Al-Megren & T. Xiao (Eds.), *Petrochemical Catalyst Materials, Processes, and Emerging Technologies* (pp. 431–458). Hershey, PA: IGI Global. doi:10.4018/978-1-4666-9975-5.ch015

Yardimci, A. G., & Karpuz, C. (2018). Fuzzy Rock Mass Rating: Soft-Computing-Aided Preliminary Stability Analysis of Weak Rock Slopes. In N. Ceryan (Ed.), *Handbook of Research on Trends and Digital Advances in Engineering Geology* (pp. 97–131). Hershey, PA: IGI Global. doi:10.4018/978-1-5225-2709-1.ch003

Zhang, L., Ding, S., Sun, S., Han, B., Yu, X., & Ou, J. (2016). Nano-Scale Behavior and Nano-Modification of Cement and Concrete Materials. In A. Khitab & W. Anwar (Eds.), *Advanced Research on Nanotechnology for Civil Engineering Applications* (pp. 28–79). Hershey, PA: IGI Global. doi:10.4018/978-1-5225-0344-6.ch002

Zindani, D., & Kumar, K. (2018). Industrial Applications of Polymer Composite Materials. In K. Kumar & J. Davim (Eds.), *Composites and Advanced Materials for Industrial Applications* (pp. 1–15). Hershey, PA: IGI Global. doi:10.4018/978-1-5225-5216-1.ch001

Zindani, D., Maity, S. R., & Bhowmik, S. (2018). A Decision-Making Approach for Material Selection of Polymeric Composite Bumper Beam. In K. Kumar & J. Davim (Eds.), *Composites and Advanced Materials for Industrial Applications* (pp. 112–128). Hershey, PA: IGI Global. doi:10.4018/978-1-5225-5216-1.ch006

About the Contributors

Ram Shringar Rao received his Ph.D. (Computer Science and Technology) from School of Computer and Systems Sciences, Jawaharlal Nehru University, New Delhi, India in 2011. He did M. Tech (Information Technology) and B. Tech (Computer Science Engineering) in 2005 and in 2000 respectively. He has worked as an Associate Professor in the Department of Computer Science of Indira Gandhi National Tribal University (A Central University), Amarkantak, MP, India. He is currently working as an Assistant Professor in the Department of Computer Science and Engineering of Ambedkar Institute of Advanced Communication Technologies and Research, GGSIP University, Delhi, India. He has more than 18 years of teaching, administrative and research experience. Dr. Rao has worked administrative works in the capacities of Member of Academic Council (IGNTU,India), Chief Warden, Head of Office, Students Welfare Officer (DSW), Coordinator University Cultural Cell, Coordinator University Computer Center, HoD of Computer Sc. and Engg., Proctor, Warden, etc. He has organized many Conferences, Faculty Development Programmes, Seminars and Workshops at National and International levels. He has delivered many Expert and Invited Lectures at National and International levels. Dr. Rao has published around 100 research papers with good impact factors in reputed International Journals and Conferences including IEEE, Springer, Wiley & Sons, Taylor & Fransise, Inderscience, Hindawi, IERI Letters, etc. His current research interest includes Mobile Ad-hoc Networks, Vehicular Ad-hoc Networks and Cloud Computing.

Omprakash Kaiwartya (M'14) is currently working as a Lecturer at the Nottingham Trent University (NTU), UK. Previously, He was a Research Associate at the Northumbria University, Newcastle, UK, in 2017 and a Postdoctoral Research Fellow at the Universiti Teknologi Malaysia (UTM) in 2016. He received his Ph.D. degree in Computer Science from Jawaharlal Nehru University, New Delhi, India, in 2015. His research interest focuses on IoT centric future technologies for diverse domain areas focusing on Transport, Healthcare, and Industrial Production. His recent scientific contributions are in Internet of connected Vehicles (IoV), Electronic Vehicles Charging Management (EV), Internet of Healthcare Things (IoHT), and Smart use case implementations of Sensor Networks. He is Associate Editor of reputed SCI Journals including IET Intelligent Transport Systems, EURASIP Journal on Wireless Communication and Networking, Ad-Hoc & Sensor Wireless Networks, IEEE Access, and Transactions on Internet and Information Systems. He is also Guest Editor of many recent special issues in reputed journals including IEEE Internet of Things Journal, IEEE Access, MDPI Sensors, and MDPI Electronics.

Sanjoy Das did his B. E. and M.Tech, PhD in Computer Science. Presently, he is working as Associate Professor, Department of Computer Science, Indira Gandhi National Tribal University (A Central Government University), Amarkantak, M.P. (Manipur Campus)- India. Before joining IGNTU he has worked as Associate Professor, School of Computing Science and Engineering, Galgotias University, India July 2016 to Sept 2017. He has worked as Assistant Prof. at Galgotias University from Sept 2012 to June 2016. Also, as Assistant Professor G. B. Pant Engineering College, Uttarakhand, and Assam University, Silchar, from 2001-2008. His current research interest includes Mobile Ad hoc Networks and Vehicular Ad hoc Networks, Distributed Systems, Data Mining. He has published numerous papers in international journals and conferences including IEEE and Springer.

* * *

Indrani Das did her B.E. and M.Tech. and Ph.D in Computer Science and Engineering. She is working as Assistant Professor in Computer Science department in Assam University (A Central University), Assam, India. She received her Ph.D. from School of Computer and Systems Sciences, Jawaharlal Nehru University, New Delhi, India in 2015. Her current research interest includes Mobile Ad hoc Networks and Vehicular Ad hoc Networks, IoT.

Udayakumar Easwaran is working as Assistant Professor in Department of Electronics and Communication Engineering at KIT-Kalaignarkarunanidhi Institute of Technology, Coimbatore, Tamilnadu India. He is an accommodating and versatile individual with 3 Years of teaching in both UG and PG courses with a solid commitment to the social, academic growth and development. He Pursuing his PhD at Anna University, Chennai. He completed his Master degree (Communication Systems) from Sri Ramakrishna Institute of Technology, Coimbatore in the year 2015. He had published 20 Papers in International Journals, 20 papers in National & International Conferences and 8 book chapters, 2 Springer Lecture notes. He had authored three books on Image processing and VLSI. He is a Life Member in various Professional Societies like IETE, ISTE, IEI, SSI, BMESI, IAENG. He is an Editor and Reviewer for many Peer-Reviewed Journals. Also received Young Scientist award 2019, Bright Researcher Award 2018, Young Researcher in Electronics & Communications Engineering Award 2019 from many societies. He had received funds from ISRO, ICMR, BMESI, IE(I), Anna university for conducting various National Seminar, Workshop and FDTP. He is also acting as Organizing Committee Member, Outreach Committee Member and Advisory Committee Member for many International Conferences. He had participated in many Workshops, Seminars and FDPs. His Research Interests includes Medical Image Processing, Wireless Communication and Antennas.

Charu Gandhi is a PhD in Computer Science from Kurukshetra University, Haryana, India. She has more than ten years of teaching experience. She is currently an Associate Professor at Jaypee Institute of Information Technology, Noida, India. She has published several papers in national and international conferences and journals. Her areas of interest include wireless networks, mobile ad hoc networks, QoS routing in MANETs, clustering techniques, energy efficiency and secure routing for MANETs, distributed and parallel computing.

Pramod Kumar Goyal received his B.E. in computer Engineering from University of Rajasthan in 1995, M.E. in Computer Technology & Applications from Delhi College of Engineering, University of Delhi, India in 2008 and Ph.D. from School of Computer and Systems Sciences, Jawaharlal Nehru University, New Delhi, India in 2018. He is working as Lecturer (Selection Grade) of Computer Engineering at Aryabhatt Institute of Technology under the Department of Training & Technical Education, Govt. of Delhi, India. He has more than 20 years of teaching experience. He has published several research papers in international journals and conferences. His current research interest includes Heterogeneous Wireless Networks, Mobile Communications, and Game Theory applications for solving problems related to these areas.

Srihari K. received the M.E. and Ph.D. degree from Anna University, Chennai. He is currently working as an Associate Professor in the Department of Computer Science and Engineering, SNS College of engineering, affiliated to Anna University- Chennai, Tamilnadu, India. Dr.K.Srihari published over 40 papers in international journals and his research area includes semantic search engines, big data and cloud computing.

Shweta Kaushik received her BE degree in Computer Science and Engineering from Uttar Pradesh Technical University, Lucknow, India in 2010 and MTech degree in Computer Science and Engineering from Jaypee Institute of Information Technology (JIIT) Noida, India in 2012. She is pursuing her PhD degree in Cloud Computing from Jaypee Institute of Information Technology (JIIT), Noida, India. In 2012, she joined the Department of Computer Science and Information Technology, UPTU as an Assistant Professor. Since August 2015, she has been with the Department of Master of Computer Application, Indraprastha University (IP) Delhi, where she was an Assistant Professor. Her current research interests include cloud computing, network security, distributed system, algorithms and big data. She is a member of ACM.

Mohd Waris Khan is currently working as a Guest Faculty in the Department of IT, in Babasaheb Bhimrao Ambedkar University (A Central University), Lucknow, U.P., India. Dr. Khan has completed his Ph.D. (Information Technology) in 2019 from the same University and M.Phil. (Computer Science) in 2013 from Dr. C.V. Raman University, Chhattisgarh. During Ph.D. work, he has worked on a Major Research Project entitled "Analysis of the impact of Ergonomic Deficiencies in Computer Workstations at Government Offices of Uttar Pradesh State". The project was sponsored by UPCST, under Young Scientist Scheme, Lucknow, India. His research interest is in the areas of Req. Engineering, Security Engineering.

Suhel Ahmad Khan has earned his Doctoral Degrees from Babasaheb Bhimrao Ambedkar University, (A Central University), Vidya Vihar, Raibareli Road, Lucknow. Dr. S. A. Khan is a young, energetic researcher and has completed a Full-Time Major Project funded by University Grants Commission, New Delhi, India. He has more than 8 years of teaching & research experience. He is currently working in the area of Software Security and Security Testing. He has also published & presented papers in refereed journals and conferences. He is a member of IACIT, UACEE, and Internet Society. Currently, he is working as an Assistant Professor in the department of computer science, Indira Gandhi National Tribal University, Amarkantak, M.P.

Arvind Kumar is B. Tech., M. Tech. and Ph. D. in Computer Science & Engineering. Presently he is Assistant Professor in Computer Science & Engineering Department at Ambedkar Institute of Advanced Communication Technologies & Research, Delhi, India. His research interest include Data Mining, Machine Learning, Computer architecture, Communication & Sensor Network.

Manish Kumar is a Ph.D. scholar in AIACT&R, GGSIPU, New Delhi. He received his M. Tech. (Information Security) from AIACT&R, GGSIPU, New Delhi, India in 2013. He is currently working as an Assistant Professor at Bharati Vidyapeeth's Institute of Computer Applications and Management (BVICAM), New Delhi, India. His current research interest includes Mobile Ad-hoc Networks and Vehicular Ad-hoc Networks.

Sanjeev Kumar is B. Tech., M. Tech. and Ph. D. in Electronics and Communication Engineering. He is working as Assistant Professor in the department of ECE at AIACTR, Delhi. He has published many research papers in international journals and conferences. He is working in the field of antenna and optical communication engineering. He is lifetime member of ISTE.

Dhiraj Pandey received his Ph.D. in the area of visual cryptography-based security schemes from Manipal University, MTech from University School of Information Technology, GGSIPU, New Delhi. He has more than 15 years of Academic experience in the institute of repute. Currently, he is working as an Associate Professor in the Department of CSE/IT at JSS Academy of Technical Education Noida. His current research interests include assistive technologies and information systems security, allied areas.

Dhirendra Pandey is an Assistant Professor in the Department of Information Technology, Babasaheb Bhimrao Ambedkar University (Accredited "A" Grade Central University), Lucknow. He is having more than 12 Years. He earned his Ph. D. from Devi Ahilya University, Indore (MP) in 2012. His research area is Software Engineering and Requirement Engineering.

Kavita Pandey received her B.Tech. in Computer Science and Engineering from M.D. University in 2002 and M.Tech. (CS) from Banasthali Vidyapeeth University in year 2003. She has obtained her Ph.D. (CS) from Jaypee Institute of Information Technology, Noida, India in January, 2017. She is currently working as an Assistant Professor in JIIT, Noida. Her research interests include Mobile Ad hoc Networks, Vehicular Ad hoc Networks, Optimization Techniques and Network Security. She has published various papers in International journals and conferences including Wiley, IEEE, Springer, Inderscience, etc.

Nithiavathy R. received the B.E. Computer Science and Engineering and M.E. Computer Science and Engineering degree from Anna University, Chennai. She is presently working as an Assistant Professor in the Department of Computer Science and Engineering, Arjun College of technology, affiliated to Anna University- Chennai, TamilNadu, India. His research area includes cloud computing storage, security.

Ram Shringar Raw received his Ph.D. (Computer Science and Technology) from School of Computer and Systems Sciences, Jawaharlal Nehru University, New Delhi, India in 2011. He has worked as an Associate Professor in the Department of Computer Science of Indira Gandhi National Tribal University (A Central University), Amarkantak, MP, India.. He is currently working as an Assistant Professor in the Department of Computer Science and Engineering of Ambedkar Institute of Advanced Communication Technologies and Research, GGSIP University, Delhi, India. Dr. Raw has published around 100 research papers with good impact factors in reputed International Journals and Conferences including IEEE, Springer, Wiley & Sons, Taylor & Fransise, Inderscience, Hindawi, IERI Letters, etc. His current research interest includes Mobile Ad-hoc Networks, Vehicular Ad-hoc Networks and Cloud Computing.

Pawan Singh received his B.Sc. from Ch. Charan Singh University, Meerut, U.P. in 2005, M.C.A. from H.B.T.I. Kanpur, U.P. India in 2009. He is pursuing Ph.D. from Department of Computer Science, Indira Gandhi National Tribal University, Amarkantak, M.P., India. He is working as an assistant professor(Senior Grade) at the Department of Computer Science, Indira Gandhi National Tribal University, Amarkantak, M.P., India. He has more than 09 years of teaching experience. He has published several research papers in international journals and conferences. His current research interest includes Vehicular Ad-hoc Network, Sensor Networks and Internet of Things.

Pooja Singh, Ph.D. from Banastahli Vidyapeeth in Computer Science & Engineering, received her doctorate (C.S.E.) and M.Tech (C.S.E) degree from Banasthali Vidyapeeth, Rajasthan and B.Tech (I.T) degree from Purvanchal University. Currently, She is an Assistant Professor, Department of Computer Science and Information Technology, at the Amity School of Engineering and Technology, An Institute of RBEF Under GGSIPU DELHI at Amity University. She has a total of 13 years of working experience in which she has been delivered her services to AKGEC Ghaziabad as a lecturer and ASET Delhi as an Assistant Professor for the past 12 years as in present. She has published many research papers in international journals including Scopus indexed, Springer and peer-reviewed journals, and in international conferences including Elsevier, IEEE and many other papers published in the IEEE national conference also some research work presented as in poster conferences at IIT-D. She also organized the college level workshop and conferences as a technical team member. She is a very active and dynamic personality, she has been delivered a seminar in different colleges and also attended more than 15 FDP/STP. Apart from this, she has various professional memberships like IEEE, IRED, UACEE, ACEEE, IAENG, IACSIT, etc. She is an active project coordinator in her institute and supervised student's major project, under her guidance more than 25 projects have been done on B.Tech (CSE/IT) level. Her responsibilities are also for the many other students' activities such as attendance monitoring, student's placement mentor, ISO committee member, and her departmental committee. Her interest area is Artificial Neural Network, Data Fusion, Wireless Sensor Network, Routing Protocols, Vehicular Network, data mining, and Optimization.

Index

A

ADS 33, 44, 204, 224, 226-228, 231
ANN 165, 170-172, 179
Aodv 44, 46, 48, 56-58, 61, 63-66, 68-69, 73, 153
audit mechanism 75

B

Bundle 80, 83, 193, 202-203, 246

C

Circular Patch Array Antenna 204, 230-231
cloud computing 75-76, 136, 146, 154, 156, 160, 166, 169, 233-240, 242-243, 248-253

D

Data Fusion 165-166, 172-175, 177-179, 183-184, 187, 189
Deep Learning 1, 6, 13, 20, 157
Delivery Probability 191-192, 195-196, 198-201, 203
Direct Delivery 191, 195, 197, 201
Discretionary Access Control (DAC) 115, 121-122, 131
Dsdv 46, 48, 56-57, 61, 63-66, 68-69, 72-73, 153, 162
Dsr 46, 48, 56-57, 61, 63-66, 68-69, 71, 153

E

E-commerce 233-234, 247-251
Effectiveness and Efficiency 203
Epidemic 191, 194-195, 197, 201, 203

F

First Contact 191, 194-195, 198, 201

G

Gamer,Ibgp 23

H

Heterogeneous Wireless Networks 90-93, 110, 112-114, 185
HFSS 204, 218, 228, 231

I

IoT 2, 75-80, 87-89, 141, 146, 156, 165-167, 169, 179-182, 185-186, 205, 232

K

KSOM 165, 170, 173-174, 176, 179

L

Latency 52, 63, 142, 156, 176, 179, 196, 198-201

M

Machine Learning 1, 5-6, 13, 20, 156-157, 160-164, 185, 188, 190
Mandatory Access Control (MAC) 115, 121, 131
Manet,Vanet,Geocast,Gps,Lar,lbm 23

N

Nash Equilibrium 94, 98-99, 104-105
Network Security 44, 89, 115-118, 120, 123, 127-128, 130-140, 162, 251
Network Selection 90-91, 93-96, 103, 111-114
Non-Cooperative Game 90, 92-94, 97-100, 102-104, 111, 113-114

O

Osm 46, 58-59, 69
Overhead 30, 64, 88, 149, 154, 157, 175, 177, 191, 195, 198-201, 203, 241, 252

P

privacy preservation 75-78
ProPHET 191, 196

Q

Q Learning 1, 13, 20
QoS Awareness 203

R

Rectenna 204, 231-232
Rectifier 204-205, 224-226, 228
Role-Based Access Control (RBAC) 115, 121-122, 131, 136
Rule-based Access Control (RuBAC), 131

S

Scalability 59, 145, 156, 159, 178, 203, 242, 250
SD-VANET 141-142, 149, 151, 153-156, 158, 160
Smart City 1-2, 22, 88, 163
Software Defined Networking (SDN) 141-142, 146
Spray And Wait 191, 197-198, 201, 203

Storage

Storage 36, 48, 75-78, 87-89, 171, 178, 192, 205, 233-234, 236, 241, 250-251
Sumo 1, 18-20, 22, 46, 58-61, 69, 71, 80, 86

T

Traffic Light 1, 4-8, 15-16, 18, 20-22
Traffic signaling 1, 4-6, 18-20

U

User Preferences 90-95, 103, 110, 113
Utility 60, 90-91, 93-94, 96-97, 99, 101, 106, 110, 112, 151-152, 156, 214

V

Vanet 23-24, 33-34, 37, 41-43, 45-50, 52-55, 58-61, 69, 71-84, 86, 88-89, 141-142, 144-146, 149-151, 153-154, 156, 158-162, 164, 185, 188, 190-191
Vehicular Sensor Network 165-166, 168, 170-171, 173, 179
Vertical Handoff 90-95, 106, 110-113

W

Wireless Sensor Network (WSN) 165

Ensure Quality Research is Introduced to the Academic Community

Become an IGI Global Reviewer for Authored Book Projects

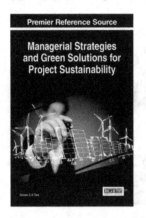

The overall success of an authored book project is dependent on quality and timely reviews.

In this competitive age of scholarly publishing, constructive and timely feedback significantly expedites the turnaround time of manuscripts from submission to acceptance, allowing the publication and discovery of forward-thinking research at a much more expeditious rate. Several IGI Global authored book projects are currently seeking highly-qualified experts in the field to fill vacancies on their respective editorial review boards:

Applications and Inquiries may be sent to:
development@igi-global.com

Applicants must have a doctorate (or an equivalent degree) as well as publishing and reviewing experience. Reviewers are asked to complete the open-ended evaluation questions with as much detail as possible in a timely, collegial, and constructive manner. All reviewers' tenures run for one-year terms on the editorial review boards and are expected to complete at least three reviews per term. Upon successful completion of this term, reviewers can be considered for an additional term.

If you have a colleague that may be interested in this opportunity, we encourage you to share this information with them.

IGI Global Proudly Partners With eContent Pro International

Receive a 25% Discount on all Editorial Services

Editorial Services

IGI Global expects all final manuscripts submitted for publication to be in their final form. This means they must be reviewed, revised, and professionally copy edited prior to their final submission. Not only does this support with accelerating the publication process, but it also ensures that the highest quality scholarly work can be disseminated.

English Language Copy Editing

Let eContent Pro International's expert copy editors perform edits on your manuscript to resolve spelling, punctuaion, grammar, syntax, flow, formatting issues and more.

Scientific and Scholarly Editing

Allow colleagues in your research area to examine the content of your manuscript and provide you with valuablo foodback and suggestions before submission.

Figure, Table, Chart & Equation Conversions

Do you have poor quality figures? Do you need visual elements in your manuscript created or converted? A design expert can help!

Translation

Need your documjent translated into English? eContent Pro International's expert translators are fluent in English and more than 40 different languages.

Email: customerservice@econtentpro.com   www.igi-global.com/editorial-service-partners

IGI Global's Transformative Open Access (OA) Model:
How to Turn Your University Library's Database Acquisitions Into a Source of OA Funding

In response to the OA movement and well in advance of Plan S, IGI Global, early last year, unveiled their OA Fee Waiver (Offset Model) Initiative.

Under this initiative, librarians who invest in IGI Global's InfoSci-Books (5,300+ reference books) and/or InfoSci-Journals (185+ scholarly journals) databases will be able to subsidize their patron's OA article processing charges (APC) when their work is submitted and accepted (after the peer review process) into an IGI Global journal.*

How Does it Work?

1. When a library subscribes or perpetually purchases IGI Global's InfoSci-Databases including InfoSci-Books (5,300+ e-books), IntoSci-Journals (185+ e-journals), and/or their discipline/subject-focused subsets, IGI Global will match the library's investment with a fund of equal value to go toward subsidizing the OA article processing charges (APCs) for their patrons.

   Researchers: Be sure to recommend the InfoSci-Books and InfoSci-Journals to take advantage of this initiative.

2. When a student, faculty, or staff member submits a paper and it is accepted (following the peer review) into one of IGI Global's 185+ scholarly journals, the author will have the option to have their paper published under a traditional publishing model or as OA.

3. When the author chooses to have their paper published under OA, IGI Global will notify them of the OA Fee Waiver (Offset Model) Initiative. If the author decides they would like to take advantage of this initiative, IGI Global will deduct the US$ 1,500 APC from the created fund.

4. This fund will be offered on an annual basis and will renew as the subscription is renewed for each year thereafter. IGI Global will manage the fund and award the APC waivers unless the librarian has a preference as to how the funds should be managed.

Hear From the Experts on This Initiative:

"I'm very happy to have been able to make one of my recent research contributions, 'Visualizing the Social Media Conversations of a National Information Technology Professional Association' featured in the *International Journal of Human Capital and Information Technology Professionals*, freely available along with having access to the valuable resources found within IGI Global's InfoSci-Journals database."

– **Prof. Stuart Palmer,**
Deakin University, Australia

For More Information, Visit: www.igi-global.com/publish/contributor-resources/open-access or contact IGI Global's Database Team at eresources@igi-global.com.

Printed in the United States
By Bookmasters